STEVE HEANEY MC
WITH DAMIEN LEWIS

OPERATION MAYHEM

THE TARGET: ONE VILLAGE.

THE DEFENDERS: 26 ELITE BRITISH SOLDIERS.

THE ENEMY: 2000 DRUG- AND BLOOD-CRAZED REBELS.

© Steve Heaney and Damien Lewis 2014

The right of Steve Heaney and Damien Lewis to be identified
as the authors of this work has been asserted in accordance with the
Copyright, Designs and Patents Act 1988.

First published in Great Britain in 2014 by Orion Books
An imprint of the Orion Publishing Group Ltd
Orion House, 5 Upper St Martin's Lane,
London, WC2H 9EA
An Hachette Livre Company

1 3 5 7 9 10 8 6 4 2

Quote on p. viii licensed under the Open Goverment Licence v2.0

A CIP catalogue record for this book
is available from the British Library.

HB ISBN 978 1 4091 4843 2
TPB ISBN 978 1 4091 4844 9

Typeset by Input Data Services Ltd,
Bridgwater, Somerset

Printed in Great Britain by
CPI Group (UK) Ltd, Croydon CR0 4YY

The Orion Publishing Group's policy is to use papers that are natural,
renewable and recyclable products and made from wood grown
in sustainable forests. The logging and manufacturing processes are
expected to conform to the environmental regulations
of the country of origin.

www.orionbooks.co.uk

To the Findermen who have paid the ultimate price, we raise
a glass in your honour. To those of you who find yourselves once
again in harm's way on active operations across the globe . . .
be safe and remember always,

'Stay low and move fast'.

'What makes the grass grow? Blood! Blood! Blood!'

RUF rebel chant, prior to battle

'Good men sleep soundly in their beds at night, only because there are rough men willing to do violence on their behalf.'

George Orwell

What Manner of Men Are These
Who Wear the Maroon Beret?

They are firstly all volunteers and are toughened by physical training. As a result they have infectious optimism and that offensive eagerness which comes from well-being. They have 'jumped' from the air and by doing so have conquered fear.

Their duty lies in the van of the battle. They are proud of this honour. They have the highest standards in all things whether it be skill in battle or smartness in the execution of all peacetime duties. They are in fact – men apart – every man an emperor.

Of all the factors, which make for success in battle, the spirit of the warrior is the most decisive. That spirit will be found in full measure in the men who wear the maroon beret.

Field Marshal The Viscount Montgomery

AUTHOR'S NOTE

I have used soldiers' real names in this book when they have been published in the press, or whenever individual soldiers have indicated to me that they were happy for me to do so. I have been asked to use pseudonyms for those serving with Special Forces and other elite units, or for operators who are still involved, or who were involved in sensitive operations. Otherwise, all aspects of this story remain as they took place on the ground.

I have done my utmost to ensure the accuracy of all the events portrayed herein. Few written records exist covering the events described in this book. Accordingly, I have recreated conversations from how I remember them and in discussions with the others who were involved. No doubt my memory and that of my fellow operators is fallible, and I will be happy to correct any inadvertent mistakes in future editions.

To all other units in the British armed forces – and those of our foremost allies – the Pathfinders' call-sign is *Mayhem*. That is how the unit is addressed over the radio net. The Sierra Leone mission related in this book remains one of the most highly-decorated in modern Pathfinder history. Accordingly, and because it seems to suit the actions portrayed in these pages, I have chosen to call this book *Operation Mayhem*.

FOREWORD

by General Sir David Richards GCB CBE DSO
former Chief of the Defence Staff

In January 1999 I led a small team of officers and marines to Sierra Leone. Our task was to assess whether the once proud little army of that tragic but spirited country had any hope of pushing back the brutal rebels of the Revolutionary United Front. I had to assess whether there was anything we could do to help them and present the case to Tony Blair's government in London.

The RUF's signature atrocity was the amputation of the limbs of young and old alike. Designed to intimidate the population, in their warped often drug-crazed minds this also had the advantage of preventing those they 'cut' from casting a vote in any future elections. We watched the Sierra Leonian army, their local Kamajor militia allies and a small contingent of Nigerian troops fight valiantly to push the RUF back out of Freetown. We departed after about 10 days but not before we had successfully persuaded the British government that these plucky people should be helped, financially and militarily.

That experience left a real mark on me and my team. We had been witness to some horrific sights, things we all hoped never to see again. We certainly never thought we would return to Sierra Leone. Little did we know.

By early May 2000, the RUF had reneged on a peace treaty they had signed the previous summer and were once again rampaging their brutal way towards Freetown. This time my ever-ready Joint Force HQ, with 1st Battalion Parachute Regiment group including the Regiment's renowned Pathfinder Platoon and some others under command, were rushed out to Sierra Leone to evacuate

British and other entitled people from the country for fear that they would be butchered by the RUF. It was a race against time. And it was vital that the RUF suffered an early blow to their morale, something that would make them pause and think twice about taking on my limited forces.

This invigorating book tells the tale of the hugely professional and courageous group of men who inflicted that blow on the RUF for me and their inspirational commanding officer Lt-Col Paul Gibson. Deliberately exposed to lure the RUF onto their positions, the Pathfinders lived up to their unrivalled reputation for toughness and professionalism of the highest order. Without a shadow of doubt, their heroic actions that memorable night was the key tactical event in what has been held up as a model intervention operation. It enabled us not only to complete the evacuation in relative security but, more importantly, allowed us to push the RUF out of Freetown and away from the vital airfield without which no operation was tenable. It buoyed up the Sierra Leonean people and crucially bought time for the United Nations forces to recover and rebuild.

Six weeks later, with the RUF essentially defeated and hugely demoralised, we were able to hand over to the UN and wend our way back to the UK. We felt good about ourselves. We had chanced our arm and more than achieved the aim. The generous-hearted people of Sierra Leone had been given their country back and could once again hope for a better future. The Pathfinders had written another stirring chapter in their short but illustrious history and Sergeant Steve Heaney was at the very centre of that story. To great acclaim he was rightly awarded the Military Cross; none can have been better earned.

Steve Heaney captures the confusion, black humour, raw courage, jargon and sheer exhilaration of combat brilliantly in this compelling and simply written book. In my judgement it is the best account of low-level tactical soldiering since Fred Majdalaney's classic *Patrol*, a World War 2 account of a fighting patrol.

But Sergeant Heaney tells a broader tale that has also rarely been captured so well. What makes an elite unit like the Pathfinders so powerful, so special? One that commanders like me loved to have under them. One that their enemies fervently wished was not opposite them. What sort of people join such a unit? What binds them together so closely that they can stay cohesive under the most stressful of conditions? What training do they go through to reach such heights of professionalism? What is the role of humour in keeping morale high when most would succumb to fear and fatigue? This classic book reveals all this and much more. I commend it to the professional soldier and layman alike.

It was people like Sergeant Heaney MC that I was thinking of when I said at my retirement parade on Horse Guards in London 'if I have seen further than most, it was because I stood on the shoulders of giants'. If you don't know what I mean, read this book and you soon will.

General Sir David Richards GCB CBE DSO

PROLOGUE: MAN HUNT

Ahead of me I saw Steve B come to a silent halt.

He dropped onto one knee, his assault rifle covering the arc of fire to the front of us. I went down into a similar stance, my weapon sweeping the arc of fire from Steve's shoulder through 180 degrees around to the operator at my rear.

He in turn did likewise, covering the arc on the opposite side of the patrol, and so it cascaded down the line, such that all areas to either side of us were being watched by a pair of unblinking eyes and menaced by a weapon's gaping barrel. We were a twelve-man seek-and-destroy patrol, hunting a vicious and bloodthirsty enemy – one that outnumbered us a hundred to one.

And right now we were ready for anything.

After weeks of living in the jungle, our unwashed bodies and unshaven faces made us appear like a band of desperadoes. But grimy, soiled uniforms blend in better with the wild terrain, as do layers of dark stubble and beards. We'd smeared thick lines of camouflage cream onto any exposed skin, to better hide ourselves. The whole effect made us practically invisible, but any sudden movement, or any sound at all from our side risked giving our position away.

When hunting an adversary in the bush and the jungle, you have to presume he is out there somewhere, hunting you or waiting in a hidden ambush position. Visibility is limited by the dense vegetation plus the impenetrable shadows. You can rarely see more than a few dozen yards. It makes spotting your adversary ever more challenging. Plus we were acutely aware that an enemy is at his most dangerous when he is injured, bleeding and badly mauled – which is what we reckoned any number of the rebels were right now.

Steve B placed one hand on his head, while the other grasped the pistol-grip of his weapon. It was the signal for me to move up to his shoulder. He raised two fingers and practically jabbed them into his eyes – the hand signal for 'look where I indicate' – then pointed to our left front. Less than a dozen yards away I could see ranks of razor-sharp points poking out from the bush. They continued onwards for a good thirty yards or so towards the ragged fringe of jungle.

It was one of our fields of punji sticks – sharpened bamboo stakes we'd got the local villagers to cut and shape and plant all around our positions, to ensnare the enemy. For a second I wondered why Steve B had pointed them out to me: there were punji pits all around us, so what was so special about this one? But as I studied those vicious bamboo blades more closely I noticed that many were splattered with a sickly red.

Rebel blood.

It had to be.

Steve B swept his hand north, pointing out the ground to the front of the punji field. The terrain was churned into a mishmash of decaying leaf matter, rotten sticks and dark, loamy soil. I could just imagine panicked feet and hands desperately trying to scrabble their way out of the punji field, rebel minds clouded with pain and agony. But it was the thick, gloopy trails of blood running from there towards the forest that really drew my eye.

That marked the way the rebels had retreated.

The path for us to track and to follow.

A wild animal is never more dangerous than when it is badly hurt. From all we'd seen over the past few weeks, the rebels here were worse than wild animals. Ahead of us danger, red in tooth and claw, lurked behind every tree and in the hidden shadows.

No words needed to be spoken between Steve B and me, the patrol commander. Clearly, our plan had worked a treat. Just as we'd suspected, the rebels had charged forward in human waves to attack us, guns blazing. Instead, they'd stumbled into the punji traps. As they'd fought to drag themselves clear of the vicious fields of sharpened stakes, a good many of them had ripped themselves to pieces.

The amount of blood alone was testament to that.

I gave Steve B the nod to push onwards.

As we set off I signalled to the operator behind me to take a good look at the blood-soaked ground, and to pass it down the line. Moving like a silent, stealthy snake we threaded our way through the bush, until the wall of thick forest was right before us – dark, brooding and hostile.

This was the rebels' domain. The Kingdom of the Bad Guys. This was their country, their backyard, the safe haven from which they launched their brutal sorties.

But this was also very much our kind of territory. We're trained to favour those areas that normal mortals shun. Bug-infested swamps, sun-blasted desert, snow-whipped mountains and impenetrable jungle – those are the areas where we expect to find little human presence, which makes them ideal for operators like us to move through unseen and undetected, into the heart of enemy territory.

Right now, we were well behind the rebels' lines. We were moving into terrain that they'd ruled for a decade or more with an iron grip of fear, brute violence and hatred. But I knew for sure that every man on my patrol – each one an elite warrior highly trained at operating in the jungle – felt quite at home here, and ready.

We were taking the fight to the enemy where they least expected it. We'd smashed them in a long and vicious firefight during the hours of darkness. Now, we were going after them in their supposed sanctuary. We'd hit them at night in the open as they tried to rush our positions, and now we aimed to hit them in the hours of daylight, in the heart of the jungle. This way, we'd keep them on the back foot – the repeated blows sending them reeling.

Or maybe not.

Maybe it had all been a feint and a trap.

Maybe the rebels knew we were coming, and were poised to unleash a scything burst of fire as we stepped into the jungle, wiping out our entire patrol.

Only one way to find out.

Push onwards into the shadows.

Steve B took a step into the eerie and claustrophobic forest interior, practically disappearing from my view as the vegetation sucked him in. I followed, each step chosen so as to avoid any detritus that might break or crack underfoot. The humidity beneath the jungle canopy was thick and it hit me like a wall. I could feel the sweat trickling down my back in rivulets, my clammy uniform sticking to the sores and welts that weeks of not washing had caused to erupt on my skin.

Steve paused for an instant, balanced delicately on the balls of his feet. He had his eyes glued to the sun-dappled jungle floor, tracing the thick, congealed strings of red goo that had been left by the rebel injured. In theory, all we had to do was track the enemy through the trees via their blood trails, and we'd have them.

I gave the hand signal for all to double their watchfulness. My adrenaline was pumping in bucket-loads, my heart pounding like a drum. Badly injured men can only move slowly through such dense terrain, so slowing the movement of the entire body of fighters.

The rebels could only be minutes ahead of us now.

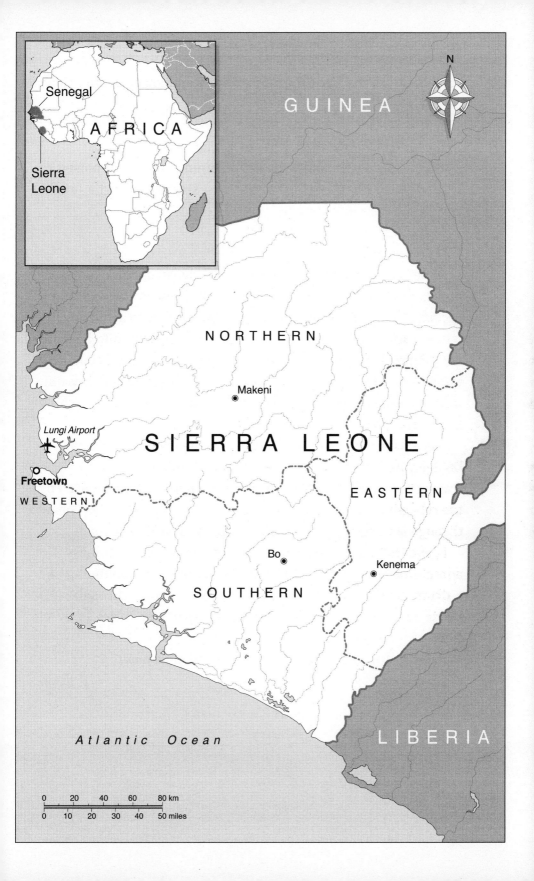

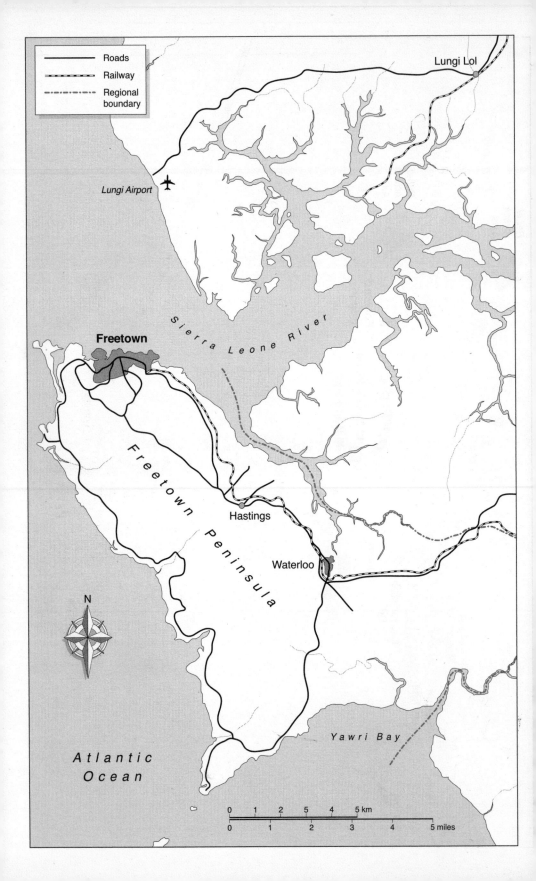

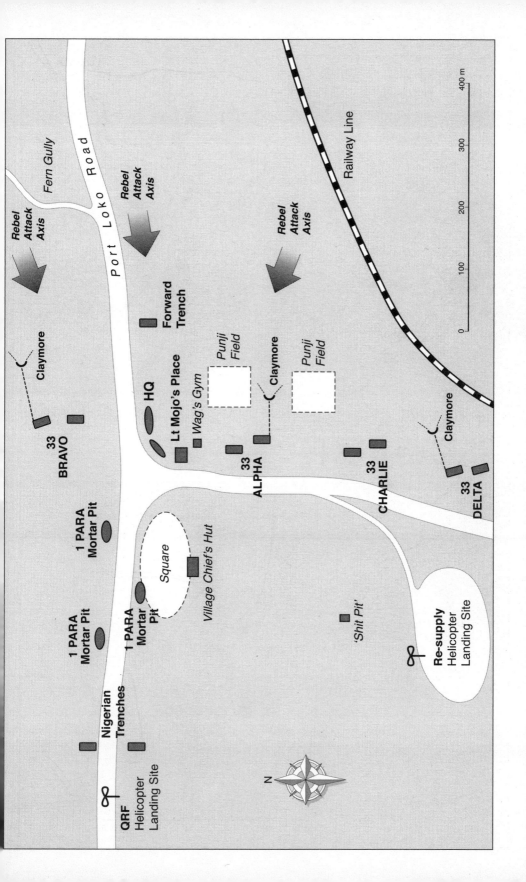

1

The day had begun just like any other. We'd started with our customary early morning run around the perimeter of the base. As usual I'd set the pace, leading from the front.

Each day we'd vary the kit we ran in. One morning it would be shorts, T-shirts and trainers; the next, boots, combat trousers and smocks. Day three we'd be kitted out the same, but carrying a 40-pound Bergen on our backs. Each of the guys had three different rucksacks permanently packed and secured: a desert pack, a jungle pack and one for more temperate climes – mountains, snow and ice.

That way, we were ready for anything.

Always.

We'd mix and match the early morning runs with gym work and sessions in the pool, doing circuit training as a cardiovascular workout and rope-climbs for upper body strength, plus a daily swim to build stamina and endurance.

At thirty-one years of age I was the seasoned platoon sergeant, and each year I led the murderous forced marches and the Endurance stages of Selection. Word was that if you wanted to pass Selection and make it into our tiny, elite unit – the Pathfinders – you needed to stick with Smoggy.

Ever since I can remember, that's been my nickname – Smoggy. I hail from Middlesbrough, a nondescript, grey industrial town in northeast England. A permanent smog seems to hang over the dark landscape, hence the nickname of those born there – 'Smoggies'.

Pathfinder Selection is similar to that undertaken by the SAS

(Special Air Service), only it's shorter – five weeks, as opposed to three months. Many claim that it's more intense, so more punishing. Others say that's bullshit: the shorter duration lowers the attrition rate. I didn't particularly care either way. Pathfinder Selection is Pathfinder Selection: it does what it says on the tin.

It begins with a pre-selection period – days of fierce punishment to weed out the weak and feeble. We'd gather the raw recruits at the Aldershot Training Area and push them through a beasting session similar to the Parachute Regiment's P Company – the fitness and endurance test required to enter the Parachute Regiment. We'd start with an 8-mile run carrying a 55-pound pack, and raise it to a 10-miler – pass time one hour forty minutes maximum. We'd intersperse that with murder runs in full kit – helmet, webbing and weapon.

If you couldn't make it through that first week in Aldershot there was no point going for the real man test – five weeks of hell in the Brecon Beacons, the rain-lashed hills in South Wales where all British elite forces' Selection takes place. Selection proper would start with Walkabout – three days hefting a massive pack across all types of terrain, to test whether individual soldiers knew how to navigate and survive on the hills.

We'd combine the brutal testing with a judicious amount of instruction, as we didn't want blokes getting killed out there – imparting such pearls of wisdom as 'Go low, stay slow; go high, stay dry'. At the end of Walkabout we knew who was capable of going on to the next stages – the Fan Dance, Point-to-Point, Iron Man, Elan Valley – heading out onto the unforgiving terrain alone and for far longer periods of time.

Selection culminates in the killer – Endurance, a 64-kilometre forced march over the highest peaks, under a 55-pound pack (minus food and water) and carrying your weapon.

Endurance has to be completed in under twenty hours.

Needless to say, it has broken many a man.

Both at Aldershot and the Brecons I was the rabbit in all of this.

I set the pace, leading the runs and the tabs. I was hyper-fit and I enjoyed the physical challenge – always have – so it made sense to make me lead man. Hence the saying: *If you want to pass Pathfinder Selection, you need to stick with Smoggy.*

That morning – as with every other 'normal' day at the Pathfinders' Wattisham, Norfolk, base – I'd put a call through to the control tower around 0645 hours. Our base was set in a secure area to one end of an Army Air Corps Apache attack helicopter facility. I'd sought clearance to run the perimeter of the airbase, after which the forty-odd lads of the Pathfinders had gathered for the off.

Oh yeah – plus the one dog.

Ben was a gorgeous chocolate Labrador. I'd had him for a year or so, and every morning he'd join us on the 6.5-mile run. We'd move off as a tight squad – all apart from Ben, who'd be away chasing pheasants and having a ball. For most of the time we wouldn't even see him. Then he'd pop his head out of a patch of bush, give me the look – *You coming, or what?* – and be off again, tracking the scent of a deer.

For the last couple of miles we'd hit open terrain, leaving behind the thick forest and scrub that surrounds the base and heading along the grass fringes of the runway. Ben would complete the last leg by my side every step of the way. First things first, when I got back to base I'd fetch him a bowl of water, then head for the showers.

Together with some of the other old and bold, I'd try to use up all the hot water, so that Grant – Captain Grant Harris, the Second-in-Command of our unit – would be forced to have a cold shower. No matter how many times we did it, it never ceased to amuse us, and Grant – God bless his cotton socks – had the strength of character to see that it was just another ragging from 'the blokes' and to go with it.

The officers who didn't get ragged were the ones we didn't rate. You only needled the good guys.

But more of that later.

After five months of running the base perimeter Ben was a four-legged hunk of rock-hard muscle and sinew. At times he looked more like a chocolate Rottweiler than a Lab. He'd grown so strong that he'd broken the metal chain that I used to put him on. I'd left him sunning himself one lunchtime, only to get a call from one of the aircrew. They'd found my dog curled up fast asleep in one of the helicopters.

From then on I'd left Ben pretty much free to roam the Pathfinders' part of the base. It was hyper-secure, ringed with razor wire and guards – a fortress within a fortress – so he couldn't get into too much trouble. He'd spend his time lounging with the blokes in the Pathfinders' Interest Room – our clubroom for want of a better analogy – snoozing on top of the grassed-over ammo bunkers, or hanging out with those working on the vehicles in the hangar.

As a unit we were constantly pushing ourselves, but the endless physical training wasn't anything about looking chiselled or Gucci. It was about ensuring we were physically robust enough to take the kind of punishment required of the insertion methods that we specialise in. Get it wrong, and the kind of means we use to get behind enemy lines could seriously injure or even kill you – and that's before you ever put a foot on hostile soil.

During that morning's run I'd been thinking about one particular jump I'd been on recently. We'd paid a visit to China Lake, the vast, one-million-acre Naval Air Weapons Station set amidst the wilderness of America's Western Mojave Desert. With 19,600 square miles of restricted airspace for us to play in, China Lake far surpasses any similar facility in the UK, providing an ace proving ground for the kind of techniques we were pioneering.

We'd been out there working with DEVGRU – America's elite counter-terrorism unit, otherwise known as SEAL Team Six – developing an ultra-high-altitude air-insertion technique, one designed to get a small body of men dropped behind enemy lines in 100 per cent secrecy.

The British military had pretty much pioneered HALO – high altitude low opening – and HAHO – high altitude high opening – parachute jumps. In the former you'd pile out of a Hercules at above 25,000 feet, plummet to earth in freefall and open your chute at around 5000 feet, so getting you fast and direct onto the ground. In HAHO, you'd jump on a static line – your chute opening automatically as you exited the aircraft – then drift for up to seventy kilometres, the idea being that you could 'fly' across an enemy's border and penetrate their airspace undetected.

But those at the helm of Special Forces had decided that a third technique was needed – one that set the 'stealth-level' even higher. This new means and technology had been labelled HAPLSS – the High Altitude Parachutist Life Support System. We were out in China Lake doing what the Pathfinders do best, putting the theory of the concept and the kit to the test of harsh reality.

When jumping at extreme high altitude the air is so thin you have to breathe from an air bottle. But unless the right type of gas is breathed at all the right stages of the jump, you can suffer from Altitude Decompression Sickeness (ADS), more commonly known as 'the bends'. So above 25,000 feet the jump becomes a medical issue as much as a set of physical challenges.

We'd pretty much mastered it for HALO and HAHO, but with HAPLSS we were going even higher and for a very specific set of reasons. Civilian airliners cruise at a much higher altitude, and HAPLSS was a system designed to enable us to jump from that kind of extreme height and survive the devastating cold, G-forces and atmospheric conditions encountered. If we could master all of that, we'd be able to penetrate the airspace of a target country in an aircraft masquerading as a civilian airliner, then jump and drift to earth with no one being any the wiser that we'd ever been there.

In theory we could even pile out of a genuine civvie airliner, leaving unseen from the cargo bay. Or if it was a combat situation, we could catch a lift on a US Air Force B-1B heavy bomber and exit the bomb bay directly after the payload was dropped – so masking our jump as a bombing run. Either would get us onto target totally undetected. But for either means to be workable we had to master jumping from the very roof of the world. That meant taking what the boffins had designed – the space-age HAPLSS survival suit, oxygen mask and protective helmet – and trialling it for real.

With HAPLSS you have to breathe a 'forced air' mixture – so the oxygen is pressurised and pumped into your lungs, as opposed to breathing on demand. You have to start breathing the pure oxygen a good hour before takeoff, to reduce the dangers of getting ADS. The standard British Hercules transport aircraft, the C-130K model, can only depressurise – open the ramp to let you jump – at 25,000 feet or less. At China Lake we'd be jumping at more than 10,000 feet *above* that altitude, and if we tried it in a standard Hercules it would fall apart in midair.

The SEALs were operating the C-130 Juliet (J-model), which had been re-engineered with a completely new set of propellers which would keep turning and providing lift in the thinner air above 25,000 feet. But even the C-130J couldn't go much above 30,000 feet, so the one we were going to be using had been modified to go higher. The only way to trial a HAPLSS jump – at air temperatures of minus 100 degrees Celsius, and in an atmosphere thinner than that on the summit of Mount Everest – was to use an aircraft specifically designed to open its jump ramp at such an altitude.

We'd make all such trial jumps with electrodes and monitors wired up to key points of the body. They'd record stresses on the human frame from G-shocks, how many atmospheres we pulled at exit from the aeroplane, respiratory and heart rate factors, plus the impact of extreme cold on the body as it plummeted through air like ice. In a 'normal' HALO or HAHO jump from 25,000 feet, terminal velocity – the maximum speed at which you freefall – is

320 kph. But the thinner the air the faster you fall. Jumping from 30,000 feet plus, terminal velocity would be considerably faster – around 440 kph.

Even at 320 kph you're plummeting through a thousand feet every five seconds. If you tried to pull your chute at the higher velocity – 440 kph – one of two things would likely happen: either you'd break your back as a result of the impact, or you'd have a canopy explosion. At that velocity, and in such thin air, the chute would come whooshing out of your backpack, and all you'd likely hear would be a massive crack and thump as the individual cells exploded, tearing your canopy to shreds. You'd be left plummeting to earth at a deadly rate of knots, with shards of torn silk flapping uselessly in the air above you.

We knew this because we'd trialled HAPLSS using a dummy – a latex model of your average bloke, laden down with metal weights to around 15 stone, and dressed in the gear you'd normally jump with (a 55-pound Bergen, plus weapons and ammo). From the dummy trials we knew that if you pulled your chute at anything above 25,000 feet, you had little chance of making it down alive – hence the default mode with HAPLSS being to freefall a good 20,000 feet prior to releasing your chute.

There was one problem with that. If you jumped and the turbulence put you into a 'spin', very quickly you'd be in danger of 'blacking out' – so losing consciousness. Ideally, you'd plummet through the turbulence of the aircraft's wake and stabilise yourself, getting into a star shape – arms and legs outstretched – for the freefall. But if you failed to achieve that and went into a violent spin you'd have just seconds in which to save yourself – and the last-ditch option is always to pull your chute before you black out.

You might have to do that at any height after the jump, so we needed to trial doing an 'unstable exit' – something that would put the jumper into a deadly spin, and possibly force him to pull his chute. We didn't even know if an operator could get out of a spin while wearing all the cumbersome HAPLSS gear ... but we still had to try.

Prior to heading for China Lake I'd gone through the necessary medical trials at the JATE – the innocuously-named Joint Air Transport Establishment; the body that oversees such high-end, James-Bond-type military air techniques – to ensure that I was physically fit and robust enough to go ahead with the trials. Hence why running the base perimeter every morning was so necessary.

The JATE is based at RAF Brize Norton. My medical trials passed, I'd got the brief on what exactly the JATE boffins wanted from me out at China Lake. They were asking me to go higher than any British military parachutist had ever gone before – so jumping from well above 30,000 feet – but that wasn't the half of it.

'Steve, we want you to do the jump, make an unstable exit and hold it for twenty seconds,' they told me. 'Then we want you to try to get out of it and we'll track whatever problems you incur.'

They made it sound so easy.

What they really meant was this: Steve, pile out of the aircraft, go into a spin, allow the spin to escalate for a good twenty seconds – or 5000 feet – of freefall, then try to save yourself. It went without saying that I'd be close to blacking out by then, so the last-resort option would be to pull the chute, with every likelihood of it exploding. But hey, the only way to perfect such techniques was to trial them, and eventually you had to switch from a dummy to a real person – i.e. muggins me.

In a way it was fair enough. As the long-serving Pathfinder Platoon sergeant I was one of the most practised military freefall parachutists in the British Army. Airborne insertion is the bread and butter of what we do: we train for it more exhaustively than any other unit in the armed forces. I had over 1200 jumps under my belt, plus I was one of only a handful of military freefall tandem masters – meaning I could freefall with another human being strapped to my person, or a piece of high-tech weaponry, or a specially-designed canister packed with 1000 pounds of ammo.

Arguably, there was no one better qualified to trial HAPLSS over China Lake.

So it was that the modified C-130J had droned up into the hot and thin air high above the wildlands of the Mojave Desert. As we neared the predetermined altitude I started to make ready. There was only one way to ensure I did what was required of me – I had to achieve an immediate 'unstable exit'. Normally you'd leap off the ramp front first, in what amounted to a long dive, arms and legs outstretched to anchor yourself in the air. By shifting an arm or a leg – drawing it closer to, or moving it further away from, your body – you could slow down or accelerate, and steer your fall.

This time, I was going to plummet from the heavens curled up into a tight ball – getting into a streamlined water-droplet or bullet shape.

The SEALs had zero idea of what would happen if a jumper was forced to pull his chute above 25,000 feet, in a desperate attempt to escape the spin. They made it clear they thought it was pretty messed-up to try, though they appreciated that we needed to know. They were pretty used to how the Brits operated by now: we had all the human potential, guts and expertise, if little of their kit or their airframes. Hence a Brit was today's fall guy, and the Yanks were providing the jump platform and the space and freedom of China Lake in which to push the limits of the known and the possible.

As I hunched on the edge of the ramp in the foetal position, the wind gusting and buffeting me like a giant tennis ball in a wind tunnel, I reflected upon how I really wasn't getting paid enough for this kind of shit. Being a Pathfinder, I didn't even get the extra £45 a week pay uplift that the UK Special Forces got. The Pathfinders don't sit within the UKSF family. We were formed as a completely black, off-the-books outfit, one that officially didn't exist. We had no budget, no personnel – every man officially remained with his parent unit – plus no kit, weaponry or ammo other than what we could beg, borrow or steal from other units.

Hence the unofficial name given to us: the X Platoon.

I couldn't see anything much while hunched into a tight ball, but I knew the red 'prepare-to-jump' light must have flickered on, for the two Parachute Jumping Instructors (PJIs) had grabbed hold of me. The PJIs are dedicated specialists whose only role in life is to oversee military parachute jumps. Right now I was going out blind, and these guys held my life in their hands.

The light must have flicked from red to green, for over the deafening roar of the slipstream I heard the voice of the lead PJI guy yelling: 'Go! Go! Go!'

I scrunched tighter into a ball, as I felt the PJIs manhandle me forwards and roll me out into thin air. For an instant I plummeted, then I felt myself sucked into the maw of the slipstream, the violent turbulence throwing me over and over and over.

Spat out of the aircraft's wake, I began to fall vertically towards earth, twisting around and around like some crazy, messed-up, man-sized spinning top. I was counting out the seconds in my head, but in the back of my mind a voice was already muttering my prayers.

'One-thousand-and-three, one-thousand-and-four, one-thousand-and-five . . . God get me out of this shit alive . . .'

I counted off the seconds and prayed for some kind of deliverance, as I tumbled through the thin, freezing blue.

The only means I had of assessing how fast I was spinning was by trying to monitor how rapidly the air around me turned from blue to yellow to blue to yellow to blue again. Blue meant I was facing the sky, yellow meant the Mojave Desert, and so on and so forth.

Had I been able to pause for the barest instant I'd have seen the clear curvature of the earth below me, but right now I was struggling to remain conscious, let alone having a spare moment to admire the view.

Being scrunched into a tight ball I was massively aerodynamic, which lowers drag and increases terminal velocity still further. I just kept accelerating and spinning faster and faster and faster, my air speed and the G-forces growing with it, the wind howling and tearing at my head like a raging hurricane.

Imagine going at one hundred kilometres an hour on a motorcycle. If you've ever done it, you'll know just how intensely the wind rips into your face and your torso, as the pressure tries to slam you out of the saddle. Now imagine going at over *four times* that speed, without even the benefit of a full-face helmet, or a set of handlebars and a seat to keep a grip on. Imagine doing so in minus 100 degrees air temperature, and with the following strapped to your person: a bulging parachute pack, a massive Bergen, your webbing stuffed with ammo and grenades, a pistol strapped to your thigh, plus your main weapon – your assault rifle – slung over your shoulder. Now imagine all of that when you're spinning crazily like a top, without the faintest clue which way up you are . . .

Sickening, right?

I was ten seconds into the freefall and the spin just kept getting worse. I could feel myself gasping for breath, as my burning lungs struggled to drag in enough gas from the bottle. My sensory awareness – my ability to judge where I was exactly, which way up I was, or who I was even – was slipping away from me.

Blue-yellow-blue-yellow-blue-yellow-blueyellow-blueyellow-blueyellow-blueeeeellooooow . . .

Argghhhhh!

The air pressure was tearing at the oxygen bottle fixed to my front, plus it was trying to rip away the heavy Bergen strapped across my lower body. I could feel my weapon slamming around in the air at my side, the butt like a baseball bat cracking blows into my helmeted head. I was on the verge of vomiting. The pressure on my heart and lungs was unbearable, and I was seconds away from losing consciousness.

At which stage I'd be dead.

With my pulse juddering inside my skull and my mind reeling horribly from dizziness and disorientation, I tried to focus on the count.

'One-thousand-and-fifteen, one-thousand-and-sixteen, one-thousand-and- . . .'

Three seconds to go and I had to try to break free and get into a stable freefall position, face to earth. I counted out the last seconds. Snap! I thrust my arms and legs into a rigid star shape, arching my back against the unbearable forces that were threatening to tear me limb from limb. I strained my muscles against the pain and the pressure, letting out a cry of agony at the top of my voice – one that I knew no one would ever hear, for I was alone on the roof of the world here.

My limbs were thrust out rigid to make four air-anchors, as I tried to grab at the thin atmosphere and slow my seemingly unstoppable whirlwind of a fall. Gradually I sensed the revolutions decrease, as the air howled all around me and my body screamed in pain. But I still didn't know which way up I'd eventually come to a halt – facing the sky or facing the earth.

Finally I stopped spinning.

I forced my frazzled mind to concentrate.

I was facing blue.

Blue meant the sky.

Wrong way round.

I was plummeting at a murderous speed with my back to the earth. If I pulled my chute in the position I was in now it would open below me and I'd fall through it. It would bag around me, doing a fine impression of a sack of damp washing, and I'd plummet to earth like a corpse entombed in a shroud of tangled parachute silk.

Not good.

I brought my right arm in close to my side and threw my opposite shoulder over, trying to flip myself so I'd end up facing yellow. *Yellow = earth.* But for some reason it just wasn't working. All it achieved was the very opposite of what I wanted – to send me back into the spin again.

For a moment I was on the verge of panic. My hand reached involuntarily for the release cord of the chute. I forced myself to stop. I forced myself to remember how we'd trialled this repeatedly with the dummy, and every single time the chute had ripped itself to shreds.

Don't pull the chute.

Pull the chute and you're dead.

There was one more thing I could try. My last option before blacking out was to do what I did now. I dragged in both arms tight by my sides, rammed my legs out straight behind me and got my back locked and arched. I was now in the Delta Track position, which should bring me into a head-down dive.

Like this I hoped to remain conscious long enough for the thickening atmosphere to slow me down to the point where pulling my chute – and survival – was a real possibility.

That at least was the plan.

2

I was three minutes into the freefall when I finally risked pulling the chute. I was at 3500 feet and I'd just completed a mega death-ride to earth. It was the Delta Track that had done the trick, getting me into a stable enough position to flick out into the star shape again, and ready myself to send 360 square feet of the finest silk billowing out above me.

It takes six seconds for the chute to deploy fully, so in reality I was at 2500 feet by the time I broke my fall, drifting silently beneath the canopy over the hot Mojave Desert. The other way to look at it was like this: I'd deployed the chute when I was a bare fifteen seconds away from ploughing into the earth at plus-320 kph. At that speed there wouldn't have been a great deal of me to scrape up amongst the cacti and the tumbleweed, so my parents – and Ben my dog – could bury what was left of me.

Still, at least now we knew.

We knew what happened when you flipped into a death spin at well above 30,000 feet while doing a HAPLSS jump.

Once I was 'safely' down I gathered up my chute and the pick-up wagon trundled over to collect me. I was driven to one of China Lake's 2000-odd hangars, halls, laboratories and other assorted buildings. There the boffins unplugged the wires, and sensors and data-recorders, to check on all the readings made during the jump.

It turned out that I'd pulled more G-forces than a top-gun fighter pilot does when putting a state-of-the-art F-15 Eagle fighter jet through its paces – and I hadn't had the luxury of a glass-and-steel airframe wrapped around me to shield me from the bitter ice and turbulence, plus the punishing air pressure and the wind speed.

Still, that was what being a Pathfinder was all about.

It went with the territory.

The day after the jump of death I felt as if I'd been in a boxing bout with Godzilla – only it had been held in a giant washing machine set to maximum spin. You only get out of shit like that when you are at the absolute peak of physical condition, hence the runs around the Wattisham airbase, plus all the other daily workouts and the intense training.

I upped the pace as we hit the final leg of that morning's run, thanking the gods or the fates or whoever for getting me through China Lake in one piece. We surged as a pack through the lines of the Army Air Corps, Ben out front, his fur sleek and glistening, his fine muzzle leading the way. This early morning ritual was known as 'running the fence', and the Apache gunship pilots had long grown used to the Pathfinder Express Train steaming through.

Of the forty men on that morning's run, twelve were at Ready Status One (R1) – which meant they were able to deploy instantly on missions anywhere in the world. Another dozen were on R2, meaning they could deploy anywhere within twenty-four hours. The rest were on R3, which meant deployment within thirty-six. On R3 you could be on a training course or on leave, as long as you could get back to the base and be good to go within thirty-six hours.

After a steaming hot shower I came into the ops room to find Graham 'Wag' Wardle, our Ops Warrant Officer, glued to the phone. From the few words that I caught of the conversation I knew that something was up. Wag and me understood each other instinctively and were the best of mates, in spite of him forever needling me about having the world's biggest ears, and me going on about him having been hit real hard with the Ugly Stick.

Wag was short and stumpy with the body of a Hobbit. He hailed from Burnley, and spoke with a thick Lancashire accent. He was shaven-headed and a walking advertisement for the world's dodgiest tattoos: there wasn't one that wasn't misspelled, off-colour or misaligned. In short he looked and sounded like a football hooligan in uniform.

To make matters worse he wasn't the biggest fan of military freefall, which was the bread and butter of our business. I used to joke that Wag had been born with four left arms. What redeemed him was that he was a total stalwart. The Pathfinders was his life. Wag was hard, robust and fit, but his real gift lay in his powers of dynamic lateral thinking. In thinking the unthinkable Wag pretty much had no equal.

At thirty-seven years of age, he was also the 'old man' of the unit. I used to joke that I'd put myself through the Military Tandem Master's course purely so I could HALO Wag in on a mission, for he was never going to make a high-altitude low-opening jump on his own. That summed up the fierce, piss-taking rivalry between us, and under our guidance the X Platoon had thrived.

As Wag came off the phone I called over to him. 'Before you get started, mate, quick question.'

'Yeah, what?'

'How did you get to be so ugly with just the one head?'

'Fuck off, go play with Noddy, Big Ears . . .'

To the rear sat Captain Grant Harris, our 2iC, and by now his shoulders were rocking with laughter. I'd made Grant sit behind me, because in contrast to Wag he was the pin-up of the unit. A youthful twenty-six, Grant was blessed with classic dark good looks and he had the gorgeous girlfriend to go with it. I hated him for it, though only in jest. Still, Wag and me were forever ribbing Grant and hitting him with the wind-ups.

The slagging stopped just as soon as Wag gave us a heads-up on the phone call he'd just had. 1 PARA had been warned off for immediate deployment to some obscure African nation none of us had ever heard of before – *Sierra Leone*. Their mission was to make a last-ditch effort to evacuate British citizens from the nation's capital, which was under threat from a bunch of rebels threatening wholesale murder and mayhem.

None of us knew the slightest thing about where or what the country was exactly, except the obvious – that this was the dark, chaotic, war-torn heart of Africa. But the best news of all was this: 1 PARA's CO had asked for as many Pathfinders as we could spare to deploy on the mission.

When I'd started that morning's run I'd had not the slightest inkling that this might be in the offing. I hadn't even known we had a spot of trouble brewing in one of the ex-colonies. But needless to say this was a very pleasant surprise. It was a golden opportunity for the Pathfinders to get some operational action in a far-flung, war-blasted, benighted corner of the world.

Top news.

Eddie 'The White Rabbit' Newell, the Platoon's Colour Sergeant, joined us in the office. Like me and Wag, The White Rabbit was a long-serving member of the unit. His role as Colour Sergeant made him a glorified stores man, but it was a necessary stepping-stone to him getting Ops Warrant Officer, once Wag moved on. With his pale, spooky, almost albino look there was no guessing how Eddie had earned the nickname; his hair was as white as snow, and his skin looked as if it never got to see any sunlight.

The White Rabbit measured five-foot-ten, weighed 15 stone and worked out in the gym a lot, but he was known as something of a tortoise-like plodder on the runs. He was no speed athlete or racing snake, yet you'd be sure of Eddie always getting there in the end. He was the third unshakeable pillar of our outfit – one of a three-cornered pyramid formed by Wag, Eddie and me.

Along with Eddie, Captain Robert Donaldson, the Officer Commanding (OC) of our unit, pitched up. They were like beauty and the beast. Tall, suave, with swept-back blond hair, Donaldson had been OC Pathfinders for the past several months, and he was approaching the halfway point in his two-year posting.

From the very first Donaldson had reminded me of Prince Charming from the movie *Shrek*. Needless to say, he and I couldn't fail to rub each other up the wrong way. Early on I'd been sent away to do a two-month Arctic survival cadre with the Swedish Special Forces, plus some other elite units. By the time I'd returned Wag had confirmed my worst fears: the verdict of the men was that Donaldson was struggling to make the grade as the Pathfinders' OC.

A quiet tension simmered just below the surface whenever we were in the same room. But right now we put our differences to one side, for we had some urgent number crunching to do on the Sierra Leone mission. The twelve men on R1 couldn't deploy. They were on standby for emergencies that constituted a direct threat to the UK. Barring those who were sick or on training, that left twenty-seven Pathfinders ready and able to go.

I headed down to the Interest Room to brief the blokes. The moment the warning went out that we were about to deploy, we'd cut all communications with the outside world. We'd go into strict isolation, with no calls or emails allowed to wives, girlfriends or family. That morning fathers had kissed their kids goodbye and gone into work expecting it to be just another day. Now all of that was about to change. This could be the start of a six-month deployment – for that's what you signed up for when you joined the Pathfinders.

I started the briefing by outlining what we knew about the mission, which was pretty much bugger all. Then I dropped the bombshell – those who were and weren't going.

'R1 guys, you know who you are – you're staying. The rest of you fit and able blokes not on R1 – *get ready*.' I read out the list of names.

The sheer elation on the faces of the chosen was a picture. By contrast, those slated to be left behind instantly started trying to jockey for a position. I silenced the lot of them with a wave of the hand. Plenty of time for that after the briefing was over.

'Right, patrol commanders,' I continued. 'Get away and get some background on Sierra Leone. Get a bloke up to the Maps Room. Do we have 1:25,000 or 1:50,000 scale, or air maps only? You'll need another guy on the local flora and fauna, plus any climatic conditions that'll dictate what kit we take. Medics – I need to know about disease types, prophylactics, malaria, and if we have the right drugs to hand . . .'

The Pathfinder medics had all attended the Patrols Medics cadre – four weeks of intensive training on how to deal with gunshot and shrapnel wounds, plus whatever else might hit us in the types of terrain in which we operate. After that, they'd completed a six-week attachment in an Accident and Emergency unit at a hospital in the UK – dealing with cuts, lacerations, burns, breaks and the like. Finally, they'd done a stint at the Army Dental Corps, learning emergency dental work – chiefly how to use Cavit, a temporary, press-in filling that hardens in the mouth.

At our Wattisham base we had a fully-fledged medical store, complete with a safe stuffed full of morphine, so we could deploy with that to kill the pain of injuries. But with Sierra Leone being cloaked in dense, steamy jungle, it was sure to offer a plethora of venomous snakes, blood-sucking bugs and nasty tropical diseases that we needed to be ready for. No point deploying to war if we all went down with cerebral malaria the moment we set foot on the ground.

If a 1 PARA guy suffered a snakebite in the field, more often than not it could be treated at his headquarters. By contrast, we'd very likely be deployed deep in the jungle where there are no such luxuries. We had to be 100 per cent self-sufficient – hence the high level of medical training, and the kind of kit we had to carry on missions. While on operations we had to presume we could only treat ourselves with what we carried on our persons.

We'd also need water purification kits, to cope with extended periods spent drinking from rivers. We'd need water purification kits such as Millbank bags, plus machetes and mosquito nets. The signallers would need to work out the right radio antennae for use under the deep-jungle canopy, likely battery life in such conditions, and how to keep such delicate kit dry and workable.

The list went on and on.

I finished my briefing with this. 'Right, we basically know bugger all about this deployment. I want blokes running down every rabbit hole exploring every possibility, so we have all kit possible good to go ... Everything else stops. Get on it and get it done.'

I had barely finished speaking when the first dissenter grabbed me. It was Roger Holt, a cracking soldier who'd taken an injury during a recent stint of training, which meant he was off the list to deploy.

'Mate, get me on it,' he begged. 'I don't care if I'm injured – with morphine and a bandage I'll muddle through.'

Our unit is a meritocracy. Those who lead do so by dint of their experience, skills and ability, regardless of rank. Everything's done on first name terms, and it's the lack of formality and Regular Army bullshit that draws a particular kind of soldier to the Pathfinders. There is no better foundation on which to build an unbreakable *esprit de corps*.

I told Holty I appreciated his fighting spirit, but he was too badly injured and he'd have to sit this one out. He gave me a look like he'd just been given a death sentence. I knew how he was feeling: a mission such as this one came along seldom, if ever, in most soldiers' lifetimes.

As blokes bolted from the room, I caught the expressions on their faces. Those who were single were buzzing. This was the chance for what they craved most – *operational action*. But for the married guys it was all just starting to sink in. It was a Friday, and God only knew what they'd got planned for the weekend. Instead, they were about to disappear with barely a word to their families. Needless to say, being a Pathfinder wasn't a recipe for a long and happy marriage.

The chirpiest bloke seemed to be H. Lance Corporal Joe 'H' Harrison – also known as 'Tackleberry', a gun-toting, shit-kicking redneck in the *Police Academy* movie series – was young, free and single. He was already counting the beer tokens, for we'd be spending nothing while out in deepest, darkest Africa. Or maybe H was dreaming about what new guns he could buy with all the money he'd save up while we were away.

H was five-foot-eleven and had a rock-hard physique, topped off with the Freddie Mercury shaven-headed droopy-moustache look. Most of the time he'd wander around base wearing nothing but a pair of shorts and a couple of belts of shotgun ammo wrapped around his person. He only seemed to own one set of 'going out' clothes – a pair of battered jeans, plus a faded green bomber jacket. Where others might buy a new set of threads, H would invest in a new gun magazine, and his room was stacked high with them.

Like many of the vagabond collection of misfits that made up our unit, H had a wicked sense of humour. Hailing from Doncaster, he spoke with a thick Yorkshire drawl. He spunked all his money on guns, gun mags and real ale, and normally he couldn't afford to drink beyond happy hour. This deployment might change all of that – at least for the few short days immediately after he got back from the mission.

H was also a superlative operator. He was a L96 AW sniper rifle guru, and the most accomplished shot in the unit. He was fit, hard and totally reliable, plus he was a demon with the general purpose machine gun (GPMG). When operating the GPMG, H was known as the 'Death Dealer'. If it all went tits-up he was the bloke you wanted by your side.

H was thick as thieves with Corporal Nathan 'Nathe' Bell, his patrol commander. Nathe was a short, stocky turnip farmer from Lincolnshire. He'd had his front teeth knocked out while playing rugby, and he wore false ones, which added a slight lisp to his slow, country bumpkin 'aarg-aarg-aarg' accent. Nathe had a boyish, prankster sense of humour. His party trick was to drop his false teeth into your glass when you weren't looking, so when you drained your pint all was revealed.

Nasty.

Nathe and H were like Laurel and Hardy. They permanently ripped the piss out of each other, but they were actually the best of mates. As two blokes heading up a Pathfinder patrol they were about as good as it gets – though it hadn't always been that way.

As a young lad on selection Nathe had missed the final checkpoint on Endurance, due to horrendous weather conditions. Being unable to pinpoint his location, we'd launched the safety procedure, which included calling out the mountain rescue team. The 'lost procedure' for those on Endurance was to head for the A470 Brecon to Merthyr Tydfil road, and tab towards the nearest checkpoint. En route Nathe had managed to find a friendly local farmer, who'd allowed him to make a call to alert us to his location.

Finally, we'd found him sitting by a roaring fire in the farmer's cottage, tucking into a bowl of his wife's finest home-made soup. From such memorable beginnings Nathe had risen to his position of patrol command admirably, becoming a superlative operator, and with H as his right-hand man he ran a tight, unshakeable unit.

The Pathfinders' numeric call-sign is *33* – so as HQ patrol, Wag, The White Rabbit, Grant and me were *33*. Nathe and H's patrol was *33 Alpha* – so the lead patrol – with the others being *33 Bravo*, *33 Charlie* and so on. Whatever shit we might be heading into in Sierra Leone, I'd put *33 Alpha* at our point of greatest vulnerability, for I had absolute confidence in them. H was extremely capable and I knew he could take over patrol command if anything happened to Nathe.

In preparation for the coming mission Grant, Wag and me broke down the blokes into four fighting patrols – with a patrol commander, a sniper, a demolitions expert and a lead scout, plus a medic and a signaller in each. That done we tried to garner some bigger picture ground truth. First off, we needed to know where the hell Sierra Leone was and what was the best weaponry to take, and whether we'd be able to use the vehicles.

Our *raison d'être* being behind enemy lines ops, that was how we had to figure Command would use us in Sierra Leone – *that's if we got used*. We needed to know the type of terrain over which we'd be operating, and the possible means of insertion. Would we be going in by helicopter, or on foot, or by HALO or HAHO means? It wouldn't be via HAPLSS, that was for sure, for we'd yet to perfect HAPLSS for use on operations.

Right now this was an 'Operation Blind' – we were preparing to deploy with next to zero Intel, and little sense of who the enemy might be, or their number or capabilities. All we knew was that it was a non-combatant evacuation operation (an NEO) and from that alone the five of us – me, Wag, Grant, The White Rabbit and the OC – tried to work up potential scenarios.

We might be inserted into the jungle to overlook named areas of interest (NAIs); in other words, positions from which rebel attacks might be expected. We might be sent forward as an early warning force, to watch for a rebel advance. With British and allied nationals needing to be evacuated from the capital, we had to presume the rebels were poised to seize it, so we might well be tasked to call in air power or artillery, raining down death on the bad guys.

Having scoped out our likely tasks, we figured we'd need specialist observation post (OP) kit – like SOFIE thermal imaging sights, night vision goggles and GPS units, plus infrared fireflies and TACBE emergency comms beacons in case we were forced to go on the run through the jungle. The list of goodies being drawn up by The White Rabbit just kept getting longer, as we tried to think of every potential piece of kit we needed to unearth from the stores.

The Pathfinders' armourer, Pete Brewster, was busy racking up a growing pile of the kind of hardware we might need when fighting in thick tropical bush. Trouble was, he had bugger all Intel to go on. Did the rebels have armour? If so, did we need LAW 80s – our 94 mm shoulder-launched light anti-armour weapons? Did the rebels have heavy machine guns? If so, we'd need the wagons with their vehicle-mounted .50 calibre Brownings to answer their firepower.

Ideally the 50-cal isn't used against human targets. The GPMG is the weapon of choice against advancing troops – used properly, it rakes down their number. The 50-cal has a slower, thumping rate of fire, and we'd normally use it with armour-piercing explosive incendiary rounds – perfect against soft-skinned or light armoured vehicles, optics or radio antennae, thermal imaging kit, satellite dishes, brick buildings and command and control nodes, and out to 1800 metres range.

It was midday when we got the call to deploy via road to the Air Mounting Centre (AMC), at South Cerney, near Cirencester – the muster point for all British military operations going out by air. There we presumed we'd get issued with our ammo and food rations, plus extra mission-essential kit prior to departure.

Heading to the AMC didn't mean that the mission was totally a 'go'. We could still get stood down. It was never actually happening until you dived out of the aircraft over the drop zone, or drove over the border into hostile terrain.

But this sure took us one big step closer to going in.

3

The modern day Pathfinders was formed in the mid-1980s to perform a role that was seen as lacking in the British Army: covert insertion deep behind enemy lines to recce drop zones and guide in the main force, and for capture, sabotage or direct-action missions. While the SAS and SBS (Special Boat Service) are trained for such tasks, their remit is multifaceted: they have to be ready to perform sneaky-beaky espionage, hostage rescue and anti-terrorist and anti-insurgent missions, plus a host of other taskings.

A guy in the SAS's Air Troop – their airborne ops specialists – has to master all disciplines required of him, which means he has limited time to train for airborne missions. Our role being purely behind enemy lines ops, we'd be doing six HALO jumps to his one, and that simple fact makes us unbeatable at what we do.

In part due to its 'black' nature, the Pathfinders has a more fluid, opaque kind of identity than Special Forces, but with that comes real downsides. Black status means no official budget. Typically, the MOD want an elite asset without having to pay for it. That means we have to fight tooth and nail for any specialist kit, training or weaponry that we need. We don't always get it – just as the Sierra Leone mission was about to prove.

Recently, we'd taken to signing off our comms with the piss-taking acronym: PF PL SFOW PMSAS. It stands for 'Pathfinder Platoon; Special Forces Or What; Poor Man's Special Air Service'. I'd done so once with a brigadier. He'd come to pay us a visit at our Wattisham base, riding his flame-red Ducati and dressed in a full set of leathers.

I'd greeted him with this: 'Sir, welcome to PF PL SFOW PMSAS.'
'Erm . . . sorry?' he'd said, shaking his head in bemusement.

I'd spelled it out for him and he'd taken it in pretty good humour.

As with all our operations, we'd deploy to Sierra Leone wearing no unit flashes or marks of rank, or anything that might identify us as an elite British military outfit. We'd sanitise ourselves still further, removing anything that might give away who we were, or what country we hailed from: photos of family, wallets, clothing brand labels, ID documents of any sort – all of it would have to go, just in case any of us got captured or killed by the enemy.

Our unit had only recently returned from a lengthy deployment to Kosovo. Tony Blair was in power, and he'd made no secret of his desire to wage 'righteous wars', as he saw them. In due course Sierra Leone would become known as 'Blair's War' – and we were about to head to Africa with no clearance to do so other than a private nod from the British prime minister.

The commanding officer of 1 PARA, Colonel Paul 'Gibbo' Gibson, had led the Kosovo mission, winning the DSO for it. He'd made a ballsy move now by launching the deployment to Sierra Leone – getting an entire British battle group, Pathfinders included, under way pretty much on the fly. He'd as good as told us he had no clear authority to move to the Air Mounting Centre, but we were going anyway, 'cause it got us one step closer to going in.

'Let's just do it,' Gibbo had told us. 'Let's just go. Get yourselves down there, Pathfinders.'

I'd barely had time to say goodbye to Ben before we swung out of our Wattisham base and hit the road. Heaping his bowl with dog-biscuits, I'd promised him I'd be back home as soon as, and in truth I'd have loved to be taking him with us. There would have been nothing better than my rock-hard chocolate Lab to give the rebels a good bite on the arse – though I had a sneaking suspicion Ben was more of a lover than a fighter kind of a dog.

Scores of military vehicles were now en route to the AMC – our open-topped Land Rovers and Pinzgauer all-wheel-drive vehicles amongst them – without anyone knowing we were on our way. Normally, some 800 men at arms undertaking a road move to deploy requires clearance from HQ Land. It requires an escort of Military Police, for live ammo is in transit, and it needs rakes of formal permissions. Colonel Gibson had had to work around all of that. Recognising that hundreds of British citizens were on the verge of getting chopped to pieces or kidnapped, he'd found the means to get the mission under way.

It was typical Gibbo: decisive action in a very unclear and fast-moving situation.

Gibbo had his priorities dead right.

Taking the bull by the horns.

Respect.

The colonel was tall, skinny and gaunt, with the physique of a long-distance runner. I'd served under him in Kosovo, and at first I hadn't warmed to him much. But with time Gibbo had proved that he knew how to play the game, and Kosovo had ended up being very good for all of us. The 1 PARA battle group had acquitted itself well, and I'd developed a grudging respect for the man. He could make gutsy, timely decisions; he was not a ditherer. His calls might be right or wrong, but either way they were timely – which was about all you could ask of a senior commander. Right now he was riding the crest of a wave, and with the Sierra Leone op we were going to have to ride it with him.

It was dusk by the time we reached South Cerney and we had to bluff our way onto the base. Normally the guard at the main gate would be told what was on its way. But right now a massive military convoy had turned up from out of the blue, and the poor corporal had not the faintest idea of what was happening. We sat in this humongous queue that snaked along a leafy country lane, as the guy tried to make up his mind whether to let us in or not.

He stood in front of the barrier with one-hundred-plus vehicles ranged before him, pumping out the diesel fumes. By now it was getting dark, and the headlights wound into the distance as far as the eye could see. Gibbo fixed the hapless bloke with a gimlet eye. The corporal quailed under the colonel's stare, eyes flicking nervously to his clipboard – like somehow he'd missed the fact that an entire battle group was scheduled to come through his gate that very evening.

'Son, open the barrier.'

No one was about to naysay Gibbo. The convoy was let through.

South Cerney is only fully staffed when there's an official airmove under way. Right now it was like a ghost town: there was no one to organise the chaos. The 1 PARA convoy got itself seriously gridlocked on the tarmac that lies between the main hangar and the runway. That done, Gibbo got the 1 PARA lads into the massive hangar and lined up by company: B, C and D in three rows, the blokes' kit piled beside them. The poor lads from A Company were on exercises in Jamaica, so they were missing out on this mission.

On the far side was the so-called 'black hangar' where we would normally gather in isolation, along with any other elite units that might be mustering. But right now the black hangar was locked, so we parked up on the approach road and kipped down beside the vehicles. I was hoping for a proper briefing on the coming deployment, but it turned out that the British military had no one on the ground in Sierra Leone. The Pathfinders were likely to be first-in, and consequently there wasn't much that anyone could tell us.

It's the Pathfinders' role to get in on the ground early and establish an intelligence picture – that way you risk sending in a few good men, as opposed to an entire battalion. Even so, it would have been nice to know the basics – the size of the rebel force we were up against, their level of training and operational capability, their weaponry, and their positions in relation to the nation's capital.

Unfortunately, no one seemed to know a thing.

HMG had been caught with her proverbial pants down.

In fact, the entire force now preparing to deploy had no maps of any sort – apart from the few that we had managed to grab from our Maps Room. There were no photos of the rebels or their bases, there was no aerial or satellite surveillance, and little info on the enemy's make-up or likely modus operandi. Worse still, no one had any food rations *or even any ammo*, because no formal orders had been given to issue any.

Each of us had packed a 'follow-on' bag, one that contained goodies to leave at a forward operating base: books, PT kit, iPods, snacks and so on. We broke out whatever scoff we had in those and got a brew going on our foldable 'hexy' stoves – ones that burn solid hexamine fuel blocks similar to firelighters. But there was sod all we could do about the lack of ammo.

No bullets with which to go to war.

It was a typical Army SNAFU – Situation Normal All Fucked Up.

Captain Donaldson, our OC, was in and out of conference with Colonel Gibson. Predictably, the mission was 'on', 'off', 'on', 'off' all night long. The rest of us got our heads down as best we could. It was the golden rule of good soldiering – always grab the chance of a feed or a sleep.

At around dawn The White Rabbit shook everyone awake, telling us there was a scoff-on in the cookhouse. From somewhere the South Cerney boys had managed to rustle up some food and someone to cook it. The queue circled several times around the cookhouse, and we were two hours waiting in line. It was like being on a conveyor belt: fifteen minutes to get as big a plate of fried bread and eggs swimming in grease down you as possible, before you were spat out the door so some hairy-arsed PARA could take your seat.

Shortly after loading up on the grease and the carbs we were given the news we'd all been waiting for: our lot would be on the first flight to Sierra Leone. We were to go in 'light order' – personal weapons, belt kit and Bergens, and no vehicles. And still we hadn't been issued with any ammo. We joked that maybe it was a good thing. Our main weapon was the SA80, a universally reviled assault rifle of sorts. When loaded, it could pose as much danger to the user as to the enemy.

The SA80 suffered from any number of horrendous faults. Worst of all was the habit the magazine had of falling off. The SA80-A1 had the magazine release button set just above the magazine housing. Because of the location and the fact that it was raised a good inch, all you had to do was go into a tight fire position and the release button would get accidentally hit, at which moment the magazine would fall to the ground, spewing out the rounds.

We joked that this was why we hadn't been issued with any ammo for Sierra Leone – so we couldn't go wasting it. But in truth, being lumbered with the SA80 wasn't very funny.

It was unbelievably prone to rust, especially around the moving parts that force the rounds into the breech. If the air was moisture-laden – if there was fog or mist even – those parts would rust up before your very eyes. Not good when we were about to deploy to a jungle with one of the highest annual rainfalls on earth. With the two main rivals – the M16 and the AK47 – if any dirt or rust got into them it would rarely prevent the internal parts from working. With the SA80 one speck would jam it every time.

As if that wasn't enough the SA80 had a safety catch that wasn't fit for purpose: it kept getting knocked one way or the other accidentally. Worse still, the weapon couldn't be operated left-handed. The cocking handle was positioned so it could only be used by a right-handed person, as opposed to the M16 or AK, which are either-handed. Once we'd been issued with the SA80 all the Pathfinders who were lefties – and we had a good number of 'em – were forced to retrain so they could shoot cack-handed, as far as they saw it.

From its earliest beginnings our unit had been issued with the M16, the superlative American assault rifle. The M16 knocks the socks off the SA80, as does the AK47. But over time our M16s had become old and worn. When we'd lobbied to get replacements we were told we were getting the SA80 instead. It was just one more example of the downside of not being part of UKSF: the SAS and SBS had a lightweight, gucci variant of the M16. We Pathfinders got lumbered with the SA80.

The SA80 was designed and built by Royal Ordnance at a cost of £850 per rifle. At the same time the M16 was actually being produced in the UK under licence at £150 a throw, but somehow the MOD had felt it better to saddle us – plus the rest of the British Army – with a costly crock of shit like the SA80.

So it was that we boarded the ageing RAF Tristars to go to war in Sierra Leone with zero ammo and decidedly dodgy assault rifles. In spite of this our morale was sky-high. Every man amongst us wanted this mission. It was an operational deployment. A combat tasking. It was a chance to get our hands dirty, to put into practice all of our specialist skills and knowledge, and to test ourselves for real against the enemy.

It was about as good as it got.

I appreciated what a blinding move Colonel Gibson had pulled here. By getting all of 1 PARA plus a good number of the Pathfinders gathered at South Cerney he'd forced the MOD's hand. As much as anything else, the force of warriors now boarding the Tristars was Gibbo and the PM's Trojan Horse. With the rebels poised to chop up a large number of British nationals, the MOD had had no option but to give us the green light. The media would have had a feeding frenzy if it had leaked out that a force such as ours had been poised to fly to the Brits' aid, but had been stood down by the penny-pinching bean counters at the MOD.

I was certain the SAS and SBS would also be deploying, though hopefully we would pip them to the post. The Sierra Leone capital, Freetown, was a hub of MI6 activity, from where they were monitoring drug-runners, Al Qaeda operatives and the trade in uncut diamonds. Al Qaeda were known to have a growing interest in so-called 'conflict diamonds' – those mined from war zones

– for money-laundering purposes, turning their dollar millions into untraceable, raw stones.

British Embassy staff – and agents from our Secret Intelligence Service – were going to be at risk if the rebels overran the Sierra Leonean capital. US nationals were bound to be working alongside the Brits, and they would be equally threatened. Securing or evacuating the British diplomatic mission was a classic SAS tasking, so the boys from Hereford were bound to deploy. It had now become a race to see which unit would get boots on the ground soonest, and be first into the action.

After a six-hour flight the Tristar touched down on a sun-blasted runway fringed with dilapidated terminal buildings and feathery palm trees. As yet we still had no ammo, so it was hardly as if we could bomb-burst out of the aircraft ready to unleash hell. In truth, I'd slept most of the flight and as we tumbled down the steps of the Tristar I had no idea where on earth we'd landed, and neither it seemed did anyone else.

This operation was moving at such a speed we were going faster than the information envelope – not to mention the ammo. We figured the Tristars wouldn't have put down in the heart of the Sierra Leone jungle, so we were likely in a transit point. But Kenya, Mauritania, Uganda – it could have been just about anywhere in Africa. Then someone spotted a sign above the control tower announcing this to be 'Dakar Airport'. Someone else figured out that Dakar was the capital of Senegal, a neighbouring West African country of Sierra Leone.

Senegal: that's where we were.

To our left two C-130K Hercules transport aircraft were turning and burning, turbines thrashing in the hot, breathless air. We were ordered to mount up the right-hand side of the two aircraft, so we sprinted across the runway with machetes in one hand and assault rifles in the other – leaving someone else to bring on our Bergens. The C-130 ramp whined closed, the turbines spooled up to speed, and we were airborne once more.

Still we had no ammo, but at least we'd got a steer as to our next destination. As we'd rushed aboard the Hercules, the aircraft's loadmaster had told us we were heading for an airfield called Lungi, which was on the coast of Sierra Leone. Other than that we had not the slightest clue what we were flying into here.

For what felt like an age the C-130 roared across the jungle low and fast, before I finally felt the lurch and the thump as it touched down. The top half of the ramp was already open, and I could see a baking hot stretch of tarmac out of the aircraft's rear, fringed by a thick, impenetrable-looking wall of green – the jungle.

The aircraft slowed, and we did a classic tactical air landing operation (TALO) – bursting out of the ramp and peeling off to either side of the still-moving warplane. By the time the twenty-seven of us Pathfinders – plus the forty-odd 1 PARA lads with us – were on the ground, the C-130 was accelerating again and was very quickly airborne.

It was midday by now, and the heat hit us like a furnace.

We made for the shallow ditches that flanked either side of the runway. I'd gone left and found myself facing a mass of brooding, tangled vegetation some fifty yards away. Wag had gone right, so towards the dilapidated and sagging airport terminal building. With bugger all ammo there was precious little we could do if the rebels were poised to smash us, but at least we looked the part.

The second Hercules came in tight on the back of us, disgorging an extra sixty PARAs. All of C Company, 1 PARA, was now on the ground, plus us lot.

I scanned the airport. There was the odd African soldier wandering about, wearing the light blue beret of a United Nations peacekeeper, plus one or two airport officials dripping in braid. There was even the one civvie airliner crouched on the baking hot runway, with passengers preparing to board. This was Sierra Leone's main hub, it seemed, and it was still in use by those trying to flee the rebel advance.

Colonel Gibson marched over to the terminal building and took command. The locals were staring at him with this slack-jawed expression, like he'd just beamed down from the Planet Zog. The airport terminal was a mass of drooping fans, broken conveyor belts and sagging plastic chairs. Gibbo seized the annexe to the fire station as his ops and briefing room, one of the few vaguely clean and functioning parts of the airport.

Within thirty minutes he had things up and running. Wag, The White Rabbit, Grant, Donaldson and me – the Pathfinders' head-shed – joined him. Gibbo ordered us to fan out onto the main tracks leading through the jungle, to get eyes-on possible routes of rebel advance. Luckily, a C-130 had just landed with a – very limited – supply of ammo, and each Pathfinder was to grab his allotted share: two mags, so sixty rounds per man.

It left us with nothing for our secondary weapons – our Browning pistols – or for our heaviest firepower, the GPMGs. But some ammo was better than no ammo at all. From somewhere a white United Nations Toyota pick-up truck had been requisitioned, to ferry us into the jungle.

'The truck will drop patrols at positions no more than two kilometres out,' Donaldson briefed us, putting some flesh on Gibbo's basic orders. 'I need *Alpha*, *Bravo*, *Charlie* and *Delta* at points west to northeast on the northern side of the runway. If the rebels are out there, that's the direction from which they'll try to hit us.'

The UN vehicle ferried us out of the airport and into the jungle. Donaldson, The White Rabbit and Wag were staying put to form our HQ element, so I set out with Grant plus four others, to form our command patrol in the field. After leaving the airport by the southern gate, we hit a dirt track lined with ramshackle stalls selling bunches of bananas, mangoes, battered cans of Fanta and sun-bleached packs of Winston cigarettes.

We drove for a good few minutes, skirting the southern edge of the runway, and the habitation petered out. We turned north into the deserted bush, following a dirt track maybe ten feet wide, hemmed in on both sides by a thick wall of jungle. We followed that track until we hit the main road leading north from the capital city, Freetown, into the country's interior. This was the Sierra Leonean equivalent of the M1, but it consisted of little more than a hard-packed gravel road maybe fifty feet wide.

We were the last patrol out and it was approaching dusk by the time we were dropped at our destination. After waiting for the UN vehicle to leave, we pushed into the jungle until we were one hundred metres or so off the main highway. From there we could get eyes-on the dirt road without being seen.

The highway had been carved out of the virgin jungle – a sandy-yellow slash cut right through it. Our mission as delineated by Gibbo was to report on any movement seen – but what movement exactly? No one doubted that the capital was under threat of rebel mayhem, but right now life seemed to be continuing pretty much as normal. There would doubtless be goat-boys, cow-herders, market traders and others moving on the road, and we had zero idea of how to differentiate the civvies from the rebels.

Colonel Gibson had only C Company plus us lot in-country, so around 125 lightly-armed soldiers. He was at his most vulnerable, for C Company had not yet had the chance to dig in and get fully armed-up, or to form any meaningful defensive positions around the airport. With an entire battalion scheduled to fly in, Gibbo would get 600 1 PARA blokes on the ground, plus 125 from 2 PARA who were coming in alongside them.

That would be a force to be reckoned with.

But right now he had 125 British soldiers in-country, and the rebels were rumoured to number in their thousands. None of us had the slightest idea what they looked like, or what might mark them out as rebels. Did they wear any form of uniform, such as armbands, a rebel flash, a badge, a logo, or any specific type of headgear?

Gibbo must have realised just what he'd flown into here, and that now was the point of maximum threat. He needed someone out there in the jungle as his early warning, in case the rebels made a rapid move on the airport.

And for better or worse, we were it.

4

We settled into our positions, each of us belly-down under the forest canopy, facing the road. Darkness comes quickly in the jungle. With it, the hordes of biting insects arrive – which right here and now included ravenous mosquitoes, eerily pulsating fireflies, and these giant flying beetles that kept cannoning into our heads, ones that we quickly nicknamed 'basher-beetles'.

I lay on the dark, musty forest floor in nothing but my combats, the scent of rot and decay seeping into my nostrils. I could feel the mozzies feasting on my blood as they forced their tiny insect jaws through my trousers and shirtsleeves and drilled into me. What made it all the more frustrating was that we'd yet to be issued with any anti-malaria pills. We knew which ones we'd needed, but no one had managed to get their hands on any prior to leaving the UK.

Still, at least we were out on active operations, and it was great to know we were first into the country ahead of any other British force.

'Any idea what's happening?' I whispered to Grant. 'What we're looking for?'

'Not a sausage, mate,' came the hushed reply.

As the darkness thickened around us even our night vision goggles (NVGs) couldn't help much. Come sundown the light level beneath the jungle canopy quickly drops to nothing. NVGs work by collecting and boosting ambient light, but with next to no illumination filtering through the vegetation above us they were barely able to function. They offered at best an unclear, wavy, fuzzy vision of the highway – little better than using the mark one human eyeball.

As far as we could tell there was zero movement out on the road anyway. Come last light everything seemed to have stopped. There were no cars, trucks, people, animals or anything. If we could have taken away the deafening beat of the insects – the rhythmic *preeep-preeep-preeep* of the cicadas above all – it would have been eerily silent. I could only presume that the rebels preferred to operate at night, so everything else stopped during the hours of darkness.

Technically speaking, what we'd formed here was a DPP – a defensive perimeter post – as opposed to a standard OP. An OP is there to observe and report; a DPP is there to observe, report and engage and fight if necessary. If we spotted any rebel movement, doubtless Gibbo would order us to slow them down as much as we possibly could, bearing in mind our tiny number – four patrols of six Pathfinders, so twenty-four men in all – plus our pitiful supply of ammo.

As I lay there in the hot and humid darkness, being eaten alive by the mozzies, I reflected on when any of us lot had last got a good feed. After fried eggs and bread that morning at South Cerney, our only other meal had been a butty box on the Tristar. Mine had consisted of a couple of soggy cheese sarnies, a packet of prawn cocktail flavour crisps, a Kit Kat and a can of Panda Cola – the cornerstones of any British Army nutritional meal. The growling in my stomach would have been audible from the bloody road, were it not for the cacophony of the insects.

Still, I loved being in the jungle. I always have. Generally speaking, it's love or hate at first sight with such terrain. As Pathfinders we'd done rakes of jungle training, and we'd tailored our tropical kit to just such a theatre of operations as this.

Each of us was wearing a very weird-looking set of headgear. The nearest you'd ever get to it in the civvie world is a beekeeper's helmet. It's basically a head-and-neck mozzie net. You pull it on like a giant sock, the fine-mesh netting bagging out around the face and fastening via elastic around the neck. We'd slapped insect repellent cream on any exposed skin, plus our combat trousers were tucked into jungle boots, to stop leeches, ants or other nasties crawling up our legs and doing damage to our manhood.

But none of this could stop the mozzies getting lock-on and chewing through our clothing – and the mosquitoes here in Sierra Leone were monsters. I could see them circling around me like mini Apache gunships, each intent on wreaking blood-sucking, disease-ridden mayhem. It wasn't as if I could keep swatting whenever I felt a bite. The golden rule of such DPP work is to remain absolutely still and silent, so as to observe the enemy without being seen.

I glanced at Grant. 'Nice here, innit, mate? We've got sixty rounds per man, we're being eaten alive, and our last feed was a butty box back on the Tristars . . . '

Grant's teeth grinned white in the faint moonlight. He eyed me through the fuzz of his mozzie net. 'They can't keep us out here forever. If we don't get eaten to death we'll bloody starve . . .'

Come daybreak we'd seen practically nothing, and certainly no movement of armed men out on the road. We needed to get a report radioed into HQ, and dawn was the time to make our first regular 'Sched' – scheduled radio call. When out on operations our patrol – headquarters – was supposed to make two daily Scheds, one at dawn and one at dusk. If we missed a Sched, that was the trigger for HQ to consider us compromised and on the run.

Miraculously, our signaller, Neil 'Tricky' Dick, managed to get a radio call through to headquarters pretty much on the first attempt. We reported what we'd seen, or rather the lack of it.

It was a marvel that Tricky had got the comms up and running amongst the thick tropical vegetation, but he was pure genius with such kit. The only way to set up our archaic Clansman 319 high frequency (HF) radios was to tie a length of string onto the end of a flexible wire aerial, fix a rock onto the string and hurl it into the treetops. When the forest canopy was up to a hundred feet or more above us that took some doing.

I'd once been on a joint exercise in the US with American elite forces. We'd been inserted via HALO parachute drop alongside a unit of Marine Corps Force Recon operators. Our mission was to mark a drop zone (DZ) for the largest airborne force parachuted by NATO since the Second World War. We'd made the long tab into the DZ, during which one of our sister units, a Navy SEAL team, had a guy badly mauled by an alligator.

When we finally got eyes-on the DZ, we prepared to radio in reports to our respective headquarters. The Force Recon signaller pressed a button on his lightweight radio backpack, flipped out a helix antenna – a collapsible, space-age dish-like aerial – and within a matter of seconds his commander was able to call in his report. By the time he was done Tricky was still trying to hurl his rock into the nearest tree, to snag a branch.

It was all the more reason to be thankful for having a guy like him with us here in Sierra Leone. A trustworthy and totally solid operator, Tricky never let the shit state of the comms kit get to him. It was all just a challenge to his ultimate professionalism.

Tricky hailed from 216 Signals Squadron, a specialist communications unit, so he was an absolute master at his chosen discipline. Pathfinder Selection is open to any soldier regardless of unit or rank. Although 216 Signals isn't a fighting outfit as such, Tricky was still a hard-as-nails operator. Five-foot-ten and blond, he was good-looking in a tough, Jason Statham-lookalike way. He could drink like a fish, smoke like a chimney and run like the wind. He loved a punch-up, but he was a thinking man's scrapper. He'd analyse a fight carefully before wading in.

Tricky was cat-like, agile and cool – a float like a butterfly, sting like a bee kind of an operator. No one ever heard or saw him coming. If I was forced to go on the run here in Sierra Leone I'd most likely choose to do so with him. Wag would get you out in the end, but Tricky would do so quickly, stealthily and in style.

Orders from Gibbo were to return to headquarters, for a re-tasking. By the time we got back there, Lungi Airport had become like a mini version of London Heathrow. Hercs were flying a relay of further men and *matériel* from Senegal. By now we'd got eight flights in, and already they were taking out the NEOs – the first British and allied civilians to be evacuated from the war-torn country.

Those who'd realised what was about to happen – that Free-town was on the verge of being overrun by thousands of rebels who had the darkest, most savage reputation of any in the world right then – had made their own way to Lungi Airport, planning to jump on whatever flight might be available to anywhere other than here. They were being shovelled onto the Hercs as fast as possible and flown out to Dakar.

To either end of the runway I could see the 1 PARA lads digging in, as they formed proper defensive positions. At the furthest western end of the runway I spotted a small vehicle-mounted unit setting up what had to be a separate, discreet base. I knew instinctively it had to be the lads from the SAS or the SBS, or maybe both of them.

It turned out it was the SAS. I knew a bunch of them, as did some of the other 'old and bold.' They drove past us in their Pinkies – lightweight, open-topped Land Rovers, similar to the ones we had been ordered to leave behind in the UK – and there was the odd wave and yelled greeting between us. We'd beaten them into the country, but now the lads from the Regiment were here it was going to be a race to see who got tasked with the first and the best of whatever missions were going.

Stacked to one side of the terminal building was a pile of British Army ration packs, so we made sure to grab some of those. That done we got issued with our first operational maps – 1:50,000 scale, showing Lungi Airport and the surrounding terrain. There were only enough for one per patrol, but that didn't stop the blokes from getting down to some serious map study and ground orientation.

In the Pathfinders, navigation is a collective art. Every man on a patrol has to know exactly where he is at any time, so as to be able to take the initiative if the patrol commander gets hit, or a patrol gets split up. Using the maps we did our first IPB – Intelligence Preparation of the Battlefield – noting key ground and vital terrain, defensive positions, routes to and from those defensive positions, likely avenues of enemy approach, possible routes of escape, and ambush points along the way.

That done, Wag, Grant, Donaldson and me got called in for mission briefing. It was given by Lewis Carson, the 1 PARA Operations Officer, and a former 2iC of the Pathfinders. It was no secret that Lewis was angling for Donaldson's job, once Donaldson had finished his two-year stint. I for one couldn't wait for him to take over. He'd proved himself a superlative operator when he'd served with us as 2iC, commanding the respect of all the men bar none.

Lewis's brief was punchy and to the point. If anything it reinforced just how little we knew: the rebels were closing in on Freetown; there was a very real fear of looting, horrific rapes and massacres if they seized the city; all British passport holders and citizens of 'allied nations' – Americans, Europeans, Aussies, Kiwis and Canadians – were to be evacuated from the country as soon as.

All of that was pretty much as we knew it. But Lewis did have one vital new element of Intel for us. Apparently, the rebels had heard about the arrival of British forces in-country, and they were determined to 'take' Lungi Airport and drive us out – and that meant that our primary objective had to be to hold it.

But for the Pathfinders mission priorities were about to change dramatically. Apparently, no one was available to secure the British Embassy or evacuate its staff – despite that being a classic SAS tasking. Hence we were to be airlifted across to Freetown, on the far side of the Freetown Estuary, in order to do so.

On hearing this we were lit up. It sure beat lying in the jungle starving hungry and getting munched on by ravenous insects, with not a rebel fighter in sight. But for some reason it didn't seem as if Donaldson shared our joy at the coming tasking.

'I really can't see the need for us,' he announced, from out of nowhere. 'I've spoken to the CO, and I've told him I don't understand the need for the Pathfinders. There's no real task for us, and we have training commitments back in the UK, and that's where we should be right now. We're wasting valuable training time and I've told the CO as much.'

Wag and I caught each other's eye. I could see the disbelief written across his features. Even Grant was struggling to hide his frustration at what he'd just heard. But as usual it was left up to me – mouthy old Smoggy, reliably blunt to the point of rudeness – to voice our collective disquiet.

'What d'you mean, boss – *we should be in the UK, training*? We're on ops here. This is an operational deployment to a war zone. This is what we live, eat, breathe and train for.'

'Smoggy's right, boss, we need to stay,' Wag added. 'We need to stay 'cause who knows what the next few hours and days may bring.'

Every bloke in the unit knew where we needed to be right now – mixing it here in Sierra Leone. But Donaldson seemed to have his mind set on getting us back to the UK, regardless. He left to go speak with Gibbo some more, leaving Wag, Grant, The White Rabbit and me to talk it over. We agreed to keep a close eye on him. If he tried doing the unthinkable and getting us off this deployment, then Donaldson would have to be stopped.

Two Chinooks from the Special Forces Flight had arrived in-country, after a truly epic journey out from the UK. They'd set out from RAF Odiham under their own steam, the UK military lacking any aircraft large enough to fly them out to theatre (C-17 Globemasters, or the equivalent). The aircrew had flown out, refuelling en route, via France, Spain, North Africa and into

West Africa. It was a 4800-kilometre flight, and it would turn out to be the longest self-deployment by helos in British military history.

We mounted up those newly-arrived Chinooks and were whisked across the water to the nation's ramshackle capital, Freetown. We touched down at the Mammy Yoko Hotel, which had been designated the rallying point for all civilians seeking to get evacuated from the country. The Mammy Yoko looked like a classic run-down, white-walled colonial-era establishment. The gardens were grand but tired and ill-kept, pretty much reflecting the look and feel of the hotel itself.

The main advantage of the Mammy Yoko was its flight facilities. Set on the ocean front the hotel has a flat, oval, gravelled area facing the sea: a helipad. It came complete with two massive refuelling bowsers, the hotel being one of the UN's main centres of operations in the country. As we'd flown in we'd noticed two massive Soviet-era Mil Mi-8 (named HIP by NATO) transport helicopters sitting on the helipad, painted in white and with 'UN' emblazoned in massive black lettering on their sides.

While the Chinooks were tasked with all military movements around the country, the HIPs were ferrying the civilians out to Lungi Airport, for onward evacuation.

From the Mammy Yoko we sent out an eight-man patrol en route to the British Embassy. It was led by Corporal Sam 'Dolly' Parton, the commander of patrol *33 Bravo*. His position of patrol command had come about by dint of his natural leadership abilities. The average face in a crowd, Dolly was married with two kids. He was a softly-spoken, quiet family man and an utterly solid operator. After Nathe and H's patrol, Dolly's was my next most capable unit, and they constituted a great backstop to *33 Alpha*.

Once Dolly's patrol had got the Embassy staff relocated to the Mammy Yoko Hotel, we'd airlift them out to Lungi Airport and onto a waiting C-130 Hercules. In the meantime, we settled ourselves in as best we could. A path from the helipad led to the centre of the hotel grounds, where there were some tennis courts, surrounded by twelve-foot-high chain-link fencing. The courts were overlooked by the hotel's bar and swimming pool, one that was built in an abstract kind of a splodge shape.

Set some seventy yards back from the pool was the hotel building itself. It looked to be about a dozen floors high, with a curved façade facing the sea. The rooms had to offer an amazing view over the Freetown Estuary, not that I figured there were many guests with the time or inclination to enjoy it. Right now, anyone with any money or sense and the right passport was getting the hell out of Freetown.

Colonel Gibson had also shipped himself over to the Mammy Yoko, and he had seized one of the hotel suites as his ops room. Donaldson disappeared to liaise with the colonel, the rest of us setting up a makeshift camp. By now our Bergens had reached us, so we were able to rig up ponchos lashed to the chain-link fence – making a series of waterproof lean-tos, which lined the edge of the tennis courts.

Our ponchos were US Army issue, for the British military didn't possess such kit. We had to buy rakes of our own equipment, including boots, rucksacks, torches, waterproofs, ammo pouches and the ponchos. The British Army doss-bag weighed in at 10 pounds. It was fine for a Regular Army unit, for their Bergens would be brought up to their lines by vehicle. For us it was 8 pounds overweight. Accordingly, every Pathfinder had a civvie sleeping bag, one that weighed in at 2 pounds and stuffed down to nothing.

If I stood every man of our force in line, I figure 10 per cent of our kit would have been standard British Army issue. Each bloke carried around £1500-worth of personalised gear, and all bought with his own money. It was a powerful testament to their dedication to the unit that each had made such an investment, and most on a private's wage of some £650 month.

Camp set, we broke open the twenty-four-hour ration packs,

got a scoff-on and waited for some kind of an update from Don-aldson. I killed time chatting with Wag. We were determined that Donaldson would deliver the right kind of an update – *that we were staying, and that we were getting ourselves a peachy tasking*. The Embassy job was clearly an interim kind of a mission. Time was ticking, and we needed something we could really get our teeth into.

Our determination to stay was just about to get a huge boost, as we got our first detailed briefing on the rebels. A military intelli-gence specialist gave us a good talking to in the hotel grounds. The rebels were known as the Revolutionary United Front, or RUF for short. Led by an ex-Sierra Leonean Army (SLA) sergeant, Foday Sankoh, they espoused no coherent political or other ideology. Their sole aim seemed to be to spread terror and mayhem across the country, and in that they had been spectacularly successful.

The rebels' 'signature' was to lop off the hands of women and children, offering them 'long-sleeve' or 'short-sleeve' style – the former being amputation below the elbow, the latter above it. They did so simply to spread sheer and utter terror across the land. Typical rebel 'tactics' involved surrounding an isolated village at night, killing all the able-bodied men, raping and mu-tilating the women, and then rounding up all the kids of 'fighting age' – the would-be child soldiers.

Boys of eleven and twelve were forced to rape their own mothers and kill their own fathers, or get macheted to death on the spot – and do so in front of the rest of the village. Thus, hor-ribly traumatised and alienated from their surviving family and community, they were sucked into the rebel ranks. With no way back to their homes or their villages, the RUF became their only 'family'. Young girls were taken in a similar way, as rebel fighters' 'wives'.

Once they were so 'recruited', the would-be rebels were fed a cocktail of crack cocaine, heroin and other drugs – 'injected' di-rectly into the blood stream via cuts made in their foreheads. The nascent child soldiers quickly became drug-addicted. To cap it all they were bathed in vats of voodoo medicine by the rebels' 'high priestesses', supposedly to make them 'bulletproof' and 'invincible' in battle.

RUF terror sorties were invariably led by these child soldier shock-troops, high on drugs and voodoo gibberish. More often than not they sported the most bizarre of 'uniforms': frilly dresses, fluorescent pink shell-suits, women's wigs, and even animal costumes made from real animal skins. Yet in spite of all of this they were a force to be reckoned with. Several times during the decade-long civil war they had seized control of the entire country, including the nation's capital, in an inconceivably dark and brutal orgy of violence that had cost over 70,000 lives.

After ten years of such warfare the Sierra Leone Army had been left largely impotent. Recently, some 17,000 United Nations peacekeepers had been drafted into the country, supposedly to keep the peace. They hailed from the Jordanian, Indian, Nigerian and other armed forces, and they very often lacked boots, radios or even weaponry to carry out their duties, not to mention a basic modicum of co-ordination, discipline or morale.

UNAMSIL – the United Nations Mission to Sierra Leone – was the largest UN peacekeeping force in history, but it had proved an utter debacle. The RUF had kidnapped dozens of peacekeepers, seized their armoured vehicles and looted their ammo dumps and their weaponry. Indeed, it was via seized UN trucks and armoured personnel carriers that the rebels were now making their final push on Freetown.

Some 800 PARAs, a handful of SAS and we Pathfinders were heavily outnumbered by the rebels. There was also increasing evidence of the RUF's links to darker forces hailing from outside the country. Sierra Leone was blessed – or possibly cursed – with a surfeit of alluvial diamonds, which occurred near the surface and could be easily mined by hand. If anything, it was lust for the diamond wealth of the country that was driving this crazed war.

Recently, terrorist franchises like Al Qaeda had started popping up in the country, looking to buy up these illicit 'conflict diamonds' and so launder their millions. Diamonds represent the ultimate fungible asset – a handful of tiny rocks that are essentially undetectable at airports and borders but remain a store of enormous wealth to whoever holds them. Factor in the hard drugs being run through West Africa, and it was a dark and dangerous mix.

It was these concerns that had prompted Tony Blair to launch the present deployment. In fact, Blair had deeply personal reasons for intervening in Sierra Leone, for his father had worked in the country as a teacher and he felt personally compelled to act. And with Colonel Gibson having moved heaven and earth to get an entire battle group in-country, we had made a half-decent start.

At the same time the overall force commander, Brigadier David Richards – who would go on to become General Sir David Richards, chief of the Defence Staff – had very much nailed his colours to the mast. In a meeting with Sierra Leone's embattled president, Ahmad Kabbah, Brigadier Richards had just made a signal promise: *he had pledged that the British military would end the war in Sierra Leone once and for all, by knocking seven bales of shit out of the rebels.*

After learning all of this I was doubly certain that this was not the time to contemplate withdrawing the Pathfinders from the country. Quite the reverse: there was a war to be fought here for all the right reasons, and against an enemy that needed to be given a right bloody nose.

I knew full well that if we jacked this mission we'd never live it down. The stigma would plague the Pathfinders for years to come, plus we'd never get another job like this. So it was just as well that we were about to get a top priority tasking – one designed to make Brigadier Richards' promise of knocking seven bales of shit out of the rebels a reality.

As the Pathfinders' platoon sergeant, I got to shape and form this tiny, bespoke unit in exactly the way I wanted. Kit failures and deficiencies apart, I didn't think there was a unit out there that could touch us in terms of the elite skills we specialised in. You needed to build a special brotherhood to succeed at our level. After the countless hours spent sprinting around the base perimeter or tabbing in the Brecons, the long overnights in OPs and on recce taskings, not to mention all the HALO, HAHO and HAPLSS jumps, I reckoned the bonds formed between us were unbreakable.

Which was just as well, for in the coming days the Pathfinders were to be tested to the limits and beyond.

5

Things began to move lightning fast. We were ordered to break camp and mount up a waiting CH-47, to be flown back to Lungi Airport. Upon arrival we were rushed in for an emergency briefing with Colonel Gibson, who'd flown back alongside us.

Humint (human intelligence) sources had reported a huge rebel force massing some seventy kilometres or so to the north of Lungi Airport. The rebels were planning to attack just as we had the NEO in full swing, loading confused and frightened evacuees onto waiting aircraft. That way, there would be hundreds of British and allied civilians milling about in the airport, and they'd be easy game for the rebels.

The RUF's intended route of advance was the dirt highway that threaded south through the swampy jungle – the one we'd kept watch over during our first night. We were getting flown far upcountry to an isolated clearing that straddled that track, near a village called Lungi Lol. The village was believed to be 'friendly', though nothing was ever certain with the ever-shifting allegiances that defined this war. Our role was to act as an early warning force, and to hold up the rebel advance for as long as was humanly possible.

The village was set deep in the jungle some sixty kilometres inland, so way beyond any British forces, which were massed around the airport and Freetown.

This was more like it. This was a classic Pathfinder tasking: an insertion ahead of British lines to recce, harass, sabotage and destroy. Colonel Gibson rounded off his briefing with this. 'Your force is very much on its own, but I have every confidence in the Pathfinders. There will be a 1 PARA QRF on standby, for I understand the danger you are going into here. If it all goes pear-shaped, make your way back to British lines by whatever means possible.'

At least we had a QRF (Quick Reaction Force) of PARAs on standby, if it did all go to rat-shit. We gathered in the ramshackle terminal building over a map, so Donaldson could brief the patrol commanders in more detail. Thankfully, the OC seemed to have got some of his mojo back, now that we'd landed such an out-there kind of a mission.

'We're going in as a platoon to form an early warning group,' Donaldson told the men. 'Intel suggests rebel forces are moving to take the airport, or at least to attack and capture British soldiers and evacuating citizens. The CO wants us out there at his furthermost point, to put a clear stop to them.'

As the blokes digested what they'd just been told, the atmosphere was electric with anticipation. This was the kind of tasking every Pathfinder dreams of.

'Our intention is to move by helo some sixty klicks northeast,' Donaldson continued. 'We'll take vehicles to give us mobility on the ground. The CO wants us in situ at this point – Lungi Lol – before last light, so we need to move it and begin liaison with the pilots. We could be going into a hot LZ. So prepare to E & E in case it does go loud. If we do need to E & E we'll move to the coast, using this dirt track, and link up with the SBS who will be patrolling the coastline.'

E & E is short for escape and evasion – our bug-out plan if we were forced to go on the run. I was hunched over the map, shoulder to shoulder with Wag and Grant, but as I traced Donaldson's proposed E & E route I didn't like what I saw. We'd be heading southwest to a chokepoint, leaving our backs to the sea, and if the SBS lads failed to show we'd have nowhere to run to but the water.

I glanced at Wag, my finger tracing the route. 'It doesn't look like we can move any further than there,' I muttered, speaking out of the corner of my mouth. 'If we get there and we're being followed by the rebels we're fucked.'

'Yep. Agreed.'

'It's not like SBS will be parked up waiting for us. It could be hours before they're tasked to us or available.'

'Agreed.'

Donaldson finished his briefing and asked for any questions.

'Yeah – just the one,' I volunteered. 'The option to move south-west to the coast if we have to E & E ...'

'Yes, what of it?'

'Boss, you do realise if we do that we're moving to a chokepoint leaving our backs to the sea. If we're being pursued and we hit the sea with no pick-up ...'

'Steve, that's what's been agreed. Move on.'

Agreed by bloody whom, I wondered? A unit like the Pathfinders operates as a meritocracy. Every bloke, regardless of rank, gets to have his say. We had a way of doing things, a collective means of decision-making that meant there were checks and balances.

'Boss, I've got to agree with Steve,' Wag volunteered. 'We'll be pinned with nowhere left to go.'

Donaldson now had his platoon sergeant and his Ops Warrant Officer voicing concerns. Between us, Wag and me had over twenty-five years' experience of elite force operations.

'It's agreed with the boss,' Donaldson countered. 'Move on. Sort the kit. Let's get on with it.'

With that he strode off to the ops room. The looks on the faces of the rest of us said it all. Small unit operations rely on command and control decisions cascading down. Officers need to trust their NCOs and patrol commanders to highlight faults in plans and identify how things can be done better. They need to earn respect. Donaldson's reluctance to use the expertise and experience of the men ran counter to everything the Pathfinders stood for, and the very soul of the unit.

I could feel Nathe, Dolly and the other patrol commanders eyeing Grant, Wag and me.

'You need to get this bloody sorted,' Nathe grumbled.

'Go brief your patrols and we'll deal with it,' I reassured him.

'Nathe, we know,' said Wag. 'Leave it with us. Go back, brief your blokes on the mission. We're going in light order for a forty-eight-hour tasking, so twenty-four hours' worth of food and water in belt kit, then a further forty-eight hours in your daysack...'

Once Wag was done the patrol commanders split. Tricky headed off to liaise with the signallers from other units, to sort call-signs, frequencies, timings of the Scheds, and the use of the Crypto – cryptographically encoded communications systems. That left Grant, Wag and me to chew over the E & E issue.

'Grant, mate, at some stage soon you need to go talk to Donaldson,' I told him. 'Officer to officer. You need to get him to listen, 'cause this is crucial shit.'

Grant nodded. 'I know. I'll have words.'

Grant was still a relatively young and inexperienced officer. I had five years in age over him, plus a decade of elite soldiering, and Wag had more. His reluctance to go against a fellow officer and the unit's OC was understandable. As NCOs, me and Wag would simply get a bollocking if we fronted up to Donaldson. If Grant was seen as undermining the command of a fellow officer it could seriously harm his career, but someone needed to get Donaldson to see sense.

It was around 1300 hours by now, and we were scheduled to get airborne at 1500 hours and on the ground at the LZ thirty minutes thereafter. In the interim we had a shedload to organise. We had to sort an air-plan with the Chinook pilots, gather all our kit, rations and water, sort the comms and the wagons – we'd just had two Pinzgauers flown in on a Hercules – load and secure them in the CH-47s, and get ourselves good to go.

But the chief worry for me right now – apart from the faulty E & E plan – was this: as the platoon sergeant I was acutely aware of our appalling lack of ammo and weaponry with which to go up against several thousand rebels. We still had just the sixty rounds per man for our SA80s, plus nothing whatsoever for the GPMGs. And there was a shedload of other assorted weaponry and explosives I'd very much like for a mission such as this one.

It was now that Wag had one of his brainwaves. Mick Robson was the 1 PARA RQMS – Regimental Quartermaster – and a guy we knew well. He was six-foot-four, blond, wiry and he was nobody's fool. Near the edge of the runway he'd established a makeshift ammo dump. He'd driven metal pickets into the ground and stretched razor wire between them, fencing off an area some twenty metres by twenty metres.

A couple of 1 PARA privates had been set to guard the ammo dump, but as Wag pointed out that didn't mean that we couldn't go on the scrounge. We hurried over. We found Mick in the centre of the Kingdom of Mick, overseeing more ammo supplies that had just been flown in. He glanced up at us with a look on his face – *here they come again, the Pathfinder likely lads on the scrounge.*

I gave him my best winning smile. 'Mick, mate, long time no see. We're heading upcountry, mate, and we could well end up in a firefight. Trouble is we've got fuck-all to fight with, so we need whatever ammo you can spare us . . . mate.'

Mick stared at the two of us, then gestured at the palettes ranged all around him. 'How long's a bit of string. Any idea exactly what you're after?'

I ran my eye around the Kingdom of Mick feeling like a kiddie in a sweet shop. One palette was piled high with metal boxes of 5.56 mm ball ammo: SA80 rounds. Next to that was a mound of 7.62 mm belted link: GPMG ammo. Two dozen LAW 94 mm anti-armour rockets were laid out nearby, along with crates of 51 mm mortar rounds.

But the real Aladdin's Cave lay on the far side of the razor wire fence: *the demolitions and explosives enclosure.* PE4 plastic explosives, timers, detonators, detonation cord – Mick would have the works in there. Being a true pro he'd sorted his ammo dump so as not to exceed the NEQ – the net explosive quantity. Under British Army rules you could only store a certain amount of explosive material – the NEQ – in one dump, hence the demolitions enclosure being placed to one side. It was set under a poncho, to keep the sun off the stuff that goes bang.

I licked my lips, wondering just how hard to push things. I opened with this. 'Mick, we've got five guns: how much ammo can you spare us for each?'

'Guns' is military speak for the GPMGs.

Mick rolled his eyes. '400 rounds.'

'How about six?' I countered.

'All right. Six – you're done. What else?'

I told him we had sixty rounds per man for the SA80s – but I wanted 330 rounds per man, so over five times that amount. Each man needed to have six mags of thirty rounds each, plus a bandolier containing an extra 150. The bandolier is a long green sleeve that you sling around your torso, consisting of five compartments each containing thirty rounds.

Mick nodded. 'Yeah, okay. Suppose you can have that. Next?'

I eyed the LAWs. 'What about four of them – them LAWs, Mick?'

He ran a hand across his sweaty forehead. 'Fuck . . . Well, okay. Take 'em. Just keep it quiet. Next?'

'Mick, any L2s or Claymores in-country?'

The L2 is the British Army's high-explosive fragmentation grenade, the Claymore a curved anti-personnel device of devastating lethality.

Mick shook his head. 'Nope. Next?'

I'd brought with me a 51 mm mortar tube from our armoury, but as yet I had no ammo. 'What about 51 mm rounds?'

'There's illume, but no HE.'

Illume are flare rounds, ones that burst high in the sky to illuminate a battlefield. Not quite high-explosive (HE) rounds, but better than nothing.

'Okay, great: how many can I have?'

He pointed to a nearby crate: 'Here – just take that bloody box while no one's looking.'

I'd open that crate later to discover eighteen rounds inside. I had no idea right now what a total lifesaver they would prove to be.

'Right, Mick, what else have you got?'

He stared at us for a long second. 'You're fucking joking me.'

I pointed to the second enclosure – the demolitions dump. 'What's that, Mick, under that poncho?'

'You lot are never bloody satisfied. It's the demms kit.'

'Let's have a look, then.'

Mick hesitated, then he stepped between Wag and me, moving towards the gate. Out of the corner of his mouth he muttered: 'You two wankers coming, or what?'

We moved around the corner to a tiny gate, then stepped inside the sacred enclosure. I pointed at a box of PE4. 'Mick, how much of that have you got?'

'About fifteen pounds.'

My mind was racing. PE4 comes in a block like a thick cigar. It's off-white, smells a bit like marzipan, and is wrapped in a kind of greaseproof paper. Fifteen pounds equalled thirty sticks.

'Mick, can I have ten sticks?'

'If I give it you, will you fuck off?'

'I will if we can have some dets as well . . .'

Behind Mick, Wag was on his knees levering open boxes. He was laying stuff on the floor, piling up a ready-made war in a box. I tried to keep Mick occupied while Wag mounded up his heap of swag.

'Mick, can we have this lot as well?' Wag piped up.

Mick turned and saw what Wag was doing. He raised his arms and cut his hands across the air – like *cut-it; cut it out; no more.*

'That's it,' he hissed. 'The fucking shop is shut – go!'

I grinned. 'Fair enough, the shop's shut. Sold out. Cheers, Mick, anyway.' I turned to Wag. 'Mate, bag that lot up before he changes his mind and I'll go get the patrol commanders. We'll need a good few blokes to carry it all.'

I called the blokes over and we began to distribute the goodies around the patrols.

I would have liked to have got our hands on a few of the folding-stock Minimi light machine guns, which the SAS had in theatre, for the GPMG was big and clumsy when patrolling through thick vegetation. I'd have liked M203 grenade launchers, although the 40 mm rounds can get deflected by thick jungle and rebound to hit your own side. But most of all, I'd have liked M16 assault rifles as our main weapon.

Yet Blair was winging it, Colonel Gibson was winging it and Brigadier Richards most certainly was – so I figured there was no reason why the Pathfinders shouldn't wing it alongside them. And with Mick's help, at least we now had the kind of ammo and explosives we needed to take the fight to the rebels.

We loaded up the waiting Chinooks, each with the one Pinzgauer strapped down in preparation for a seat-of-the-pants kind of a ride. The 'Pinz' is a four-wheel-drive all-terrain vehicle, with a cab sitting over the front wheels and an open rear. The two vehicles were there to provide us with a fast and mobile means to escape and evade, with greater reach than going on the run on foot. Wag, Grant and me got our heads together with the Chinook pilots over the air maps. There looked to be nowhere to land to the south or west of the village. The best bet seemed to be a small clearing to the northeast, adjacent to the road. We figured it was just about large enough to land the pair of Chinooks, but by anyone's reckoning it was going to be a tight fit. We decided they'd go down as a pair facing northeast, ramps open towards the village.

We agreed actions-on if the LZ turned out to be 'hot'. If the pilots encountered heavy ground fire, we'd abort the landing and search for an alternative LZ. If we put down, disgorged and took heavy fire, the helos would fly a holding pattern, providing cover with their door-mounted, six-barrelled Miniguns. We'd only call the helos back in to extract us if the resistance proved too fierce, and if they stood a decent chance of getting in and out without being shot down.

As the aircrew readied themselves to get airborne, Lewis, the 1 PARA Ops Officer, pulled me off for a last word.

'Steve: over here, mate!'

'Wag and Grant?' I yelled back.

'Yeah, bring 'em too.'

We gathered in a huddle, Lewis with a worried expression in his eyes. 'Look, guys, just to warn you, 'cause you need to know: Donaldson's still arguing to the CO to get you sent back to the UK. He's saying he doesn't see a role for the Pathfinders and that you've got training scheduled with air assets cued. Guys, you're on the verge of being pulled out. Be wary.'

Having given us the warning Lewis split, leaving Wag, Grant and me to digest the news. Donaldson had seemed reinvigorated, our unit having landed the present mission. There was no way we could allow ourselves to get pulled off this one at the eleventh hour.

I eyed Grant. Wag was staring at him too. He held up his hands in a gesture almost of surrender. 'All right, guys, it's out of order and don't I know it. But look, we're flying out of here and once we're airborne we're committed . . .'

Donaldson was scheduled to fly in with us, this being a platoon-level op. The White Rabbit had drawn the short straw and was remaining here as our liaison with Colonel Gibson, along with one of our radio operators. We figured we needed to get Donaldson on the Chinook and airborne as quickly as possible, at which stage we were pretty much past the point of no return.

As we waited on the apron for the final 'go' an unmarked HOOK helicopter flew in low and fast. It looked exactly like the HIPs the UN were using, except it had a shorter body and was painted a dull khaki green. It landed beside us, and eight operators dressed in black jumpsuits dismounted, each carrying an AK47. The only clue as to who they were was the American flag sewn onto the shoulder of each of them.

We'd had no warning they were inbound and I presumed they had to be either Delta Force or from the CIA's Special Activities Division (SAD), its paramilitary wing. I figured they'd be here to help deal with any US nationals holed up in Freetown. Being Pathfinders, we'd trained with Delta, but there was zero time to go have words with the new arrivals. Our priority was to stay on the helos and get out of Lungi Airport before anyone could put a stop to us.

At 1500 we got the final 'go'. The Chinooks' giant twin rotors spooled up to speed and finally we were airborne. We were whisked over the thick jungle that fringed the runway, clipping the treetops in an effort to avoid being detected by the rebels or getting hit by any ground fire. I felt this massive surge of elation as we left Lungi Airport behind us: at least now the mission was a go.

We had fourteen Pathfinders on our Chinook, ranged in two ranks of seven, seated to either side of the aircraft's hold. The Pinz was fastened to the metal lugs at the front of the hold, tight against the metal compartment that sealed off the cockpit. Beside me the Chinook's loadmaster was strapped to the aircraft's side, hanging out of the two-part rear ramp, the upper half of which was folded inwards to offer a view over sky and jungle.

As the Chinook gathered speed the ground sped past beneath the open ramp. I gazed out. The terrain below looked utterly horrendous – patches of thick, dense forest interspersed with wide expanses of tropical swamp and mangroves. Here and there water glinted in the blinding mid-afternoon light, revealing the bend of a river, a lagoon or a quagmire. Away from the one dirt highway there looked to be no easy way through such terrain.

I'd plugged into the Chinook's comms system via a set of

headphones, ones that linked me to the cockpit. I could hear the pilot and co-pilot calling out landmarks and flight details to each other plus the navigator, who was perched on a fold-down seat to the rear of the cockpit crouched over his air maps.

Pilot: 'Boomerang-shaped turn in dirt track, port side of aircraft, three hundred metres.'

Navigator: 'Check. Thirty klicks out of village.'

Pause.

Co-pilot: 'Speed: a hundred and fifty knots. Direction of travel: zero three five degrees.'

Pause.

Pilot: 'Passing moon-shaped lagoon to starboard side of aircraft, two hundred and fifty metres.'

Navigator: 'Check. ETA LZ twenty minutes. Look for bend in track five hundred metres on left, then clearing a hundred and fifty metres ahead of that.'

Pilot: 'Roger that.'

By now I'd pretty much realised there was no end to the swamp, wetlands and mangrove forests flashing past below. This wasn't the odd, isolated patch of waterlogged terrain that you could skirt around. I'd trained and operated in the lowland forests of Belize, Brunei and elsewhere, so I'd experienced wet jungle ground before – but I'd never set eyes on anything like this.

With the terrain to either side of the road being impassable, the only viable escape route was going to be that one dirt highway. It snaked south, passing through a series of villages, ones that were totally uncharted territory: they could be friendly or they could be rebel bases. Even if we got the Pinzgauers going on the road and could get through the villages okay, we couldn't load all twenty-seven of us onto the wagons, because they couldn't carry that many.

It would be easy enough to get into the dense, waterlogged terrain to either side of the road and disappear on foot. We could go to ground and hide, but what then? No one was about to come into that kind of terrain to lift us out, and at some point we'd be driven to leave – by hunger, disease, or the snakes and crocodiles that would infest the badlands. In the meantime the rebels would be able to motor ahead on the dirt road and get us outflanked and surrounded.

We were twenty-seven against God only knew how many thousand rebels, and we were heading into a green hell.

6

We closed in on the LZ. There was a high-pitched whine and the bottom half of the helo's ramp folded down, hot jungle air and burning avgas fumes barrelling in through the opening. On the port side of the Chinook the hatch was open, the door-gunner manning the six-barrelled .50-calibre Gatling gun readying himself for action. If there were hostiles on the LZ we were relying in part of his firepower to provide cover for our extraction.

I took one last look at the terrain as we thundered in. We were hammering along at fifty feet above the jungle canopy, below which there was an endless seam of glistening swamps and rivers feeding into the Freetown Estuary. I glanced around the faces of the men, trying to give them the kind of reassuring look that I figured they expected from their platoon sergeant. The lads were utterly silent, and I could feel the tension and apprehension sparking in the air.

No one was breathing a word, but we all knew. It was a water-logged, jungle hell down there and we had not the slightest idea of what we were going to encounter at the LZ. But over and above the fear and apprehension, I sensed something else – a real confidence and self-belief. Every man aboard the Chinook shared a unique bond: each of us had made it through the brutal Pathfinder Selection course, bonding us as brother warriors. There was an inner strength, one grounded in the conviction that we could take care of ourselves come what may.

We were also acutely aware of how Colonel Gibson had shown absolute belief in us by sending us on this mission: *Your force is on its own, but I have every confidence in you, Pathfinders.* Those words were balanced by what we could see of the ground now, but we were determined to prove the colonel right in putting us out here as his vanguard.

He could have sent another unit forward. He could have chosen to use the SAS boys operating out of Lungi Airport. He hadn't. He'd chosen us.

That was what we had to live up to.

The loadie raised two fingers and waved them in front of the faces of the blokes: we were two minutes out from the LZ. The guy allotted to drive the Pinz mounted up the vehicle and the engine coughed into life. To either side of him, guys prepared to loosen the quick-release straps and get the wagon rolling.

The loadie held up his thumb and index finger in a sideways U-shape, signalling we were half a minute out.

'Thirty seconds!' he yelled above the noise of the screaming turbines.

The guys were on their feet now, ready for the go.

I could feel the Chinook descending through the hot and humid air, the arse-end of the helo dropping more quickly than the front. The pitch of the turbines changed as the pilot feathered back on the rotors, the beat going from a rhythmic *thwoop-thwoop-thwoop*, that sliced the air apart, to a crazed *brrrrrrrrrrrzzzz*, as we flared out to land.

As the Chinook dropped, I felt a series of powerful, juddering shock waves reverberating through the airframe. For a moment I feared we were taking fire, before I realised what it was: the rotor blades were slicing into the jungle at the outer edges of the LZ, the space was so tight. This weird, rhythmic ripping sound bounced back at us – as if some giant chainsaw were tearing into the vegetation to either side of the aircraft.

I prayed the rotors held up. If they hit any major trees then they'd shear, sending us into the hell of a crash-landing. All of a sudden there was a massive *Bang*! – as if the rear rotor had struck a tree trunk. An instant later I realised it was our back wheels slamming into the deck as we landed. I felt the aircraft pivot forwards, and then the front pair were down.

The instant they were the loadie was screaming: 'GO! GO! GO! GO! GO!'

We piled off in two sticks, those on the left-hand side of the aircraft going left, and those on the right going right, until we had a ring of blokes strung around the Chinook, guns levelled at the jungle to their front, the twin rotors thrashing in the air above us. The Pinzgauer followed on our heels, roaring out of the Chinook's belly and onto the rough ground, the two blokes who had released the fixing straps piling down the ramp last-out.

Thirty seconds after touching down the loadie yelled into his intercom: 'Troops off! Ramp clear!' It was the call for the pilots to get airborne. Turbines screamed into a deafening howl as the pilots hit full throttle, and the pair of Chinooks rose as one, rotors tearing at the air as they clawed skywards, banking towards the east. We were left in a wind-whipped chaos – vegetation, grass, leaves, rotten wood and dirt howling all around us.

The bellies of the helos were swallowed up by the dust storm. We stared down the barrels of our weapons into a blinding whirlwind of debris.

I couldn't see a bloody thing.

Gradually the air cleared, revealing the wall of vegetation that surrounded the clearing, rotor-strikes clearly showing in the white scars of shattered branches.

The helos weren't taking any fire above us.

We weren't taking any fire on the ground.

Not a muzzle sparked amongst the shadows.

Right now, there was zero sign of the enemy.

As far as we could tell there wasn't a thing moving out there. We were down on our belt buckles 300 yards to the north of the village of Lungi Lol, and there wasn't a soul to be seen – villager or rebel fighter.

The patch of ground that we'd put down on looked as if it had been cleared via slash-and-burn – a method by which locals cut the jungle, leave it to dry, fire the vegetation and plant crops in the ash-rich residue. The first things to move off were the Pinzgauers, bumping and lurching across the uneven ground. They made for the dirt highway some thirty yards from where we'd landed.

We joined the Pinzgauers on the main track. They began chugging their way towards the village, as we skirmished through the jungle to either side on foot. All the while I was thinking: *Where the hell is everyone? The locals must have heard the Chinooks come in, so where the hell are they?*

We hit the northern edge of the village. I noticed the first of these mud-walled and grass-thatched huts lining the road, interspersed with cleared areas for gardens and patches of thicker vegetation. Then I spotted the first of the locals. Here and there wide, frightened eyes peered out of a shadowed hut doorway. They were staring at us like the Martians had just landed.

We reached the T-junction of dirt tracks that marked the centre of the village. I gave orders to the patrol commanders to take up positions facing the wall of jungle to the northeast of us – the most likely line of any rebel attack.

We went firm.

To the east I could hear the pair of helos flying their prearranged holding pattern. They'd orbit there for five minutes, in case we needed to call in their fire support. We checked the vegetation to our front for anything untoward: the glint of sunlight on gunmetal; a muzzle flash; urgent or rapid movement through the trees. Our eyes scanned for targets, all the while knowing that just as the villagers had heard us fly in, so would any rebels – that's if there were any hereabouts.

While the villagers wouldn't have a clue as to who we were or where we'd come from, one thing would be crystal clear: *we weren't rebels*. We were clearly foreigners and we were clearly soldiers, but that would be about as much as they could know right now. It was no surprise that they were keeping to the cover of their huts: in a country such as this, men with guns were so often the bad guys.

For a good five minutes we scanned silently for targets. It was starting to look like ours had been an unopposed landing, as if the rebels hadn't reached this far south yet. We'd touched down at 1530 hours, so we had around three hours remaining until last light. The village was now loosely secured. We were in occupation, we'd yet to get shot at and we were not aware of any immediate threat.

Wag, Grant, the OC and me decided to do a walkabout, to get a sense of the lie of the land. We got the Pinzgauers parked up on an open area of hard-packed dirt, one ringed with huts, just to the west of the T-junction. I figured this was something like the village square. There was a clutch of ramshackle wooden stalls ranged down one side, which had to be the marketplace.

A smaller track branched off from the main highway, slicing south through the jungle. That had to be Donaldson's intended E & E route. The track ran for 12 kilometres, before it reached a dead end – the sea. Our flight over the jungle had only reinforced in my mind how defunct was any escape plan based upon heading that way. We'd be hemmed in on three sides – by sea and impenetrable jungle – and with the rebels at our backs.

Walkabout done, Wag and me began siting the individual patrols, while Tricky, Grant and Donaldson established comms with headquarters back at Lungi Airport. All we had to go on when choosing patrol locations was the lie of the land. We needed maximum cover from view and from fire – from being seen and being shot at – while at the same time being able to put down rounds on the most likely avenue of enemy approach – the dirt highway. With the terrain being impassable off-road, we presumed the rebels would have to come at us straight down the main drag.

We sited the HQ patrol in a couple of shallow craters, some thirty metres to the east of the village square. That way, we'd be pretty much at the heart of things so we could co-ordinate any action. We put Nathe and H's patrol – *33 Alpha* – some ninety yards to the east of us, facing down the throat of the dirt track. From there they could put down accurate fire onto the road, as far as we could see to the front of us.

Dolly's patrol – *33 Bravo* – we sited in a patch of thick bush a hundred yards or so to the far side of the highway, so protecting our left flank. The patrol commanded by Dale 'Ginge' Wilson – *33 Charlie* – we placed a hundred yards to the south of Nathe's patrol, with *33 Delta* – Taff Saunders' patrol – a hundred yards to the south of that. We now had the entire front of the village covered by our defensive positions.

Ginge Wilson, *33 Charlie*'s commander, was a northerner with a distinctive Mancunian accent. Around five-foot-ten, with a whippet-like runner's physique, Ginge had the impulsive ways typical of a 'racing snake'. He had only recently been promoted to patrol command, and was one of the least experienced and most excitable of the lot – hence my decision to sandwich his patrol between Nathe and Taff's, putting an experienced pair of hands to either side of him.

Taff Saunders – *33 Delta*'s commander – hailed from the Royal Regiment of Wales, and he was a five-foot-ten, 15-stone, hard-as-nails Welsh rugby player. He had a thick Welsh accent – he called everyone 'bud' – and he would only ever refer to God's own country – England – as 'the annexe', a carbuncle on the otherwise unblemished face of the Welsh motherland.

Taff hailed from the Rhondda Valley – the heart of the land of myths and dragons. The blokes ripped the piss constantly: *How can you be under cover behind enemy lines with an accent like that? Guys from the Rhondda all marry their sisters.* We did a lot of our training in South Wales, and you have to cross the Severn Bridge to get there. It's a toll bridge, but you only pay the one way, going from England into Wales.

Taff would torture us with that. 'Hey, bud, you only pay to get into Wales, not the other way around. No one pays to get into England.'

I referred to Taff as my 'yeah-but' man. He was a natural-born brawler and great in a bar fight, but he always had an answer for everything. A typical conversation with Taff went like this.

Me: 'Right, Taff, what I need from you is . . .'

Taff: 'Yeah, but, it'd be far better, bud, if we . . .'

I'd sited Taff out on our right flank – one of our most isolated and vulnerable positions – for a very good reason: I knew that the tough little Welsh git would never back down from a fight.

Wag and me left the lads to dig themselves some hasty shell-scrapes – the fastest way to get a bunch of soldiers below ground. A shell-scrape is a hole some two metres long, one and a half wide and three-quarters of a metre deep. It's big enough for two men to lie side by side facing the enemy, along with their kit – Bergens, webbing and weaponry. Shell-scrapes provide decent protection against fire, and limited protection against a nearby ground-burst explosion.

If the men had the time, they'd create additional cover by build-ing up a 'bullet mantle' – using the soil they'd dug out of the hole to mound up around the front and sides – and then camouflaging that with local vegetation. That would provide the kind of defence that is our minimum for a twenty-four- to forty-eight-hour mis-sion such as this one.

For the moment everything was going like clockwork. From an insertion onto a potentially hot LZ we'd formed a front line of de-fence across a village that seemed to be largely peaceful. Having sited the patrols, Wag and I made our way back to the HQ pos-ition. But before we could get much of a heads-up with Grant and Donaldson, the first figure to appear emerged from the bush.

He wasn't quite what we had been expecting.

He was tall and ebony-skinned, and dressed in a spotless set of combat fatigues, topped off by a pair of enormous mirror shades, plus a distinctive light blue beret. It seemed as if there was at least one UN peacekeeper based here in the village of Lungi Lol.

We beckoned him to approach. His sunglasses were so completely black that you couldn't see his eyes, and they had massive Foster Grant golden frames. They covered his face from his eyebrows to his cheek-bones, but other than that he was parade-ground smart. He was freshly shaven, his combats had sharp creases down the front and his boots were polished to a gleaming, mirror finish.

Impeccable.

He opened his mouth to introduce himself and out came this educated, public school English. He sounded posher than any of us lot – Grant and Donaldson included.

'Good afternoon, gentlemen. I am Lieutenant Oronto Obasanjo, from the Nigerian Army, forming up part of UNAMSIL, the United Nations peacekeeping mission here in Sierra Leone. You are most welcome. You are from which nation's military – Her Majesty's Armed Forces, if I am not mistaken?'

Grant and Donaldson recovered pretty well from the shock and did the introductions. Meet and greet done, we asked him for a ground orientation brief – a talk around the position. He proceeded to outline the lie of the land. The village was maybe eight hundred yards from end to end, with some fifty huts scattered along its length. There was little evidence of furniture or other material possessions amongst the villagers, and between each of the huts lay a swathe of thickly-vegetated farmland, where they grew most of their food.

Our two Pinzgauers parked up on the village square were the only vehicles in the entire place. At the southern edge of the square was a more substantial hut, and that was the village headman's place, the lieutenant explained. It was something like the mayor's office, and from there the chief oversaw everything that happened in his domain.

That was about all Lieutenant Obasanjo had to tell us. Apart from this: he'd been deployed to Lungi Lol six months earlier leading a force of sixteen fellow Nigerians. In the entire time he and his men had been here they had received not one visit from their commanders in UNAMSIL or even a set of orders. They had no food rations, they hadn't been paid for months and they had very limited supplies of ammo. In short, this was a typical UNAMSIL operation – chaotic, dysfunctional and forgotten by everyone in command.

Under the circumstances, what the lieutenant told us next was hardly surprising: his men had gone native. They'd discarded their uniforms in favour of T-shirts and sarongs, and shacked up with local village ladies as 'wives'. It was only Lieutenant Obasanjo, it seemed, who had refused to let standards drop. A true blue officer, he was determined to keep up appearances come what may.

'What, if anything, has happened in the village in terms of the rebels, the RUF?' Donaldson asked him, once he'd finished telling us about his posting. 'Have you had any encounters with the RUF while you've been here?'

The lieutenant shook his head. 'No. We have seen no sign of the RUF. In fact, we have had very few if any visitors.'

This was bizarre, way out left-field kind of shit. We'd flown into what we'd been warned was potentially a hot LZ, only to be met by a Nigerian officer fresh from the parade ground, with seemingly not a worry in the world. More bizarre still, his was no UN checkpoint keeping watch for rebel movement: it was sixteen blokes who'd discarded their uniforms, got married to the locals and become a part of village life. And if the lieutenant was to be believed, he and his men were quite happy thank you being left here to rot by the UN.

In a sense you had to take your hat off to the guy. He wasn't moaning or feeling sorry for himself. He and his men had adapted to the situation as they'd found it. Abandoned by all, they'd done what they had to in order to survive. And if the lieutenant didn't have a local wife then he was up all night washing and starching his uniform and polishing his boots, which I didn't think was very likely.

'Can you fucking believe it?' Wag remarked, once the lieutenant had left us. 'Fucking Lieutenant Mojo and his Gone Native Crew – chilling out in Lungi Lol?'

I laughed. *Lieutenant Mojo.* That was it – the name stuck.

We set about building an ATAP at the HQ position – a simple wooden frame thatched over with branches and leaves. It was a temporary structure designed to last the next forty-eight hours – the supposed duration of the mission – and was for shelter and camouflage only. Then we slung our hammocks from the nearby trees. Sewn from parachute silk, they are incredibly strong, light-weight and versatile. But as with so much of our gear we had to buy the raw materials and get a wife, girlfriend or mother to sew it for us, for the British Army didn't possess such kit.

The cost of getting one of those para-silk hammocks made was a considerable burden and many – especially the married blokes – simply couldn't afford it. They came complete with a para-silk mozzie net, one that pulled over the top, and a waterproof poncho above that. Half a squash ball threaded onto the cords at either end stopped any water running down or insects getting in. The hammocks were perfect for deep-jungle missions, yet the entire lot weighed less than two pounds.

The hammock situation typified how ludicrous was the British Army's kit-procurement system – the same system that had endorsed the SA80 over the M16. The British Army did issue hammocks, but they were made from thick nylon, came complete with collapsible aluminium struts, and were designed to double as a stretcher. Great idea on paper. Shit in reality. They were imposs-ibly heavy, rattled as you moved and took an age to erect and take down.

They typified the Army's egghead mentality, whereby kit was rarely if ever tested by those who would use it at the hard end of soldiering. The trials and development unit of the British Army should have been manned by soldiers who'd served on operations, and had the experience and ingenuity to make kit workable in the field. Instead, it was staffed by SO1 (staff officer 1) colonels who'd rarely if ever been out at the dirty end of ops.

Normally, we'd set trip flares around positions such as those we'd taken up at Lungi Lol, to warn of any hostile forces creeping forward under cover of darkness, plus we'd position motion sensors on the ground to detect any movement. The motion sensors consist of a transmit–receive module that looks like a transistor radio, plus eight individual sensors each the size of a 12-bore shotgun cartridge. You'd hollow out a small hole and bury each sensor just below the surface, in areas you couldn't cover by fire, or to plug gaps in your defences.

There are eight LEDs on the transmitter–receiver. The buried sensors can detect seismic activity – so ground disturbance within a twenty-metre radius. If someone walks past, the sensor picks up the movement and transmits a message back to the receiver, at which point the LED corresponding to that sensor lights up. With each sensor's location plotted on your map, you'd then know you had something moving at position X.

But with none of that kind of kit available in Lungi Lol, it was up to human watchfulness to detect any rebel approach.

Just prior to last light we called the patrol commanders in for 'prayers' – a communal heads-up, and to set the routine for the coming night hours. We gathered in a circle – Nathe, Dolly, Ginge, Taff, Wag, Grant, Tricky, Donaldson and me. Prayers is a concept that lies at the heart of the Pathfinders: it's supposed to be a time when all ranks are free to contribute to whatever is being planned.

Donaldson began by outlining our mission. 'Now, the reason why we are here is to observe for any rebel movement and to stop them infiltrating further south,' Donaldson began. 'The threat is from rebel attack, which makes holding the village key. We need to presume the rebels' approach will be via the main track from the northeast. They've got the same constraints as us, so they can't move unless using that dirt highway. We'll set stags through the night keeping watch, two on and two off . . .'

'We need to make the ERV west along the main track,' Grant piped up, once Donaldson was done. 'Then we can E & E to Lungi Airport that way.'

ERV stands for Emergency Rendezvous – the point at which we'd come together if we were on the run. Behind Grant's seemingly innocuous comment lay a whole change of plan. He was suggesting that we E & E down the main highway to Freetown and Lungi Airport – in other words, abandoning Donaldson's plan that pitched us directly into the sea.

Donaldson stared at his fellow officer for a second, before nodding his assent. 'Okay. Good one, Grant. We'll do that.'

A silent sigh of relief went around the men. At least we'd got the E & E sorted.

We discussed actions-on if the rebels hit us in overwhelming numbers and we couldn't hold on for the QRF. If we had to bug out we'd try to use the vehicles and keep together as a unit. We'd move fast down the main drag, using the Pinzgauers to carry our wounded, and with the rest of us beasting it on foot. If we got split up the ERV was set as a point on the map 1.5 klicks down the dirt highway. Those already gathered at the ERV would sit on a standoff bearing, allowing them to watch the ERV unobserved, and check if any new arrivals were 'friendlies'.

We'd keep the ERV 'open' for two hours following the time of first contact with the enemy, giving every man that long to make it – at which point everyone gathered there would bug out. Our next ERV was the 'War RV' – the point at which we had entered the country as a unit – so Lungi Airport itself.

'To help keep watch on the main highway I want some early warning out front of the patrols,' Donaldson announced. 'Steve, Grant: you two take a couple of blokes and a Pinz and push forward five hundred yards out on the track.'

I glanced at Grant, worriedly. We'd sited the patrols well and got our defences sorted. We were ready. Sending four guys alone and unsupported at night into unknown terrain, and into the teeth of a rebel advance – it didn't make any sense. Not in my book, anyway.

I gritted my teeth. 'Boss, in light of everything we know, do we really want four blokes five hundred yards out there and at night? Especially as that's the way the rebels will come. We'll be isolated, unsupported, and in unknown territory.'

'Yes, we do. I need eyes out there.'

'I understand that, boss, but any movement to our flanks and we'll be cut off.'

'No, 'cause you'll be covered from the village.'

Covered from the village? We'd be a good half a kilometre out from our forward positions. The accurate range of an SA80 is far less than that, even if the lads could see in the darkness to aim and to shoot properly. More to the point some three hundred yards out from the village the track kinked northwards, putting it out of sight beyond. I figured we'd be unseen, out of range, and cloaked in darkness.

To my mind, we'd be lacking proper cover and support.

If an order or direction is delivered in a way that is rational and sensible, and I can understand why it needs to be done, I will embrace it. But as far as I was concerned this was none of those things. Pathfinder prayers always ends with 'going around the bazaars' – getting input from each of the men present.

'Anyone got anything else to say?' Donaldson asked. 'Dolly? Taff? Ginge? Nathe? Nope? Okay, get ready in your positions for stand-to.'

At first and last light we do stand-to. Militaries the world over have worked out that those times are the best at which to launch an attack. At first light men are likely to be sleepy and less alert, but there is enough light to see and fight by. At last light they are likely to be tired from the day's activities, and looking forward

The Fan Dance. Pathfinder selection is a tough five-week trial, culminating in Endurance, a 64-kilometre forced march under extremely heavy loads over the notorious Pen-y-Fan, in the Brecon Beacons – terrain known to test many a man.

Pathfinders deploy deep behind enemy lines with the kind of specialist light weaponry – like sniper rifles – to take out strategic enemy targets.

Riding the tube. As one of the British military's most experienced Tandem Masters, I got to jump with a massive canister of heavy equipment strapped to my person. Landing it was spine-crushing work.

Once you pull the chute, your world goes from the adrenaline-pumping rush of the freefall to one of comparative silence and stillness, as you drift under silk towards the landing zone below.

Bergen first. Just prior to landing, you let your Bergen drop on the extension rope, so it lands ahead of you, taking the impact of its own weight and saving your legs.

Touchdown. Gathering in the silk after a monster freefall to earth, in a HALO – high-altitude low-opening – jump.

HALO. Diving off a Hercules ramp into the howling void as a four-man patrol, in a HALO – high-altitude low-opening – parachute jump, with yours truly leading the stick.

In formation. Seconds later in the freefall on the same jump, myself in centre of photo. Note the M16s strapped to our left sides, in case the landing proves 'hot' – occupied by the enemy. You stick together close in the freefall, so that when you pull the chutes you can follow the lead jumper – me – into the drop zone.

Freefall. Same HALO jump as opposite, from above 25,000 feet, in full oxygen-breathing, parachute, survival and combat gear.

Solo. A different HALO jump, with yours truly flying high, with a General Purpose Machine Gun (GPMG) strapped to my left side, barrel downwards.

Desert rats. Pathfinders are tasked to go deep behind enemy lines in all kinds of terrain. On desert operations, *shemaghs* – traditional Arab headscarves – are vital for keeping sun and sand out of mouth, nose and hair. They're also great for anonymity. I'm in the vehicle commander's seat, so left of driver.

Sandy wanderers. Pathfinders in the North African desert, operating a mixed bag of Pinkies – desert-adapted, open-topped Land Rovers – and Armstrong 500cc motorbikes. I'm on the far right of the photo, leaning against the vehicle. All the others in this photo are now serving with Special Forces, hence faces being obscured.

Two wheels good. Yours truly, deep in the North African desert where we used Armstrong 500cc off-road motorbikes to act as an outrider force, scouting the route ahead and searching for the enemy.

The jungle is neutral. It's neither inherently hostile nor friendly, but only by becoming as one with it will you defeat an enemy. Wag is standing on the far left of photo, yours truly is far right, also standing.

Down 'n' dirty. The 'briefing room' for jungle training and ops in Belize, in the Central American rainforest. Wag's ever-friendly mug is in the centre of the photo, front row, with me peeping out from behind him on far left of the back row.

Home sweet home. A *basha* – a jungle sleeping platform made from cut bamboo and wood, with A-frame supports at either end, and a waterproof poncho thrown over, and tethered to nearby trees.

to a good feed and a rest. Accordingly, we get locked and loaded and on high alert at first and last light, with every man ready to rumble.

After stand-to we'd adopt 'night routine', with sentries set all through the hours of darkness. We'd have two men in each patrol standing watch, with the changeover times staggered, so there was always one set of eyes out on stalks. Staggering sentry changeovers also provides for continuity, so one sentry can report to the next all that has been seen.

But as for Grant and me, it was time to head east into the brooding darkness and the unknown. Donaldson ordered us to push out in one of the Pinzgauers, in case we had to make a 'rapid withdrawal'. We chose to take Mark 'Marky' Lewis and Steve B with us, a couple of solid operators whom we'd pulled in from Nathe and Dolly's patrols.

To my way of thinking it made little sense to send four men into the unknown with several thousand rebels massing. Right now Donaldson was ignoring one of the cardinal rules of the Pathfinders – that critical decisions are discussed and decided upon collectively, and based upon experienced-based reasoning, using the input of all the senior blokes.

But making an open stand against Donaldson now, in front of the others, would only damage us, and at the very moment when we needed to perform at 101 per cent. We prided ourselves upon tight cohesion, trust and faith in each other, brotherhood and *esprit de corps*. Having made it through Selection, the aspiration of every man was to become a patrol commander, and then make platoon sergeant. If right now they were forced to witness Sergeant Heaney ripping into their OC – that would be very bad news indeed.

So we mounted up the Pinzgauer, pushing north, with dark walls of jungle hemming us in on either side.

7

Half a kilometre out from the village we pulled to a halt.

We'd made the drive showing no lights, and navigating by the faint moonlight that filtered through to the dirt track, so as to have a greater chance of remaining unseen by any watching enemy. Our natural night vision had kicked in. We'd spotted a small, open area to one side of the track, one devoid of any vegetation. It was maybe ten feet by twenty and it formed a kind of a lay-by.

Using that we spun the Pinz around and got the nose of the wagon pointing back down the track towards the village, in case we had to make a run for it.

The cleared area had a bank of earth about four feet high running around it, where the bulldozers had pushed back the dirt and vegetation. Grant and me said we'd take the first stag, leaving Steve and Marky to try to get some sleep. The back of the Pinz was lined with bench seats, making it too cramped to doss in. So Steve and Marky bedded down on the dirt, lying in the lee of the earthen bank, which at least provided some cover from fire.

On the far side was the jungle.

It loomed before us like a dark and impenetrable cliff-face – one-hundred-foot-high forest giants, fringed with smaller palm-like bushes, tree-ferns and vines, where the dozers had torn a jagged edge through the mass of vegetation. Mature rainforest – growth that has remained undisturbed for centuries – generally consists of a high forest canopy, with little greenery on the dark forest floor. But where such virgin jungle has been disturbed – like having a highway slashed through it – secondary vegetation springs up in the sunlit clearings so formed.

The dirt highway had cut a tunnel of sunlight through the forest, and on each side of the road was a riot of greenery. While it is relatively easy to trek through mature jungle, such secondary vegetation is thick, tangled and more often than not full of horrendous thorns and spines. If the rebels hit us, it would take an age to cut through it with our machetes. In reality the only escape route was to drive hell-for-leather back the way we'd come.

With Steve and Marky bedded down on the deck, Grant and me took up a position by the rear of the wagon, weapons pointing eastwards – the direction from which we presumed the rebels would come – eyes scanning the night-dark terrain.

'I know why I'm here,' I muttered to Grant, not taking my gaze from my weapon's iron sights. 'Gets mouthy old Smoggy out of the way.' I jerked my head in Marky and Steve's direction. 'But why are those two here, plus you?'

Grant shook his head imperceptibly, eyes showing white in the darkness. 'I've no idea. None, mate.'

We were keeping our voices low, partly in case any rebels were within hearing distance, but partly so we wouldn't be overheard by Marky and Steve. We didn't want our doubts and apprehension cascading down to the blokes. They had to believe the links in the chain of command were strong, although none of the guys were stupid. They would know there were tensions.

I tightened my grip on my weapon. 'You know, this doesn't make any sense . . . Sending the four of us out here . . .'

'Mate, don't I know it,' Grant cut in. 'But right now there's not a lot we can do about it.'

Having talked it over some more, we agreed that the only thing to do was for Grant and the senior NCOs – me, Wag, The White Rabbit – to go direct to Colonel Gibson if this continued. And with Gibbo a whole world away back at Lungi Airport, we were pretty much stuck with things as they were right now.

It was far from perfect, but what other options were there?

The night proved warm and sticky, with a lot of ambient light from the moon and stars. It meant our view northeast up the road was pretty good, without having to use any NVG. No one could make much progress through the jungle or down the road without making considerable noise, so we'd most likely hear 'em before we'd see 'em.

Or so we hoped.

If they skirted by us undetected in the deep jungle, they could get between our position and the village, at which stage we were toast. We'd be surrounded by rebels on all sides. We'd be killed or captured – and if the latter, presumably we'd be offered amputations, 'long-sleeve' or 'short-sleeve' style. Or maybe something even worse. But there was sod all we could do about that now – four blokes set a half a klick out from any support.

We focused our every molecule on our senses – chiefly hearing and sight – our early warning systems. The key to survival here was watchfulness in every sense of the word, and tuning in to the natural environment. Once we'd familiarised ourselves with the regular beat and rhythm of the jungle, we could filter out those sounds and scan for ones only a human might make: the crunch of boots on leaves; whispered voices; the *clatch-clatch* of a bolt being pulled back on an assault rifle.

It was like a form of meditation, this tuning in to the night environment. I opened up my mind and senses to any changes in the setting here, and I was hyper-alert to any sense of threat. If my ears caught the faintest sound – anything distinct from the deafening night-time beat pulsating out of the forest shadows – my eyes immediately swivelled around to focus on that point.

We had with us one Clansman 349 VHF radio, which was set to 'listening watch'. This meant we had an open line of comms to Tricky, back in the HQ ATAP, and we'd keep it live all night long. That way he would hear if we were under attack the moment it happened. We'd only speak to him if we had to – if there was something vital to report – and vice versa.

All that night the tension rippled back and forth, as we sensed movement out there in the darkness. Every noise from the brooding bush sent my pulse racing. I'd soldiered in many of the world's jungles but this was something different. We were four against several thousand, and we stood out like the proverbial dog's bollocks with the wagon parked on the dirt roadway.

First light was about the most welcome sight that any of us had ever seen. Imperceptibly the jungle brightened, and I felt the tension of the long night's watch draining out of me.

Almost as the first rays of sunlight filtered over the horizon, Tricky came up on the air. '*33, Zero*. Move back into village.'

Zero was the OC's call-sign, 33 was us.

'Roger, out.'

Never has a short drive down a dirt track been so enjoyable as that one back into Lungi Lol.

We parked the Pinz on the village square and made our way to the HQ ATAP, leaving Marky and Steve to head back to their patrols. We'd been out there for nine hours straight and I'd managed four hours' fitful sleep, lying in full belt kit on the dirt with my weapon only ever a hand's reach away. With the constant buzzing of the mozzies that were feeding on me, plus the tension, I'd never really been fully asleep. There was always an edge of wakefulness.

After stand-to we got a brew on, tucking into some ration packs over a nice cup of tea. All around us I could hear the village starting to come to life. None of the patrols had much to report, our first night in Lungi Lol being seemingly a quiet one.

Around 0800 hours Donaldson gathered the head-shed. 'Right, I'm heading back to Lungi Airport,' he announced. 'I need to speak to the CO. I'll need a driver, so I'm taking Marky with me.'

Utter silence.

No one said the barest thing in response. This was so totally and utterly unexpected we were at a complete loss for words. The OC radioed for Marky to join him, and the two of them made their way across to one of the Pinzgauers. With barely another word they mounted up the vehicle and drove west out of Lungi Lol.

The four of us in the HQ ATAP – Grant, Tricky, Wag and me – were stunned. It was as if we were all waiting to see who was going to be the first to break the silence and say something.

It was Wag. 'What – the – *fuuuuck*?' he asked, incredulously.

I shook my head in disbelief. 'Mate, I have no idea.'

'But what the *fuck* is that all about? Tricky – has he said anything to anyone on the comms?'

Tricky shook his head. 'Nope. Not said a word all night long.'

There weren't the words to express how we were feeling right now. We were utterly dumbfounded. The ramifications of this were unknowable. Was Donaldson gone for good, or just paying Gibbo a temporary call? Did command now pass to Grant, or not? Was Grant now *Sunray*, the OC Pathfinders' call-sign? Or was Donaldson somehow still in command – just that he wasn't with us any more?

Who fucking knows?

Why did Donaldson need to speak to the CO in person anyway, instead of via the radio? No one had the faintest idea. Equally importantly, would they even make it? They had several dozen kilometres of uncharted territory to get through, with no known friendly forces between us and Lungi Airport. Plus we were left with just the one vehicle in Lungi Lol, which greatly lessened our ability to escape and evade via the wagons, for one Pinz could carry no more than a dozen men.

We took stock. We had another thirty-six hours max of the mission ahead of us, and we were determined to make the best of it. We decided to use the time well. First off, we'd get the patrols to build up their defences still further. Wag and I got them busy doing that, then we went to have a further chat with Lieutenant Mojo, to try to get a better sense of whether his men might be of any use to us in a fight with the rebels.

Just to the south of the HQ ATAP Mojo had his own quarters,

encircled by a palisade of wood driven into the ground. We'd yet to see inside, for the fence was ten feet high and blocked all view. It was around 0900 hours when we knocked on the small wooden door. Mojo appeared dressed as immaculately as he had been on day one, and gestured for us to join him.

'Please – this is where I live.'

We poked our heads inside. Immediately to our front was a large hut, one made out of a wooden frame plastered in mud and with a grass-thatch roof. To the right was the weirdest sight of all – a rickety post, with the distinctive light blue flag of the United Nations hanging limply. The palisade was so high and the flagpole so low that you couldn't actually see the flag from outside. But what struck me most powerfully was what was *lacking from the place*: I couldn't see a single radio antenna, no sign of any radio, nor any solar panels with which to charge one.

It looked as if Mojo and his men had no way of making comms back to UN headquarters, that's presuming the UN had such a thing. They had no way to receive orders, Intel updates, schedule resupplies or to get relieved, and no way to call up reinforcements when several thousand rebels came charging down their throats. In the circumstances, going native – as Mojo's men had done – seemed about the smartest option in terms of trying to stay alive.

Having been shown around the Kingdom of Mojo, it struck me that the lieutenant mightn't even know that a battalion of British PARAs – plus elite forces – had jetted into the country. We invited him over to our place for a brew and a chat. It quickly became clear that Mojo had not the slightest idea about pretty much any-thing: he had no idea that the British military had intervened in the war, occupying Lungi Airport and most of Freetown. He'd pre-sumed we were British soldiers somehow working with the UN, as fellow peacekeepers.

He knew of the RUF's existence, but he had zero idea of their proximity, or that they were massing to assault Lungi Airport and Freetown – so aiming to usher in another dark chapter of murder and mayhem across the country. In fact he had absolutely no idea of the kind of danger he and his men were in – largely because he had no way of making contact with, or getting updates from, the UN.

Incredible.

Grant proceeded to enlighten him. 'Lieutenant, you need to know that there is an imminent threat and that this village is in danger. There are several thousand RUF advancing on Freetown and the only way they can get there is via here. Right now they could be any distance away – from a few dozen kilometres to spitting-distance close. The updates we're getting are that they're on the move, and we thought we were flying into a hot LZ.'

Lieutenant Mojo looked suitably taken aback. He'd had six months of a peaceful posting, without the slightest hint that the villagers of Lungi Lol were about to get butchered, along with all of his men.

'Ours is only a forty-eight-hour tasking,' Grant continued. 'We envisage we will be gone in two days maximum. We're here as a blocking force, to provide security while we evacuate our nationals from Lungi Airport. But while we're here we'll assist you with your mandate, which I presume is securing the village.'

Mojo gave a confused shake of the head. 'I had heard reports of villages getting attacked, of women being raped and of villagers being put to work by the rebels – but this was all upcountry and a very long way away. If the rebels are poised to take Freetown that means the UN operation here ... well, it has been a very big failure.'

'That's as may be,' Grant replied. 'It's not our concern. You're the UN and you have your roles and responsibilities. Our tasking is to ensure that the ongoing evacuation of civilians from Freetown goes ahead unhindered. We are not – *repeat not* – a peacekeeping force. We will use lethal force if fired upon or if the need arises. Do you understand the difference between us?'

Mojo glanced at Grant. 'I do. But it doesn't seem as if there is much peace to keep any more.' He paused, then fixed Grant with this earnest look. 'If things are as serious as you say, you need to meet the village chief. Let me take you to him. He needs to know this.'

We figured this was a smart idea. The more local connections we could forge here in Lungi Lol, the more Intel we might garner.

Mojo led the way to the village square. It was around 1030 by now and the marketplace was getting busy. People were milling about carrying baskets of mangoes and trays of tomatoes and bicycles were criss-crossing to and fro. There was even the odd guy on a moped pootling about. To one side of the square lay a larger building raised up three feet or so on wooden stilts. Its walls were made from a woven latticework of branches plastered with mud, and it had the obligatory grass-thatch roof. Six wooden steps led up to a veranda that ran along the front of the building, plus a wooden door.

To the left of the door sat an old, balding, wiry-looking man on a straight-backed wooden chair. His poise and bearing marked him out as a man of substance. The chair faced onto the village square, plus the T-junction. From this vantage point he could observe all who passed through his domain. To the right of the door was a younger dude – clearly the village chief's lackey.

It struck me as odd that the chief hadn't been over to see us yet, to ask what we were doing in his village. But we'd learn with time that the chief never stirred from his chair. Everyone went to him. People came to ask a favour, or to air a grievance, or to sort a feud, whatever.

Grant, Wag, Mojo and me gathered at the bottom of the steps, with Mojo slightly in the lead. He began to address the chief, speaking some language that we couldn't understand. I caught the odd English word, but otherwise it was gibberish. We'd learn in time that this was Pidgin English, a blend of English mixed with Creole – a West African dialect dating back to the times of slavery.

The chat went on for a good few minutes, Mojo doing the talking and the chief listening. I saw him gesture at the three of us, as he gabbled away. Every now and then the chief would glance at his lackey, the lackey would say a few words, and then the chief would nod for Mojo to continue.

I gave chiefy a good long study. I figured he was around seventy-five years old and thinning on top, with wispy hair flecked with grey. He was lighter-skinned than Mojo and several of his yellowing teeth were missing. An all-in-one robe fell from his shoulders to his feet, which were shod in worn leather sandals. In his right hand he had a lighted cigarette and every now and then he took a drag.

We were doing our best to be culturally sensitive – hearts and minds stuff and all that – but still Wag couldn't resist making the odd comment.

'What d'you reckon he's saying now?' he muttered, out of the corner of his mouth. 'Let's kill 'em all?'

Mojo still had his massive Foster Grant shades on – in fact I'd never seen him without them – but his tone and attitude was now one of total respect. When the chief raised his hand in a gesture for silence Mojo shut it immediately, leaving the big man free to talk. The chief said a few words, his eyes flickering from Mojo to us and back again, and Mojo translated.

'Okay, he says he is happy that you are here. He welcomes you on behalf of the village. He says if you need anything while you are here you must come to him. He is very glad you have come.' Mojo paused. 'So, he would like you to introduce yourselves.'

Grant glanced at the veranda. 'Hi, I'm Grant.'

Mojo: 'Grant!'

I was trying not to crack up. 'Right, I'm Steve.'

Mojo: 'And Steve!'

'Aye, and I'm Wag,' said Wag.

Mojo did a double take: 'Wag?' he queried, in a high-pitched voice of surprise.

'Mate, just this once how about being Graham?' I muttered.

Wag glared at Mojo. He was crouched there like a Hobbit, his weapon in one hand and his torso wrapped in bandoliers of ammo. Correction. Right now he didn't remind me so much of a Hobbit, as of Gimli the Dwarf in *The Lord of the Rings*.

Wag scowled. 'Not Wag like that,' he said, mimicking Mojo's high-pitched whine. 'It's *Wag*,' he growled. 'Wag.'

Mojo turned to the chief and shrugged: 'And . . . Wag.'

The chief nodded gravely. Introductions done, Mojo chatted some more, then turned to us. 'Okay, so we're done. Let's go.'

On the way back to HQ ATAP Mojo told us it had all gone very well. 'Any assistance the chief can give – anything – just let me know.'

'We're fine for the time being,' Grant replied. 'We've got the men on the ground and the patrols are well bedded in.'

'How many of you are there?' Mojo asked.

'Twenty-seven.'

Mojo stopped dead in his tracks: '*Twenty-seven*?'

We'd spent all morning warning him about the danger of getting massacred by thousands of rebels. I guessed he'd imagined several hundred British troops had thrown a wall of steel around Lungi Lol. Now we'd revealed our true numbers – *twenty-seven*. Correction: twenty-five with Marky and Donaldson gone.

Mojo hurried off towards the Kingdom of Mojo looking decidedly worried. We turned left to where Tricky was hunched over the radio. Right now he had a bunch of kids crowded around him. Our ration packs contained bags of boiled sweets, and Tricky had started doling them out to the boys and girls of Lungi Lol. Each time he handed some out a kid would start cavorting about and yelling for joy. *Yippeee!* Compared to back home in Britain these poor little sods had next to nothing, and the looks on their faces would have melted the hardest of hearts.

'So, how did it go with the chief?' Tricky asked.

'Yeah, we just met The King,' Wag replied. 'He never said a lot. Happy for us to be here . . . yada, yada, yada.'

Tricky grinned. 'I've just sent the morning Sched. Told 'em we are on the ground with nothing to report on rebel movements . . . so far.'

It was a good three hours since Donaldson had left us, so unless he and Marky had been hit en route and were lying dead in a ditch they would be back at Lungi Airport by now. I checked with Tricky if he'd had any news, but there was none. There was bugger all we could do about it, so we settled down to priority number one – stopping the RUF at Lungi Lol.

Grant, Wag and me got our heads together, talking through how best to cement our positions. First priority was to map the ground over which we would be fighting. That done, we could hone our defences to better suit the threat. We'd need to ensure each patrol knew its left and right arcs of fire, beyond which they shouldn't put down any rounds – for they'd be straying into the neighbouring patrol's domain. That way, we'd have interlocking arcs of fire covering all potential avenues of approach.

There was no way we could target any rebels massing in the tree line – the fringe of jungle that hemmed in the village on all sides. It was too dark and vegetated to see clearly, and that meant we only had a limited amount of open ground in which to stop them. That in turn meant that we'd have to make every shot count once the rebels were in the kill zone.

We got Dolly, Nathe, Ginge and Taff to draw up detailed sketches of the terrain within each of their patrols' arcs of fire. Any land-marks or reference points – a burned tree stump, a distinctive termite mound – were marked up. That way, fire could be called in instantly: 'Bring to bear, twenty yards right of burned tree!' Everyone in the patrol would know exactly where the enemy was.

Range cards were put together, on which we measured out the distance to each marked point. Below 100 yards the trajec-tory of fire isn't affected by wind or distance, but above that it is. With the range cards, we'd know exactly when to compensate and by how much: we'd automatically aim off the correct fraction for wind speed and distance. Finally, a 'dead ground' study was added to the mix – identifying areas that were hidden from view and from fire, where the enemy could go to ground, regroup and attack.

Those areas were shaded on the sketches, with the entry and exit points identified and named. Fire could then be called instantly onto any of those points. The GPMGs were repositioned to cover the dead ground, while the SA80s would be used to hit individual targets in the open. This was all about increasing the accuracy and intensity of the fire we could bring to bear.

In spite of our mega-blag with Mick back at the Lungi Airport weapons dump, Wag and me were painfully aware of our limited supplies of ammo: there would be no 'fire for effect' on this mission. So at its simplest, this was also about ensuring that every bullet found a target.

When the rebels hit us we needed to make sure one shot equalled one kill.

8

We figured we also needed to up our profile and our visibility with the locals. All morning we'd had people moving along the main highway into and out of the village – presumably traders, family visitors, farmers, whatever. Everyone stopped to stare at these strange white soldiers who'd occupied Lungi Lol. But it was clear as day that any number of them could have been rebels posing as villagers.

The rebels might be recceing our positions, or even infiltrating the village so they could hit us from the rear. Their ranks were made up of scores of child soldiers, so in theory even the kids could be the bad guys. We knew they had used villagers as human shields – forcing them to march in front of their fighters – in previous battles. We had to presume they were pretty much capable of anything, and if they were getting in amongst us undetected it wasn't good news.

As a priority we needed to push out roving foot patrols to keep a watch on the comings and goings, and to establish stop and search checkpoints. The more we could get the patrols on the move the more ground truth we'd garner, plus the harder it would be for any of the bad guys to figure out our exact positions or our numbers.

That afternoon Wag and me did a walkabout to check on the patrols. It was the hottest part of the day by now, and out from under the tree cover the sun was merciless. We headed first for Dolly's position – *33 Bravo* – on our left flank. By the time we had reached the shade of the thick bush we were soaked with sweat. I had beads of it dripping off the rim of my jungle hat in a constant stream.

What made matters worse was that we'd been issued with just the one litre of drinking water per man per day. As with ammo, weaponry, maps, anti-malarials and so much else, someone had forgotten to add water to the list of supplies we might need in Sierra Leone. While we had the kit to filter and purify water, the village appeared to be totally dry. We figured they'd built it on a patch of the highest land available, so that it didn't flood too badly during the rains. But that meant there wasn't a ready supply of water anywhere nearby.

Ideally, we needed to drink several litres per day, to keep properly hydrated. Dehydration causes listlessness and the lack of ability to focus. Right now we'd not had a single shot fired at us or seen the slightest sign of any rebels, and village life seemed to be proceeding pretty much as normal. We needed to get around the blokes and reinforce the need for watchfulness.

The threat was very real: we just didn't know when or where exactly they'd hit us. We needed heightened alertness, measured with sustainability. The blokes couldn't be staring down their rifles all day long or they'd go stir crazy. We needed to balance getting good rest, eating properly and trying to keep actions to a minimum during the heat of the day, with a permanent readiness to do battle. That was the message we spread around the patrols.

The plan in the case of an overwhelming assault was to hold the village for as long as possible. We agreed three trigger points for us to go on the run. The first was taking unsustainable casualties (i.e. more than we could evacuate). The second was facing the serious danger of being overrun. The third was when two-thirds of our ammo had been exhausted. If that stage was reached we'd be left with around a hundred rounds per man with which to do a fighting withdrawal.

It was late afternoon by the time Wag and me were back at the HQ ATAP. Mojo must have had a word with his blokes, for several of them had pitched up, dressed in a hodgepodge of mixed combats, T-shirts and sarongs. In contrast to their leader's parade-ground perfection, these guys were tatty and unkempt, and their weapons looked similarly ill-maintained. They carried Belgian-made FN assault rifles, but one look at them and I doubted if they would be much use in battle.

Wag was obviously thinking along the same lines. He approached one of them, feigning interest in his weapon, as if he'd never seen the likes of it before. In reality Pathfinders are trained to use just about every kind of small arms invented, in case we have to disarm the bad guys, or scavenge their weaponry and ammo when in a situation like the one we were in now.

'What kind of gun is that, then, mate?' Wag asked. I wondered if the Nigerian would understand his thick Burnley accent. 'Can I have a look at it then, mate?'

The Nigerian handed it across. The FN looks like the old British Army self-loading rifle (SLR). It has a fully-automatic function and packs a 7.62 mm round. Wag removed the magazine, unloaded the weapon, cocked it and got a good look at the working parts. Simply by listening to the action as he moved it back and forth, he'd be able to tell if it was smooth and well-oiled, or stiff and gravelly.

'Oh yeah, this is a nice weapon, like,' Wag remarked. He turned it around as if admiring it, before replacing the magazine. 'Is it yours like? All yours?'

The Nigerian smiled proudly as he took back his weapon. It was his all right, and by the look on Wag's face it hadn't seen a clean or an oil in the six months the Nigerians had been here.

'The mag was dented and battered,' Wag reported, once Mojo's men had gone. 'Looked to be about half a dozen rounds in it, max. And did you hear the crunching of the working parts? Horrendous . . .'

We could assume that if one was like that, they likely all were. If and when the rebels hit us, we'd not be relying on Mojo's men for back-up, that was for sure.

Prior to last light Tricky radioed through the second Sched

of the day. We got a surprise message from The White Rabbit in return: '*Sunray* will not be returning to your location. Repeat: *Sunray* will not be returning to your location. There will be a re-supply tomorrow morning: send HLS grid.'

Sunray was the code-name for Donaldson. As no further information was provided, no one had a clue what had happened. But we could make a good guess about how Donaldson's surprise re-appearance would have gone down with Colonel Gibson. In any case, he was gone and we had a job to get on with here.

During that afternoon's walkabout we'd realised there was a far better HLS – helicopter landing site – than the one we'd flown in on. Due west of Taff's position was a large, open, sandy bowl some seventy metres across. The surface was hard-packed like concrete, and there was little vegetation to obstruct a landing. That was now the preferred HLS. Tricky called through its grid to The White Rabbit, and we got confirmation that a Chinook would be inbound the following morning.

We didn't know what the resupply flight was for exactly, as we were scheduled to be out of Lungi Lol sometime tomorrow. The White Rabbit rounded off the comms with an Intel update for us.

'Information suggests significant rebel movement towards Freetown, and that *it will have to come through you*. Repeat: rebels moving in significant numbers and coming via your location.'

Comms done, we took stock. We could easily have been scouted by the rebels posing as villagers during the day. Even if they hadn't infiltrated Lungi Lol, we had to presume that word of our presence had spread like wildfire. In Lungi Lol and its environs we had to be this year's biggest ever news.

The rebels would know we were here. For certain.

And now we were doubly sure that they were coming.

We called prayers. Having passed the new Intel around to the blokes, Grant delivered the news that Donaldson was gone. He did so in as easygoing a tone as he could muster, but the looks on the patrol commanders' faces said it all.

Nathe gave a snort of derision 'So where's he fucking gone to, then . . .'

'It doesn't matter where he's gone,' Grant interjected. 'He's gone, so let's kill it there. Let's get on with it.' He paused to let the words sink in. 'Right, night-time routine, and I don't need to warn you about the threat level . . .'

No one appeared to dwell on the OC's departure too much, and morale seemed high. This was the 'train hard, fight easy' mentality: the more you drilled down into your skills, the more confident you became in your abilities. When you trained relentlessly, when you were twenty-five guys at the zenith of your abilities, then you could have total faith in those to either side of you. And you could face odds like these with steel in your eyes – not to mention losing your OC.

With dusk came all the noises from the jungle. But tonight there seemed to be more than the normal amount of weird squeals and squawks from out of the tree line. No one had a clue what they were exactly, but we knew of the rebels' habit of signalling to each other at night, using the calls of jungle animals.

'What the fuck's that?' Wag muttered. We'd taken the first stag. 'Was that an animal? Doesn't sound like any I've ever 'eard of.'

To our left people were trickling down the darkened road into the village. We spotted a crowd of a dozen or more moving steadily towards the square.

'Who the hell're that lot?' Wag growled.

I studied them via my NVG. 'Can't see any weapons. I can see a kid, plus a couple of women.'

'Right, well if it's blokes only we stop and search 'em. Agreed?'

'Agreed.'

By the time Wag and I came off stag the village square was filling up. We did a short walkabout, and it turned out that more people were expected. Word had spread on two fronts: one, that the RUF were poised to launch an attack characterised by all the usual bloody murder and mayhem; two, that the British Army were in Lungi Lol to stop them. People were flooding in from all around and kipping down on the village square, *for protection*.

The village chief was vetting each new family arrival, giving them permission to stay, and allocating an empty space for them to sleep. Most were women and children and they were terrified of the horrors they feared were coming. They bedded down on straw mats that they'd carried with them, with blankets thrown over families huddled together, for the added sense of security. The village square was some seventy yards wide and it was already half-full.

It was our second night in Lungi Lol, and we were counting down the hours until our withdrawal. But in truth, no one was particularly keen to leave. Hardened from years of soldiering in Northern Ireland, where so many of the locals hate British soldiers, it felt great to be on the side of the angels for a change.

We returned to the HQ ATAP. In addition to our sentries, our patrol had a 24/7 watch to keep over the radios. New orders, plus intelligence updates on rebel movements, might be radioed through at any time, and it was vital to keep a listening ear.

Those of us not on watch dossed down, fully dressed in boots and belt kit and with a machete strapped to our side. A grab bag made a passable pillow, with any extra kit stuffed inside it in case of the need to go on the run.

At the crack of dawn I got Tricky to radio Nathe's patrols and get a couple of blokes sent to me. We then headed down there. At 0700 hours dead the distinctive form of a Chinook swooped in low over the treetops and put down in the clearing. The White Rabbit came off the open ramp, along with Marky, the guy who'd driven Donaldson out in the Pinzgauer. I ran across in a crouch to meet them.

'Mate, this is open-ended now!' The White Rabbit yelled in my ear-hole, above the deafening noise of the helo's turbines. 'No idea how long you'll be here!' He jerked his thumb towards a heap of stores lying under a cargo net in the hold. 'Load more supplies in there – water jerries, food, anti-malarials . . .'

I signalled to the guys to get unloading. Eddie and I moved away from the helo, whose rotors were still turning and burning, as the blokes started ferrying kit out from under the downwash of the thrashing blades. We got ourselves a good twenty metres away from the noise and the dust, so we could get a proper heads-up. Even so, Eddie still had to yell to make himself heard.

'Steve, Donaldson's gone. He flew out on a Herc yesterday back to the UK. He's on a compassionate. Jacko's been made stand-in OC Pathfinders.'

A 'compassionate' is military speak for going on compassionate leave – so if you had extraordinary personal or family reasons that meant you had to get home. If Donaldson had gone on a compassionate, at least that would help make some sense out of all that had happened.

Jacko – Mark Jackson – had been the 2iC of the Pathfinders prior to Grant taking over. He'd served under Johnny Allem, the superlative OC we'd had prior to Donaldson. He was the son of Sir Mike Jackson, the high-profile ex-commander of KFOR (Kosovo Force), the force that had liberated Kosovo in 1999. Needless to say, we were in good hands if Jacko had taken over command.

'Mate, the NEO is almost done,' Eddie continued, 'but the op is evolving and the Intel we're picking up indicates serious rebel movement towards your position. The CO wants you here for the duration.'

Intel was flooding in thick and fast, Eddie explained. Largely it was from humint sources – paid informers – within the rebel ranks, but also due to our electronic warfare people having cracked the rebels' communications, so we could listen in on their conversations. From that they figured some 2000 rebels were massing to the north of us. They were armed with small arms, rocket-propelled grenades, light machine guns, and 12.7 mm DShK heavy machine guns, plus they had captured UN armoured personnel carriers and trucks.

'Make no mistake: holding this place is key to everyone's plans,' Eddie continued. 'The rebels have to be stopped here, otherwise they'll make it into Freetown and we all know what follows. The CO doesn't have anyone else who can do the job.

'Now that you're here for the duration, the SAS lads will come through you and recce your flanks. That's about it. Oh yeah, apart from this.' Eddie handed me a large, bulky mobile-phone-like device. 'We figured you might need this. We've got another back at base so we can do satphone-to-satphone comms, just in case the radios aren't working.'

Our 319 HF radios were dodgy as hell. All it generally took was a good soaking and the 319s would stop working. By contrast, the Thuraya satphone that Eddie had handed me was a bulletproof system. A purely civvie piece of kit, it was 100 per cent reliable, versatile and fast. A tenth of the size and weight of our 319s, it was also perfect for going on the run. They were like gold dust, and getting our hands on one meant the nightmare scenario of getting hit by the rebels and not being able to call in the QRF was pretty much over.

Eddie and me chatted for a few seconds more as the blokes finished unloading, running through various scenarios of how the twenty-six of us lot were going to stop 2000 rebels armed to the teeth.

He signed off with a bemused shrug. 'Mate, fuck knows.'

With that he turned and took a crouching run back up the Chinook's open ramp. The loadie hopped on after him, gave the thumbs-up, and almost before the ramp started to whine shut the Chinook lifted off. They'd been on the ground for four minutes max before they were heading back towards Lungi Airport.

The White Rabbit had flown in with three days of rations per man – all they could spare from stores. He also had a few jerry cans of fresh water. Being Pathfinders, no washing was allowed when on operations, so this was for drinking only.

The reason you don't wash is if you cut your face shaving you can get an infection, which in conditions like these could turn nasty very quickly. Plus our aim on a mission such as this one was to take on the look, the feel and the smell of the jungle, so as to become invisible to the enemy. If we were forced to go on the run we would be living like animals anyway, so the transition would be that much easier if we'd started it early.

In short, we didn't have the water to waste washing and couldn't take the risk of doing so. The only exception to the no washing rule was teeth. The body can cope with being dirty – just. But gum disease or rotting teeth is an endex (end of exercise) issue – you'd be pulled off the mission.

I fetched the Pinzgauer. We loaded up the supplies and drove back to the HQ position. It was the start of our third day in Lungi Lol, and we'd been in-country for six. Finally the British Army had managed to get its act together on the medical front: the resupply included some packs of Lariam, an anti-malarial pill.

I sent the guys back to their patrols, then gave Wag, Tricky and Grant the news.

'The op's evolving and we're here for the duration, to protect the only viable route into Lungi Airport and Freetown. The task is open-ended, and this is it: the rebels stop here. Oh yeah, and Donaldson's gone back to UK on a compassionate, and fucking Jacko's taking over as acting OC.'

As I was telling them about Donaldson being gone for good, I was watching the guys' expressions. Wag's face would become all puckered-up whenever he was annoyed, which was exactly what it had done now. He looked like a size ten bloke in a size eleven skin. As for Grant, he actually seemed relieved.

'At least now we can get on with the job in hand,' he announced.

Wag grunted a bunch of curses in agreement.

Tricky, meanwhile, was in sheer ecstasy at having got himself a Thuraya.

We called the patrol commanders in and Grant briefed them in turn. They took the news about Donaldson's compassionate pretty well. No one spared much of a thought about the OC any more. There were other priorities right now. We were twenty-six against two thousand, and we'd be here until battle was joined.

We had no heavy weapons, one thin-skinned vehicle, and with only two Chinooks in theatre we suspected the QRF might take a little longer to get to us than the thirty-five minutes we'd been promised. The chances of a helo plus a platoon of PARAs being kept permanently on standby to come to our aid were just about zero – especially with the evacuation of hundreds of civilians under way.

To make matters worse we had no access to any fire support. We had no air assets in theatre capable of doing danger-close air strikes in the thick of the jungle. And while we did have British warships steaming off the coast, ones boasting guns with the range to reach Lungi Lol, there was no one in theatre capable of orchestrating such complex naval fire support. In short, we were pretty much unsupported and on our own out here.

Eddie's Intel brief had contained one other, distinctly worrying, snippet of info: one of the chief aims of the rebels was to capture some British soldiers. No one needed telling what would happen to any so taken. If they could capture some elite operators like us, it would serve to humiliate the entire British military. It would also big-up the rebels' own reputation, and very likely turn public opinion in the UK against intervening in such a far distant war.

As the rebels had advanced towards Freetown they had already started to achieve their aims. They'd surrounded and laid siege to some 500 Indian peacekeepers upcountry in an isolated UN base. Parachute Regiment Major Andy Harrison had been captured, along with fourteen Indian troops. Major Harrison had only just been posted to Sierra Leone. He'd been sent here to try to turn the UN mission around, but before he could get to work the rebels had struck.

That was only one in a wave of such kidnappings, all of which were being targeted chiefly at British troops. The RUF had surrounded and laid siege to a second UN base, this one staffed by seventy Kenyan peacekeepers. Inside the base were Royal Marine Major Phil Ashby, plus Royal Navy Lieutenant-Commander Paul Rowland and Major Andrew Samsonoff of the Light Infantry. It was those British soldiers that the rebels were hell-bent on getting their hands on.

The RUF had vowed to spill British blood in Sierra Leone. As of yet, no British soldiers had been killed, but Andy Harrison had fallen directly into their hands, and had been savagely beaten and threatened with execution. The rebels had a habit of giving their missions darkly bizarre names: Operation Cut Hands; Operation Kill All Your Family; Operation Kill All Living Things. They had named their present mission 'Operation Kill British'.

The overall aim of Operation Kill British was apparently to turn Sierra Leone into 'Britain's Somalia' – a reference to the American military's defeat in the Somali capital, Mogadishu, immortalised in the book and the movie *Black Hawk Down*. Via Operation Kill British the rebels would drive us out of Sierra Leone, and their victory – plus the humiliation of Her Majesty's Armed Forces – would be complete.

And all that stood in their way right now were the twenty-six of us.

9

In light of Operation Kill British we figured better and stronger defences were in order, and for what we now had in mind we'd need the village chief's help. Around midday we paid a visit to the Kingdom of Mojo. The lieutenant invited us in – his gate was always open – and Grant proceeded to brief him on how we were here for the long-term.

'We need to go see the chief, 'cause we need a workforce,' Grant told him. 'The incentive for him to provide one is that there are two thousand rebels moving on Freetown and they are coming through his village. For us to be able to help him and his people, he is going to have to be ready to help us.'

Mojo must have realised the seriousness of the situation. He seemed more alert and his whole pace had quickened. 'Okay, I understand. Let's go.'

We made our way directly to the chief's place and found him already holding court. Two women with a young boy were in a conflab with him.

Mojo held out a hand to stop us butting in. 'Okay, just wait.'

We took a ticket and joined the queue.

When they were done Mojo launched into one. He was the most animated I'd ever seen him, and while I couldn't understand what he was saying I could sense the urgency, as if he was really trying to drive his points home. He finished speaking and the chief had a few words with his lackey.

Then: 'Okay, we will help.'

Via Mojo we told the chief we'd work out exactly what we needed, now we knew he was able to assist. Then we said our thank yous and returned to the HQ ATAP.

Tricky got a brew on – he was the master of the brews – while Grant gave Mojo a good talking to. Bearing in mind the state of their rifles and their drills, we didn't want Mojo and his men any-where near us when the bullets started to fly. But we did need some kind of force to man a line of defence to the rear of the vil-lage, in case the rebels managed to get around the back of us. We didn't have enough men to mount a 360-degree defence, so maybe the Nigerians could act as an early warning force if the rebels were attacking from the rear.

'Once we sort out the battle plan we may need you and your men to be involved,' Grant told Mojo. 'No longer can you just sit on the sidelines.'

Mojo's response was muted. He knew full well that the long, lazy months of summer were over and that he and his men were going to have to either shape up or ship out. But still he seemed reluctant to get involved.

'But we are here only on peacekeeping duties,' the lieutenant objected. 'Our role is to keep the peace . . .'

Wag and me waded in. We soon convinced Mojo that there was no f-ing peace to keep. If and when the rebels hit Lungi Lol it was kill or be killed – and that was the same for the Nigerians in their natty blue berets as much as for us. Grant told Mojo we'd come back to him on exactly what we needed, when we'd worked out the wider plan.

With that Mojo left, shoulders bowed and heading for the pri-vacy of his compound. Presumably, he was trying to think up the words to tell his men that the Lungi Lol Sunny Vacation was over, and that Armageddon was only just around the corner.

With Mojo warned off, Grant, Wag and me gathered over the maps. It was time to drill down into the threat – to establish exactly what it was and where it would come from. As always, we would afford the enemy the ultimate respect until proved other-wise. We had to think along these lines: *If I was advancing with*

2000 men and that kind of firepower, how would I launch an attack?

If the rebels chose to rush us in a full-frontal assault we'd face 2000 coming at us in human waves. With 300 rounds per man, we could in theory kill 7800 enemy fighters – but that's if every round equalled a kill. As it was, we'd have to average one kill per 6.66 rounds fired, if we were to account for 2000. But *my* favoured plan of attack would be far more sophisticated than that, and we had to work on the presumption that the rebels would come up with something equally subtle and sinister.

By now we'd had foot patrols out, pressing into the edge of the forest. One of those patrols had stumbled upon a feature that worried me perhaps more than anything. To the far side of Taff's position – so on our right flank – there was a railway line. It wasn't marked on any maps and we figured it was disused. But it constituted a clear line of advance through the jungle, and it ran pretty much parallel to the main highway.

In short, it provided the rebels with a second line of march, in addition to the dirt track. If I was attacking Lungi Lol, I'd put a force on the main road and make it look as if I was launching a full-frontal assault. But at the same time I'd send a second force down the railroad, moving silently and stealthily through the jungle. I'd use that to outflank us, and hit us from the side and the rear – just as the feint from the front drew all our fire.

From all that we could see, the first thing that was obvious was that we needed Claymores. They could be planted covering key avenues of approach – the worrisome railroad first and foremost. Triggered by a command wire, a mass of shrapnel would fire out in a 180-degree arc, scything down anything in its path. Claymores would be a game-changer. We didn't have any, of course, but with the chief's help we figured we could likely cobble some together.

Top of our shopping list with chiefy went: 'Find raw materials for making Claymores.'

With a 1 PARA QRF being thirty-five minutes' call away – plus add another ten to muster them – we'd need to hold out for forty-five minutes before a platoon of PARAs flew in to reinforce us. We needed to block enemy approach routes with Claymores and channel the rebels into massed groups, where we could mow them down with our heaviest firepower – the GPMGs. That should hold them off for long enough to get the QRF in.

In order to channel them we needed to create obstacles that would slow them down and cause injuries, and put large swathes of terrain off-limits. We needed to squeeze them into kill zones. We needed to clear the vegetation around those kill zones so they had not a scrap of cover to hide, and so we could see them to shoot them.

Second on our shopping list with chiefy went: 'Get villagers to clear kill zones out to forest edge.'

But the biggest challenge was how to channel the rebels into those kill zones. The Claymores would stop them in their tracks on the main approach routes. From there we needed physical barriers to corral them into death traps. The question was, what raw materials were available in and around the village to create such barriers? We had an abundance of wood. Most of the village buildings – Mojo's palisade included – were built out of one particular type: bamboo. This wasn't like the bamboo you get in your garden back home: here it grew to sixty feet in height and the thickness of a man's arm.

We had an abundance of bamboo, plus we had machetes and knives, and from what we'd seen the locals knew how to work with bamboo to build pretty much anything. It was Wag who first gave voice to the idea that was coalescing in our minds: *could we get the locals to make and plant fields of 'punji sticks'?* Done properly, they'd trap and injure the rebels, corralling them into zones where we could cut them to ribbons with the guns.

Wag and me had been on several joint training exercises with the SAS in the rainforests of Borneo. The aim was to operate for long periods as isolated groups deep in the jungle. We'd learned how to move through the forest without leaving telltale signs; how to track an enemy, and how to lose one that was tracking you; how to engage in close-quarter battle in the thick bush; how to cache weapons and food supplies; and how to survive in the jungle.

As we contemplated the coming battle at Lungi Lol we realised there was one lesson from Borneo that we could well use here. The native tribes that live in the rainforests have a tradition of raiding each other's villages. As a defence against such attacks, they plant fields of sharpened bamboo stakes around their settlements – so-called 'punji sticks'. They're lengths of bamboo honed to a razor sharpness, and they are as lethal as a steel blade.

There are several variations on the basic punji theme. The stakes can be placed in the base and walls of a 'punji pit', so that when one of the enemy steps into it his leg is pierced in many places. They can be set in pits with their points facing downwards, so if he tries to pull his leg out the punjis will tear the trapped limb to pieces. They can even be arranged as a latticework of spikes and suspended from a tree, being triggered to drop on anyone passing below.

In terms of winning a battle, wounding the enemy is often more effective than killing them outright. Generally, wounding one opponent takes three out of the fight – because two are needed to evacuate the injured man. Punji sticks were the ideal means to wound, and there was no reason why what works for the natives of Borneo wouldn't work here. We were twenty-six facing 2000. We had very limited firepower. The rebels did not. Desperate straits called for desperate measures. The punji stick proposal got an enthusiastic response from all.

We sketched out the ideal areas in which to plant the punji fields. We'd need two work parties from the village: one cutting bamboo in the forest and shaping and sharpening it, another clearing vegetation and driving the sharpened stakes in. We needed the punji fields to be well-hidden, so as to ensnare the rebels. We didn't want twelve-foot-high monster spikes that were visible from a mile away. We wanted them hidden at around knee or thigh height, and maybe the odd punji pit dug as well, to really scare the shit out of the bad guys.

Third on our shopping list with chiefy went: 'Get villagers to make and plant punji fields.'

Finally, we needed trenches dug, to get the lads below ground. The rebels boasted vehicle-mounted heavy weapons – namely 12.7 mm DShKs, the Russian equivalent of the NATO .50-calibre heavy machine gun – plus belt-fed support weapons. That kind of firepower would chew through the vegetation and the built-up earth banks around our shell-scrapes. We needed proper battle trenches, two to each patrol, sited so they mutually supported each other, in case one was in danger of being overrun.

In addition to the two trenches per patrol – eight in all – we decided we needed one trench set forward on the main highway to control access into the village, and to ID any enemy forces massing to attack. We'd site that trench a hundred metres ahead of the village, and it would be manned by two guys on a 24/7 watch. It would also require some kind of cover constructed over it to provide shade, for it would be well out in the open.

We also figured we needed two further trenches set to either side of the road at the rear of the village. Presuming Mojo and his men agreed to play ball, those would be manned by the Nigerian peacekeepers – who we hoped had been persuaded of the urgent need to move onto a war-fighting footing.

Of course, if we sited the Nigerians in those trenches and we did have to fall back through the village, Mojo's men would likely be trigger happy and firing at shadows. They could end up killing some of us – that's as long as their rifles still worked. We decided the only way to prevent this was to ban Mojo and his men from firing back into the village. They would only be allowed to open fire towards the south and the west, so away from the centre of Lungi Lol.

Last on our shopping list with chiefy went: 'Get villagers to dig battle trenches.'

The reason why we needed the villagers to do this, as opposed to us, was simple: while they were building the defences, we'd be keeping watch for the rebels.

I figured now was also the time to radio in a request to The White Rabbit for trip flares and motion sensors. Those would be a total game-changer, in terms of stealing the enemy's element of surprise. The British military had them, that was for sure. We'd used them countless times on exercises. But whether they'd actually got any into theatre was a different matter entirely.

Priorities sorted, Wag and me went and fetched Mojo. We explained exactly what we needed the village chief to organise, plus we outlined the role we'd allocated to Mojo and his men.

'We need you to provide security to the rear of the village,' I told him. 'We'll need you to man one trench set to either side of the track. Your aim is to stop the rebels advancing from that direction. If the rebels attack you stay there and you do not leave and you hold that end of the village. Can you do that?'

Mojo nodded. 'Yes, okay. We can.'

I fixed Mojo with a very direct look. 'Right, so you are now involved in the active defence of this village, unless you tell us otherwise – at which stage you are on your own.'

'Right, okay, I understand,' Mojo confirmed. 'We are in.'

'What are the UN's Rules of Engagement?' I asked.

Mojo looked at me like he didn't understand the question. Our ROEs were tight: *do not engage the enemy unless fired upon; continue to fight until that threat is eliminated.* But ROEs seemed to be a totally alien concept to Mojo and his UNAMSIL force.

'Okay, breaking it down: at what stage are you as the UN allowed to open fire?'

Mojo glanced from me to Wag and back again. He shrugged. 'I don't know.'

'Right, our ROE is fire when fired upon; maybe you should do the same. But one thing: if you see battle being joined, you never fire up into the village, not under any circumstances. You only ever fire west and south – *away from the village*. You must brief your men never to fire into the village, okay?'

'Okay. But why?'

''Cause at the moment we have no way of ID-ing friend or foe and there could be villagers moving through. Secondly, our plan is that if we are overrun, then we withdraw from the village and we will be coming along the track passing by your positions. And we strongly recommend that you withdraw with us.'

From the look on his face I could tell that it was finally dawning on Mojo what a shitty situation we were all in.

'Our plan if we get overrun is we will be bugging out,' I reiterated.

'Okay, but we will need to stay,' Mojo remarked, quietly.

Wag and I exchanged glances. 'But Mojo, you'll be fucking massacred,' Wag objected. 'Mojo, mate, they will chop you up and eat you for breakfast.'

The Nigerian lieutenant's nickname had stuck so well that Wag had started calling him 'Mojo' to his face. I was slipping into the habit too, not that Mojo seemed to mind.

He remained inscrutable behind his massive Foster Grant shades. 'This is my post. Those are my orders.'

There appeared to be nothing we could do to persuade Mojo that staying put in the face of being overrun by the rebels would not be very good for the health or longevity of him and his men.

The British Army thrives on the concept of 'mission command': you are given an order and you do what is necessary to complete that order, but only up to the point when you realise that it needs to be adapted. Individual commanders of Mojo's rank and higher are given the freedom to make appropriate decisions on the ground. Most other militaries don't really have that concept, certainly not with their regular forces. As to the Nigerian military . . . Well, enough said.

Mojo only ever turned up to speak with us alone. His pride in his dress and appearance plus his educated English set him out as a man apart. The Nigerian military – as with most third world armies – was clearly rigidly hierarchical. In the British military you'd always have the 2iC, and maybe some patrol commanders, sitting in on the kind of briefings we were having. The ability of NCOs to provide ideas and input is unique to the British military, and especially to units like ours.

I figured we needed to shore Mojo up a little. 'Don't worry, mate, it'll never happen. We'll never get overrun. We've got a QRF on standby at Lungi Airport 24/7. People will be coming to our aid.'

Mojo forced a smile.

'Mojo, it's gonna take forty-five minutes for that QRF to get here,' Wag added. 'That is how long we need to make a stand.'

Mojo nodded. 'Okay, okay, I understand.'

'What kind of ammo do you have for your men?' I asked.

'Two magazines. Two magazines.'

Two FN mags should have meant forty rounds per man, but Wag had checked one of their mags and it contained six rounds. So, they'd most likely got a dozen rounds each. Even so, we couldn't afford to spare them any, for we didn't have enough ammo ourselves.

'So, if that's agreed we need to go ask the chief for some work parties,' I concluded. 'Lead on, Bonaparte ... Onwards and up-wards, mate. Off we go.'

Mojo had woken up now to how much he'd been left to rot and stagnate, abandoned in his jungle outpost with no Intel updates or warning of what was coming. In the nick of time we'd pitched up and he'd learned just how dark and shitty his situation was. We were now talking about planting punji fields, siting Claymores, cutting the bush to clear kill zones and creating interlocking arcs of fire.

I could see this light in Mojo's eyes, a kind of realisation: *Oh my God, this is how you do it. This is how you fight the rebels.*

Maybe with these guys we just might get out of this alive.

He set off like the Pied Piper, taking us to see the village chief. It was pretty much the same routine as before – us standing off to one side not saying a word, while Mojo delivered the briefing. He must have done a great job describing what would happen to the village if we didn't get the assistance we'd requested, for within a matter of minutes the chief was in.

Mojo turned to us. 'Yes, he understands, and he will help you. He will gather the people you need. He will assign a head of the workforce, so you can show him what you want.'

'Top job,' Wag enthused.

'Mojo, get him to send the head of the workforce to us at the HQ ATAP,' I said. 'We'll brief him there on what we need. And Mojo, we need to start on this asap.'

We thanked the chief and walked away. It was now 1430 hours on day three of our mission in Lungi Lol, and with the chief's help we planned to turn this remote African village into Sierra Leone's version of the Alamo.

Within the hour this guy pitched up at the HQ ATAP. We were in the midst of having a brew and a snack, and in truth we hadn't expected chiefy to get his act together so quickly. The new arrival was this incredibly tall and lanky beanpole of a bloke who looked about nineteen or twenty years old. He was dressed in a green T-shirt over a green flower-pattern sarong, plus open-toed sandals, and he had a massive machete dangling from one hand.

'I am Ibrahim,' he announced. 'I have been sent by the chief to help the British. What you need?'

His English was pretty good, and this was clearly the chief's chosen foreman. Leading him off to Dolly's position on our left flank, we explained we'd start with vegetation clearance. We wanted the bush cleared back 200 yards to the edge of the jungle. We didn't need it cleared to ground level: just the taller foliage gone, so we could see the rebels as they advanced, to kill them.

Wag used a hand-cut gesture to show the kind of thick bush we needed cleared. 'Get this down. Get this down.'

Ibrahim nodded enthusiastically. 'I do! I do!' He motioned to a palm tree with his machete. 'And cut this too?'

'Yes, yes – shooting through there.' Wag made a rifle gesture with his hands, complete with pulling the trigger. 'Bang, bang. Kill the man through here. Need to see.'

Wag seemed to have struck up a real rapport with Ibrahim, just as he seemed able to do with any average working bloke from Burnley to Bombay. Next we showed Ibrahim the battle trenches we needed dug. Dolly had scratched out a shallow furrow in the ground using the blade of his machete, marking out two rectangular outlines.

'This wide and this long, and up to here,' Wag motioned at neck height. 'Dig 'em so deep.'

'I dig! I dig!' Ibrahim confirmed, mimicking Wag's up-to-the-neck height gesture. 'Up to here.'

'No, no,' Wag shook his head, laughing. 'Up to *my* neck height. Not yours. Ibrahim very tall. Otherwise, men cannot see over top to shoot!'

We did a repeat performance with Ibrahim all along our front, and we were back at the HQ ATAP by around 1600 hours. The sun was already low in the sky and in two hours it would be completely dark.

I glanced worriedly at the ragged line of jungle to our front. 'Nothing much is going to get done tonight, is it?' I remarked to Wag.

Wag shrugged. 'You never know with that Ibrahim bloke. The guy's a fucking human dynamo.'

A few minutes later Nathe came up on the radio. 'Guys, they're chopping. They're out front chopping.'

Grant, Wag and me hurried over to take a look. Out at the front of Nathe's position around thirty villagers had gathered. Mostly they were women and children. Ibrahim was striding about in their midst, shouting orders as they bent to their task. They wielded whatever tools they had – machetes, hoes and picks. Some were even using their bare hands to rip up the vegetation.

For several long minutes we stood there under the trees that shaded Nathe's position, watching in amazement.

Wag emitted this long, low whistle. 'Wow. Will you look at that? People power.'

'Take a look at Ibrahim,' I remarked. 'He's the foreman all right. There he goes – look at him chopping . . .'

Wag grunted in agreement. 'Yeah, no-nonsense – he's the big man now. About as good as it gets.'

Grant smiled. 'I guess that's what you get when you wield the authority of the chief . . .'

The villagers would be out there chopping until close to midnight, opening up our first field of fire. They'd clear from the left edge of Nathan's position – the highway – right across to the right edge of Ginge's arc of fire, then move on to the next position.

By the time they were done cutting, *33 Alpha*, *Bravo*, *Charlie* and *Delta* would be cleared to unleash hell.

10

While Ibrahim's army was busy clearing the bush, Wag and me did a walkabout, brainstorming every possible means of defence with the blokes. Nothing was beyond due consideration, but we were partly in reassurance mode as well.

'This is it, lads, we're in here for the duration,' I kept telling them. 'Everything you've ever trained for, every one of your skills that you've honed and honed – this is where they'll get put to the test.'

The attitude amongst the guys was fantastic. Feedback was great and the blokes were buzzing. Getting Ibrahim's army on the job seemed to have given them a real boost. The feeling seemed to be – *If the rebels are coming, let's get it on.*

Walkabout done, Wag and I launched the next stage of 'Operation Alamo' – as we'd nicknamed the defence of Lungi Lol: fashioning some DIY Claymores. When manufactured in an armaments factory the Claymore is a rectangular device about eight inches across and five inches deep, with a gentle curve in its face. The casing is packed with a mass of plastic explosive and ball-bearings. When triggered it fires horizontally in a solid wall of destruction, cutting down anything in its path.

Luckily, when Wag had blagged his pile of swag from Mick, back at the Lungi Airport ammo dump, he'd pulled together the basic raw materials to make some Claymores. First off he'd got the sticks of PE4. The plastic explosive is fairly inert. It can be moulded like Plasticine, and detonation cord – or detcord – is one of the few things that will set it off. Detcord explodes at a rate of 6000 metres a second: in other words, a length 6 kilometres long goes up in one second flat.

Detcord is highly volatile, and a length slung around a small tree will fell it. But it's PE4 that actually has the real killer punch behind it. It's a dynamic high explosive – the sheer magnitude of the blast and the shock wave so created will drive a scything wall of metallic death out of a device like a Claymore.

Wag had also scrounged ten mixed L1A2 and L2A2 electric detonators, to trigger the detcord, plus 100 metres of electronic firing cable. So all we were lacking were some containers to set the explosives in, plus some 'shipyard confetti' – any form of projectile to take the place of the standard ball-bearings.

Via the chief some empty cooking oil containers were scavenged from around the village. These were about the size of a five-litre fuel can, and made of thick tin-plated steel. They were the right dimensions for us to cut down and mould into shape. After doing so we ended up with a series of shallow tin trays, each eight inches long, six wide, and about two deep.

Perfect.

Next, we sent a couple of the blokes to scour the length and breadth of Lungi Lol, searching for shipyard confetti. Ably assisted by the village kids they came back with handfuls of old nails, bolts and screws, broken bits of machinery, old car parts, plus assorted other bits and pieces that could be used as improvised shrapnel. When the metal ran out we could even use shards of razor-sharp bamboo – the offcuts from the punji sticks.

Then we cut a small hole in the back of each tin tray, and moulded a slab of PE4 into a tennis ball shape. We placed the snowball of plastic explosive in the base of the tin tray over the hole, and kneaded it into a convex dish – so it would have a cone blast effect when detonated. A length of detcord – knotted twice to lend it extra umph – was pushed through the hole into the PE4. It was left hanging out of the rear of the device like a rat's tail.

Finally, the shipyard confetti was pressed into the convex face of the PE4. A length of cardboard cut to fit was laid over the front, and sealed in place with gaffer tape. We'd used the same weight of PE4 (about one and a half pounds) as a standard Claymore would be armed with – so we could pretty much rely on our DIY ones having the same kind of kill-range. At the apex of the blast – so fifty metres out from the device – the cone of destruction would be two metres high and fifty metres wide.

The next challenge was placing them. Claymores have a sixteen-metre back-blast. Anyone caught in that zone could be maimed or killed. We had a limited amount of firing cable, and we had to be able to see the enemy to be able to detonate. We were using Mini Shrikes to do so – a hand-held device about the size of an iPhone. Into that we'd plug the two leads – one black, one tan; a positive and a negative – which make up the firing cable.

We couldn't just blow the Claymores as soon as we detected voices or movement out there in the dark. If we triggered them blind we might kill innocent villagers, plus you needed to be sure the enemy would be caught right in the cone of the blast. The guy operating the Mini Shrike had to be able to see both the Claymore and the target, while not getting caught in the back-blast, or shot by the enemy.

We left it up to the patrol commanders exactly where to position their DIY Claymores. They would only be set in place after last light, so if there were any rebel spies in the village they wouldn't be able to see where we'd sited them.

That evening's Sched contained a crucial Intel update: the word was that the rebels had shifted their objective completely now. Rather than seizing Freetown and laying it waste, their main focus was on joining battle with the British military and capturing some British soldiers. Their push was to be wholly against Lungi Airport, where most of our forces were located.

Operation Kill British had truly come of age.

We called the patrol commanders together for prayers, and took a good long look at our situation. Priority one was to defend and hold this position. If we could hit the rebels hard enough and kill enough of them in the first contact, it might be possible to stop them. With the kind of defences the villagers were working on, we might hold out for long enough to turn the rebel tide.

But if they penetrated our perimeter then we were pretty much done for.

The feelings amongst the men cut both ways now. On the one hand Colonel Gibson and Brigadier Richards had shown absolute faith in our ability to make a stand here – and above any other force at their disposal. That alone was gratifying. But on the other hand it was becoming ever more clear what a massive barrel of shit we'd been dropped into. If we failed to stop the rebels and were forced to go on the run, the wounded would be piled onto the lone Pinzgauer, which would make a mad dash for Lungi Airport. The rest of us would attempt to E & E through the jungle on foot, but no one particularly rated our chances.

As if to reinforce the sense of impeding doom, the trickle of villagers who had started arriving the previous night had swollen into a veritable flood. We'd figured then that we had maybe two hundred sleeping on the square, ranged mostly around the edges. By midnight on our third day in Lungi Lol the open space was packed from end to end. Several hundred people, mainly women and children, were there – and all of them seeking the sanctuary provided by twenty-six Pathfinders.

With darkness the jungle came alive. There were sounds tonight that we didn't seem able to recognise. My mind was a swirl of thoughts. Were the rebels out there, lurking unseen in the fringes of the forest, getting eyes-on our positions and readying themselves to strike? Had they been in amongst us during the day, counting us and sketching out our whereabouts?

As the darkness thickened two blokes from each patrol crept forward of their positions, trailing out the electrical firing cable. On the far west of the village Dolly set one of his DIY Claymores to cover a V-shaped gully that ran from the dark fringe of jungle almost to the brink of his trenches. Thinking like the enemy, that was the point via which he would launch an attack, getting his men as close as possible before breaking cover.

To the front of H and Nathe's position, their target for the improvised Claymores was clear: it was the dirt track itself. Any rebel vehicles advancing on our position had to come that way. The Claymores were powerful enough to shred any soft-skinned trucks or pick-ups, but would have little effect against armour. If the rebels came forward in their captured United Nations APCs, we'd have to rely on our shoulder-launched LAW 94 mm rockets to smash them.

To the south lay perhaps our greatest threat after the dirt road – the railway track. Moving through thick jungle at night is noisy, slow work, even for those as highly trained as Pathfinders. That railroad offered a silent means of advance right up to the very edge of the village. Taff laid out his own roll of firing cable, setting his DIY Claymore to cover that point of silent ingress – the steel tracks.

The night passed. Long hours on sentry dragged by as tired eyes stared out into a dark, featureless mass of jungle. Sleep snatched here and there in two-hour chunks is never enough. The blokes were building up a sleep deficit, and fatigue was becoming a real issue. Crouched in the damp earth of the trenches, with every crawling-slithering-sliding thing dropping in on us, sentry duty was a shitty business – but that pretty much went with the territory.

But tonight was different. Every one of us could feel it in our bones: a hostile force was out there in the darkness, probing, watching and waiting to strike. The rebel commanders would know for sure there were just over two dozen British soldiers – plus a dodgy Nigerian UNAMSIL contingent – holding the village. With a couple of thousand rebel fighters under their command, their options in terms of how to launch the attack would be legion.

No matter how good we were, twenty-six blokes couldn't mow down hundreds of fast-moving targets at night, and the drugs and voodoo would drive their fighters forwards. But our real worry was that the rebel commanders would be far more capable than that. If they mounted a feint – a move to draw our fire, to mask the real thrust of their attack – we had no force in reserve to deal with it.

No rebel assault materialised during that dark night of tension, but none of us doubted that it was coming. It was only a matter of when the RUF commanders decided they were ready to smash us.

Just after first light the unmistakable figure of Ibrahim re-appeared. 'I am ready. We good? We start?'

'Ibrahim, you happy?' I asked.

'Yes, very happy.'

'Ibrahim, today we finish?'

'Yes, today we finish.'

'Ibrahim, very important we finish today cutting the bush and digging the trenches.'

'Yes. Today I do. I do.'

He was very enthusiastic and definite. I didn't doubt him for a moment, either.

'We've got one more thing on the to-do list, though,' I added.

'What is this?'

'Punji fields.'

Ibrahim looked confused. 'Poongy field? What is this?'

'We cut bamboo, Ibrahim, maybe five feet in length and this fat.' I used my forearm to indicate the width we wanted. 'One end we make a spike – very sharp, Ibrahim.' I grabbed my rifle to demonstrate the next bit. 'The blunt end we drive into the ground at a forty-five-degree angle, with the spike facing upwards. We need the spikes set this far apart, and not in lines or regular. Put them so a man cannot run or move through . . .'

Ibrahim's eyes had lit up. 'I know! I know!' he interjected. 'This is "poongy field"?'

'Yeah, punjis. When you're ready we'll show you where to place them, okay.'

Ibrahim nodded happily. 'I do! I do!' He was practically dancing from foot to foot with excitement. The idea of the punji fields clearly tickled his fancy. With that he turned and was gone.

Ibrahim set to work, and Wag and I wandered off on our early morning walkabout. As Pathfinders, we never move in less than a pair no matter where we might be going. Even if paying a visit to the shitters we still had to do so in twos. This is the buddy-buddy system, one that guarantees you'll never be jumped by the enemy without having a buddy to provide back-up. Hence Wag and me moved as a pair as we went to check in with Dolly's patrol.

We got there to find a couple of blokes on stag, one brewing up, and another sleeping.

'See anything last night?' I asked Dolly.

'Nope. Just all those weird noises all night long.'

'Yeah. We heard them too. Did you see all the civvies coming into the village?'

'Yeah. Sleeping in the square?'

'Yeah. It was chocker.'

I heard a light rustle of vegetation from behind me and three young lads emerged from the bush. One was a carrying a battered old axe, another a worn machete, the third a shovel with a broken stump for a handle.

The boys smiled nervously. 'We dig? We dig?'

Dolly returned the smile. 'Yeah, lads, go for it – dig.'

We watched for a while as the boys got to work. Clearly experts at this digging business, they had the vegetation cleared in an instant above the outline of the first trench. After a few seconds' work with the shovel they were through the thin, sandy surface and into a thicker, clay-like subsoil. It was criss-crossed with tree roots, and I could now understand the mix of tools the lads had brought with them. While shovel-boy lifted out the soil, axe-boy and machete-boy hacked out the roots.

We left the lads working away, and as we crossed over the road to check on Nathe's position we spotted the familiar figure of Ibrahim, surrounded by his army. The work party was out front of Ginge's patrol now – *33 Charlie* – clearing away the bush. Ibrahim was dressed exactly as he had been on day one – he was tall and green, like a willow tree. He was barking orders and leading by example and he'd got his workforce out real early.

We paused to have words with Nathe. 'How're the blokes getting on, mate? Bollocksed?'

'Yeah, mate, getting pretty knackered.'

'Right, make sure when the locals are out doing their stuff you get as much rest as you can. Make like a vampire, mate. Daylight's the time to catch up on the sleep. Keep two on stag and four off, and get as much kip as you can.'

We moved on to Ginge and Taff's positions, and all the time we could hear Ibrahim shouting his instructions, and the dull thud of trees and bushes getting the chop. It was around 1000 hours by the time we were done. Turning back towards the HQ ATAP, we saw a thin line of figures threading through the bush. We were on the alert for a surprise attack – always – so our first thought was: *rebel column.*

Then we noticed it was all women. They were making their way back into the village, and they had thick bundles of bamboo balanced on their heads.

There was a grove of bamboo to the west of Dolly's position, and that was where they'd chosen to cut the first of the raw materials to make the punjis. More groups of women started to appear from various directions. Two hundred metres to the west of Ginge's position there was a real boggy area, and it was from there that they seemed to be getting the peachiest lengths of bamboo. It was coming out in pieces as thick as your biceps, and in sections that were as long as your average scaffold pole.

All morning the work continued: kids digging trenches; women hauling bamboo; and all and sundry clearing the vegetation to the front of our positions. I didn't figure anyone was getting any work done in Lungi Lol, other than that connected with Operation Alamo. But the most amazing thing of all was this: *these people were singing as they worked.* This wasn't some dire dirge either: it was a rhythmic, lilting, soulful chant that sounded almost joyful. And whenever they took a break from the singing, this animated chat and laughter echoed back and forth through the trees.

We joked amongst ourselves about what we'd nicknamed 'Ibrahim's army', but in truth we were hugely impressed. This was hard, tough physical labour under a beating sun, but the villagers seemed to be driven and almost happy to be doing it. It was seriously impressive. I mean, in what village in Britain would you get young boys, girls and women clearing the bush, digging battle trenches or cutting bamboo punji fields, *and all voluntarily?* Forget it. They'd be too busy watching the Shopping Channel or gaming on their PlayStations.

We figured the people of Lungi Lol had to know what would happen if the rebels made it into their village. Everyone knew. In Freetown and neighbouring areas there were these so-called 'Amp Camps'. They'd been set up by the international aid agencies and charities, and they were peopled by the RUF's victims – from kids as young as toddlers to ancient grandmothers, and all with hands, arms or legs amputated.

So it was all hands to the pump here in Lungi Lol, because no one wanted to lose theirs to a drug-crazed rebel's machete. But that didn't make it any the less impressive.

I could hear the giggling of the kids who were digging the battle trenches, as they larked around with the blokes. It was a boiling hot day – the hottest yet in Lungi Lol – but those kids never once complained or flagged. And each time I heard it their laughter sent cold shivers up my spine – for I couldn't help thinking what would happen to those kids if we failed, and the rebels made it in here.

I'd had a tough childhood growing up in smoggy Middlesbrough, but compared to these kids it had been a party. School had never really worked out, and by the time I was in my early teens we'd had the police around the house numerous times. I was forever stealing milk floats and selling them as scrap to the gypsies, or climbing derelict buildings and ending up in hospital. I'd broken about every bone in my body and had got a reputation for scrapping.

There was no military tradition in my family – my dad was an electrician, my mum a barmaid – and we were seriously at loggerheads over my wayward ways. Then at the age of thirteen I happened to see a news report about the Parachute Regiment's famous stand in the Falkland Islands.

That changed everything.

Having seen the PARAs in action I knew what I wanted to be: I was going to win the right to wear that famous maroon beret. I was going to join the PARAs.

More or less everyone said I stood zero chance of making it. I was stringy and thin, with barely a muscle on me. But my dad stood by me. There was never a lot of money in the Heaney household, though what there was my parents spent on me and my younger brother, Neil. Dad took me to the local charity shop. He got me an old pair of Army boots and a pair of knackered combat trousers, plus he forked out for a brand spanking new bright orange rucksack from Millets. We nicknamed it 'the Satsuma'.

I started running for miles on end through the back streets of Middlesbrough. It was like a scene from *Rocky*, but with me a slim, wiry drink of piss with a giant satsuma strapped to my back. My schoolmates thought I was cracked, but my dad was rock solid. I started running the hills that ring the city. Dad would drive me out there and sit in the car reading the *Mirror*, while I tore up and down the slopes.

People still said that I'd never make it, but my reaction was – *sod them*. I *did* get accepted into the Junior PARA, which turned out to be like torture without the water-boarding. Most found it utter purgatory, but I loved it. I thrived on the physical challenges, and it quickly straightened me out. I even got selected for the Junior PARA's boxing team.

I'd just turned seventeen and Andy Gow – the guy who raised the 3 PARA flag over Port Stanley – was our CSM. He threatened to kill anyone who didn't win his bout. I put my opponent down in the third round, so Andy spared my life. I went on to the Parachute Regiment's P Company: six days of charging through woods and stagnant bogs, of log and stretcher races, the Trainasium (designed to test your fear of heights) and finally The Milling – where you stand face to face with another recruit and have to smash the fuck out of each other.

I passed P Company as the Champion Recruit, so I guess I did okay. Having joined 3 PARA in 1987 I got my first sight of the lads of the X Platoon. I was mesmerised: this was the mysterious unit I'd heard referred to as the Shadow Force. These were the guys who were always away overseas – whether on training or ops no one seemed to know. They wore their hair longer, showed no marks of unit or rank, and everyone – even the officers – addressed each other as 'boss' or 'mate'. I knew their role was supposedly to HALO behind enemy lines on clandestine taskings, but other than that I knew next to nothing about what they really got up to.

I was drawn to them like a moth to a candle flame.

But never once when I'd contemplated joining their number did I ever envisage being on a mission as out-there as this one – twenty-six blokes tasked with saving an African village from total mayhem and carnage . . . For that's what this mission had become to us. We'd been sent here to stop the RUF, but over the past few days we'd realised what the reality would be for the people who lived here if we failed.

The rebels would rape the women who were cutting the bamboo to make the punjis for us. They'd gun down Mojo and his men, or machete them to pieces. They'd murder Ibrahim and most likely the village chief too. They'd chop the hands off the kids who were digging our battle trenches, and doing cartwheels of joy over a packet of British Army boiled sweets. They'd take the survivors and drive them before their forces as human shields, as they advanced on Lungi Airport – to make Op Kill British a bloody reality.

And right now, for every one of us here failure to stop them was not an option.

11

It was late afternoon when Ibrahim turned up at the HQ ATAP once more. He didn't appear to be particularly tired, sweaty or dirty. In fact he looked full of beans and in the thick of it.

He approached Wag, whom he seemed to have identified as the guy in charge of the work gangs. 'Hey boss! Hey boss!'

Wag grinned a welcome. 'Ibrahim! Come on – take a load off. Take the weight off, mate. Sit down.'

Ibrahim folded up those long legs of his and sat cross-legged on the ground.

Tricky threw a packet of British Army ration biscuits at him. 'Here! Ibrahim, catch! Get those down you.'

Ibrahim didn't seem to want to drop the machete, so he could catch the biscuits more easily. Instead, he tried to catch them with the machete still gripped in his hands, and ended up slicing the packet in two in midair.

'Whoa ... Ibrahim, mate, watch it!' Tricky exclaimed. 'You'll have someone's eye out with that ...'

Ibrahim started to munch on the biscuits, but Tricky hadn't seen fit to warn him they were 'hard tack'. Hard tack biscuits taste pretty good, but they're impossible to eat without water – worse even than cream crackers. They're so bad we used to play a game: *bet you a tenner you can't eat six hard tacks without taking a drink of water.*

As Ibrahim munched away we started a wager on how many he'd manage before he was desperate for some fluid. There are six in a packet. He got one down him, then two. He was onto his third by the time his chewing got noticeably slower, as the hard tack glued his jaws together, drying up his saliva like a sponge. By now he was incapable of talking, but still he kept eating.

'That's his fourth,' Wag commented. 'Here goes . . .'

We'd been watching him for five minutes or so, and finally he'd got to the point where he could barely open his mouth any more. Being on his fourth hard tack – well, for a novice we figured he'd done pretty damn well.

Tricky waved his water bottle at him. 'Ibrahim, you want some water? Water?'

Ibrahim, nodding: 'Hmmm. Hmmmm.' He couldn't speak.

Tricky threw his water bottle over. Ibrahim didn't seem to want to let go of the killer biscuit packet, or the machete, so he tried to catch the water bottle in the crook of his arm. He got the water bottle wedged between his knees, and managed to lever it open with his elbows. He tipped it back, raising it to the vertical, and drained it in one.

Ibrahim threw the empty water bottle back to Tricky, picked up the two remaining biscuits and started eating again.

'He ain't getting any more bloody water,' Tricky muttered.

Unbelievably, we were still on the one-litre ration per man per day, and Ibrahim had just drained Tricky's dry.

We were all of us laughing now.

'Fucking hell, Ibrahim, nice one,' I remarked. 'So, are you finished? Not so much the biscuits, mate, but the work?'

In answer Ibrahim brandished his machete, and grabbed the one remaining hard tack biscuit: 'Yes, finished! Come check! You come check!'

He led off, Wag and me following after. Ninety per cent of the clearance was done. He still had people out chopping, and as we walked up and down the line of our positions we showed where we needed a bit more done.

'Little bit more here, Ibrahim,' Wag indicated. 'Cut a little here, okay.'

'Yes, yes, no problem!' He clicked his fingers, called some of his people over and they started to slash at the offending patches of vegetation.

That done he led us over to this massive pile of cut bamboo. 'This, now? This good?'

Wag picked up one of the lengths of bamboo. 'Make this end sharp; very sharp.'

Ibrahim: 'Yes, yes, yes! Very sharp!'

'This much,' Wag measured off a foot, 'into the ground.'

Ibrahim: 'Yes, yes! In the ground!'

Wag placed it at a forty-five-degree angle, pointing away from the village. 'Like this, Ibrahim. Not like this.' He placed it vertical. 'And not like this.' He placed it horizontal. He returned it to the forty-five-degree angle. 'So, it gets the man in here – it pierces his thigh . . .'

'Yes, yes, I do!'

'Wag, you mark out the one patch,' I told him, 'and I'll do the other.'

I headed down to where we wanted the southern punji field sited, while Wag dealt with the northern one. We each drew a furrow in the ground indicating the perimeter, marking out an area twenty metres deep by thirty-five metres long.

Punji fields mapped out, Wag explained exactly how we wanted them positioned. 'Not in straight line, Ibrahim. Random. Not in straight line.'

'Yes, yes, yes. Random. I do!'

Ibrahim had half his people busy putting the final touches to the cleared fields of fire. The other half were watching us.

'The man, he must run this way and this way,' Wag indicated, doing a little jinking dance with his feet. 'Back and forth. Back and forth.'

'Yes, yes. To and fro! I do!' Ibrahim turned to his people and beckoned them over. 'Come, come!'

He was now in the centre of his army, demonstrating with his monster machete how to fashion a punji stick, while talking his workers through how to plant them. It looked as if we'd left the building of the punji fields in very capable hands.

As we headed back through the trees that fringed the outskirts of the village, Wag and me chatted about the 'I-man' – Ibrahim. He had great man-management skills. Single-handedly he was overseeing half a dozen construction projects, with maybe a hundred villagers at work across them. No doubt about it, the I-man was a damn good bloke to have on our side.

We came up to Nathe's position, and we could see yet another work party at it – mattocks going up and down as a dozen boys cracked into their battle trenches. They were up to their shoulders in the dirt, six of them in each hole, *33 Alpha*'s trenches being a good halfway down.

We paused to have words. 'Nathe, how's it going, mate?'

Nathe shrugged. 'Nice to see someone else on the blister end of a shovel for a change.'

I tried not to laugh. 'Mate, they're kids.'

'Yeah, but look at 'em – they're loving it.'

Nathe did seem to have a point. As long as he and his men kept feeding them the boiled sweets, his trench gang seemed more than happy to keep shovelling.

We got back to our position, and the four of us took stock over a brew. We couldn't help but marvel at what the village chief, plus Ibrahim and the people of Lungi Lol, had got sorted over the last twenty-four hours. It was easy to see how these people were able to build their own houses, dig their own wells and carve out their very lives from the bush. They had nothing else, so they crafted their lives around what nature provided.

More to the point, they'd dropped everything to help us. The community spirit and cohesion here would put any English village to shame. We'd yet to hear a single gripe or complaint, yet back home we whinge and moan when our bins aren't emptied on time. The people of Lungi Lol were an example to the rest of us.

Being here had also given me a real insight into my fellow

operators. I'd always known Wag was a man of the people, but here it had truly come to the fore. Somehow, the stumpy Hobbit-man had really charmed the I-man, Mojo and the rest of 'em. I was more fiery and likely to flash than Wag was. If someone stepped out of line I'd be – *You fucking what?* Wag was far more of a mellow fellow: *Come on, lads, screw the nut.*

I guess that's why we made such a great team. Wag was the persuader, me the enforcer. Plus with Grant, we had a commander who truly got the ethos of our unit. He was the officer with the education and the gravitas, but it was the NCOs and patrol commanders who had the operational experience. Grant knew that. He got it and he was cool with it. The three of us together made a fine team, and that positive attitude was cascading down to the men on the guns.

Ibrahim's army were chopping away at vegetation, sharpening punji sticks and driving them into the ground well into the hours of darkness. Eventually, the patrol commanders had to ask the I-man to call off his work gangs, because the lads couldn't hear properly if the rebels were out there massing to attack.

By now Dolly's trenches were done, and the rest were at least usable, so we were in a good place. Confidence was growing that we could mount a blistering defence of the village. We hadn't asked for any trenches in the HQ position, for our fold in the ground was deep enough to lie flat in and avoid most of the fire, plus we were surrounded by thick vegetation and pretty much hidden from view.

We passed that night – the fourth of our mission – hunkered down behind our strengthened defences and watching for an attack. Still none came. But the stress of being always on the alert, plus the lack of sleep, fresh food or being able to wash was starting to take its toll.

The following morning the I-man had his people out as soon as it was light. The clearance out front was now so impressive you

could see all the way across from Nathe's position to the railway embankment, which lay a good three hundred metres to the
south of us.

As we admired the view, I noticed the flash of what had to be
lightning to the north of us. A roar of thunder rolled across the
village. Thick, boiling clouds piled up on the horizon, and when
the storm broke it proved to be a monster. The rain swept in like
a sheer wall of water, pounding across us in waves. I'd never seen
anything like it. It was so dense I couldn't see more than ten feet
in any direction, and even Ibrahim's army had ceased work under
the onslaught.

We sat there in the HQ ATAP almost feeling glad of the soaking. The rain was warm, and it was like being under the world's
biggest power shower. I could feel it washing the shit out of my
combats, and scouring some of the worst of the grime off my exposed skin. At the same time my SA80 was going rusty before
my very eyes, and the 319 radio would see the rain as the perfect
excuse to stop working. Thank God for the Thuraya satphone that
The White Rabbit had given us.

For the first time since we had got here the village was eerily
deserted and silent, apart from the pounding of the rain. It poured
off the main track in muddy orange torrents, and within minutes
the village square was flooded. But the storm was over as quickly
as it had begun: one hour after the first drops had started to fall it
abruptly ended. We were left with the pitter-patter of drops falling from the leaves of the trees, as the sun burst out from behind
the clouds and began to dry out the terrain.

The villagers emerged, and the I-man got his army out putting
the finishing touches to the punji fields. As the rainfall evap-
orated the humidity grew to unbearable levels. It felt as if we
were in one massive sauna, and I couldn't imagine what it was
like for those slaving away cutting and driving in the punjis.

Wag and I wandered down soggily to check on the patrols. We
figured the battle trenches had to be flooded, and sure enough

Dolly's had two feet of water standing in the bottom. It was half-way up to the knees of the guys on stag – like Glastonbury Festival in the African jungle. We just had to hope that by tonight the sun would have dried the trenches out enough for them to be good to fight from.

We headed for Nathe's position. 'All right, Nathe? How's it going? Survived the storm?'

'Wet.' He pointed to something on the ground nearby. 'You seen the fucking size of them?'

I looked where he was indicating, and to his right was the trunk of a massive forest giant, complete with buttress roots around four feet high. All around the base of the tree were these big holes like burrows. Above the nearest two I could see these enormous beasts glued to the tree bark, with their glistening heads poking out and antennae waving spookily.

I stared at them. 'What – the fuck – are they?'

Nathe shrugged. 'I dunno. Snails?'

'Well, you tell us,' said Wag. 'You're the fucking farmer.'

'Snails,' Nathe repeated. He pointed at a neighbouring tree. 'Yeah, and they're over there look and all.'

These things were like no snails I had ever seen. Their shells were dark brown, shiny and conical, spiralling up to a point at the back, and each was the size of a baby's head. We stood there for a good couple of minutes or more, wondering what planet we had landed upon.

Nathe voiced what had to be the obvious question to him. 'Reckon you can eat 'em?'

Wag glanced at him. 'Yeah, *you* probably could.'

I snorted with mirth. 'Ben would give you a run for your money, though, mate.'

My chocolate Labrador was infamous for eating everything and anything. He'd once broken into the Pathfinders' stores and got his teeth into the exercise mats we used to do our fitness. This wasn't just having a good chew: he'd devoured his third mat by the time someone managed to stop him. No doubt about it, Ben would have given Nathe a bit of competition on the scoffing-giant-African-beasts front.

The snails – if snails they were – must have been drawn out by the rain. All around us they were munching happily on vegetation and leaves, and they were clearly oblivious to Nathe's culinary intentions.

We got back to the HQ ATAP to find Tricky entertaining the I-man. He'd learned not to give Ibrahim anything that wasn't water-soluble. Each twenty-four-hour ration pack contained three sealed metallic bags – one with a breakfast like sausage and beans, the others containing main meals like meatballs and pasta, Lancashire hotpot, or beef stew and dumplings. In addition there was a tub of cheese spread, a small bar of chocolate, chewing gum, assorted drinks packs (tea, coffee, hot chocolate) and biscuits.

Sensibly, Tricky had opted to try Ibrahim on the Garibaldi-type fruit biscuits – ones that didn't require washing down with a litre of water. Just as soon as he spotted Wag and me the I-man jumped to his feet, cramming down the remainder of his Garibaldis.

'Come, come – come see! Finish! Finish!'

Tricky being the signaller, he was glued to the radio 24/7, so Wag, Grant and me followed the I-man down to the punji fields. Each contained around one hundred stakes honed to a dagger-like point.

The I-man waved his machete in the direction of the nearest punji field. 'You like? You like? Good?'

Under Ibrahim's instructions the villagers had done pretty much exactly as we'd asked.

Wag nodded enthusiastically. 'Yeah, fucking love it.' He bent low so he could get a good look across, checking for any potential routes through. 'But that one there – move it there, okay? And put another there, to even out the spread a little. Okay?'

'Okay, I do.'

'Then it'll be perfect, Ibrahim. Perfect.'

'I do! I Do!'

'Tell you what,' I observed to Wag, 'I wouldn't like to have to cut through that under fire.'

Wag smiled, evilly. 'Too right, mate.'

Ibrahim ordered us to follow him, as he set off towards the southern punji field. He was so proud of his work that he more or less force-marched us down there.

'Woah, Ibrahim, slow down a little, pal,' Wag remarked, as he struggled with his stumpy legs to keep up.

'No, no – come, come! You see!'

Punji field number two was pretty much a repeat of field number one. A bit of tweaking here and there, and Wag declared it to be a top job.

Ibrahim beamed. 'Is good, yes?'

'Ibrahim, mate, it's class,' Wag confirmed. 'Listen, we're going to speak to the village chief for you. Maybe for you a very big house now, very big house.'

Ibrahim's smile grew even broader. It was about to split his face in two. With that he tottered off into the tree line and was gone, leaving us in the midst of the punjis.

We made our way back via Nathe's position, pausing to check on their battle trenches. The blokes had topped them off with camouflage, spreading moss, dry leaves and other vegetation around the lip, rendering them practically invisible. You had to be standing right on top of one before you realised it was there.

To the rear of the trenches Nathe was hunched over a big black cooking pot. It was simply massive and it dwarfed the tiny, fold-up hexy stove that was heating whatever it contained. Nathe stirred away, like a wizard at his cauldron. Crouched next to him was one of his trench-digging gang. The boy had a snail gripped between his knees, and was levering out the flesh with a sharpened stick.

'All right?' Nathe grunted.

He was 100 per cent focused on the task in hand. The pot was bubbling away, and I could see the individual snails turning over and over as it boiled.

Nathe glanced at the boy and nodded to the pot. 'Go on, then, get another in.'

Beside me Grant's chin was practically on the floor. 'Nathe. What. The fuck. Is that?'

'Dinner,' Nathe replied, matter-of-factly. 'Mate, food is fuel. You don't eat, you die.'

Grant gave a snort of revulsion. 'Well, I won't be fucking eating with you, that's for sure.'

We were six days in now, and after that many days on British Army ration packs you did get a bit desperate for some 'fresh'.

Each day we'd had the village kids come and sit with us, throwing around a few words of English as we doled out the goodies. The relationship between them and us was becoming one of real camaraderie, and Nathe had clearly built up a friendship that was closer than most. The kid from Nathe's trench-digging crew seemed oblivious to Grant's obvious revulsion. He was totally focused on hooking out the next snail and adding it to whatever concoction Nathe was brewing up here.

'Tell you what,' I remarked to Grant and Wag, as we moved onwards. 'Let's give it twenty-four hours, and if Nathe's still alive we'll try some of the stew.'

Wag chortled. 'Aye, sounds good to me.'

Grant made a T-sign with his hands. 'Time out, lads. You're on your own. I'm strictly a boil-in-the-bag man.'

I figured Nathe's snail stew was going to prove the real man test here in Lungi Lol. Nathe wasn't the real wilderness man amongst us – he was just the hungriest. H was the hunter and survivalist par excellence. For sure, H would probably eat the snails raw, but only if he'd caught 'em with his bare hands. H's mantra was – *if it moves, kill it*. Once it was dead he could rely on Nathe to eat it, and that's why Nathe and H were such good mates.

Dolly and Ginge would force themselves to eat Nathe's snail hotpot, but only because of peer pressure. As for Taff, all we had to do was tell him they were from the Rhondda Valley. 'They're Welsh snails, mate.' Taff would be right into them. 'Oh, fuck-aye, bud, they'll be lovely, then.'

But there was also a serious side to Nathe's culinary experiments. Self-reliance is the mantra of the Pathfinders. There is no other way. Practically all of our kit was from non-British Army sources. The Army didn't provide a usable machete, so each of us had picked one up from a civvie store. We'd put together our own rifle-cleaning kits – crucial when using a temperamental piece of crap like the SA80. Our kits were waterproof, and had triple the capacity of cloth and gun oil – enough to last a long mission isolated in the jungle.

Likewise, there were no guarantees when our next resupply of rations would be flown in to Lungi Lol. We were running low already, and learning what local flora and fauna were good to eat was a sensible move – even more so if we were forced to go on the run. At that point we'd be living off the land, and Nathe's snail goulash might be all we could rustle up between us – boil-in-the-bag Grant included.

We'd spent just under a week in Lungi Lol by now, yet oddly it felt as if we'd been here forever. This mission was turning into one of those incredible, once-in-a-lifetime experiences – a view into a world and a way of life so different from our own as to be almost unrecognisable. As we worked with the villagers on Operation Alamo, and scavenged the local flora and fauna to supplement our rations, the mission was proving utterly unforgettable.

But nothing was to prove as unforgettable as the dark murder and mayhem that was coming.

12

In recognition of how we were now pulling together as one, in a united village defence force – Pathfinders, Mojo and his men, plus Ibrahim's army – I figured I'd get the blokes to set aside all the chocolate, sweets, biscuits and other goodies they could spare from the ration packs. Presented to the villagers, it would be our way of saying a heartfelt 'thank you'.

I called the patrol commanders in. 'Listen, lads, you need to get your blokes to surrender any scoff – anything you don't need – and bring it back to me. After what the villagers have done for us we need to repay the favour; so any goodies, hand 'em in.'

Nathe, Dolly, Ginge and Taff handed over stacks of biscuits, drink kits, boiled sweets and chocolate. I threw it all into a big box – one that had originally held ten of the twenty-four-hour ration packs. When I was done it was brimful with goodies, and Wag and me carried it over to the Kingdom of Mojo.

I showed him the box. 'Look, we want to give this out to the villagers, but we don't want to upset the chief. So what's the protocol? How do we best go about it?'

Mojo studied the box for a few seconds. 'Well, you must give it to the chief, and let him be seen to give it out.'

We headed over to the chief's place to do so. Wag and me placed the gift box reverentially at the foot of the wooden steps, as Mojo launched into one of his speeches, pointing at the box and miming eating and drinking. There was a bit of general chat, plus smiles all around, before Mojo turned to us.

'The chief, he says – thank you very much; this is very kind. This will be very good for him.'

'Please tell him thanks for all the work,' I said. 'Plus a special thank you for Ibrahim. They've done a fantastic job, all of them. The village is strong now, with good defences.'

Mojo translated what I'd said.

'Please also tell the chief this,' I added. 'We need to know if people come to the village and tell him anything about the rebels. Or if he sees people in the village he does not recognise – young men who may be rebels – then he must also tell us.'

Mojo related all of that, then translated the chief's response. 'Yes, he will tell you. They are watching very closely and they will see and warn about any rebels.'

We left the box lying at the foot of the stairs, suspecting that we'd pulled off some great hearts and minds work here. Sure enough, over the course of the next few hours we spotted villagers wandering around with stuff from the goody box, proving that the chief had been true to his word. And we passed our fifth night in Lungi Lol feeling a tad more secure behind our seriously beefed-up defences.

It was mid-morning the following day when the I-man rocked up at our position. He pointed at the ground where we'd been sleeping and started gabbling away.

'This here, you?' He made a load of snoring noises. 'You that here?' He made some digging and cutting motions, and repeated the snore noises again.

None of us had a clue what he was on about, but it had been all good so far with the I-man, so we figured we'd go with it.

'Yeah, Ibrahim, we kind of snore there, mate,' Wag confirmed, 'so crack on.'

With that Ibrahim was gone. He was back a few minutes later carrying an armful of cut branches. Having dumped them on the floor where he'd made the snore noises, he disappeared once more.

'What's he up to now?' I asked Wag. 'What d'you reckon they're for?'

Wag shook his head. 'No idea, mate, not a Scooby Doo.'

When Ibrahim returned he had a length of rattan – a strong jungle vine – coiled around his shoulder, like a cowboy with a lasso. He'd obviously been to different parts of the jungle cutting the bits and pieces for whatever he had in mind. Question was, what exactly was he building for us now? A garden bench? A gazebo? Toilet maybe? I hoped not, not with Wag's bowel movements being such as they were.

A few days back we'd asked Mojo the obvious – where did he and his guys go to answer the call of nature? Mojo had explained to us where the village shit-pit was situated, which appropriately enough was as near to Wales as you could get in Sierra Leone. It was just to the rear of Taff's battle trenches, on the edge of the trees that fringed the village.

'Go down to the end of the side track and turn right,' Mojo had explained. 'You will know where it is when you get near enough.'

He was damn right.

You could smell it from a good fifty metres away. It consisted of a hole in the ground four feet square and about fifteen feet deep, complete with a complimentary swarm of botflies – and it was filling up quickly. All around were these mounds of earth where other latrines had been dug, then filled in and topped over. This was truly shit city.

The only way to relieve yourself was to grab hold of a post planted for the purpose, and hang your ass out over the stinking hole. The first thing Wag and I did – we'd gone there buddy-buddy fashion, of course – was to test the pole for strength and stability. Wag promptly nicknamed the post 'the lean-tree'. British ration packs seem designed to make you constipated, which meant an age spent hanging onto the lean-tree. The only way to cut time at the pit was to get some fresh down you – hence the draw of Nathan's snail curries.

'How the hell d'you keep one hand on your weapon, one hand on the lean-tree, and wipe your ass at the same time?' Wag demanded.

It was a good question. I couldn't think of an answer. I was too busy trying not to laugh at the expression on Wag's face as he tried to go.

Ibrahim had dumped his building materials to the right-front of the crater-like depression that made up our HQ. No doubt about it, if Ibrahim was building us our own, private latrine here, it was going to be far too close for comfort.

We watched in fascination as the I-man proceeded to scoop out four narrow holes with his machete, each about twelve inches deep, so it swallowed the entire blade. Ibrahim was 100 per cent focused on his task, and we in turn were glued to whatever he was doing.

Next he took one of the long branches, stood it vertical and chopped it into four pieces, each two feet long. He slotted those pieces into the four holes he'd dug in the ground, then he took the soil he'd scooped out and tamped it around them, until he had four rock-solid posts arranged in a rectangle. He cut more lengths of wood, to make crosspieces at either end of the rectangle. Then he bent the rattan vine over the machete blade, sliced off a length, and lashed the two crosspieces to the uprights.

'Maybe it's some kind of evil trap to ensnare the rebels,' I suggested. 'One we haven't thought of.'

'Bollocks,' Wag snorted. 'But whatever it is, it sure beats going to Ikea.'

Next, the I-man took a long length of wood, stood it upright, marked where his shoulder came to with his fingers, and lopped off the excess. He then repeated the performance with another pole. That done, he knelt down and lashed the poles to the long side of the uprights, using the rattan to do so.

He now had about twenty feet of the vine remaining. After tying one end to the corner of the rectangular frame, he started to thread the rattan back and forth, looping it around the wood twice as he went. He worked his way from one end to the other. Once he was done he threw his machete down, point into the soil.

The whole process had taken about forty minutes, during which he'd never said a word to us – not even cracking a joke about what he might be up to.

With his back to us he sat on the rattan latticework, and took a bounce or two, clearly testing its strength. Maybe it was some kind of a garden bench? Then he swung his legs up and laid his whole body flat on the construction. He bounced and wriggled and shuffled about a bit and went: 'Hmmmmm ... Hmmmmm ... Hmmmmm ...'

With a seriously happy expression on his face he sat up and turned to us. 'Try! Try!' He made the snoring noises again. 'This very good here.'

Ah, so that's what it was – *a bed.*

I glanced at Wag. 'You're the heaviest – get on.'

He shrugged. 'Yeah. Fuck it. Why not?'

Wag got up, removed his belt kit and climbed on. He did a repeat of the I-man's performance. He rolled to the left and went: 'Hmmm ...' Rolled to the right: 'Hmmm ...' Rolled back again: 'Hmmm.' I was half expecting him to go crashing through, but the I-bed didn't shift an inch. Wag climbed off with a big smile and Ibrahim picked up his machete and started the whole process all over – making us bed number two.

Forty minutes later it was done, and there was a three-foot gap between the two of them. Ibrahim had never taken one proper measurement the entire time. No tape measure for the I-man. As Wag had said, it sure beat going to Ikea, where you'd spend an hour reading the instructions and then build it almost to completion before realising that some bits were missing and you'd fixed half of the others the wrong way round.

Ibrahim pointed at a clear patch of ground adjacent to the two I-beds: 'There? Another?'

Wag shook his head. 'No, no, no, mate, two is more than okay.'

Ibrahim, pointing at the four of us: 'No, no, no – *four.*'

Wag, pointing at the two beds already built: 'No, no, no – two Ibrahim is fine.'

There was a bit more toing and froing before Ibrahim finally seemed to get it that as two of us would be on stag, we didn't need any more I-beds. That understood, he collected his things and wandered off happily. It was early evening by now and we were all curious to have a proper go on the new furniture.

I tried one of them. 'Hmmmm ... Bit stringy on the back. I tell you what. We'll cut up the ration boxes, flatten them out and lay the cardboard ... Look, I'll show you ...'

The beaten flat ration boxes provided enough of a cardboard layer to cover the torso area of both beds, and the legs were fine anyway.

'Perfick,' I announced. 'The dog's nads mate.'

Wag's eyes glittered. 'Fucking 'ell, we've got two peachy beds. Wait 'til the blokes come for prayers and see 'em.'

The patrol commanders filtered in one by one. We gathered in a circle around the rim of the depression. We were waiting to see their reaction over the I-beds, but although Nathe, Dolly, Ginge and Taff were now all present not one of them had said even a word.

'They're just trying to ignore it ...' I mouthed at Wag. 'Fucking blokes.'

Wag decided to make a pre-emptive announcement. 'Look, before anyone says anything, yes we do have two very fucking nice beds, thank you.'

We were expecting a massive chorus of: *You wankers*!

Instead, Nathe just shrugged. 'So what? They're just like ours.'

'What, you've got beds as well?' I asked.

'Yeah.'

'What, like those?'

'Yep. The same.'

'Really?'

'Yeah.'

I turned to Dolly. 'Have you got two 'n all?'

'Yeah, two.'

'Ginge?'

'Yeah. Two as well.'

'Taff?'

'Two, bud.'

'How the fuck did you get beds? Ibrahim can't have been in five places all at once.'

'Nah, it was the kids,' said Nathe. 'We told 'em to build 'em set back from the trenches, in the shade of the canopy. Ibrahim turned up rattling his sabre and cracking a few heads and did an inspection. He found the beds fit for muster and left happy.'

Dolly nodded. 'Yeah, he turned up and did the same with us and all.'

Ginge and Taff had a similar tale.

The beds issue pretty much dominated that evening's prayers. Other than that, the patrol commanders reported that all the defences we'd asked for were present and correct – punji fields included. Now, it had become a waiting game to see who would be the first to blink and take a bullet: us or the rebels.

It was around seven that evening, so just getting properly dark, when Mojo pitched up unannounced. He was sporting shiny boots and a beret, and amazingly his Foster Grant shades were still in place. Balanced on his shoulder was a large cardboard box, like a fruit tray. He proceeded to deposit the box on the lip of our depression.

Inside it was a heap of fresh bread rolls. I could smell them from where I was sitting, and after a week of British Army rations the aroma was mouth-watering. I glanced at the others. This was way out left-field kind of shit. I mean Mojo wasn't exactly the Hovis boy on his bicycle, and this wasn't quite the cobbled streets of Shaftesbury's Gold Hill, in Dorset, where the Hovis ads were filmed.

'A gift from the chief,' Mojo announced. 'You will get one bread delivery every evening.'

For a moment we were speechless.

Then Wag posed the obvious question. 'Mojo, where the fuck did you get fresh bread?'

'They made it for you. The villagers. And also from tomorrow the ladies will fetch your water, as well.'

'What d'you mean – *the ladies will fetch us water*?'

'Every morning they will go to the water source and bring you drinking water.'

'Really?'

Mojo nodded. 'Yes. This also is from the chief.'

With that he about-turned and drifted into the shadows. We counted the bread rolls. There were twenty-six, one per man. We were flabbergasted. How the hell had they managed that? We removed our four, then Wag and me did a walkabout of the positions, starting with Dolly's.

'Here you go,' Wag announced, as he counted out six bread rolls from the tray under his arm. 'One, two, three ... that's six. One each.'

Dolly stared at the rolls in disbelief. 'What – the fuck – are those?'

'Bread rolls.'

Wag was being mega-straight-faced, which made it all the funnier. I was having to tighten my belt to stop myself from laughing. If I so much as sniggered the wind-up would be over.

'Where in God's name did you get those?' Dolly demanded.

'The shop,' said Wag.

Dolly stared at him. 'What shop?' The rest of his blokes were staring now too.

Wag jerked a thumb over his shoulder. 'On the corner. The baker's.'

Dolly had the hook deep in his mouth now. 'What baker's? I've been here seven days and ...'

'The corner shop at the end of the road,' Wag cut in.

Dolly shook his head. 'I haven't seen no baker's.'

Wag shook his head, in mock exasperation. 'Look, stop asking so many fucking questions. D'you want 'em or not?'

Wag was the past master at these kind of wind-ups. He was brilliant at acting as if all was completely normal. I was stood behind him desperately trying not to laugh.

'And if you're good lads you'll get the same again tomorrow,' Wag added. 'Plus I'll be sending someone in the morning to fill your water bottles.'

'Fuck off,' said Dolly.

But he still grabbed his ration of bread rolls.

The joke got repeated all down the line. It didn't get any less funny with each rendition. It took Wag and me an hour to get it done, for no one could quite get their heads around the bread delivery.

Like everything else we do, we also eat in pairs. Most blokes were having one major meal in the evening and making it an 'all-in'. You'd save up your boil-in-the-bag meals and mix in your hard tack biscuits, making one big gloppy stew. A little bit of fresh like those bread rolls provided a massive boost to morale. They were a little taste of home, of family, of the familiar – and maybe even of safety.

By the time we got back to the HQ position it was fully dark. Tricky had just got an Intel update via the Thuraya satphone, for the 319 radio was still kaput after the rainstorm. He'd taken the radio set to pieces, removed the batteries and left it all to dry in the sun, but still it wasn't playing ball.

The Intel update was as follows: 'Be aware the rebels are coming. All Intel suggests two thousand plus. All comms inter-cepts suggest they will come through your position. Repeat: they will be coming through your position.'

That night was one of sleeplessness and high tension, in spite of the luxury of having the I-beds. Something was different about the jungle. The noises had changed, and we were becoming in-creasingly convinced it wasn't animals making most of them any more. We figured the rebels were using the hours of darkness to do their close-target recces – so scoping out our defences and the best potential routes of attack – and were signalling to each other via their spooky 'animal' cries.

Just after stand-to the following morning two women appeared at our position. They wore bright scarves tied around their heads, and multicoloured wrap-around sarongs knotted over one shoulder. Each had a five-gallon cooking-oil container perched on her head – the clear plastic ones. They were using them to carry water. Each must have weighed a good forty pounds and God only knows where they'd had to go to fill them – most likely the wetland area from where they'd cut the best of the bamboo.

They plonked their burdens down on the lip of the depression, gave a shy kind of a smile, then turned and wandered off. As promised, this was our early morning water delivery.

Amazing.

I didn't doubt that all the patrols were getting their water delivery – and so it proved. Once it was put through the Millbank bags to rid it of any sediment, and treated with Steritabs – a sterilising tablet that kills most nasties – it would be good enough to drink. Until now we'd been on seriously tight water discipline. We'd been rationed to seventeen one-litre bottles per six-man patrol, to last three days – so slightly less than one litre per man per day.

It was nowhere near enough in the gruelling heat and with guys on stag or out doing their foot patrols. We were getting seriously dehydrated – suffering lethargy, exhaustion and pounding headaches. This early morning water delivery was going to be a lifesaver. With two jerry cans per patrol, we now had an extra sixteen litres a day – or four litres each, which was more like the kind of amount we needed to be drinking.

But equally importantly, this was classic hearts and minds stuff. Somehow, we'd really started to win the battle on that front, and there were few militaries in the world that could have done this.

The villagers had taken us into their hearts, built the defences we needed, started a regular water and bread delivery and shown us how to harvest and cook the local fauna. They had their eyes and ears out scanning for the enemy, and the best Intel you can ever get is good local humint.

Nathe's snail baltis were part and parcel of the whole hearts and minds process. The most insulting thing you can ever do is refuse to eat the locals' food, or turn your nose up at it. We'd achieved all of this while looking and smelling ever more like a bunch of street hobos. In spite of our rain-shower, we were grimy as hell. During the heat of the day we were attracting swarms of flies. They'd settle on our sweat-soaked shirts in voracious clouds, eating us alive.

It would have been impossible for us to dig the battle trenches, clear the vegetation, and make and plant the punji fields on one litre of water per man per day. We'd managed to make the villagers feel as if we were here to protect them, and that if we worked as a united team we could win this thing – because if we didn't we were all getting slaughtered anyway. If we had for one moment appeared like a force of occupation, we'd have lost the battle before we even got started.

More rain fell that morning, and this time it just kept coming. Pathways turned to raging torrents, and within seconds just about every piece of kit we possessed was soaked. In addition to the dodgy Clansman 319 HF radio, we also had Clansman 349 VHF radios for short-range communications between patrols. The 349s consisted of an earpiece, plus a throat-mic to speak into and send. But they were almost as vulnerable to moisture as was the 319. Much more of this kind of rain and it'd put an end to them as well. This was a real issue, for we had decided upon a single code-word to be given over the radios if the rebels were spotted: *maximise*.

If *maximise* was given, all would know we were about to be hit and to stand-to in our fighting positions.

13

The formal role of the Pathfinders is to 'cue the deep battle'. In theory, we go forward into enemy territory to guide in the main force, and bring in battle assets: fixed-wing warplanes, helicopters, mortars, artillery, rocket fire. We also act to sabotage and divert enemy forces, by hitting their command nodes and key personnel – using sniper rifles and other precision weaponry.

Accordingly, Pathfinders have to be mentally and physically tough enough to operate as small teams in isolation over protracted periods of time. The twenty-six of us positioned in Lungi Lol were capable of doing all of this and more – if only we had the kit to enable us to do so. But right now, with our main radio kaput and our personal radios on the blink, that was looking decidedly doubtful. The call to *maximise* might well never be heard.

With only the one set of clothes we sat there soaked to the skin after the cloudburst, and set about stripping down and cleaning our SA80 rifles. We did so two on and two off, so those on sentry were always ready to fight should the rebels appear. As the sun dried the clothes to our bodies, so the danger of 'prickly heat' intensified – whereby dirt and shit blocks up the pores, causing unbearable rashes and itching. With the lack of hygiene, boils were starting to form on our skin, and our feet were rotting in our warm and damp socks.

A week in by now, part of the danger had become the routine: sentry, sleep, eat; sentry, sleep, eat. Routine leads to boredom and in a situation like this boredom can prove lethal. Now we had a reliable supply of drinking water I figured we could do more. I decided to push out the foot patrols beyond the village clearing.

They'd search for signs of the enemy that we figured were out there in the forest fringes, scoping our positions.

I told the patrol commanders to take time to sit at the edge of the jungle looking back into the village, assessing where and how they would launch an attack.

'You've got to think like the enemy,' I told them. 'Think like the enemy and pay them the respect they deserve.'

H came in from one such patrol having spotted a route through the punji fields. New bamboo stakes were planted to block it. Taff came in from another patrol suggesting we thread a running track around the village perimeter, so we could start 'running the fence' again. It was partly in jest, but the point was well made. With all the lack of physical exercise blokes were losing their edge – and so was planted the idea of building some makeshift gyms.

That morning Wag made the announcement: 'Right, I'm gonna see if I can make some weights.'

He vanished into the small patch of woodland that lay adjacent to our position, and I could hear him chopping away with his machete. After five minutes or so curiosity got the better of me. I found him hacking up various lengths of wood, trying to fashion some makeshift dumbbells.

Halfway through the chopping he paused: 'Fuck it – I need a weights bench.'

In a brazen attempt to copy the I-beds, Wag started to try to build an exact reproduction – but one set within the shade of the woods. He began by planting a couple of uprights, each branching into a V-shape at the high end, forming the rest to lay the weight bars on. Then he started work on the weight bench itself. He got about halfway when he realised he had a problem.

'Fuck it – I've run out of rattan!'

By now Wag was a man on a mission. He went and fetched a length of paracord, one that was rolled up into a dog's-bone shape, like you buy washing line in a hardware store. He switched to using that to lash the framework together. I was assisting as best

I could, cutting down branches here and there, and two hours in the bench was done.

Next, Wag set about hacking out some massive blocks of wood, to make the weights on the end of the bar. But now he faced a problem. He rubbed his hand across his shaven head, glancing from the bar to the weights and back again. The problem was how to attach one to the other.

'Fuck it – what now?' he kept muttering. He paused for a second, then looked at me. 'Right, you seen the fucking I-man anywhere?'

'Nah, mate, I've not seen him. But he'll be about, won't he?'

'Come on, let's go find him.'

Wag shrugged on his belt kit and off we went. Generally, if you walked up and down Lungi Lol's main drag a couple of times you'd find just about anyone. Sure enough we spotted Ibrahim, still in his green shirt and flowery sarong, pottering about on one of the pathways just off the track.

Wag marched over. 'Ibrahim, mate, we need a hammer and nails. Bash, bash. Nails. Pointy object.'

For a few moments Ibrahim stared at Wag uncomprehendingly, before he finally seemed to get the idea. 'I fetch! I fetch!' With that he was gone.

We returned to the HQ ATAP and a few minutes later Ibrahim appeared. In one hand was a rusty-headed hammer with a wooden handle and in the other was an assortment of fifty different bent and blunted nails.

'I have! I have!' he announced, excitedly.

Wag held out his hands. 'Right, okay, give us them here then.'

Wag hurried off towards his woodland gym, tools in hand. I followed, telling Ibrahim that he'd better come with us.

We found Wag surveying his enterprise. He bent to pick up the bar, with the weights, hammer and nails balanced in his free hand.

From behind me Ibrahim came barging through. 'You want this fix here?'

'Yeah,' Wag nodded. 'Yeah, yeah.'

Ibrahim gestured at the hammer and nails. 'Give me, give me.'

A little reluctantly Wag handed them over. Ibrahim hammered away for a few seconds and the lump of wood was attached to the bar. Wag told him we needed another lump on the far end the same size. Within minutes Ibrahim had found one, made a few alterations with his trusted machete, and hammered it on. We now had a bar with a lump of wood nailed to each end, ready for use.

We hefted it between us. I figured it had to weigh a good forty pounds. It was clear the I-man didn't have the slightest idea what we were up to here. He most likely figured we were building some kind of cunning trap akin to the punjis.

'You want me to give it a try?' I asked Wag.

'Yeah. Go on. Go on.'

I took off my webbing, laid my weapon on top to keep it out of the dirt, then lay on the bench. I could hear it creaking and groaning horribly under my weight. No doubt about it – this was not a genuine Ibrahim. It was a cheap Western copy. Wag was stood over me staring into my face, the weights bar between us.

I reached up for the bar. 'Fuck it – in for a penny, in for a pound.'

I was looking up Wag's nostrils as he leant over, preparing to help me lift it.

My fingers closed around the bar. 'Mate, you'd better get ready to catch it if it snaps.'

'Fucking get on with it.'

I eased it off, so I had it held above my head, and started to bench press. After half a dozen pushes, I said: 'Here, mate, grab a hold.'

Wag took the weight and put it back on the rests.

I sat up facing Ibrahim. He had his machete dangling from his hand and was staring at us in total disbelief. He started doing these slow, silent shakes of his head. They just kept coming. He did one final shake – *the white men have finally lost it!* – then turned around and left.

From behind me Wag said: 'Here, let's have a go.'

We reversed the procedure, the bench creaking and grinding but somehow holding fast under Wag's bulk, and that was it – gym sorted. We returned to the HQ ATAP, got a brew on and told Tricky and Grant all about what had happened.

Wag's gym had to be worth it just for the laughs we got out of it. It was impossible to remain laser sharp and focused if all you ever did was stare down the barrel of an SA80 into a wall of jungle. After a while you'd go stir crazy. I added to the list of desirables that we'd radio through to The White Rabbit some alternative fresh food – as opposed to giant African snails – so Nathe and the other masterchefs amongst us could keep themselves busy.

A local cycled through the village with one bloke perched on his battered handlebars and another on the seat behind him, while he himself was standing on the pedals. Three on a bike – it was like Billy Smart's Circus. A call was made for everyone to be eyes-left and have a good laugh. Anything to break the routine. And as it happened, our biggest ever routine-breaker was just about to emerge from the jungle to the south of the village.

It was around lunchtime when a white Lada taxi puttered into Lungi Lol from the direction of Freetown. We were sat in our depression finishing off our brews, and Tricky was the first to spot it.

'What – the fuck – is that?'

Wag glanced over. 'It's a white Lada taxi.'

We stared at it. We'd had practically no vehicular traffic through Lungi Lol, and certainly no taxis pottering out from the nation's capital. It came crawling along the road towards us, as if the driver was highly unsure of where he was going. Once opposite the chief's place it slowed to a snail's pace, then pulled to a halt beside our Pinzgauer.

The back door swung open. I watched in disbelief as a tall, sandy-haired fellow emerged from the rear. He was dressed in neat chinos and a crisp white shirt, and he had a camera slung around his neck.

He stood by the Lada and practically sniffed the air – as if he was saying; *I say, anyone here speak the Queen's English?* He held onto the car door with one hand and peered all about. Unless you knew exactly where we were positioned you'd never be able to see us.

'Better go see who it is,' I announced. 'Grant, you coming?'

We rose as one and went to investigate. The moment the stranger spotted us emerging from the bush, his face broke into an expression of sheer unadulterated joy. It was like all his Christ-mases had come at once: *the taxi driver hasn't screwed me; I am not about to get kidnapped, tortured, buggered . . . and ransomed for a million dollars.*

He bent down, reached inside the Lada, pulled out a daysack and slung it over his shoulder. By the time he'd done that we were pretty much on him. Neither of us had the slightest idea who this might be, except for one thing: he was a prize-winning A1 lunatic.

'Ah, I am in the right place then!' he announced, as an opener.

I stared at him. 'That depends what you're looking for.'

He shut the door, stepped towards us with real purpose and shot out his hand: 'Tim Butcher.'

I put out my hand. 'Steve. And this is Grant.'

'Ah. Steve and Grant. So, are you guys 1 PARA?'

'No.'

'Are you SAS?'

'No.'

'So who are you?'

'We're Pathfinders.'

'Great,' he enthused. 'Great. Great. Pathfinders.'

We were stood at the front of the Lada taxi, and we were still none the wiser as to who this guy was or what he was doing here.

'Sorry, Tim, but you do know where you are, don't you? Where you're coming from . . . Where you're going to . . . What planet you're on . . .'

'Ah, erm, I was trying to find the furthermost British position, actually.'

I shook my head in disbelief. 'Well, mate, you're standing on it.'

'Great. Great. Am I? Superb.'

When anyone has done anything completely and utterly insane, a phrase comes into my head: *When God gave out heads, you thought he said 'beds' and said I'll have a big soft one . . .* That was exactly what I was thinking now. What on earth was this crazed loon doing here, alone and unarmed and riding in a Lada taxi cab?

'Oh, erm, I'm from *The Daily Telegraph*,' he added, almost as an afterthought. 'The newspaper? It would be great to get an interview with you guys and some pictures.'

Grant and I exchanged glances. 'Okay, you'd best come with us.'

We led him in silence down the track and through the bush towards the HQ ATAP. We threaded between some trees, to where Wag and Tricky were draining the last of their brews. Our surprise guest laid eyes on them, kind of jumped backwards a step and stared.

'Urgh . . . Ah! There are more of you!'

Tricky being the brewmaster had a giant metal mug perched on the hexy stove between his legs. Both he and Wag were a week into Lungi Lol, and neither had had a wash or a shave in that time. They – like Grant and me – were stinking. Our mystery guest stared at them for a long second, before running his eyes around the position. His gaze came to rest on the I-beds.

He glanced up at Grant and me in disbelief. 'Erm . . . How long . . . How long have you guys been here?'

'A week.'

'Really?'

'Yep. Really.'

'So, how many of you are there?'

Grant gave me this look: *Mate, time to read him the riot act.*

'Look, Tim, we cannot stop you from having access to this village,' I told him. 'You are free to walk around. In fact, I'll take you around. But we're going to have to place some restrictions on you, and agree some ground rules, okay?'

'Right. Right. Okay, fine.'

'Okay, so, we'll let you speak to people and show you around the village. But no photos of the blokes, and especially no facial shots. No photos of defensive positions, and no talk about our strengths, weaponry or numbers. Agreed?'

'Yep. Fine. Understood. Got it.'

Tricky had finished brewing up. He held out the battered, dirty, gungy mug to our visitor. 'Brew?'

Tim stared at it. 'No, erm, thanks – I'm fine.'

He removed his daysack from his shoulders, bent down, un-zipped it and pulled out a ring-bound reporter's notebook. As he did so I spotted what looked like a Thuraya satphone in the depths of his pack.

'Is that a Thuraya?' I asked.

Tim nodded. 'It is.'

I smiled. 'I do for you, you do for me.'

He looked a bit confused. 'Sorry?'

'We'll give you full access to the village bar the restrictions al-ready stated, if you let me have use of that phone while you're here. You know – calls home.'

'Calls home?'

'Yeah – let the married guys have five mins each to speak to their wives. They've not spoken to them for nigh-on ten days.'

'Oh, yes, I see.' Tim smiled. 'Deal.'

I turned to Tricky. 'Mate, take the Thuraya, cut around the mar-ried guys, five mins each on the blower. Do it.'

Tricky grabbed the satphone and set off towards Dolly's pos-ition going like the clappers.

'Wag, go lend Tricky a hand, will you?' I added.

Wag grunted an acknowledgement and set off after him. I fig-ured it made sense to keep Gimli the Dwarf and the press as far apart as possible.

We had our own Thuraya, of course, courtesy of The White Rabbit, but its purpose was strictly military.

I gestured towards the patch of trees to our front right. 'Okay, let's start the tour.'

Tim set off after me, daypack on his back and notebook in hand, with Grant bringing up the rear. We threaded through the trees, Wag's gym lying ten feet off our line of march. I pressed on, but behind me I sensed Tim come to an abrupt halt. He was staring at the makeshift weight bench and dumbbells.

He pointed. 'Erm . . . what's that?'

'Oh, yeah, we've just finished it. It's a gym.'

'Sorry?'

'Yeah, it's a gym.'

'A gym?' Pause. 'You've *made* a gym.'

'Yeah, Wag and me made it this morning.'

He kept glancing at the gym, back at me, then back at the gym again, as if waiting for some kind of a sensible, credible explanation.

'Well, we've been here a week and we were getting lazy . . .'

He shook his head in disbelief.

'You know, big arms for the summer, mate.'

'Big arms for the summer,' he muttered under his breath. 'Oh yeah . . . Working out. Ho, ho.'

I waved him on. 'Come on, come on. Lots to see.'

I walked on, glancing behind me to check on Tim. He wasn't looking where he was going any more. Instead, he was sketching out Wag's gym in his notebook. From there to Nathe's position was sixty-odd metres, and Tim was busy drawing and scribbling away the entire distance.

I spotted Nathe up ahead of us. He was in his regular pose – seated, with his arms resting on his knees and bent over the dirty cauldron, which was three feet in front of him, steaming away. Gripped between his knees he had a tree stump, and in his hands he had a big, very sharp-looking knife.

'All right, Nathe?' I called out.

He glanced up. 'Yeah, all right, mate.'

Then he was back to his chopping.

On the block he had a new one on me – a massive, black-topped mushroom. The rain had brought the fungi out big time, but I hadn't quite realised that Nathe had moved on to snail and mushroom baltis by now. He sliced the stem off, leaving a cap about the size of his hand. It was spongy underneath, not gilled, and glistening like a fresh cowpat. Nathe started slicing chunks off it and tossing them into the pot.

Presumably, snails alone had proved a tad too bland, so Nathe had decided to add some local flora. This didn't surprise me in the least: this was Nathe. Likely as not the boy from his trench gang had suggested that the giant black fungi with fluffy white edges were particularly tasty, so in the pot they went.

I figured Nathe would have done all the usual edibility tests. The first is the allergic reaction test. You rub the fungi or flora on an exposed part of your skin – say the back of your hand. Then you wait fifteen minutes to see if you get any kind of adverse reaction – like a rash, lumpiness, redness or itching – which might indicate it was toxic. No reaction seen, you break off a small piece and place it on your tongue, then spit it out. You wait fifteen minutes and if you experience no bad reaction you move on to stage three: breaking off another piece and eating it. You'd have to wait a full hour to see if you had any stomach pains, cramps or vomiting. If you had none of those, you could be pretty sure it was safe to eat, and cooking it would generally add another layer of safety.

I came to a halt beside Nathe, quietly relishing what was coming. Mr Tim Butcher was closing fast, head down writing. Nathe finished the mushroom, grabbed himself a freshly deshelled snail, and nailed it on the chopping block. He was living the village good life, and it was close to his lunchtime.

I spoke to the top of his head. 'Nathe, there's this British journalist called Tim has pitched up. He wants to talk to the blokes.'

Jungle ops. Pathfinders taking a breather, in the heart of the Central American rainforest. Even in virgin jungle like this, remarkably little sunlight filters through the forest canopy, making dark and dirtied-up uniforms and blackened-up faces the best camouflage.

Kaboom. Moving deep into enemy territory, small lightly-armed elite forces such as ourselves are bound to come up against far larger and better armed enemies. The one advantage we normally have is the ability to call in air-power, using lasers to mark targets and steer in precision-guided air-strikes.

Smoking hot. Deployed on small-unit actions behind enemy lines, Pathfinders are trained to return fire with maximum aggression and speed, then to break contact as soon as possible, so as to avoid being overrun, killed or captured.

Graham 'Wag' Wardle, trusty GPMG in hand, carrying a crushing load. We were best of mates: I was always twisting his arm about being the Brigade's ugliest man, while he would hit back about the size of my ears.

Captain Grant Harris, then second-in-command of the Pathfinders. A young but very capable officer, he did a sterling job when the shit hit the proverbial fan in Sierra Leone.

Jacko. In spite of not being able to get his swearing right, Jacko was a top operator, and there was no one better to take over command in Sierra Leone.

Nathe. He had somehow made it from turnip farming in Lincolnshire into the Pathfinders – and a better patrol commander I couldn't have wished for. He was also the king of bush tucker: if it moved Nathe would eat it.

Taff Saunders. Like many a Welshman, Taff believed that England was a carbuncle attached to Mother Wales. But never a better bloke in a punch-up. Here he is flanked by two of the Nigerian United Nations troops, who joined forces with us in Sierra Leone.

Tricky. In action on the ranges putting down intense fire during live contact drills training.

The architect of evil. Foday Sankoh, a former sergeant from the Sierra Leone Army turned founder and guru of the Revolutionary United Front (RUF) rebels – known as 'Africa's Khmer Rouge'. By the time our operation was finished, Sankoh had been captured and the rebel resistance broken. Sadly, he died in custody before he could stand trial for mass war crimes.

The bad guys. Rebel fighters of the Revolutionary United Front – those who had declared they were launching 'Operation Kill British', to force us out of the country. We were outnumbered 100-1 and heavily outgunned.

Battle Group. With hundreds of British citizens about to be kidnapped, tortured and slaughtered by the rebels in Sierra Leone, 1 PARA jetted in to Lungi Airport to evacuate them, and halt the rebel advance. As luck would have it, we were to be placed at the tip of the spear.

A pair of CH47 Chinooks from the RAF heading low and fast over the Sierra Leone capital, Freetown – the means via which we would deploy on operations deep into the jungle.

Going in. You could cut the atmosphere with a knife as 26 Pathfinders flew into the teeth of the rebel advance, and with no idea what we'd meet on the ground in the jungle.

Going in hot. Sweeping across the jungle at tree-top level, the Chinooks put us down in Lungi Lol village with no idea where the enemy might be. It was a case of poke the hornet's nest, and see what response we might get.

Armed and dangerous. Gripping a six-barrelled Gatling-type mini-gun, a door gunner scans the jungle below for rebel fighters, as the Chinook flies in low and fast.

Nathe didn't even pause the slicing. 'Yeah, all right, mate.'

Tim walked in still scribbling away, and an instant later he'd all but kicked over Nathe's cooking pot. He dragged his notebook to one side, finally got a look at what was in front of him, and jumped backwards.

'*Fuck!*'

Nathe glanced up at him. 'Hey, mind the pot.'

Tim shook his head in consternation. 'Sorry, sorry.'

He took a couple more steps backwards. He stared at the concoction that he'd very nearly kicked over. It was bubbling away and hissing like the world's most evil brew. Nathe meanwhile was back to his task, tossing glistening chunks of sliced mollusc into the cauldron.

'What – is – that?' Tim finally managed to choke out, his voice like a strangled whisper.

I guessed to him deshelled giant African snail probably looked a bit like sliced child's brain . . .

Nathe didn't miss a beat. 'Lunch. D'you want some?'

Tim visibly blanched. 'Erm . . . Erm . . . Erm . . . I think I'll pass.'

I was massively intrigued about what exactly Nathe had in there. 'Let's have a try, then, Nathe.'

I retrieved my spoon from the side pouch of my webbing. It was a massive metal one – a classic 'yaffling iron' as we call them. Normally, you cook in pairs, so the bigger the spoon the more you're able to get down you. I bent, scooped, and managed to land a lump of glistening flesh, a chunk of brown stuff that looked like . . . tree bark, plus a slice of what I figured was fungus, all of which swimming around in a thick black gravy. I raised the yaffling iron and in it went.

It tasted particularly salty.

I smacked my lips. 'Mate, well done. A bit chewy. A bit too much seasoning. But not bad.'

Tim Butcher was rooted to the spot. I could hear him almost retching, as he stared at Nathan and me in revulsion and horror.

I replaced my yaffling iron. 'Okay, Tim, if you're not feeling hungry best go speak to the blokes.'

'Great . . . The blokes,' he mumbled. 'Not particularly peckish . . . Great, great, thank you.'

I backed off to let him through, without him having to pass too close to the cauldron, and he hurried off in the direction of the battle trenches.

He passed by *33 Alpha*'s I-beds as he went, giving them a good long stare. By now he was convinced we had gone 100 per cent native – Nathe's Lungi Lol balti being the *coup de grâce*. I presumed he'd been flown in by 1 PARA to report on the conflict, so he would have come through Lungi Airport – which would be a place of shower blocks, mess tents, and clean-shaven smart young soldiers by now. From there he'd arrived at . . . this. We were like Kurtz and his band of renegades in *Apocalypse Now* – eating whatever we could scavenge in the jungle . . . Clearly, if we hadn't already started, cannibalism was only a short step away.

We left him free to chat to the blokes. He asked them all the usual kinds of question: What's life like here? How are you coping? What have you seen of rebel activity? How are the villagers? When do you expect an attack? He was very respectful of the reporting restrictions I'd placed upon him. I guessed he feared he might be for the cooking pot himself if he stepped out of line.

It was in Kosovo that I'd first come across the media and begun to appreciate their hunger for the story. I'd also witnessed the insane risks individual journalists took to get it. They'd push themselves into situations of enormous danger. But this guy – he was out on a limb as never before. If he hadn't spotted the Pinz, God knows where he would have ended up, or in whose hands. We were twenty-six elite operators trained to survive in the jungle, and packing some real firepower: he was one guy with a camera in a white Lada taxi cab.

We bounced him around the patrols, but we didn't show him the punjis or the Claymores or any of our other less orthodox Op

Alamo defences. Meanwhile, Tricky and Wag were buzzing about with his Thuraya, getting around the married guys. They didn't manage much in the time allotted to them: *Yeah, I'm all right, love; don't believe all you see on the news; love to the kids and I'll see you soon.* But even that was pretty special.

I didn't bother to call home, because the only one I had to speak to was Ben, and I figured he'd get a right arse-on when he heard about all the lovely scoff he was missing out on here in Lungi Lol.

We managed to spin Mr Butcher's tour out to a good two hours, by which time Tricky gave me the thumbs-up that all the lads had got to make a call. I reminded Tim he was at the furthest forward position of any British forces in Sierra Leone, and that he'd best be getting back to Freetown. Otherwise, we'd invite him to stay for dinner, and no guessing what was on the menu.

At that he reclaimed his satphone, we walked him to his taxi and he got the hell out of Lungi Lol.

14

Bang on schedule that evening Mojo turned up with our bread delivery. He had some worrying news for us. 'You need to come and speak to the chief. He has something important to tell you about the rebels.'

Mojo led the way, as Grant and me went to have our audience. Just as we'd hoped, the chief had got his people out watching and listening, and he'd secured some peachy humint as a result.

'People arrived here today who come from a village five kilometres northeast along the main track,' Mojo translated. 'They saw the rebels coming to attack their village and they ran for their lives. They came here for safety and asked for the chief's permission to stay.'

We asked about rebel numbers, weaponry and the like, but the answers we got were pretty sketchy. Hardly surprising, considering the villagers had been running for their lives. But at least now we knew: the rebels were 5 klicks away and closing.

'Tell the chief to get as many people as he can inside the village tonight,' I advised. 'Spread the word that if the rebels come there will be fighting. No matter what happens he must make sure the villagers stay in their homes or under cover. If they are seen running around they could get mistaken for the bad guys and we do not want to end up shooting them by mistake.'

Mojo translated and the chief confirmed that he understood.

I fixed Mojo with a look. 'We hope we can count on you and your men, mate, to respond as we've asked.'

Mojo nodded. 'Okay, yes, yes – I understand. We will help. We will help.'

We thanked the chief, hurried back to the HQ ATAP and briefed Wag and Tricky. Tricky had just received that afternoon's Sched, with an Intel brief that pretty much confirmed what the chief had told us: 'Highly likely your position will face a rebel attack tonight. The force is 2000 strong.'

Tricky called the patrol commanders in. H had been put in charge of the lone battle trench situated on the main highway, so he would be joining us. We gathered in a circle and Grant set about the briefing.

'There is a very strong indication the rebels are as close as five ks out. If they are that close they may be making a move on us tonight. Priorities: ID your targets, maintain battle discipline; fire control; management of ammo. And remember, keep us informed of all that's going on at all times, if you can.'

'Right, guys, remember what we decided,' I added. 'The fallback plan has not changed. If you're overrun make your way back to the fallback point. And remember, if you're coming in – clear and loud: "We're coming in! We're coming in!" The radios are shite and we can't rely on them in a firefight: I will not be listening to them. So, shout like fuck. Make doubly sure weapons are prepped and ready.'

I finished with this. 'Right – this is it. *Showtime*.'

'Fucking let 'em come,' Nathe grunted. 'About time.'

H: 'Yeah. Pissed off waiting.'

Dolly: 'Yep, no problem – let 'em come.'

Ginge and Taff confirmed they were likewise ready.

To our left we were aware of this massive influx of people. As we'd talked, silent crowds of mainly women and children had been moving in towards the village square. Somehow, their silence was oppressive. It spoke volumes. They were clearly shit-scared. Petrified.

Our chief worry was that rebels were mingling amongst them, weapons hidden under their clothing. It would only require half a dozen to do so, and start firing from inside the village as the main force attacked, to really mess us up. We'd be facing an attack from without and within, which would not be a top fluffy feeling. But there was fuck-all we could do about that right now.

As dusk faded into full-on darkness we were on an absolute knife-edge. No one would be getting any sleep tonight. The quiet in the village only served to accentuate the increase in noises from the jungle. There were more weird animal-like yells and shrieks, and here and there the snap of a branch rang out like a pistol shot. Plus there were the low murmurs coming from those villagers still making their way in to join the hundreds gathered on the square, huddled together for safety.

We spent our time with safety catches off and fingers on the trigger, waiting for what was coming. We could sense that the jungle was alive in a way it hadn't been before. It felt thick with malice. It was watching and it was hostile. I could sense the enemy presence, and feel the threat hanging heavy in the air.

By first light we'd still not been hit, though I didn't doubt the rebels had mapped our positions comprehensively. As the early rays of sunlight streamed through the uppermost branches, I felt a wave of relief wash over me. We had fourteen hours of daylight ahead of us, and if they hit us during that time the advantage switched to us. We'd be able to see clearly, and we'd be fighting over ground we'd prepared exhaustively. The chances of scoring a first-round kill were greatly increased, which meant ammo became less of an issue.

If they wanted to hit us during the hours of daylight – *bring it on*.

'The following stuff's just come in,' Tricky announced, once he'd scribbled down that morning's Sched. After he'd read it out he'd destroy it, so nothing useful could ever be captured by the enemy.

'The Amphibious Readiness Group has moved into a position where 42 Commando can be put ashore. The intention is that 1 PARA will be withdrawn and the Royal Marines will RIP those

positions held by 1 PARA, and by us. Be prepared for an RM dele-
gation to come in by helo to your resupply LZ, to scope out your
positions.'

'RIP' stands for relief in place – when one unit comes in to
relieve another in their positions. It stood to reason we'd get relieved at some point, but as of yet we'd been given no timescale to
expect the Royal Marines (RM) to fly in and check out our positions. In any case, our mindset remained this: *the rebel attack is
imminent; they're five klicks or less away; they had eyes-on us last
night; they'll hit us within the next twenty-four hours, which means
it ain't gonna happen on the Marines' watch.*

Wag and me did our morning walkabout. Doubtless the blokes
hadn't slept during the night, so we needed to reiterate the need
to get some rest during the daylight hours.

'We need the same level of alertness as ever,' I told Dolly, 'but
those not on stag need to get as much sleep as possible, plus get
some food in your stomachs. If we end up on the run we won't be
stopping to eat, so get as much scoff as you can on board.'

We repeated the message with all the patrols, and the chat
and the banter was all good. Morale seemed amazingly high in
the face of a force that outnumbered us pretty much a hundred
to one. As we moved through the positions, we'd seen the odd
villager going about their business, smiling and waving. By now
they were utterly convinced that the twenty-six of us were their
saviours: *The British are here; God's on our side* ... That in turn
served to strengthen our resolve and the sense that we were all
in this together.

As we returned to the HQ ATAP, I made a comment to Wag.
'Mate, the blokes are holding up well. We're as prepared as we'll
ever be. If it's going to come let's just get in amongst it.'

'Aye.' Wag nodded. 'It's time.'

We got back to the HQ position, only to have another vehicle
roll in from the same direction as Mr Butcher had come. But this
time it was very different from a lone Lada taxi cab. It was some

of the SAS from Lungi Airport, driving their open-topped Pinkies. There were eight Regiment lads in two wagons. We invited them to partake of whatever hospitality we could offer. Oddly, they didn't seem too partial to a Lungi Lol balti, but they were happy to share a brew.

For some reason they had no weapon mounts on their wagons, so they could carry no machine guns. All they had were their personal weapons, but those we eyed with great envy. Being official UK Special Forces they had all the usual Gucci kit. Six of the blokes had the lightweight M16 variant with M203 40 mm underslung grenade launchers attached. The other two hefted Minimi SAW (squad automatic weapon) light machine guns, a beautiful little drum-fed LMG perfect for fighting in close jungle.

What we wouldn't have given to have been equipped with Minimi SAWs and lightweight M16s.

We did loads of joint training with the SAS. Right now, I was involved in several cutting-edge equipment development programmes with the Hereford boys, HAPLSS being one such enterprise. Now they'd pitched up in Lungi Lol with their top-notch weaponry, while most of us were holding the line with precious little ammo and the cursed SA80.

Because we did training and ops together, we had loads of friends in common. Blokes migrated from the Pathfinders to the SAS for the extra pay, the kit and the career stability. In UKSF you got a better pension, better chances of promotion, plus job security. None of that was available in a black outfit like ours. We exchanged news over a brew, swapped stories, and then the SAS lads told us they were moving ahead to get 'eyes-on' the bad guys.

We warned them the rebels were less than five klicks away. Having agreed to keep in touch via the radios – that was when they were working – the SAS guys mounted their Pinkies and set off on the highway heading out of the village. It was day nine of our mission by now, and still we'd not taken one round of fire from the enemy. But the SAS lads had reiterated what every man and his dog was telling us – that the rebels were preparing to steam-roller through Lungi Lol and surge south to take the airport.

Around lunchtime we got a warning via the Thuraya that the Royal Marines were on their way to scope out our positions. Grant and I headed down to the LZ. By now the Chinook pilots knew what they were flying into here, but the RM guys would be coming direct from their ship. Most likely, all the RM pilot would have been given was a grid in the midst of the jungle. From his perspective he was flying into a gap in the canopy, so it made sense to help guide him in.

I stood with my back to the wind holding up an orange air marker panel (AMP) to my front. Every Pathfinder carries an AMP: it's a foldable piece of fluorescent vinyl that collapses to the size of a deck of cards. I could hear the distinctive beat of the rotor blades already, though this sounded like a Sea King, as opposed to a twin-rotor Chinook.

The helo appeared over the ragged fringe of the jungle. I saw the pilot spot me and my AMP and adjust his line of approach, and then he was flaring out to land. He came down nose-onto me, fifteen metres in front. I gave him the thumbs-up, signalling they were down safely, and got the same in return.

I moved around to the side door, knelt down with Grant, and waited for the RM advance party to disgorge. We were expecting several marines, but when the door swung open just the one figure dismounted. He jumped down and ran in a crouch to join us, the Sea King already winding up for takeoff. Because I'd air-marked the LZ I was slightly closer, which meant that the RM bloke greeted me first.

He thrust out a hand. 'Captain Richard Cantrill, 42 Commando.'

'Steve Heaney, Pathfinders.'

Grant joined us and shook hands. 'Grant Harris, Pathfinders.'

Neither of us had given our rank, and I could see the guy searching our uniforms for any rank slides. The Sea King was now at treetop height and pretty much gone.

'Just the one?' Grant asked.

'I'm OC 42 Recce Platoon. Been sent in to get a feel for the lie of the land and your positions. Intention is Recce Platoon will come into here to relieve you guys.'

The RM captain's accent was southern English and well-bred, with a bit of a lisp thrown in for good measure. He looked to be in his mid-twenties and was around six-foot-one, with close-cropped hair. His uniform was spotless, his boots were gleaming, and he seemed fit, athletic and purposeful, not to mention scrupulously clean.

His visit was scheduled to be a short one, and he was carrying nothing but his SA80 and his webbing. I figured he was doing his best to ignore our ten days of facial growth, mixed with sweat, shit, piss and general grime. But still there was the hint of a look that he flashed at Grant and me: *You've let yourself go there a bit, haven't you, lads?*

If Mojo was up there with Guardsman standards of parade-ground smartness, Captain Richard Cantrill was immaculate. He'd out-Mojo Mojo. I could smell the soap and the aftershave, and his Combat Soldier 95 (CS95) uniform had knife-edge creases ironed into it. Combat 95 was notorious. It was made from a thin and flimsy nylon in Disruptive Pattern Material (DPM), which cuts into you and doesn't breathe. We might wear it around camp in the UK, but as soon as we deployed anywhere we'd ditch it for some cotton jungle fatigues – just like we were wearing now.

They were durable, reasonably breathable, and nice and baggy. By contrast, Captain Cantrill's Combat 95s were bordering on the figure hugging, if not skintight. He was wearing standard British Army boots, ones that would be next to useless in this kind of environment. They were rubber-soled, with leather uppers, and great for yomping across the rain-and-wind-swept Brecons – but in this kind of heat and humidity your feet would roast, sweat and rot to pieces in them.

The American military made the perfect jungle boot – one with a hardened sole, sporting a metal spline that would stop punjis from piercing it. The bottom half of the boot was made of leather, but with drainage holes in it, complete with perforated metal covers like mini-grills. They allowed the boot to breathe and drain when filled with stagnant water, after wading through swamps. Above the leather was canvas that came up high around the ankle, and it was dryable and easy to move in. They were designed for the jungle, and each of us had managed to get our hands on a pair.

The nearest the Royal Marines have to a unit like the Pathfinders is their Brigade Patrol Troop (BPT). The BPT boys are a pre-assault force, consisting of Mountain Leaders trained to scale cliffs and fix lines, to enable the main force to come behind them and assault a coastal position. They're superlative at what they do, but their specialism is vertical assaults up rock faces – not going beyond an enemy's front line as a deep battle asset, or operating in isolated jungle.

We had two Pathfinders that had qualified as Mountain Leaders. It stood to reason that scaling cliffs and mountains had to be a part of your skill-set if you were operating deep inside enemy territory. In 1994 a British military expedition had gone missing in Lowe's Gully, a notorious jungle chasm in Malaysia. A mixed force of SAS, SBS and Pathfinders were sent in to find them. The only way in was to rope down a one-thousand-foot waterfall at the head of the gully. It was two Pathfinders who led the way, for our blokes had the greatest capability and experience.

Royal Marine Captain Cantrill had flown in to get a sense of what exactly they were about to take on here in Lungi Lol. To be fair, he'd come direct off a ship, and hygiene is such a key part of living in the close confines of a Royal Navy vessel – hence his squeaky clean appearance. But I wondered what he'd make of things here. As we walked him up to the HQ ATAP, Grant pointed out our various positions, explaining how long we'd been on the ground and describing the integration of the locals into the village defences.

'Recently, there's been a significant increase in the threat level,' he explained. 'We thought we were going to get hit last night, so it will more than likely be tonight. Intel says it's a force of some 2000 RUF rebels, so those are the numbers.'

As Grant spoke I was monitoring the captain's facial expressions. I'd noticed a distinct change come over him. He'd gone from this smart, shiny, über-confident, thrusting figure to something very different. He looked visibly shocked by what we were facing here, and what he was supposed to be flying his men into in due course. It was clear that no one had briefed him on the isolation of our position, the threat level, or the unorthodox measures we'd adopted to defend this place.

Captain Cantrill seemed particularly taken by the punji fields. I couldn't wait to offer him my yaffling iron, so he could have a go at Nathe's snail-and-fungi balti.

We reached the HQ ATAP and introduced him to Tricky and Wag. He took a seat on the edge of the depression in between Grant and me. Tricky passed a brew over, and it did the rounds clockwise, everyone taking a sip. When it got to Cantrill, I could see him having to force some of it down him. Sharing a brew with a bunch of evil scumbags like us was clearly not to the captain's liking.

'So, explain to us what's happening with the Marines and the 1 PARA RIP,' I prompted. 'What's the timeline for the handover and is it the same for us getting RIP'd here?'

'All I've been briefed is that 1 PARA will leave and 42 will come in and take up the mantle of those positions. I'm here to scope out RIP'ing you guys from here.'

We spent fifteen minutes sketching out the village on a hand-drawn map, and explaining all the nuances of the village defensive system that we had set in place, and the chief's pivotal role. We briefed him on Mojo and his men and the role they'd play as a back-stop force, and then we took him on a walkabout.

We ended up at Dolly's position, across the highway and out on our left flank. In the interim, Cantrill had got to see the punji fields, the DIY Claymores, the cleared arcs of fire, the battle trenches, the works. Plus he'd got a good eyeful of how the men had adapted to village life. He was scheduled to leave on a helo at 1630, so it was a whistle-stop tour, but even so he appeared somewhat disturbed.

What really seemed to have got to him was how the blokes had settled in to living under such conditions, and yet how upbeat and positive they remained. The highlight had been Nathe waxing lyrical about the joys of jungle cuisine, as he crouched over his bubbling cauldron. We got back to the HQ ATAP shortly before his helo pick-up was due, only to learn from Tricky that it was all-change for Captain Cantrill.

'We've had a message in from Lungi ref "our guest",' Tricky announced. With nearly all comms being done via Thuraya by now, The White Rabbit had adopted a kind of coded way of speaking. The Thuraya was 'insecure means' – unencoded and vulnerable to intercepts – and in theory anyone might be listening in. Tricky eyed Cantrill. 'I guess "our guest" has to mean you. Message is there will be no pick-up today: earliest 0800 tomorrow.'

Cantrill nearly coughed up a lung. He had absolutely nothing with him for overnighting with us lot: all he had were his personal weapon and his belt kit, two water bottles and zero food. Glancing around, he practically begged if he could have one of the I-beds. I did a long intake of breath, commented on how good he smelled with all the aftershave, and said he was welcome to share mine...

The slagging really started now. We slipped into Navy-speak, just to really twist him.

'So, it's turning out to be a nice run ashore for you, eh?' I needled. 'Don't worry, we've got a wide and varied menu on offer in the galley.'

'Can you imagine how smelly you'll be, after a night with us lot?' Wag gloated. 'Got your toothbrush?'

'Want us to have words with the village chief, to see if he can set some showers up?' Tricky threw in. 'You got your foo-foo powder? You do know it's hands-to-bathe, don't you?'

Hands-to-bathe is Navy-speak for when a vessel gets into port and all aboard are permitted to dive off the ship for a mass swim. Foo-foo powder is talcum.

'Fuck off, fucking pongos,' Cantrill muttered. 'The fucking Army.'

He was sat there eyeing the four of us like he was surrounded on all sides by pure evil . . . and we hadn't even got to show him the village shit-pit yet. It struck me that he had an expression on his face similar to the one Tim Butcher – the newspaper reporter – had worn, when I'd given him the village tour.

'D'you want me to get a wet on – cheer you up a bit?' Tricky added. 'Sippers?'

A 'wet' is Navy-speak for a brew. Sippers means sharing between all. We always did that – passing the one massive mug between us. Navy types never did.

'Like I said, you can sleep next to me tonight,' I added. 'You fucking smell lovely.'

That was it. Cantrill was staring at me like I was the Antichrist. Sharing an I-bed with me was clearly his worst ever nightmare.

The torturing only really stopped when the SAS lads came beetling back through the village. They pulled over in their Land Rovers to share their news over a brew – sippers, naturally. From all that they'd been able to glean, the rebels were massing some serious firepower just to the north of us. They asked us what our drills were if we got overrun. I joked that we were going to hand over the lone Royal Marine as a sacrificial peace offering.

Joking aside, I told them that our plan was to hold firm at all costs, or at least until our meagre supplies of ammo ran out. But if the rebels got around the back of us and hit us from the south and the west, we'd have problems. If that happened, we'd try to fight through their number and E & E through the jungle.

At that the SAS lads wished us luck, then set off en route to Lungi Airport.

15

That evening Mojo pitched up with the bread delivery, and now there were twenty-seven rolls, one extra for Cantrill. The Marine captain's eyes were out on stalks. Suffice to say the poor bloke didn't know what to make of it, particularly when we invited him to sit down and dunk his roll in one of Nathan's balti specials.

In fact this one was *really* special. Today, Nathe had somehow managed to get his hands on a giant African pouched rat – a rodent about the size of a small dog. Nathe argued that the locals ate this kind of shit so why shouldn't we? *A lovely bit of fresh.* But strangely, Captain Cantrill didn't seem to be hungry.

I asked him what he had with him ammo wise. He had two mags, so sixty rounds for his SA80. It was approaching stand-to and time to slip into night routine. We called prayers and briefed the patrol commanders that we were shortly to be RIP'd by Captain Cantrill's boys from 42 Commando, but to remain eyes-peeled while we still held the village.

That done, I said to Cantrill: 'No point you stagging-on or being on the comms, mate, 'cause you don't know the routine. May as well get your head down.'

With our levels of fatigue – not to mention malnutrition; in spite of Nathan's curries, the weight was dropping off us – a fresh pair of eyes might well have been very useful tonight. But we were so into our stag rosters by now that it was too much hassle to slot Cantrill into the rotation of sentry duties. The Royal Marine captain bedded down on some cardboard left over from the ration boxes, as the rest of us settled into dark routine.

My first stint on stag was tense, but relatively uneventful.

My second sentry duty was scheduled to last from 0100 to 0230 hours, when I would go to wake the next man. I joined Grant on watch and asked him what he'd seen. He told me nothing as such. But there were loads of those weird animal-like noises echoing through the jungle, and tonight he was 100 per cent convinced they were human. He did some whispered impressions. I ripped the piss a bit, but we both knew exactly what it might mean.

Not only did the RUF use those chilling 'animal cries' to signal to each other as they moved through the bush – they also made them to terrify those they were about to attack. Their targets were almost invariably villages full of women and children. Well, if they were out there massing to hit us right now, they were going up against a very different adversary to their normal fare of de-fenceless civilians.

I gazed into the darkness, straining my ears for any weird or unusual sounds. Sure enough I detected these odd, inhuman, piercing shrieks and wails coming from out of the distant tree line. A lot of jungle animals make calls like that – troops of monkeys in particular. But somehow I didn't figure this was any group of primates moving through the darkness. These weren't like any normal cries of nature that I'd ever heard.

Instinct told me these were the bad guys.

Their unearthly cries sent these icy chills up my spine.

At 0230 hours I woke Tricky so he could take my place on stag, then returned to my watch for a further thirty minutes, while he got himself ready. We staggered the changeovers, so you never had two blokes going off sentry at once and a position left unmanned.

By now I was really struggling to keep awake and remain alert. Pathfinder Selection needs to be as rigorous and brutal as it is – failure rates are normally in excess of 90 per cent; on one recent Selection we had thirty-five start and only three make it through – because these were the sort of operating conditions blokes had to be able to handle day after day after day.

When Tricky was ready to take over I went to get some shut-eye.

Wag had already replaced Grant, and he'd brief Tricky on whatever we had seen or heard. I collapsed onto the I-bed, and swung my legs onto the rope mattress with my boots still on, lay back and closed my eyes.

I was looking forward to getting a good few hours' kip before stand-to. Mine was the second bed out from the depression, with Cantrill on the floor next to me, and Grant on the I-bed beyond. I lay there for a while trying to get comfortable, before gradually drifting into semi-consciousness.

The next thing I knew I had Tricky kneeling beside me, shaking me violently awake.

'STEVE! MAXIMISE! MAXIMISE! MAXIMISE!'

Instantly I was up on the bed, feet swung down. I elbowed Cantrill in the ribs. 'Get up! Get up! Get up and get your kit on!'

Cantrill was wide-eyed awake now. He shrugged his webbing on, and joined Grant and me in the depression, facing east towards the silent threat. I had no idea what time it was exactly, but the absence of any noise felt all wrong. The jungle had gone unerringly quiet.

The stillness felt crushing.

Claustrophobic.

Suffocating.

The intense, eerie quiet was broken by a single shot. It had the unmistakable dull thud that a low-velocity round makes. It was one single low pop – the signature noise of anything above 7.62 mm in calibre, and more than likely the sound of a pistol being fired.

It had come from the front and slightly to my left, so from the direction of the track leading into the village. There was just the vaguest possibility that someone might have had an ND – a negligent discharge (firing their weapon accidentally). It was extremely unlikely with one of us, but quite possible with Mojo and his men. Still, the way things were feeling right now I really didn't think so.

The next instant the darkness to our front was torn apart by a long, punching burst of fire. I caught the instantly recognisable hammering crack of the GPMG, as it unleashed a savage volley of rounds. It was a ten- to fifteen-round burst – *zzzzzzzztttttttt* – and it was pretty obvious it had come from the single battle trench to our front, the one manned by H. It could only be H letting rip with his favourite weapon – the Gimpy.

We weren't using tracer, so it wasn't as if I could follow H's rounds into target. All I could see was the flash of his muzzle, as he unleashed hell. Tracer rounds have the advantage of pointing out the enemy's position. All a soldier has to do is follow his own side's tracer to the target, but likewise the enemy can also follow the tracer back to find and target you (unless you're using modern delayed action rounds).

The roar of the GPMG was answered almost instantly by return fire. It wasn't automatic shots at first, but very repetitive single shots and lots of them: *crack, crack-crack-crack, crack-crack.* It sounded like bigger calibre weaponry than 5.56 mm, so it had to be AK47s as opposed to our own SA80s – and that had to mean the rebels.

Maybe twenty seconds had passed since that first single low pop, and it was now that all hell was let loose. There was a massive eruption of fire from the jungle. The entire forest seemed alive with it, muzzle flashes lighting up the ragged fringe of trees in all directions. We knew in that instant that this was it: the rebels had launched a human wave assault from all along our front.

I could feel the rounds tearing through the branches above us, and I could see the tracer streaking through the night sky like swarms of giant, supercharged fireflies on acid. With the fire came a roaring wave of sound that washed over us, as if one long continuous tsunami had us gripped in its depths.

The nearest rounds went buzzing past my head like angry wasps – *bzzzt-bzzzt-bzzzt-bzzzt-bzzzt* – barely inches away. The next instant the roof of the ATAP above us was ripped apart, as a barrage of incoming tore through it, scattering wooden splinters and shredded leaves across the lot of us.

I saw Tricky's radio shack disintegrate under a murderous blast of fire. Then I saw trees to either side of us juddering under the impact of rounds, trunks blasted asunder with the sheer volume of leaden death that was pounding into them. I shuddered to think how many rebels were out there.

I'd never known a rate of fire like this. There is one particular exercise that involves crawling on all fours, with scores of machine guns zeroed in and firing above your heads. We had Overhead Fire and Flanking Fire guns zoomed in on us, and it was designed to make us get used to being under murderous levels of fire.

This was far worse.

NATO 5.56 mm rounds make a distinctive *pop-pop-pop* sound as they scoot past your head. This was very different. Much of the fire coming our way was 7.62 mm short – the calibre of bullet fired by the AK47. It makes a much heavier *chthud-chthud-chthud* as it rips by. And from the rate of fire the rebels were unleashing it was clear that they suffered none of the shortages of ammo that we did.

Amongst the AK47 fire I could make out the heavier crack and thump of bigger calibre weapons opening up now, as the rebels' machine guns kicked into action. Just as we'd feared – they outgunned us as well. This was sheer fucking murder. Either we started to get the fire down and kill them, or they'd be on top of our positions, swamping us.

Right at this moment they'd have their fighters surging forwards, using the cover of the hail of fire to rush us. I figured I could hear rebel voices screaming out of the darkness, plus more and more of those weird, animal-like cries – although now there was no doubt who was making them. The savagery and blood lust embodied in those ghostly howls was spine chilling. I knew now what the rebels were trying to do: *they were baiting us.*

In theory, this was an Operation Other Than War (OOTW) that we were on, and under the rules of engagement we could only open fire in response to being fired upon. Well, we'd just been given every excuse possible to let rip, if only we had the ammo to do so. Instead, our priority was going to have to be to *conserve* our ammo, but still kill a shedload of the bad guys.

That first, single, low-velocity pop had sounded like a rebel opening fire, but getting an immediate stoppage. The instant re-action from H suggested he'd had the guy in his sights and was just waiting for an excuse to open up on him. But almost imme-diately H's GPMG had been drowned out by the sheer volume of return fire.

In fact, several minutes back H had spotted two columns of fig-ures creeping down either side of the main highway, sticking to the drainage ditches for cover. H had given *maximise* as soon as he'd identified them as rebels, so dragging those of us asleep to instant attention. That done, he'd continued to watch the rebels as they'd drawn closer, keeping them nailed in the stark metal sights of his machine gun.

The lead rebel figure had raised himself into a crouch, and opened fire with his AK47 – the signal for the rest to launch the attack. He was the one who'd had the stoppage – so firing off the single shot. The fact that his gun had jammed had enabled H to get the drop on them, and open up with the GPMG, mowing down that first rank of RUF fighters. But the advantage had lasted barely moments. Hordes of rebels had crowded in from behind and let rip.

During the hours since last light the rebels must have filtered into the jungle all around us. They'd sited their machine guns all across the forest to our front. In every direction I looked I could see muzzle flashes sparking under the canopy, and I could feel the rounds tearing past just a couple of feet above the HQ depression, the trees and vegetation getting torn to shreds.

I glanced behind me at Tricky and Wag. Tricky was crawling

towards the 319 radio, trying to reach it before it got shot to pieces. Wag was on his hands and knees and had somehow managed to grab the Thuraya, which was a massive fucking relief. I knew he'd get a contact report away – format: what had happened, where and when, and get the QRF scrambled.

Behind us the village was utterly deserted. The noise was enough to wake the dead, but the villagers had clearly decided to stay put and hunker down, which was exactly what we'd told them to do should the rebels attack. Any shadowy figures moving through the open we'd treat as hostile, and they'd very likely get gunned down.

I turned back to the front. Time seemed to have slowed into an agonising stillness. I had Grant kneeling to one side of me, Captain Cantrill to the other, his eyes like bloody saucers. I guessed this wasn't quite what he'd bargained for. He'd flown in for a short recce in his nicely-pressed uniform, only to have to bed down in the dirt, and get woken to seven bales of shit breaking loose all around him.

The rebels were unleashing with tracer rounds and where they were firing high their trails were arcing into the heavens way beyond the village. Tracer takes a good kilometre or more to burn out fully, and the night sky over Lungi Lol had erupted into Sierra Leone's most fearsome ever firework display.

The number of weapons hammering rounds into us was unbelievable. Terrifying.

As our fire rose in volume to meet theirs I could hear the pop-gun bark of our SA80s, as the blokes out front gave their all. They were letting rip with four- to six-round bursts – aimed deliberate shots – mixed in with longer eruptions from the GPMGs. Trouble was, at this rate of fire we'd soon be out of ammo, let alone keeping a third in reserve so we could make a fighting withdrawal.

I couldn't let that happen. I needed to take immediate action. I needed to take control of the battle, or we were done for. As platoon sergeant my place was forward with the guys. I had to get there and I had to make the move now.

I heard Wag's voice screaming from behind me: 'Steve! I've got the Thuraya! Sending contact report now!'

I yelled a reply. 'Got it! Wag! Wag! I'm going forward!'

Every night I'd slept with my weapons beside me: my SA80, my Browning pistol, the 51 mm mortar, plus the bag of mortar rounds that Wag and me had scrounged off Mick, back at Lungi Airport. My plan if we were hit during the hours of darkness was to use the 51 mm to put up illume, so as to light up the battlefield. I'd expose the rebels in the kill zones – the areas where the villagers had cleared the vegetation – so the lads could see to shoot them. Plus I'd make them visible at a far greater range, so we could kill them before they overran us.

Putting up the illume was crucial to our defence of the village. The lads would all be expecting it. It was part of our game plan for a night attack. But to get the mortar rounds up I had to move forward, and that meant into the teeth of the enemy fire.

I reached for the 51 mm mortar, then glanced to my immediate front, checking the route via which I needed to crawl. I could see a line of muzzle flashes sparking out of the dark jungle to either side of the track. I counted a good dozen, and each had the fast, rhythmical *fzzzt-fzzzt-fzzzt-fzzzt-fzzzt* of a belt-fed 7.62 mm machine gun.

I yelled at Grant to stay put and keep a grip on things from here. I grabbed my SA80 with my other hand, but I needed someone to bring the mortar rounds and act as my loader. Wag was busy sending the contact report, Tricky needed to stay on the comms, and Grant was here to make command decisions.

That left only one possible candidate.

I locked eyes with Captain Cantrill.

He was lying on the ground, mouth hanging open. His expression said it all: *I didn't expect this when I came ashore!*

I tossed the daysack of mortars across to him. 'Here you go, mate! Grab that and follow me!'

I got into a belly-crawl and prepared to move. At night an attacking force tends to aim high, for they can't see where the ground starts. Right now rounds were hammering past maybe four or five feet above us, for the rebels had yet to adjust their fire to ground. Cantrill and me had to remain below that level if we were to stand any chance of making it forward without being hit.

I had the pistol-grip of the SA80 grasped in my right hand, the butt resting on my right forearm. The barrel of the 51 mm was gripped in my left hand, the base plate resting on my left fore-arm. Plus I had a bandolier of 150 extra rounds for the SA80 slung around my neck.

I started the crawl – right arm forward, left leg up, and vice versa. I was on my belt buckle as I inched over the lip of the de-pression and into the more open, bullet-blasted terrain beyond.

I glanced behind me for Cantrill. Sure enough he was on it. He was a foot away from my right boot. His SA80 was gripped in his right hand, plus the bag of mortars in his left, so he could drag its 40-pound weight behind him.

I turned back to the front. My eyes traced the route ahead of us, but the trees and thick vegetation to either side were rocking and rattling with the weight of fire tearing into them. I found myself thinking: *Fuck me, that's accurate and sustained fire . . .*

Having crawled out of the cover of the depression the sound of battle came to me much more clearly now. I could hear H in his fire-rhythm, squirting out eight- to ten-round bursts. He was unleashing a volley, breaking fire, then letting rip with an-other. The barrel of the GPMG tends to climb to the left the more rounds that are fired, so after each burst he was bringing it back onto target.

They didn't call H the 'Death Dealer' for nothing.

No doubt Tackleberry was in the zone right now, and his with-ering fire would be hammering into the waves of rebel fighters.

All to his front they would be dropping like flies, but it didn't seem to be having the slightest effect on their rate of fire.

Beyond H's trench I could hear blood-curdling screaming and shouting – but not the screams of agony that I'd been hoping for. This was very much yelling – in drugged-up, bulletproof, voodoo-frenzied attack mode. Long banshee howls echoed from the forest, as if we had the devil and all his minions at our front.

I could hear this weird, wild chanting in the background, interspersed with what sounded like jungle drums. It sounded utterly crazed and fucked up.

The rebels had a motto that they'd shout before battle.

'What makes the grass grow?' one would shout.

'Blood! Blood! Blood!' would come the answering chant.

What makes the grass grow?

Blood! Blood! Blood!

What makes the grass grow?

Blood! Blood! Blood!

What makes the grass grow?

Blood! Blood! Blood!

By the time they'd got into their stride, most sane people would have fled in terror – those who could run. If the rebels had got a village surrounded, those trapped would have nowhere to flee, and they'd be imprisoned in their fear. Imagine that happening. Imagine if you were a mother or a father with children trapped in such a village. And that's what the rebels had come to Lungi Lol aiming to do – spread sheer terror and savagery.

Instead, they'd run smack bang into H on the Gimpy.

As I listened to the light *pop-pop-pop* of our SA80s answering the rebel war cries, I cursed the fact that most of the blokes were using 5.56 mm. The British military had switched from 7.62 mm to 5.56 in 1987, when it became standard across all NATO forces. The Yanks had used 5.56 mm in Vietnam, and they were sold on the smaller calibre. The upside was that a man could afford to carry far more of the lighter ammo, but the downside was the sheer size and velocity of the round.

We'd learned all about the lack of stopping power of 5.56 mm in Northern Ireland and Iraq. It fires with a greater muzzle velocity and has less drag. It hits a target with such speed that it punches through tissue pretty cleanly. As a result it can take two or three rounds to stop a man, and especially one high on drugs and voodoo gibberish. By contrast, one round of 7.62 mm drops a man pretty much instantly, wherever he's hit. With its lower velocity and larger head it rips flesh and shatters bone.

With 5.56 mm you needed to score a head shot or hit a vital organ to be sure to stop a man. Facing 2000 drug-and-adrenaline-fuelled RUF rebels, how many bullets could we afford to waste trying to put each of them down?

I forced myself onwards, getting into the rhythm of the crawl. Arms and legs were pumping. I bulldozed over tree stumps and whatever unidentified crap was jabbing into me and tearing at my combats. After all the torrential rain of recent days I could feel thick soggy dirt and shit under me. I tried to concentrate on keeping the barrels of the mortar and the SA80 out of the worst of it. With both weapons resting on my forearms, my points of contact were elbow, stomach and knees.

Cantrill and me had made about twenty yards when I stopped dead. I'd sensed the fiery *pshusshshh* of an incoming projectile. Only one weapon makes such a distinctive sound – the rocket-propelled grenade (RPG) – and we were well within the RPG's maximum 500-yard range.

I saw the projectile come flaming out of the darkness – like a road-cone laid on its side and trailing fire, but one packed with high explosives and wrapped in razor-sharp steel. It was flying high, but if it hit the branches above us it would detonate, peppering the ground below with a lethal spray of shrapnel and splintered wood – which would be me and Cantrill pretty much done for.

I dropped my head as it tore past six feet to the right of us with a deafening *whoooosh*. Miraculously, it went roaring through the tree branches and on into the night *without exploding*. It continued across the village and didn't appear to hit a thing. I figured it must have buried itself in the jungle somewhere out the back, where Mojo and his men would be positioned. *That's if they had got into their positions* . . . But no point worrying about that now.

I set off at a crawl again, eyes scanning the darkness for further RPGs. How that one hadn't detonated I just didn't know. The RPG-7 is designed with a 'graze mode', so that the minute the warhead touches anything it explodes. It doesn't require full impact to do so. I glanced back at Cantrill, fearing that the Marine captain might have gone to ground. But he was right on my heels, God bless him, dragging the mortar pack behind him.

So far, he was doing a sterling job.

Rounds snickered off the vegetation to the left and right of me, as a rebel gunner hammered in a horribly accurate burst. Not for the first time I cursed the fact that none of us had body armour. It existed. The Yanks had the best body armour money could buy, plus the SAS lads had it. Just someone somewhere within the MOD had decided that the X Platoon could do without. In this kind of climate you'd never wear it all day long, but once the fire started you'd want to have it on.

Cantrill and me had to push right forward if I was to get a grip on this battle. As the adrenaline pumped through the system, young lads not long into the Pathfinders would be tempted to let loose with the ammo, or even to break cover to try to better target the enemy. If we allowed ourselves to get carried away in the rush, we'd start running out of rounds and we'd get blokes killed.

Cantrill and me needed to move as far and fast as we could, to have any chance of winning this one.

16

I belly-crawled ahead, arms scrabbling amidst the filthy under-growth and the squelching dirt. My mind was a whirl of thoughts. *What if this was just a probe, one designed to sacrifice a few hundred rebel fighters for the bigger prize? What if they'd sent hundreds more to one or both flanks, to encircle the village?* They had enough men to do it, and it's what I would have done if I'd been their force commander.

I was trying to second-guess what was happening. Was this really only a tidal wave onslaught – hitting us with a human wave directly to our front? Or were they smart enough to use the railway track – this being a feint while they hit us from the side?

Right now all I could be sure of was that it was dark, with bugger all ambient light, and it had to be tough as hell for the lads to ID their targets. I needed to get the illume rounds up, but I was still under the canopy of trees that surrounded the village. I figured I needed to push on for another thirty yards or so, at which point I'd hit open terrain.

Every ten or twelve pumps of my elbows and knees I paused to check on Cantrill. No point reaching a position from where I could fire if I was minus a loader and rounds. He wasn't breathing a word but he was right behind me, glued to my heels. I could hear the spud-gun *pop-pop-pop* of SA80s directly to my right now, which had to mean I was drawing level with Nathan's battle trenches.

I flicked my gaze in their direction, and I could see the blokes of *33 Alpha* hunched over their weapons, pouring fire back at the enemy. I just knew for sure we were burning through the ammo, and I hoped Nathe could keep a grip on the fire discipline. There was no shouting or cries of alarm yet, and there was no panic in the air – which was reassuring. But I could tell the lads were waiting for me to put up the light, and I knew I had to cover more ground more quickly.

I had to get further forward. I needed to be somewhere where I could see the enemy and use the mortar to best effect, but most importantly where the lads could see and hear me, so as to take my lead. I needed them to slow the rate of fire, get one shot to equal one kill, and get the fire discipline tight. But I was tiring under the exertion. The sweat was pouring off me in bucket-loads. I was soaked with it, and my arms and shoulder were sore and burning with agony, my breath coming in sharp gasps.

I paused to wipe the slick of sweat from my eyes. It was half blinding me. I glanced forward and I could just make out a glint where the darkness of the foliage was broken by moonlight filtering through. That was where I had to get to. Once I was out from under the trees I'd be in the clear to send up the mortars. But it didn't escape me that once I left the cover of the foliage I'd be completely exposed: the rebels would be able to see me, and target me with fire.

There was bugger all I could do about that. You can't put mortars up when you're under tree cover, or they'll very likely burst in the branches above you – end of story.

There was a solid stream of bullets hammering past just inches above me now, and I could feel the pressure waves thrown off by the rounds thumping into the back of my head. The rebels were bloody good: they were adjusting their fire, dropping it to meet ground level, leaving Cantrill and me less and less of a margin for error.

No ifs or buts, I was fucking terrified, but adrenaline was driving me forwards. More to the point, I'd been here for days readying myself for just such a battle. Poor bloody Cantrill had flown in on a short recce jolly, and now this. He had to be totally shitting himself. I knew I was basically pulling him forward with the sheer effort of my concentration and my force of will.

I crawled on for another ten yards, dragging Cantrill with me. I was 60 yards to the south of the track, with H's trench lying to my front left. We had to be on our own front line now, and this was as good a place as any to set up the mortar. But as I glanced upwards I cursed. Above me there was still thick vegetation – the spreading canopy of a grove of fruit trees – and that meant I couldn't use the mortar.

If I sent up rounds here they'd detonate in the branches, which would be no good to anyone but the enemy. I steeled myself. Gritted my teeth. We needed twenty more yards, maybe thirty, and we'd be out from under the branches ... and right under the enemy guns.

I paused for an instant longer. I needed to gather my thoughts, get a sense of the battle space, and orientate myself to make sure we didn't crawl off at a tangent. We'd come forward maybe sixty-five yards. I knew Wag would be back there with Tricky and Grant, getting the message through to headquarters. Already the gears would be turning at Lungi Airport to rack up the QRF. The 1 PARA duty signaller would be waking Gibbo, so he could issue the order for them to launch. In my mind's eye I could see a platoon of paratroopers gathering their weapons, the fire in their eyes. *Fuck it, let's go!*

We just had to hold out for long enough to get the QRF in. We'd then be sixty-odd blokes facing a couple of thousand rebels – so odds down to 33–1 – which was much more like it.

To my left I heard H screaming out targets. 'Right of bent tree, two o'clock, a hundred and fifty yards!'

To my right Nathe was yelling out similar fire orders to his blokes, and Cantrill and me were sandwiched in between. I couldn't hear Dolly, Ginge or Taff, but their voices were very likely drowned out by the horrendous rate of fire going in both directions.

Then I heard the cry: 'CHANGING BELT!'

H was yelling out a warning, so the lads could keep the fire going with the SA80s as he changed a belt on the GPMG. That meant he was 200 rounds – or a third of his ammo – already gone.

Nathe and the lads from *33 Alpha* opened up with long bursts from their SA80s. And then I heard that worst of cries: 'STOPPAGE!'

There was the stark steel-on-steel *clatch-clatch* as whoever it was tried to clear their weapon. I just hoped to fuck another of our SA80s didn't go down. We'd kept the assault rifles scrupulously clean and rust free. We'd never stopped polishing and oiling the fucking things. But the SA80 was just a heap of shit whichever way you treated it.

An instant later H had sparked up the GPMG again, which meant the worst of the moment was over. He'd have one further belt of ammo laid out next to his weapon, on a waterproof poncho to keep it off the dirt. As he fired he'd keep one eye on the ammo level, to check how close he was to needing to do another belt change. But all we needed was H's GPMG to run out of rounds and we were going to be seriously buggered.

H was pushing the weapon to the very limits. The normal rate of battle fire on the GPMG is twenty-five rounds a minute in short, three-round bursts. The rapid rate of fire is a hundred rounds a minute, in four- to five-round bursts. H was unleashing in eight- to ten-round bursts, so he'd upped the fire to cover the mass of rebels he was facing. The GPMG pumps out rounds in a cone-like spray, and is ideal against bunched-up targets at shorter ranges. H had to have the enemy charging down his very barrel right now, with the rate of fire he was unleashing.

Trouble was, under heavy fire you are supposed to change the barrel of the GPMG, or it gets red-hot and you get a cock-off, or breech explosion. The working parts get so hot that when you feed a round into the breech it ignites with the heat, exploding in your face. With the rate of fire H was putting down he knew what he was risking – but no way could he afford a barrel change any time soon.

If H tried that, he'd be overrun.

Likewise, if he ran out of rounds.

Right now the blokes were targeting whatever they could see: muzzle flashes, the glint of moonlight on gunmetal; movement; rebel war cries. It was far from being the best way to use up our limited supplies of ammo.

We needed the light.

I forced myself to cat-crawl onwards into the face of the enemy. Above the gunfire, I could hear blood-chilling rebel yells coming from all directions. It was as if they were getting us surrounded and deliberately *taunting us.*

I was thrusting forward with my elbows when all of a sudden I sensed the ground in front of me give way. I half-tumbled into a stinking, muddy ditch. For an instant I feared I'd fallen into one of our own punji pits. Those fields of sharpened bamboo spikes were just forward of our front positions. I'd figured the nearest one lay off to my right, but maybe I'd miscalculated.

Fuck, the punji fields are just around here.

Fuck, I've drifted too far right into the punjis.

I felt around myself gingerly, but no spikes had pierced my combats or torn into my flesh, so I figured the punjis had to be a fraction further forward and off my line of march. Rolling half around, I checked on the canopy of vegetation above me. As I did so I realised I was lying in twelve inches of stagnant, shitty, putrid water that filled the bottom of the ditch. Doubtless, it was infested with every kind of sucking, biting, slithering thing the jungle had to offer, and right now they were having a good feed.

I cursed. We were still under the bloody trees.

There was no option but to push on.

I elbowed ahead through the dark and fetid water.

I must have cat-crawled a good thirty yards beyond our line of battle trenches when I finally emerged from under the trees.

Glancing behind, I saw Captain Cantrill was still with me, though he was hanging back a good few feet, the poor bastard.

Directly to our front lay the enemy.

The ragged fringe of jungle was dead ahead, and I didn't doubt that the rebels were getting right in amongst us. Just to my right lay this dark, shadowed mass – the sweep of the nearest punji field. It was good to know that it was there. To my left I could just make out H's silhouette, crouched in his lone battle trench adjacent to the main highway – which showed as a barely-visible yellow slash cutting through the darkness.

From where I was lying I could hear figures thrashing about in the bush ahead of me, and blood-curdling cries. All around there were the flashes of weapons firing, as unearthly shadows and shapes flitted through the darkened terrain.

I heard cries from behind me, voices tinged with panic. 'STOP-PAGE! STOPPAGE!'

They were coming from Nathe's position. Like H's, it was right in the line of the rebels' mass attack, and it had to be in danger of being overrun. The priority was to get the light up now, but that meant raising myself into the level of the rebels' fire.

I could hear the bullets scything through the vegetation a foot or more above where Cantrill and I hugged the earth. I could fire the 51 mm from the prone position, that I knew. I could slam the base plate down, level it with the spirit level built into the tube, grab a round from Cantrill, reach forward and drop it down. It was all doable lying prone as I was, and I'd be far safer that way. But like this I couldn't see properly to target the enemy with the light.

If you can't see you can't fire accurately, I told myself. *Get on your knees, Heaney.*

Decision made, I laid my SA80 on the dirt – no other place to put it – and levered myself up into a kneeling position, all the while trying to blank out the hiss and crack of rounds tearing past to either side of my head and shoulders. I cursed again the lack of any body armour. Right now if an accurate round came my way I was taking it with no protection, and it would likely kill me outright.

I stole a glance around me to sight my targets. We were right in the heart of the battlefield – the no man's land between the two sides. It was carnage. Streams of tracer fire were pouring out from the jungle, from where the rebels had sited a good dozen or more machine guns. To either side of me I could see scores of AK47s spitting flame, as rebel fighters probed forward, unleashing long, savage bursts.

To the southeast of the village I caught a momentary glimpse of distant moonlight glinting on a pair of linear objects – the railway tracks. *Fuck me.* I was so far forward I could actually *see* them, despite the darkness. On the opposite side of me and just to my rear I had the reassuring sight and sound of H's lone GPMG pounding out the rounds.

I heard H yelling out target instructions: 'Sixty yards! Dead ground exit *Lowe*!'

Sure enough the rebels were closing in for the final push, and they were doing so via the dead ground – where we couldn't see clearly to shoot them. If they were at dead ground exit *Lowe*, that meant they were just dozens of yards away from Nathe's battle trench. For an instant I wondered how the other patrols were faring, and if any of those had yet been overrun.

I told myself to keep one hand on my SA80, in case the rebels swarmed us. They would know where our main positions were by now: our muzzle flashes would have given us away. But we couldn't know where they were unless we saw them firing or moving – and for that we sure as hell could do with some flare rounds.

Siting the mortar base plate was key to accuracy, so the first thing I did was swipe the ground with my hands, to clear it of any rocks, roots or other obstructions. That done, I placed both hands on the tube and drove it down as hard as I could, slamming the solid base plate into the earth to anchor it. The kickback from the first round would really bed it in, and stop it skidding around or jumping.

I moved my right knee back, in case the tube jumped with the first round, smashing the base plate into my kneecap, which could easily break it. With my left hand on the heavy mortar sleeve – a tough canvas shield that protects the operator's hand from getting scorched – I glanced behind for Cantrill. He was flat on his belly, bang on my right heel. Good positioning. His rifle lay to one side of him, the daysack full of rounds right next to him. I reached out with my right hand palm upwards, feeling for the mortar that I needed him to deliver, like a relay baton.

'Round!'

He flipped open the top of the pack, reached in, dragged out the first mortar and slapped it into my hand. As it went past my face towards the mouth of the tube I did a quick visual inspection, just to check that it hadn't been damaged during the long crawl forward. Last thing we needed now was a dud round getting stuck down the tube.

I raised myself on my haunches, reached forward and dropped it down the tube, tail-first. I heard it slide down the barrel and make a hollow thunk as it hit bottom, coming to rest on the firing pin plate. I aimed by sight and feel. The 51 mm has a sighting mechanism, but I had neither the time nor the light to use it. Instead, I was aiming by intuition. The higher you angle the tube, the higher the round goes, but the shorter the trajectory.

From long practice I knew that at a 45-degree angle the round would burst 500 to 600 metres in front of me, which was just where I wanted it. I needed the light behind the enemy, throwing them into silhouette against its glare but leaving us cloaked in darkness. I needed the rebels smack bang under its 200-metre cone of light, and us well out of it. That way, we would be invisible, and they'd be pinned under the blinding glare.

Being this far forward I needed to let the lads know it was

Cantrill and me opening fire, otherwise they might mistake us for the enemy and slot us.

'STEVE HEANEY – PUTTING UP ILLUME!'

I repeated the yell in both directions, to our right and left front. I saw the silhouettes of two heads nodding their acknowledgement from H's trench, so at least those guys had heard. I was also giving the lads a warning: *Prepare for the rebels to be lit up, and be ready to put down aimed shots to smash 'em.*

I left a second for the lads to prepare, checked the orientation of the barrel one last time, grabbed the dick-like handle to the front and slammed it down, hammering the firing pin into the rear of the mortar. It emitted a loud *phuuttt* as it fired, the flash of the thing throwing Cantrill and me into sharp relief. If the enemy hadn't known we were here they sure as hell would now. They could range in on us, using the noise and the thick plume of smoke hanging in the air to target us.

I blanked my mind to the threat and gazed skywards, following the trajectory that the mortar would have taken. The fire from the rebels was as intense and murderous as it had been from the start. A great deal of it was zipping past to either side of my head now – so I guessed they'd seen the telltale signs of the 51 mm firing.

Everyone on our side knew a mortar was in the air. They were poised for the burst and what it would reveal. But the level of fire from the enemy and their wild shouts and screams continued unabated, so hopefully they hadn't a clue what was coming.

The 51 mm illume fires to a height of 250 metres. It detonates to leave a flare drifting beneath a parachute – one that looks like a giant roman candle. It burns with a 350,000 candle-light power – illumination by which the lads could see and kill. But it would also signal that I was here, taking charge of the battle.

If we'd had HE rounds I'd have got an illume up, nailed the enemy positions, then hammered them with HE to tear them to pieces. On a good day I could put down six to eight HE in sixty seconds.

But right now we didn't have any HE. We didn't even have 40 mm grenade launchers to mallet the rebels, putting ten rounds into them on the back of the illume. All we could do was get the light up so we could better call down the GPMG and SA80 fire.

I waited the last few seconds it took for the round to reach height, and then *pop!* – it hung there like a tiny sun burning in the heavens. It had burst just where I wanted it: bang above the line of the jungle, throwing light over all the ground to the front of it. Just for an instant I sensed the enemy fire falter, the pounding percussions from their machine guns seeming to stall in mid-fire.

They hadn't been expecting that – not to be pinned under the fierce, fluorescent daylight of the illume. For an instant we had them foxed. We had to seize the advantage. A sense of euphoria swept over me that maybe this was all doable – *we still could win this one.*

'PICK YOUR TARGETS!' I yelled. 'PICK YOUR TARGETS! PICK YOUR TARGETS!'

In spite of having rebel gunmen charging down their very throats, the guys had refrained from using rapid fire. They'd been aiming at shadows. Now they had the light, all of that had changed. All to our front rebel fighters were frozen under the glare, and trying to find some cover to go to ground. Thanks to the villagers cutting the vegetation, they had precious little foliage in which to take refuge.

I glanced behind me for an instant, and in an arc bending around to my right I could see a solid line of muzzle flashes, as our guys opened up. In an instant the goading, animal cries from the enemy died. Instead, I could hear screams of agony as rebels went down. Voices started yelling out what had to be orders, as their fighters scrabbled to get out of our line of fire. But the ground from the dirt highway across one hundred yards or more to our front was lit up like a football stadium under floodlights.

For the rebels, there was nowhere much left to run or to hide.

17

I straightened up, so more of the lads could see me: 'USE THE LIGHT! USE THE LIGHT! DELIBERATE FIRE! DELIBERATE FIRE! PICK YOUR TARGETS! PICK YOUR TARGETS!'

A rapid rate of fire with the SA80 – when it doesn't jam – is thirty rounds a minute. Ten minutes and you'd be 300 rounds down – which was all each of us had. That's why I'd called for 'deliberate fire'. With deliberate fire the lads would put down controlled, aimed single shots – so around ten a minute. Even so, some of the lads were very likely pushing 150 rounds down already.

I remained on one knee as that first illume round drifted to earth, long bursts of machine gun fire kicking up mud and shit all around me. I was spotting for rebel movement in the light, and yelling out the fire instructions like a madman.

We also needed the illume so badly because most of the blokes didn't actually have workable night vision equipment, or at least not gear you could rely on. Each patrol had been issued with one common weapon sight (CWS) – a long, black night vision unit that screws onto the SA80. Trouble was, here in the soaking wet and humid tropics it would rapidly steam up, which made it unusable.

All across our patrols I could hear more of the lads having problems with their SA80s. 'STOPPAGE! STOPPAGE! STOPPAGE!'

Those with a stoppage they couldn't immediately clear would try to use the CWS sight to help direct the GPMG fire – yet there were no guarantees that the CWS would be working properly. Without the light from the illume, any number of us were going to be left fighting blind.

I went down on my belt buckle again. Illume round up and

targets spotted – I could afford to hit the dirt for a good few seconds. Rounds were coming in thick and fast, so the rebels must have switched on to where Cantrill and I were positioned and what we were up to. To my left H was hammering away like a good one, slamming fire into the bunched-up fighters caught under the harsh glare on the main highway. The rebels were being cut down as the Death Dealer got to work.

But then I heard him screaming out a warning: 'MOVEMENT! By the railway track! By the railroad!'

Pinned under the illume to our front, the rebels were desperately trying to get away from its murderous glare. But just as I'd feared, they were also trying to hit us from over on our right flank, and that's where the Death Dealer had spotted them.

That's where they needed the light.

I forced myself into the kneeling position again, getting my head and shoulders up above the surrounding foliage and fully into the enemy's line of fire. No other way to do it. I swivelled my body through 90 degrees, until I was facing southeast. I dragged the tube around with me and slammed the base plate down again. The 51 mm tube is fixed to the base in such a way that you can only adjust elevation – hence the need to haul it around every time you seek a new target bearing.

My arm shot back towards Cantrill: 'Round!'

The guy had anticipated the move, and the cold steel of the mortar slapped into my open palm almost before I'd asked. Good lad. The railway line was 450 yards away, but I needed the illume a good 100 yards beyond that, so we were talking a 550-yard shot. Working on muscle memory and instinct alone, I lowered the barrel to the 35-degree angle, dropped the round in and checked the alignment one last time.

I hit the firing lever. *Phuuttt – the second mortar was away.* It left Cantrill and me enshrouded in the telltale pall of smoke billowing out of the muzzle. I hit the deck again, and lay there tracing the mortar's trajectory, staring into the dark night and trying to ignore the bullets zipping past to the left and right of us. We now had one mortar shell to our front, hanging under its chute and gently oscillating as it drifted towards the forest canopy, and another about to burst over the railroad.

The second illume popped a good 150 metres beyond the railroad, casting a cone of brightnes like daylight across the ground a hundred metres to either side. It hung lower in the sky than the first – I'd had to fire it on a shallower trajectory, to achieve the range – so it would have less than the optimum burn time, but there was nothing I could do about that.

I yelled out the fire instructions, screaming at the top of my lungs to try to get heard by Ginge and Taff's patrol. 'PICK YOUR TARGETS! PICK YOUR TARGETS! PICK YOUR TARGETS!'

Almost before I'd finished I heard Ginge's distinctive Mancunian accent cutting through the night: 'Two hundred metres, half right railway track – rapid fire!'

In the light of the illume they'd nailed the rebel figures advancing stealthily along the steel tracks. Patrol *33 Charlie*'s GPMG spat fire, a long burst hosing down the new rebel target. I saw figures diving for cover, as the GPMG rounds tore into them. Once hit by a GPMG's 7.62 mm bullet you weren't getting up again, no matter where it tore into you.

Or at least normally you weren't . . .

Here in Lungi Lol things were a little different.

We were facing hordes of drugged-up fighters who truly believed they were invincible in battle. The rebels gave themselves *noms de guerre* – war names – like Baby Killer, Belly Slasher, Colonel Savage and the Born Naked Squad (those who stripped their victims naked before abusing and killing them). They were infamous for 'playing' the Sex The Child 'game'. A pregnant woman would be captured, and her belly slashed open with a machete – the rebels placing bets beforehand on the sex of the unborn child.

'Bathed' in their voodoo 'medicine' prior to going into battle, they truly believed they were bulletproof. The voodoo priestess would promise them: 'With this I make you invincible in battle! The bullets will flow off you like water!' Doubtless they'd have done just that in preparation for the first major battle of Operation Kill British, and in part it seemed to be working.

I saw rebel fighters get slammed to the ground by a round from one of the guns, then clamber to their feet and start charging forward again, screaming maniacally. Some took three or four rounds from the SA80s before they finally went down and stayed down.

Not good for conserving limited supplies of ammo.

Right now the main thrust of the assault seemed to have shifted to the railroad. But no matter how much light I put up the rebels just seemed to keep coming. It was sheer suicide to charge ahead when the cover of darkness was ripped away, but I guessed the rebel commanders could afford to sacrifice any number of fighters ... and over on our right flank serious battle had now been joined.

The battle trenches of *33 Delta* lay some three hundred and fifty yards away, and I could see the long tongues of fire spitting out of them towards the enemy massing along the railroad. I could barely hear Taff's dulcet Welsh tones – he was too far away for his voice to carry properly above the deafening noise of battle – but I presumed he was calling out the targets to his blokes.

For an instant my mind flashed to fears of the rebels totally outflanking us and getting round our rear. That must be what the move down the railroad was meant to achieve. Just as I would have done it, they'd sent in one force on a full-frontal assault, while filtering their main body of fighters silently past our right flank. It was only getting the light up over the railroad that had blown their cover, and I didn't figure any of the rebel commanders had been expecting us to have flare rounds.

Right at this moment we'd seized a slight advantage. But I was certain of one thing now, more than ever before: the RUF commanders were no slouches. In fact, for all the voodoo crap and the taunting animal cries they'd launched a textbook attack. If I was in command of their forces I knew what I'd try next: I'd go for an outflanking manoeuvre further to our left or right flanks, one that would get my forces in to our rear. Then I'd hit us from behind.

All we had to hold them off with were sixteen Nigerian peace-keepers with very likely a dozen rounds per man.

That's if Mojo and his men had even got into their positions.

Wag was back in the HQ ATAP, so hopefully he'd overseen the Nigerians rallying under Mojo and getting into their battle trenches. *Hopefully.* But right now I had no guarantees that Mojo and his merry band were in position and every man ready to fight, and no way of knowing. Our rear could be wide open. Unwatched and undefended. That's just how it was.

The rebel commanders were moving to outflank us, that much I was sure of. Plus they had the numbers to do so on *both sides*. That meant Dolly's patrol – *33 Bravo* – could well be in their line of march. Dolly's lot were way out on our left flank on the far side of the highway. Were they in action too? If so we were getting hit all along the 600 yards of our front, meaning they were coming at us from all sides.

Risking a peek, I levered myself up into the kneeling position. I glanced over the top of H's trench, and sure enough I could see the guns at Dolly's trenches spitting fire.

Fuck me, that was everyone in action.

The entire platoon was sparking.

The highway effectively split the rebel formation, for H had that nailed as a kill zone. I'd seen him blast apart any number of rebel fighters as they'd tried to move across that open patch of dirt. Ginge and Taff's patrols had the railroad similarly covered. So, in effect, the rebels were split into three units: those north of the highway facing *33 Bravo*; those sandwiched between the highway and the railroad, facing H and *33 Alpha*; and those south of the railroad, facing *33 Delta* and *33 Charlie*.

We could kill them in their droves as they tried to cross those open areas under the light.

But if they filtered through the thick jungle to one or the other side of us, we were going to have problems.

The first flare was about to fizzle out, going dark as it hit the jungle. I figured Dolly's was the patrol most in need of light right now. The vegetation was closer and thicker around *33 Bravo*'s trenches, the terrain being wetter and more swampy, which had made it harder for the villagers to fully clear *their* arcs of fire. Plus there were folds in the ground – ditches and hidden gullies – for the enemy to use to mask their advance.

I felt it in my bones: *Dolly was the one who most needed the light.*

I took hold of the 51 mm, hefted it up and swung it through 180 degrees, pivoting on my right knee. I got it in position and drove it down again, base plate smacking into the earth with a heavy thud. It was now orientated towards the north, with *33 Bravo* being some three hundred yards away from me. I angled it at 45 degrees, to get the range, and reached behind me.

Cantrill was still lying prone on the deck and I didn't blame him. With all the fire we were taking, it made sense to keep lower than a snake's belly. The air was thick with the peppery, firework smell of cordite, and a haze from all the gunfire lay low across the village. But still he had a fresh mortar round ready and waiting, and he slapped it into my hand. The Royal Marine captain was doing me proud.

I yelled like a madman. 'DOLLY! YOU'RE GONNA GET ILLUME! PICK YOUR TARGETS!'

With Dolly being so isolated out on our left flank, I wanted him and his boys to have plenty of prior warning. I let the mortar fly. It flew on its silent trajectory, before bursting to the front of *33 Bravo*'s trenches, throwing the ragged jungle into stark relief.

I straightened up: 'USE THE LIGHT! PICK YOUR TARGETS! PICK YOUR TARGETS!'

The moment I'd finished yelling I heard a massive upsurge in fire from Dolly's battle line. There was the *pop-pop-pop* of controlled SA80 fire, plus long, punching bursts from *33 Bravo's* Gimpy.

To my immediate left a second GPMG joined in the fire, hosing down the rebel fighters massing at Dolly's position. It was H. Due to the fact that all the other friendly positions were behind him, H could cover a 180-degree arc from due south to due north. Or at least, all friendly positions *should* have been well behind him. Right now he had us two lunatics bang out in the open on his right and with not even a shell-scrape to hunker down in.

H kept ramping the Gimpy to left and right. He was dropping rebel fighters as they tried to sneak along the drainage ditches to either side of the main highway, then pivoting left to give Dolly supporting fire, hammering rounds into those trying to rush *33 Bravo's* trenches. On H's right shoulder he had James 'Bucks' Roebuck, the second guy manning that lone trench, and I could see Bucks likewise blasting away with his SA80. That was one assault rifle we didn't want having any stoppages.

Their position had borne the brunt of the battle since the opening shots had been fired. I'd heard H make the one ammo belt change already on the GPMG. He had to be burning through his second belt. Firing ten-round bursts, it only took twenty pulls on the trigger and that was a belt of 200 rounds of link exhausted. With sixty bursts, that would be all his ammo finished – and then H and his wingman were either going to get overrun, or they'd have to bug out and abandon their position.

'H! Watch your ammo!' I yelled across to him. 'WATCH YOUR FUCKING AMMO! WATCH YOUR AMMO!'

I turned in the direction of Nathe's trenches. After H, they'd taken the next greatest volume of enemy fire, and they had returned it with good measure.

'Nathe! Watch your ammo! WATCH YOUR FUCKING AMMO! WATCH YOUR AMMO!'

I'd fired three of the illume rounds now, meaning I had fifteen remaining. With the light up our fire was fearsome and precise, if only we could keep a careful watch on the ammo. But when you could see your targets under the light, the temptation was to let rip on auto. What I wouldn't give now for some HE rounds for the 51 mm. In the time it took one illume to drift to earth I'd get four to five HE mortars launched in quick succession, smashing the enemy apart.

I'd be calling out to Cantrill: 'Illume! HE! HE! HE! HE! HE! Illume!' And so on and so forth.

But even without HE, the 51 mm was still proving a game-changer. Getting the light up had tilted the balance of things maybe just in our favour. The battle was balanced on a knife-edge still, but at least we had deliberate aimed shots going down, and we were getting pretty damn close to where we needed to be: *one shot = one kill*.

The first illume round went down and out now, fizzling to darkness in the jungle. Round two was only seconds away from plunging into the forest to the far side of the railroad. Round three was halfway to earth above Dolly's position. It was time to light them up again.

I swung right 90 degrees, hefting the mortar with me, so I was facing to my front. The extreme exertion of the long crawl, followed by the sheer physical effort of ramping the 51 mm tube around was half-killing me. I felt as if I'd been sitting under one of Lungi Lol's drenching tropical rainstorms, my combats were that soaked with sweat. I was literally steaming with it – clouds of water vapour evaporating from my body into the cool night air.

The fourth illume went up without a word having been spoken between Cantrill and me, other than: *Round!* I sensed it was a nice, long, deep shot, one that would burst a good two hundred yards beyond the fringe of jungle. The moment it ignited my eyes were drawn to flashes of movement out on the main highway.

In the few short moments of darkness since that first illume to our front had died, the rebel commander had got his men on the move. Scores of heavily armed figures were darting across the dirt track, heading in the direction of Dolly's position. Being the man furthest forward, there wasn't anyone better placed to spot the rebels, or to call down the fire.

I could see fighters armed with AK47s, plus others hefting RPGs and belt-fed RPK light machine guns, the Russian equivalent of the GPMG. H had his focus on targets to the front of Dolly's trenches, which he was blasting apart with his gun. His wingman, Bucks, was likewise smashing fire into them with his SA80. I needed them to swing right ninety and mallet the rebels surging across the highway.

'H! Bucks! Target movement on track four hundred metres! Bend in track! Bend in track! RAPID FIRE!'

H tensed his shoulders and swung his gun east. The muzzle spat out a long burst of flame, as he hammered out the first burst. It tore into the ditch to one side of the track, where the rebels were mustering to make the dash across the open road. We weren't using tracer. We had none. We'd have used it if Mick had had any – packing each 200-round belt with four normal ball rounds to a fifth of tracer. At night, the first tracer round gives you your line to aim for: *fuck, I'm high, drop down three.* The second confirms you're on target.

In daylight you can see the strike of bullets on the ground. You can gauge from that the need to adjust fire: *drop ten and come right five.* Fighting in the dark and with no tracer, the only indication we had whether our rounds were on target was seeing people get hit and fall. The way the rebels on the roadside were going down, H had to be hammering in the rounds bang on the bull's-eye.

I saw figures get smashed to the ground and struggle to get up again, but before they were halfway to their feet the Death Dealer had cut them down once more.

Some three hundred yards out from the village the main highway kinked north, beyond which it lay out of our line of sight. The rebels were surging across it at the bend in the track. I figured they had to be planning to move to our far left flank and advance on Dolly's position from there. At 300 yards' distance from us, it was well within range for engaging with the GPMG, which is accurate up to 1000 yards or more.

With the SA80, 300 yards was about the limit of its accurate range, even if every weapon had been fitted with a night optic sight. As it was we were using the basic iron sights – the metal V at the rear of the carry handle, which you line up with the nipple on the muzzle-end – which meant Bucks was having to operate at the very limit of his marksman's skills.

I remained in the kneeling position, scanning the terrain 180 degrees to our front and trying to get a sense of what the rebel commanders were going to try next. The light over Taff's position spluttered out, throwing the railroad back into shadows and darkness. I checked the one above Dolly's patrol, where I figured the rebels had shifted the present thrust of their attack. Their fighters had got well malleted to our front and on our right flank, so it made sense to shift well left.

I figured the railroad had to be littered with bodies – rebel dead and injured – as was the highway. I could see the corpses littering the dirt road ahead of us. Any rebel commander worth his salt would have learned a vital lesson by now: Operation Kill British was going to be no pushover. Wherever he got his men moving out in the open we were getting the light above them and they were getting smashed. Hence the need to stick to the cover of the jungle and the darkness, and to try to hit us from fronts we least expected.

Hence the need on our part for maximum vigilance.

As I knelt there eyeing the distant fringe of jungle, I was scanning for any close movement as well. Surely the rebel commander would have sent some of his fighters forward to take out Cantrill and me. With the state of mind his fighters were in, he was sure to have no shortage of volunteers. *Oh, take me, me, me! Take me! I'm bulletproof!*

If he managed to take us out – by either killing us or worse still capturing us – in one fell swoop he'd have half of his problems sorted: *no more light*. With the threat from the rear as well, I felt like I needed eyes in the back of my bloody head.

But as luck would have it, the rebels were about to hit Cantrill and me right from our very front.

18

I caught the flash of fiery movement even as the noise washed over me: *pshshuuusshshh*!

RPG launch.

From somewhere to the southeast of us the fiery trail of an RPG cut through the blinding darkness. The high-explosive projectile came barrelling towards us, with me and the 51 mm tube bang in its line of fire. Time seemed to freeze. I hit the deck in slow motion, even as the express-train *whooooooooossh* of the thing drilled into my head.

At the very last instant the increasing velocity of the RPG round must have forced it to climb a fraction higher, and it tore over the top of my head, missing me, the mortar tube and Marine Captain Richard Cantrill by bare inches. I was left enveloped in the back-blast of its rocket motor, fumes billowing around my ears and a choking, burning smell hanging in my nostrils.

It screamed onwards. I figured it would smash into the trees around the HQ ATAP, which lay next in its line of fire, I tensed for the blast, but none came. I didn't hear any explosion at all – fuck knows why. All I did know was this: *that had been no lucky shot.* It had been targeted directly at Cantrill and me. The rebel commander knew where the battle was being orchestrated from, and killing us had to be his number one priority now.

'What – the – fuck!' I exclaimed.

Cantrill was lying face down in the dirt. He didn't so much as raise his head to acknowledge me.

For a good thirty seconds the fire from the enemy side slackened, as if upon orders to do so. From the positions to our front I figured that as few as three belt-fed machine guns were lancing in the tracer now. The rest had ceased firing. Then even those few remaining guns fell silent.

All quiet on the Lungi Lol front.

What the fuck were the rebels up to now?

In the eeriness of the comparative silence I heard cries of 'MAG CHANGE!' Blokes to either side of us were shoving fresh magazines onto their SA80s.

The loud click and slide of a fresh bullet being rammed up the barrel was followed by a tense, expectant stillness, as we waited for whatever the rebels were going to try next. I figured we'd just survived their first two major pushes – one a feint to our front, the other along our right flank on the railroad. I didn't think for one moment the rebels were done with us. Without doubt they'd be regrouping in the jungle for a third try.

I flicked my eyes back to Cantrill. We hadn't spoken a single word since the RPG had torn across us. Apart from the fact that we were still alive, the amazing thing was how we'd somehow been working faultlessly as a team. He hadn't fumbled even one of the mortar rounds; each had been ready and waiting where and when I needed it. I gave him the faintest of nods. He forced a smile in return.

We had to win this thing in the time the light would buy us, for sooner or later we were going to start running out of illume. Somehow, I needed to keep the light up, while rationing the mortar rounds. I'd dived onto my front to avoid the RPG, which meant I was pretty much unsighted right now. I risked bobbing up again to get eyes-on the silent battlefield.

I got on one knee, glanced north and I could see the flare round drifting earthwards over Dolly's position. Bare seconds now and the light over *33 Bravo* would go dark. Directly to my front, the most recently-fired illume round was still riding high above the main highway, oscillating gently from side to side. But over Taff's position on the right flank all was very dark.

I grabbed the 51 mm tube, twisted 90 degrees right, planted the base plate, took a baton from Cantrill and fired. Even before the round had burst over Taff's position I swivelled through 180 degrees, sighted over Dolly's patrol and got a second round airborne. They burst in quick succession, throwing a burning halo across the sky to either of our flanks, Cantrill and me sandwiched in the centre of the glare.

We were six illume rounds down now. Twelve remaining. Or four more blasts of three across our front.

My gut instinct was telling me that the bad guys were heading for Dolly's position, way out on our left. I'd spotted the rebels surging across the main highway in that direction. At the distance they were out from the village, I figured they had to be heading for a distinctive feature that we'd already scoped out as a major threat. The blokes had discovered it via the probing patrols that we'd pushed out from the village, and they'd given it the nickname Fern Gully.

Fern Gully was a knife-cut ravine some seven to eight feet deep. It ran from the fringes of the main highway out towards *33 Bravo*'s front. Come one of the torrential rainstorms we'd been having, the gully would fill with water, draining off the road and the surrounding terrain. But right now it was comparatively dry. Fringed with thick bush, it provided great cover to mask the movement of a large body of men at arms.

It was the perfect feature via which to advance on *33 Bravo*'s battle trenches unseen, and get in amongst Dolly and his blokes. I risked raising myself still higher, getting into a half-crouch so I could check for any enemy movement through Fern Gully itself. It was only the fact that I was fractionally higher than I'd been before which alerted me to the threat to Cantrill and me: the rebels were danger-close, creeping through the bush to overwhelm us.

From the corner of the punji field nearest to us I heard a distinctive *crack* – dry vegetation crunching under the weight of a human footfall. My head darted around, my eyes flicking towards the noise, my ears straining. I figured I could detect rustling in the low undergrowth now – all that had been left standing by the villagers who'd cleared out the arcs of fire. We hadn't got them to cut to ground level: we'd only asked them to clear anything that might hide a man from our fire.

Then I heard an unmistakable sound: the hard clink of metal on metal. It rang out through the silent darkness like a gunshot. It was the kind of noise a spare magazine makes when banging against a rifle, or a grenade against a steel webbing buckle.

Either Nathe's blokes had moved far forward of their trenches without giving warning to anyone, or we had rebels between Nathe's position and ours. I spotted a shadow creeping forwards. This wasn't fucking Nathe's lot. It couldn't be. If they were coming in the least they'd have done is yell out a warning: *Steve! Steve! Nathe plus one coming in!*

The rebels were there – right fucking on top of us.

They were so far forward that they were well out of the cones of light cast by the illume rounds. Now I understood the silence: the rebel commander must have sent a hunter unit forward to nail Cantrill and me. Smash the guys putting up the light, so he could launch his next offensive in total darkness.

I let the mortar tube fall from my grip, and in one smooth movement I grabbed the SA80 in my right hand, lifted it from the dirt and brought it into my shoulder.

Bang-bang-bang-bang-bang-bang-bang-bang-bang-bang!

I let rip with a savage ten-round burst, aiming at the movement and the flitting shadows. Thank fuck that even after laying my SA80 in the dirt for so long I hadn't had a stoppage. I paused for a second, watching like a hawk. Cantrill was down on his belly and I'd not breathed a word to him of the threat. I figured he had to be wondering who the hell I was shooting at, though surely he could hear them.

More movement.

Hordes of shadowy figures rushing us.

Bang-bang-bang-bang-bang-bang-bang-bang-bang-bang!

Shifting my aim left and right, I hammered rounds into them. I heard the hollow, soggy *thuttd-thuttd* that 5.56 mm rounds make when they tear into human flesh at very close range. Any nearer and we'd be poking the fuckers with bayonets. They were so close I didn't need the SA80's metal sights: I was scanning the darkness with the weapon in my shoulder, sighting down the length of the barrel.

I heard screams now, agonised screams.

I realised how dark it was.

It was pitch black.

Dark, dark, dark.

More movement. *How many of the fuckers were there?* I saw figures rear up from the bush in front of me, eyes white in the darkness and wide with ... what? Adrenaline? Drugs? Voodoo-bulletproof-madness?

Muzzles sparked from barely a few dozen yards away.

I answered fire with fire: *Bang-bang-bang-bang!* Four more rounds.

Bang-bang-bang-bang! Another four.

More screaming.

Deafeningly close.

I was dripping in sweat, my heart was going like a jackhammer, and I was high as a kite on the adrenaline.

I heard these spine-chilling cries of agony rend the darkness, this time a little further to my right. It had to be from where the rebel fighters had blundered into the punji fields. My fire must have driven them back that way, the injured and the survivors fleeing into the safety of the open darkness, only to get stuck with bamboo spikes honed to a razor sharpness.

For an instant I wondered what it had to be like stumbling through the darkness, only to get stuck by those bamboo staves. I figured I could almost smell the rebels' confusion and fear. They were in amongst the punjis – I was sure of it now. And once you've stumbled into punjis in the pitch darkness, your greatest fear is you don't have a clue where to go next. *They could be anywhere all around you.*

Generally, if you've fired more than six to ten rounds you slot on a new magazine, grabbing any spare moment in which to do so. That way you always have a full mag on your weapon. I'd fired off far more than that by now, more like close to a full mag, so I used the momentary lull in close-quarter battle to do a lightning-fast change.

I made a mental note to try to grab a few seconds to recharge my mag from the bandolier of ammo that I had slung around my torso. That way, I'd have as many mags as possible fully bombed up and good to go. But right now I didn't have a spare moment, for the battle was balanced on the very brink.

I could sense it. *Feel it.*

Right now, in the next few minutes, we would either win or lose this thing – Operation Kill British vs. Operation Alamo.

Or at least we'd win or lose the first battle in what promised to be a far longer, wider and bloodier war.

All to our front I heard probing bursts of fire, signalling the rebels were back on the offensive again. I had to get my focus off the enemy, danger-close to Cantrill and me, and back on the wider battle and the light. But I felt frozen by indecision: *If I put the fucking rifle down, to fire the mortar, I'll be defenceless – and they're fucking right on top of us. But if I don't get the light up, they could creep through our positions unseen and get in amongst the lads, not to mention the village.*

For several long moments I kept the SA80 hard in my shoulder, my focus on the rebels barely spitting-distance away. Time seemed to have slowed to an agonising, slowmo loop. A second seemed to last a lifetime, as I scanned the spectral battleground. The night was thick with the scent of adrenaline, blood, hatred, pain, aggression and fear.

If I dropped my weapon and they rushed Cantrill and me, we

were done for. But to my left I could hear H rattling through the ammo big time. Beyond him, I could hear Dolly yelling out urgent fire instructions from the direction of his trenches. I figured the rebels were in amongst Fern Gully in serious numbers now. At the same time they'd sent a force forward to hit Cantrill and me and keep us from putting up the illume rounds. The fuckers.

What the hell was I to do? Get up the light? Help the lads conserve the ammo? But I had enemy engaging us in close-quarter-battle. Ammo? Light? CQB? Which was the fucking priority? And where the fuck had the rebels gone to who were right on top of us?

Should I get Cantrill to cover me? Get him under orders. *Get your SA80 going and cover me, as I use the mortar.*

I was so focused on my weapon I'd almost forgotten he was there. Then I remembered his pitiful lack of ammo. He only had the two mags. That's what he'd flown in with. *No way could I rely on him alone to cover us.*

The illume round to our front – the fourth that I'd fired – drifted silently into the trees and went dark. The darkness became thicker, as illume rounds five and six floated earthwards. Soon they would be snuffed out in the thick jungle. *Decision time.* Either I discarded the SA80, took up the mortar tube and fired more illume, or all along the battlefront it was going very, very dark.

I heard Dolly's voice screaming fire control orders, his words laced with desperation.

'Fern Gully! FERN GULLY! FIRE! FIRE! FIRE!'

Fuck it, the lads needed the light.

I dropped my rifle, grabbed the mortar tube, brought it up in the aim and punched a hand back to Cantrill.

'Fucking round!'

He slapped it hard into my palm. With my SA80 resting on my jungle boot I shifted 90 degrees to my left and launched the illume. I was aiming up and out beyond the gully, over the terrain that Dolly's blokes were hammering the rounds into. That was where they most needed the light.

As the mortar flew to height my mind flashed to the HQ ATAP, and what Tricky, Wag and Grant would have been doing while we were having the fight of our lives out here. I'd left Wag on the Thuraya, so I figured he'd have got a contact report through, while Tricky would have been trying to work his magic on the 319 radio. So even now the QRF should be riding to our rescue in a Chinook.

It was a fine feeling: *the cavalry are on their way.*

We just had to hold on.

The illume burst blinding-white over Dolly's position.

Almost simultaneously, the enemy redoubled their fire from the jungle directly to the front of us, just to remind H, Nathe, Cantrill and me that they hadn't gone away. The deafening eruption of violence underlined just how much we needed the QRF. The rounds screamed in, and the night sky above me was rendered into a blinding latticework of tracer.

If they were firing one tracer per five – 'four bit'; four ball rounds to one tracer, as we would – that meant there was practically a solid wall of bullets whipping past across us. The upsurge of fire was met with an instant response from our side – blokes hammering in short, aimed bursts. Seconds later the fire to our front petered out. I heard the odd *pop-pop-pop* of an SA80 from our side, before it went completely quiet again, the fire dying down over at Dolly's position as well.

The eerie silence drew out: ten seconds became twenty … There was the odd single shot from out of the tree line, but not a sniff of return fire from our lads. They were holding their fire, which meant they were keeping great discipline with the ammo.

Eventually, the rebel fire petered out completely.

Silence.

Nothing moving.

Stillness like the grave.

I grabbed the opportunity to yell around for any casualty stats. I figured we had to have injured, but with all the chaos and the deafening noise of the firefight no one had been able to report in via the Clansman 349 radios. If anyone had called 'Man down!' on the net, I wouldn't have had the slightest chance of hearing them.

Nathe yelled across confirmation that all were okay in his trench, but I couldn't get a sniff of a response from the others.

The seconds dragged into minutes, as the tense silence settled heavy and ominous all around us. The rebels weren't even making their evil animal cries any more.

Where were they?

And what in hell were they up to?

The silence was deafening. Eerie. Spooky. Unsettling. In a weird way I'd felt happier when we were under fire: at least then we could see the enemy and know where they were trying to hit us.

One minute stretched into two, and still the empty, ringing quiet. For a moment I wondered if that was it: *battle over.* Maybe we'd given them the shock of their lives, and they'd withdrawn to lick their wounds and count their dead. But something – that fail-safe soldier's sixth sense – told me that wasn't so. The night was rippling with menace. It pulsed back and forth through the trees, like a palpable evil.

Two minutes became five. Still nothing. For a moment I wondered whether Cantrill and me should pull back, getting ourselves into a position of relative safety. We'd had the enemy charging down our gun barrels. There was nothing to stop them doing so again. Out here we were prime targets for Op Kill British – or rather for getting bound, gagged and dragged off into our worst ever nightmare.

But if we pulled back and my sixth sense was right, the lads would have no light for when the rebels hit again. *No: we had to stay put.*

I wondered if the rebel commander might have sent his men in covertly, which might account for the quiet. Were they even now belly-crawling through the bush to get right in amongst us? In which case, did I put up some more light? But I only had a limited amount of mortar rounds remaining – and my priority, as with all of the blokes, had to be to conserve our precious supplies of ammo.

Five minutes became ten, or at least it felt that long, what with the weird, otherworldly slowing down of time that comes with ferocious battle and the adrenaline rush of combat. I'd reclaimed my SA80 and I was scanning my arcs all around me, but each second staring down the gun barrel into the silent night felt like an hour.

For a moment I heard this faint rustling and scrabbling in the bush just to my front. My rifle barrel nailed it, finger bone-white on the trigger. *Come on – fucking show yourselves.* I tensed to unleash hell. Then a centipede the size of a prize-winning Lincolnshire carrot came wriggling out of the vegetation, crossed the dirt in front of me, and slithered away on the far side, moving in the direction of the punjis.

What the hell was that doing scuttling about in the midst of a firefight like this?

As with their snails, they built their insects big here. The giant centipedes came complete with a nasty, venomous bite. They were one of the few species of wildlife Nathe hadn't got into his cooking pot. Apparently, they were crunchy as hell and the venom wasn't good for the digestion, or so his trench-digging lads had told him.

I went back to scanning the empty darkness. For a moment my mind drifted. During a lifetime spent soldiering the only time I'd ever remotely felt as on-the-edge as this was on a previous jungle operation – one of my first ever with the Pathfinders. I was a twenty-three-year-old lance corporal, with three years' experience in the PF, and I was the lead scout of a four-man patrol. We'd been sent to Rideau Camp, in the Belize jungle, to run six weeks' training for the Gurkhas.

The CO of the Gurkha unit was ex-SAS, and one morning he'd called us in to tell us we were getting retasked. On the remote border with Guatemala a lawless rebel drugs gang was preparing to ship a consignment of heroin from one of their refineries to the US. Our mission was to get inserted by Puma helicopter into the jungle, then trek to a ridge overlooking the drug gang's operation, where we'd set up an OP. We were to go in with five days' food, ammo and kit, to get eyes-on the bad guys.

We were issued with live ammo – as opposed to the blanks with which we'd been training – for our M16s, food rations, thermal imaging optics, the works. Our patrol commander was a very capable bloke called Andy Parsons, plus there was a signaller called Bill Basha Barnes and a medic, Johno Smith. Having studied the maps, we chose a clearing for the helo insertion 5 klicks from our intended OP. We got dropped by the Puma, and then began the killer trek through the jungle.

It was typical 'egg box' terrain: thick forest and vines cloaking a series of egg box-shaped ridges and gullies. The loads were crushing. As well as oxygen bottles, we had eighteen batteries for the thermal imaging kit, each battery weighing a pound. We couldn't guarantee there would be any water on the ridge, so we were carrying all of that, plus food, ammo and survival gear. We'd been warned that a Gurkha patrol had been ambushed here by the rebels just a few weeks earlier. They'd got badly shot up and had been forced to go on the run.

The rebels funded their insurgency via drugs, and they didn't want any pesky British soldiers poking their noses in. It could easily take a whole day to cover 5 klicks moving tactically through such appalling terrain, and we only made the high point – our intended OP – at last light. We prepared to hunker down for the next five days, with the rebel drug-runners' den in clear sight below us.

Carved out of the forest was this deep-jungle clearing. It contained a dirt street lined with gambling dens and whorehouses, with some massive, warehouse-like buildings that had to be the drugs refineries. Badly distorted Mexican-style music drifted up to us, and with darkness the boozed and drugged-up partying began. Gunshots rang out every few minutes, blending in with the Mex-beat and the *put-put* of the generators. This was a lawless Wild West Dodge City, financed by a rebel mafia drug-running operation, and we really did not want to be discovered spying on this little operation.

From here mule trains carried the white powder out via the Belize jungle, and then by boat to Miami and the wider USA. We set up the OP, then got to study the place via a tripod-mounted Swift scope. Our first task was to log key points of interest: guards' posts and numbers; mule-train routes in and out; locations of refineries; vehicles on the move. We were on strict hard routine – so bedded down on the rock, with no washing or hot food or drink allowed. To avoid detection, we were shitting in cling film and pissing in coke bottles, so we could carry it all out with us.

One thing struck us immediately: the place was much bigger than our maps and satphotos indicated. We sketched it out in more detail: it had expanded massively since it was originally mapped, and it was creeping towards the Belizean border. Dodge appeared to be booming, and due to its enlarged size we couldn't see enough from our elevated position. Andy knew we couldn't complete the task as given from here. We'd do a 70 per cent job, and 70 per cent wasn't good enough. He figured we needed to move closer, but that would mean crossing the border into Guatemala.

The CO hadn't told us explicitly to 'do whatever it takes', but that is what lies behind every Pathfinder tasking. This being a very sensitive op, if we did get scarfed up in Guatemala our own people would very likely deny those were our orders, for it would cause a massive political shit storm if they didn't. No one underestimated the dangers of what Andy was proposing.

We were a four-man patrol, and our heaviest firepower were the 40 mm grenade launchers slung beneath our M16s. Ranged against us were several hundred drug-running rebels, and if they got wise to us we were not trained to wound. The ensuing firefight would be fast and brutal, and for us capture would lead to torture, abuse, death or worse.

Andy wasn't about to order us to go in, especially as Basha was totally against it. He reckoned the risks were too great. I said I'd back Andy, and Johno went with the flow. It was three against one, and so the decision was made. We stashed our gear, and at last light we headed down through the jungle, crossing into another sovereign nation's territory and past the point of no return. Johno remained behind as our backstop, 100 metres into the forest, and we laid a string from there to the edge of the canopy, where we left Basha as our fire support.

Andy and I headed out into Dodge, under the glare of the flood-lights that ringed the place. Every inch of our exposed flesh was blacked-up, so as not to catch the light. The only way to pene-trate further unseen was by the cover of these drainage ditches that ran around the base. We slid into the first: it was three-foot deep and full of stinking, stagnant water. I was on point. As I belly-crawled in, unidentified slithering and sliding things went 'plop' and 'sploosh' all around us.

We crawled onwards for three nightmarish hours, covering a good five hundred yards. Dodging guards by keeping submerged in the festering water, we got to a point where we could see and hear just about everything. Andy opted to take the people as his targets, me the buildings. Wriggling forward, we did our close-target recces, our faces barely peeping from the stink-ing swamp water. We were trying to imprint everything on our minds, for we couldn't write anything down.

We were right in the chaotic heart of the place: gunshots kept ringing out on all sides and there were open street brawls. I could see the front gate that led into Dodge, and the path heading off into the jungle, which had to be the mule-train route. I counted the big, metal-roofed structures that had to be the refineries. The drug-runners were dressed in a mixture of combats and local dress. They were armed with AR15 assault rifles – the predecessor of the M16 that the Americans used in Vietnam – and they looked serious and businesslike enough.

We'd reached Dodge Central around midnight. By now we'd discovered just how many leeches had got into our combats and were feasting away on our blood. Scores had worked their way into my groin area. They'd got lock-on and were making themselves very comfortable. But there was nothing we could do to fend them off: one false move and we'd be spotted.

We lay in the fetid murk getting drained of our blood, trying to keep bodies and minds sharp as a razor blade, as we waited for the rebels to show us what we really needed to see: a mule train laden with bales of drugs, revealing just what kind of gear they were refining, and smuggling out of here.

We'd lain unmoving in the swamp in the very heart of Dodge and we'd waited to get the killer shot . . . For how long were the rebels going to make us wait here in Lungi Lol, I wondered? How long before they showed themselves? How long before they made their killer move?

I flicked my eyes away from the stark metal sights of my SA80 to the horizon towards the east. Was I just imagining it, or did I detect the faintest skein of light – just the barest hint of the coming dawn? First light was what – maybe sixty minutes away? A lot could happen in that time, but come sunup the advantage shifted to our side – to the village defenders.

I got my answer about the rebels' intentions pretty quickly now. As if on one word of command from their leader, the enemy just seemed to open up on us with everything they'd got. After the long and deafening silence, the sudden eruption of violence was stunning in its intensity. The incoming fire was fearsome, yet now it was coming from one main direction and was concentrated pretty much on one single target.

Our far left flank.

Dolly's position.

33 Bravo.

To the north of us, the lads at *33 Bravo*'s trenches were taking a massive pounding. Dolly's lot were getting totally smashed, tracer like a solid stream of flame scorching into them. It was like a dragon was perched at the jungle fringe due east of *33 Bravo*, mouth open and streaming fire into their battle trenches. During the long minutes of silence the rebel commander must have shifted hundreds of his fighters that way, in preparation for his final big killer push.

I dropped the rifle and rose on one knee, mortar gripped in hand. But I didn't need to yell out any fire instructions any more. Instead, the response from the lads was instantaneous. I saw this sustained volume of rounds smashing back from our side and tearing into the enemy. But our rate of fire was really scaring me now: *it was too much, too fast*. Keep this up and pretty soon we'd be down to fighting them with our pistols, machetes and bare hands.

I reached behind me: 'ROUND!'

Cantrill scrabbled forward and thrust the mortar at me. I dropped it down the tube, fired it, and seconds later I'd got light bursting over the far side of Dolly's position.

I started screaming: 'WATCH AND SHOOT! WATCH AND SHOOT! PICK YOUR TARGETS! WATCH YOUR AMMO! WATCH YOUR AMMO! WATCH YOUR FUCKING AMMO!'

As I yelled out instructions I spotted scores of figures sprinting across the dirt highway at the fringes of the jungle. More and more of the rebel fighters were pouring north to join the killer thrust of the assault, which had turned against *33 Bravo* big time.

I screamed out a warning: 'REF TRACK TWELVE O'CLOCK AT TREE LINE ENEMY – RAPID FIRE!'

An instant later the guns in H's trenches swivelled around and unleashed hell, scything down figures on the highway. I grabbed my SA80 from where I'd laid it on my boot and joined them. As I opened up I could see rebel fighters taking hits, getting smashed and stumbling to the ground. I was halfway through my thirty-round mag within seconds.

As I fired I started yelling at Nathe's position to my right: 'NATHE! CAN YOU SEE THEM? CAN YOU SEE THEM?''

'YEAH! ON! ON! ON! ON!'

The lads at *33 Alpha* opened up on the rebel targets, adding their firepower to mine and H's. I was firing by 'battle-sighting' now – looking over the top of my sights and sighting down the barrel alone – so as to allow me to maintain my peripheral vision. The last thing I needed was to get tunnel vision, and miss some rebel fighters creeping up to hit Cantrill and me.

From my vantage point I spotted a new threat now: hordes of shadowy figures surging through Fern Gully to swarm Dolly's trenches.

I screamed out a further warning. *'33 BRAVO* DUE EAST – WATCH AND SHOOT! WATCH AND SHOOT! NEAR END OF FERN GULLY!'

Barely had I finished yelling when a savage burst of rounds sparked out from Dolly's position. It was their GPMG tearing the night apart, signalling that their gunner had spotted the enemy fighters all but on top of their positions. This was it now: this was where the rebel commander had chosen to make his die-hard push. This was where they would overrun our first positions, or die trying.

Then I heard it. Desperate cries of: 'STOPPAGE! STOPPAGE! STOPPAGE!'

More SA80 bullshit, but this time from over at Dolly's trenches, and with the rebels surging out of Fern Gully and spitting-distance close.

Then, even worse from H: 'CHANGING BELT! CHANGING BELT!'

An instant later H's Gimpy ceased fire, the solid stream of rounds that he'd been hammering into Fern Gully coming to an abrupt end.

A mixed bag of Nigerian and Jordanian United Nations peace-keeping troops, plus villagers. Trouble was, in Sierra Leone there was no peace to keep – as our mission was about to prove.

By strength and guile. The SBS – Special Boat Service – were out patrolling the rivers and estuaries that criss-cross the jungle, and our first escape and evasion plan had us getting picked up by their boats.

The SAS and the SBS deployed alongside us in Sierra Leone, but as luck would have it we would get to see the real action.

Long-sleeve style. The rebels' speciality was lopping off the hands of women and children, using axes or machetes, to spread a dark reign of terror. They gave their victims the choice of long- or short-sleeve style – amputation above or below the elbow. How could we do anything else but fight to the last man to stop them?

Mango, anyone? Barefoot angels – that's how the kids in the village of Lungi Lol struck us. No rebels were kidnapping them, lopping off their hands, or forcing them to be child soldiers – not on our watch.

The kids are all right. We were 26 Pathfinders facing 2,000 rebels. But with smiles like these from the local kids, how could we do anything other than smash the rebel advance and stop them butchering the village?

Having decided we were their heaven-sent saviours, the locals scavenged food from the jungle for us and fetched our daily water – as we waited in our trenches, poised to kick seven bales of shit out of the rebels.

Village people. This is why it mattered. We flew into the jungle to smash the rebel advance, and stop them wreaking carnage in the capital city and at the airport. We ended up in the fight of our lives to save an entire village.

Bush tucker. When it rained in the jungle, snails as big as your fist came slurping out of their tunnels to munch on the wet vegetation. Nathe being Nathe, he decided they were for the pot, and so his legendary Lungi Lol Snail *baltis* were born.

The bunker. The forward battle trench manned by 'H' – 'The Death Dealer' – with his tried and trusted GPMG. No rebels were sneaking past when 'H' was on duty.

Front toward enemy. A factory-made Claymore – a convex wad of plastic explosives, primed to blast out a wall of ball-bearings at the enemy. We were forced to manufacture our own from old food tins and 'shipyard confetti' – any make-do 'shrapnel' we could scavenge around the village.

With a 51mm mortar like this, I was able to crawl far forward and put up illume rounds – flares that drift under a parachute – so lighting up the entire night-dark battlefield. Light for the lads to see and to kill by.

Digging for victory. Pretty quickly, we realized that unless we recruited the locals to help us defend the village we were all going to end up butchered by the rebels. Young village kids dug our battle trenches, made beds and shelters for us to sleep on, and cut bamboo to make sharpened punji sticks.

Brigadier Richards, our overall force commander, sent us in to stop the rebels in their tracks. This we had done. Here villagers gather up the rebel dead, after the first night's combat.

Calling prayers. Prior to sending out Pathfinder patrols to go after the rebels, we got a collective heads-up with all patrol commanders, to work out how best to track, find and kill them.

Ready for anything. 1 PARA mortar crews load up the 81mm rounds, to beat back the rebel forces massing in the jungle.

Fire! Once we got the 1 PARA mortar teams in, with their 81mm mortar tubes, we could really take the fight to the rebels.

Hunter-killer. After the initial massive firefight, we knew we'd given the rebels a bloody nose. Next we did the utterly unexpected: we left our battle trenches and went into the jungle on a hot pursuit to track them down.

X Platoon at end of Lungi Lol Op: The A-team. The 26 Pathfinders at Lungi Lol, plus5 support staff from Lungi Airport. Rear row, from left: 4th, Taff Saunders (*33 Delta*); 9th, Ginge Wilson (*33 Charlie*). Middle row, from left: 4th, Eddie The White Rabbit Newell; 5th, Grant Harris (*Sunray*); 6th, Mark 'Jacko' Jackson; 7th, Graham 'Wag' Wardle; 8th, Neil 'Tricky' Dick; 9th, Nathan 'Nathe' Bell (*33 Alpha*); 10th, Sam 'Dolly' Parton (*33 Delta*). Front row, from left: 5th, yours truly; 6th, Joe 'H' Harrison; 10th, Bryan 'Bri' Budd VC.

For a long-drawn-out moment Dolly's lot were on their own, guns malfunctioning and the enemy right on top of them. H must have done the fastest GPMG belt change in history. Barely seconds later he had the weapon up and into action again. He hammered in the rounds up and down the length of the target, saturating Fern Gully with leaden death: from his position he could pretty much fire into the entire length of it.

But H was on his last belt of 200 rounds of link now, and if Dolly's lot lost H's fire support, they were pretty much finished.

'H – FUCKING WATCH YOUR AMMO!' I yelled. 'WATCH YOUR FUCKING AMMO!'

By rights H was now eating into his escape and evasion (E & E) rounds. We'd agreed that when we got down to the last third of our ammo it was time to get the hell out of Dodge. I didn't doubt that there were a whole lot more blokes who'd passed the same point – but now was hardly the time to turn and run. If we tried to bug out right now, Dolly's lot were going to get slaughtered.

The illume over Dolly's position was drifting low towards the trees. It'd soon be gone. I reached for another, then hesitated. By firing this one, I was about to eat into our E & E ammo for the mortar. We'd fired twelve: we had six remaining. I was about to cross the same line as H, and any number of the other lads.

Over the raging din of the firefight I could hear Dolly yelling desperate fire orders at his blokes. Though I couldn't make out the words, right at this moment I knew how much he needed accurate supporting fire, and for that he needed light.

I said a quick prayer, gave Cantrill the nod, then dropped the round down the tube.

19

There was a pop in the sky as the illume burst right over the top of the deep, V-shaped gully, throwing the length of it into this harsh, phosphorescent glare. I yelled out the fire instructions, but there was almost no need: from every position that could get eyes-on Fern Gully the lads were smashing in the rounds. It was getting hosed down by a murderous barrage of fire.

Fuck rainwater: right now the Gully had to be churning with rebel blood.

All of a sudden a voice rang out from behind me, tearing my mind away from the brute savagery of the fight.

'STEVE! STEVE! STEEEEEVE!'

I glanced over my right shoulder, thinking it had to be Cantrill. Maybe he was warning me that the rebels were rushing our position again. The Royal Marine captain was lying there staring up at me, next round held at the ready, and it clearly wasn't him doing the yelling. I glanced over my other shoulder and there was Grant. He was a few feet back from Cantrill, lying prone on the man's heels.

'STEVE! RIGHT – LET'S GO!' he yelled. He jerked a thumb over his shoulder. 'MATE, LET'S GO! COME ON! LET'S GO!'

I stared at him, caught in a moment of confusion. *What was he saying? Who should go? Just me and him, or all of us?*

'Mate, let's withdraw!' Grant yelled. 'We need to withdraw!'

It suddenly dawned on me what he was saying: *Time to get the hell out of Lungi Lol.*

I didn't know how long we'd been fighting for now, but it felt as if we'd been battling for a lifetime. I figured Grant's rationale for withdrawing had to be this: me, Dolly, H, Nathe and the others were so far forward and absorbed in the firefight that we'd lost any perspective. We'd passed the one-third of our ammo limit, the trigger to bug out and start the E & E; we'd been hit all along our front line positions, so very likely we were getting surrounded. I could understand how Grant had made the judgement call that now was the time to go.

'Mate, withdraw!' he yelled again. 'Mate, let's withdraw! Let's go! Bug out!'

But I hadn't been expecting this. A chaotic jumble of thoughts crashed through my head. I figured I had a better sense of the battle, being so hands-on as I was. I figured we could still win this, that we had the measure of the rebels now. If we could hold on for just a few minutes more we'd get the QRF in, and sooner or later we'd start to get a little light. Come first light we could see the rebels properly to kill them, and we wouldn't need any more illume.

Sure, we were well down on the ammo. I figured H, Nathe and Dolly's lot were well past the one-third mark. I was taking a wild stab in the dark, but maybe Taff and Ginge would be better off on the ammo front. I didn't know what casualties we'd taken, but I hadn't heard a single cry of 'man down' – the call for a wounded man needing urgent evacuation and treatment. We still held our defensive positions, and we'd be more exposed if we abandoned those and went on the run. Who knew what we'd stumble into if we tried to E & E through the jungle?

Those thoughts flashed through my mind in microseconds. If we pushed the rebels back from Dolly's position they'd be forced to regroup, having taken scores of casualties. That meant we could get the QRF inserted into our battle trenches, which meant thirty fresh blokes from 1 PARA plus shedloads of ammo. Time becomes hugely warped and confused when drugged out of your mind on adrenaline, but either way the QRF could only be minutes away now.

If we tried to withdraw right now, we'd be doing so with Dolly's lot still under a murderous siege. If we ceased firing and pulled back we'd be leaving them to face the brunt of the rebel assault, and I didn't figure they'd make it. Plus we still had a village to protect here. The villagers of Lungi Lol fucking needed us.

Decision made.

I shook my head violently. 'NO, MATE! No fucking way! We're staying! We stay! We're staying!'

I didn't have the time to give Grant a detailed heads-up as to my reasons why. But Grant and me had such a relationship that I figured he'd trust my call on this one. He could rest assured that I'd considered all the options and made my decision accordingly. Grant would trust my call, I was sure of it.

'Mate, we're staying!' I repeated. 'We stay!'

'Okay, mate, okay. I hear you!'

Grant was good with it. He didn't know my reasons, but he knew I'd have them. That was why Grant was such a great bloke to have in command.

Dolly's patrol was still in the thick of it. I could hear their guns hammering away. They needed light up over them pronto, for the last illume that I'd fired was well down by now. Turning to Cantrill I reached for another round, and within seconds I had it winging into the air high above Fern Gully. As it burst bright and angry in the dark night sky it was like a signal: *No one fucks us out of Lungi Lol; we're staying.*

The firefight raged on. I fired another illume and another, as the ones before them faltered. As a final flare round burst, throwing its harsh light down the length of the battlefield, the firing from the rebel side ceased abruptly. One moment, all hell was letting loose – the next, almost nothing. I could hear the odd *pop-pop-pop* of an SA80 firing from out of Dolly's trenches, but it was as if they were chasing after fleeting shadows.

In the near-silence I could hear Dolly yelling at his blokes, checking they were okay.

I heard Grant's voice from behind me again. 'Steve, I'm gonna move back to Tricky! I'm gonna send a full contact report!'

'Got it.' I gestured at Cantrill. 'Mate, go with him.'

Cantrill eyed me for a long second, before nodding his understanding. 'Yeah, okay, fine.'

I gestured for the daysack, and he thrust it into my hand. Taking the mortar tube in my left and the rifle in my right, I slung the sack of rounds over my shoulder. Like that I doubled over, sprinting in a crouch for H's trench. I needed to stay forward, but we'd been exposed in this position for far too long now. If I could make it to H's trench, I could get into some cover, rest the mortar on the lip, and still put up the light. Like that I could self-load, so I wouldn't need Cantrill any more.

As I thundered through the bullet-riddled bush I yelled out a warning: 'H, it's Steve! Steve! Steve! It's Steve! I'm coming in.'

H barely grunted an acknowledgement. His eyes were glued to the sights of his GPMG. To one side of H his wingman – Bucks – was likewise eyes-down his weapon. I tore across the last few yards and leaped in. Then I hunkered down, so I was sandwiched between the two of them. I threw the bag of remaining rounds onto the forward lip of the trench, laid the mortar tube next to the bag, grabbed my SA80 and took up a position leaning on the revetment, my eyes down the barrel of my weapon.

To my left H had the GPMG menacing the length of Fern Gully, but right now there were bugger all targets to fire at in there. Bucks was to my right, SA80 likewise in the aim. I could hear the odd burst of fire from the direction of the jungle, from where the latest rebel assault had been launched. Somewhat ominously, there was nothing much in terms of return fire from *33 Bravo*.

For a moment I had this horrible thought: *What the fuck's happened to Dolly's lot?* I had visions of them being captured and dragged off into the heart of rebel hell.

The final illume round spluttered out into darkness, the last of the gunfire seeming to die with it. For a moment there was complete silence, and then I heard this new noise start up – these agonised groans and moans coming from the direction of the gully. No matter what a bloke's nationality the language of pain, agony and dying is pretty much the same. *Aaarrrggghhh.*

For two minutes or so these horrible cries rent the darkness, before they too died into silence. All I could hear now was the *brrsst-brrsst-brrsst* of the basher-beetles, as they bumbled about in the vegetation to either side of us.

H let out this nervous laugh. It began as a faint chuckle deep in his chest, before creeping up out of his throat. He still had his eyes-down his gun, but from the corner of his mouth this thick Yorkshire accent went: 'Fooking hell, mate.'

'Yeah, fuck me,' I confirmed.

Silence.

Observation.

Watchfulness.

Where will they come from next?

And what the hell's happened to the lads at 33 Bravo?

I figured the QRF could only be minutes out, so we had to have a helo inbound. At the same time I figured the rebels had withdrawn with the aim of getting into our rear. They'd hit us left, right and centre and been smashed. That only left one avenue of attack. They'd probed our positions, in what amounted to a series of savage recces-by-fire, losing dozens of blokes killed and injured – but in doing so they'd discovered the limits of our defences and how to skirt around them.

That meant we had to get the QRF down on an LZ that was least menaced by the enemy. No point getting thirty-odd PARAs flown in, if their Chinook got blasted out of the sky and all the blokes were killed.

There was a bit of whispered chat between H and me as to where the enemy had gone to, and where to get the helo in. Wherever the rebels had pulled back to, we knew in our bones this was only a temporary lull. The rebel commanders had vowed to take

Lungi Lol and execute Operation Kill British. They'd keep coming.

They'd regroup in the jungle, patch up their wounded, and decide upon a new plan of attack. And here in H's position, plus in *33 Bravo*'s trench at least, we were down to less than a third of our ammo, and I figured we had to have wounded.

For a moment I wondered what we'd do with our casualties. Most minor flesh wounds we could treat in the field. But anything serious would have to get a casevac – a casualty evacuation back to Lungi Airport. It made sense to get any injured blokes out on the same Chinook that would fly the QRF in. In which case I figured it was time for me to get to the HQ ATAP, so I could get a sense of things, and liaise with the helo that was flying in.

'I'm going back to the HQ ATAP,' I grunted at H.

He nodded a silent acknowledgement.

I told him the obvious: to keep watching the track and the gully, scanning for movement. Grabbing the daysack of 51 mm rounds plus my SA80, I clambered out of the trench, retrieved the mortar from where I'd laid it, and began a hunched run the 70 yards back towards our HQ.

As I neared it, the village ahead of me seemed alive with figures. It was still dark, so I couldn't make out a great deal, but it sounded like complete chaos in there. I guessed we had to have dead and wounded villagers – those who'd been caught in the crossfire – and some of those might well need casevacing, alongside our blokes.

As I thundered into the HQ position I yelled out a warning: 'It's STEVE! STEVE! I'm coming in!'

I crashed through the foliage and sprang into the depression. Grant and Cantrill were there, with Wag and Tricky to the rear crouched over the Thuraya and the radio.

I locked eyes with Wag. 'Anything in from the patrol commanders? Wounded?'

I was expecting him to say: *33 Bravo* report three casualties, and so on and so forth all down the line of patrols.

He shook his head. 'No, mate, nothing yet.'

'Any update on QRF?'

'Yeah, initial contact report's gone and received. Sending more detailed one right now.'

We didn't need a confirmation message that the QRF were inbound. Our first contact report would trigger their launch, in which case they could only be bare minutes away now.

At that moment an unmistakable figure appeared from the direction of the village. It was Mojo, and following in his wake were his men. I counted eight blokes in all. I'd just presumed that Mojo's lot were in position in the trenches at the rear of the village. In which case, what were nine of them, their commander included, doing here?

Grant got to his feet and turned on Mojo. He simply exploded. 'What the fuck are you doing here? Why the fuck are you not in your positions? Get the fuck down to your trenches, or else!'

Mojo had a look on his face like he'd just shat his load. He didn't have a weapon with him, but then again he never seemed to carry one. At least his blokes appeared to be armed. I saw him bark some orders at his men. They turned almost as one and started sprinting down the road towards the rear of the village.

'Tricky! Wag!' Grant called over. 'Heads-up.'

We knelt in the HQ depression, the four of us facing inwards. We huddled together cheek to cheek in the cover of the earthen bowl. Cantrill was down in the prone position on the lip of the depression, looking back the way we'd crawled, his SA80 in the aim. But I could tell he had one ear cocked at the four of us.

'Right, guys, decision time,' Grant announced. 'What are we doing? Those attacks were most likely a probe, so there's still an argument that now is the right time to get out. Do you think we should go?' he queried. 'There's a lull in the battle. We're not under fire. So do we get out now? Steve?'

'No, mate, we stay.' I was adamant. 'We've repelled the attack. We've re-bombed our mags. We're in good defensive positions.

We've inflicted serious casualties. The plus points of staying outweigh pulling out, putting half the blokes on the Pinz and running down an open track. Mate, I reckon in these initial stages we've stemmed the tide. I'm taking it that the QRF are inbound, and unless someone tells me different we haven't took any casualties.'

Grant shrugged. 'Too early to say.'

'Agreed, mate, but with our position being as it is I still reckon we stay.'

'Okay. Wag?' Grant prompted.

'Agree with Steve. For the time being we've held 'em off. But I need to get around the blokes and do ammo stats and check on casualties. But for me, for now, we stay.'

Grant glanced at Tricky. 'Tricky?'

'We stay.'

Despite doing an ace job as my mortar loader, Marine Captain Cantrill didn't – with all due respect – get to cast a vote.

Grant nodded. 'Okay, agreed, we stay.'

'Right, I need to get around the blokes,' Wag repeated.

'Coming with you,' I volunteered. 'Grant – you good to stay with Tricky and monitor the net?'

Grant confirmed that he was.

Wag and me crept through the trees that surrounded the HQ ATAP. We broke cover and sprinted across the dark void of the track, filtering into the bush on the far side.

Wag let out a yell of warning as we approached Dolly's position. 'Dolly, it's Steve and Wag! Coming in!'

We got the shout back: 'Okay!'

We scuttled up to the back of their battle trenches and Wag and me knelt down. Dolly turned to face us.

'We've made the decision to stay,' Wag whispered. 'You happy to hold your position?'

Dolly looked surprised that the question was even being asked of him. 'But fuck, yeah. Fucking right I am.'

'Right, any casualties? Plus what's your ammo stats?'

'No casualties. We're three hundred rounds remaining for the gun. Each bloke has around five full mags including the bandolier.'

'They were last seen at your location, so the fuckers could be going round the side and back of us,' Wag continued. 'They haven't fucking gone yet, mate. Keep a very close eye.'

Dolly nodded. 'Yeah. Got it, mate. No worries.'

Dolly had had the rebels practically on top of him, their fighters spewing out of the V-shaped gully to his front. It was amazing that no one had been wounded. We'd been incredibly lucky. It was equally amazing that they'd held the rebels off, yet still had some ammo remaining. There wasn't a great deal, but maybe enough for one more sustained firefight. Plus Dolly hadn't fired his Claymore yet, so they had one last layer of defence they could fall back on.

We did the rounds of the other patrols, moving across Nathe's, Ginge's and then Taff's, over at the railway line. As we flitted from one to the other, Wag briefed me in on what had happened with the comms, and the likely status of the QRF. The signaller back at Lungi Airport had been manning the 319 radio when the firefight had kicked off, so Wag's initial call via the Thuraya hadn't got an answer.

As a result, Tricky had been forced to radio through the contact report on the dodgy 319, with the added delay of having to encrypt the message (the 319 uses cryptographic coding to make the communications secure). The Thuraya, being a satphone, bounces the message up to an orbiting satellite and back down again pretty much instantaneously. By contrast, the 319 sends an HF signal up into the ionosphere, the idea being that it bounces off that down to the recipient. The transmission is very susceptible to climatic conditions: cloud cover, moisture in the air, and even a wet jungle canopy can stop the message getting through.

Eventually, even via the water-damaged 319, Tricky had got the message through, whereupon both sides had switched to using the Thurayas. In spite of the delays, by my and Wag's reckoning the QRF should be with us any moment now.

The news from *33 Alpha*, *33 Delta* and *33 Charlie* was that they too were well down on their ammo, but with a bit of cross-decking from one patrol to the other we should be able to hold on for a good while longer. More importantly, none of the patrols had taken any serious casualties. Amazingly, not one single bloke needed casevacing.

It was little short of a miracle.

With the QRF inbound, someone had to get down to the landing zone and clear the Chinook in.

'We'll go back via Grant and I'll make for the LZ,' I said to Wag.

'Got it, mate.'

We headed back to the HQ at a crouching run. I told Grant what I was planning, then asked Tricky to get one bloke from each patrol sent across to me, as security. We'd chosen to use a clearing at the far rear of the village – so beyond even Mojo and his men in their trenches – as the LZ for the Chinook to come down on. We'd scoped it out as the safest place to get the QRF into, but with the rebels getting around and behind us maybe it wasn't any more.

There was just no way of knowing.

I gathered the blokes, then had a final word with Grant. 'Right, I'm off. We'll take the Pinz, mate, 'cause I don't want to head out of the village on foot facing the number of rebels that are out there.'

'No problem,' Grant confirmed. 'Call me if you hit any difficulties.'

The five of us ran for the Pinzgauer. As we scurried through the predawn village the square was a mass of confusion, with groups of shadowy figures screaming and wailing. I could see a body lying on the ground, surrounded by weeping women. Clearly, we had dead or injured amongst the villagers, but we had zero time to deal with that now.

We reached the Pinz and I told Marky – the guy who'd driven Donaldson when he'd bugged out – to get behind the wheel. I jumped into the passenger seat and the others climbed into the rear. The Pinz had been parked for days with the keys in the ignition, but thankfully it fired up first time. We screamed down the track heading west out of the village, passed by our rear battle trenches and there was Mojo in position with his men.

They'd got there . . . eventually.

We pushed on for another 250 yards, heading for the dark fringe of jungle, then came to a halt. We parked up and went into all-around defence, lying prone at the side of the track. I found myself looking back at the village, with the faintest hint of breaking dawn on the distant horizon. A tinge of fiery pink was just starting to touch the high clouds.

Bring it on, I told myself.

With sunrise the advantage would shift to us big time.

I told the guys to listen out for any noises from the jungle. If, as I suspected, the rebels were moving to outflank us, now was when we'd detect the signs of their presence.

We lay there in utter silence, straining our ears for the faintest hint of any movement in the tree line. It was quiet. Deathly quiet. It reminded me of the seconds before the firefight had first kicked off, when the air had been thick with the tension of the coming battle. If we had a major contact here, we'd have to jump back in the Pinz and head hell-for-leather back to the village, and abort the landing.

I readied my night-time air-marker – an infrared strobe – to guide the helo in, and scanned the skies to the southwest of us. We'd yet to have a helo land on this HLS, so it was crucial I steered them in. I warned the blokes to keep focused on the jungle.

Last thing we needed right now was to get jumped, and just before we got the QRF landed.

20

We'd been waiting for ten edgy, nervous minutes when we heard the distinctive, juddering *thwoop-thwoop-thwoop* of a Chinook inbound. *Oh yeah.* There is no feeling like knowing the cavalry are on their way. The beat of that helo's rotor blades was the most welcome sound any of us had ever heard.

I spotted the helo silhouetted against the faint blush the coming sunrise had thrown across the heavens. Getting to my feet, I switched the IR strobe to pulse mode. I knew immediately that the pilot had spotted my marker – flying on NVG as he would be, my IR strobe would beat out like a lighthouse. He banked hard to starboard and swung the helo's nose around to my heading.

I brought the pilot in front-on to me, backing down the track away from the Pinz to give him room to land. He came in at real speed, and dropped the helo to treetop height with the aircraft's nose fifteen feet away from me. As it settled into the clearing, the thrashing rotor blades clipped the trees and the thick vegetation on either side. I could see the two pilots in the cockpit, the weird green light of their NVG casting their faces in a ghostly glow.

Going down on one knee, I switched off the IR firefly, and saw the pilot drop the arse-end of the helo onto the ground. There was a loud bang as it made contact. Orientated like this, the PARAs would be able to pile off the rear, and remain shielded from any enemy that were still to the east of us. But if we had rebels in the jungle around here now, the PARAs would be disgorging right into their line of fire.

I saw the ramp go down and waited for the surge. But nothing. I was thinking they should be off by now, so why hasn't the

helo gone? After thirty seconds or so I ducked under the forward
rotors, hurrying down the side of the Chinook to try to find out
what was causing the delay. By rights, thirty seconds was more
than enough time to get a platoon of PARAs off a helo.

I came around the back and glanced into the Chinook's dark
hold. I spotted two lonely figures inside. One was the Chinook's
loadie, the other was Captain Chris James, a guy I knew well. He
was a former Second-in-Command of the Pathfinders. I'd taken
him through Selection and for a while I'd had him in my patrol. He
was now serving as 1 PARA's Adjutant.

I had one thought, and one only, crashing through my head
right now: *Where the fuck are the fucking PARAs?*

Clambering aboard I closed in, so I could have words in Chris's
ear. 'What the fuck is going on?' I yelled above the deafening
whine of the turbines. 'Where's the fucking QRF?'

'Steve, I've been sent to have a look,' he yelled back. 'I've been
sent to do a recce.'

I exploded. 'A fucking recce! Mate, we have just been in a fucking horrendous contact, we have no idea where they fucking are
now, we're down to our last mags of ammo and there's *no fucking
QRF*? What the fuck?'

'I hear you, mate, but I've been sent to have a look, to assess
things.'

'Assess this, Chris: I don't give a fuck what you've been sent to
look at, you need to get the fucking QRF in – *NOW*.'

I backed away in a seething cloud of rage, but he reached out
and stopped me.

'Steve, we'll fly around and take a look! Fly over the village.'

'Mate, I don't give a fuck where you fucking fly – just get the
QRF sorted.'

I stormed off the back. The red mist had well and truly come
down. I felt waves of frustration and anger washing over me.
We'd been promised a QRF on thirty-five minutes' standby. Those
were the conditions on which we'd gone in. Instead, we'd just had

possibly the entire RUF try to rush us, and they were very likely still out there getting us surrounded – and now this.

The Chinook took off.

I ordered my blokes back to the wagon. 'On the fucking Pinz! Let's go!'

The guys stared at me, confusedly.

'Steve, where's the QRF?' Marky queried.

'They ain't fucking coming,' I snapped. 'Let's go!'

We drove back in a taut silence. Not a single word was said. I had blokes in their early twenties with me, and I could sense their frustration and their anger. But what the hell was I supposed to say? *Yeah, lads, I know you've just given your all facing odds of 100–1, and we're running out of ammo, and we were promised a QRF and no one's fucking turned up; but wrong decisions get made; shit happens.*

That was about the truth of it, but it wouldn't exactly help much to give voice to any of that.

Above us the Chinook climbed to altitude, then followed the track out over the village, pushing east across the terrain from where the rebels had first hit us. It flew a circuit over that area, as I sat in the speeding Pinz trying to get my temper under some form of control. *But fuck me, Chris hadn't even brought us any re-supply of ammo . . .*

We parked up the Pinz and I ordered the guys back to their patrols.

As I headed for the HQ ATAP a local woman ran over and tried to accost me. In Pidgin English she started yelling: 'Ma dauter – she been shot! She been shot! She . . .'

The woman was trying to drag me towards the village square. I got both my hands up and forced her away: 'Get back! Away! Away!'

With no QRF having materialised, I couldn't deal with this kind of shit right now.

I stormed over to the HQ ATAP. I had had steam practically

coming out of my ears. The four of them – Grant, Wag, Tricky, Cantrill – were staring at me in amazement. I got lock-on with all four, and from a dozen yards away I yelled out the good news.

'There's no fucking QRF!'

I could see the looks of total disbelief on their faces. They had these blank expressions, as if they couldn't comprehend what I'd just told them; as if this couldn't be for real. They'd heard the helo come in. They'd expected me to come storming back with thirty paratroopers in my wake. And now this. It just didn't compute.

Tricky held up his hands, almost in a gesture of surrender. 'Mate, I fucking sent the contact report. I got confirmation ...'

'What, they think we sent a contact report 'cause we were fucking homesick?' Wag snarled. 'Wankers!'

'When you say there's no QRF, d'you mean it's delayed or it's never coming?' Grant asked. The voice of reason, he'd posed the million-dollar question.

'No fucking idea. It was fucking Chris James on the helo, and he'd been sent out to *take a look*.'

'A look!' Wag exploded. 'A look at fucking what?'

I held my hands wide. 'I have no idea, Wag, mate, no fucking idea.'

Right at that moment you could cut the atmosphere with a knife.

I tried to get my anger under control. I tried telling myself that wrong decisions did get made at all levels of the chain of command. God knows, I'd made a good few in my time. The strength of a unit like the Pathfinders lay in how we responded to such bad decision-making. If we sat and stewed in our anger, spitting vitriol at whoever had fucked up, we'd fester and spoil. What we had to do now was deal with it, get over it and get sparking.

'Right, what the fuck do we do now?' Grant prompted.

We got our heads together for our second Chinese parliament of the morning. Decisions had been made in the first one based on the assumption that we only had to hold out until the QRF got here, with bucket-loads of fighting men and extra ammo. Grant laid it out for us how things had changed.

'Right, we have to work on the assumption there may be no QRF. They may not be coming.' He paused, letting the words sink in. 'On the upside, it's nearly first light and we can already see a good way into the jungle. This being the case, what do we do? What are our options?'

This was it now: life or death decision time. We'd had no further information from headquarters, and not the slightest hint that any help might be on its way. We had to call this for ourselves: *do we stay or do we go?*

'Option one is to stay and defend,' I volunteered, 'in the knowledge there may be no QRF at all. In my opinion, okay – there's no QRF. But on the ground nothing's really changed. We've got the same number of blokes, same ammo stats, the same defensive positions. We just readjust the plan. We've got the added advantage of daylight, plus no serious casualties. Let's stay and do this.'

Wag nodded. 'I've got a good handle on the ammo situation, so I can get it redistributed across the patrols.'

'For me we stay and defend this place,' I reiterated.

'Agreed, I reckon we stay,' said Wag.

Tricky nodded. 'I say we stay.'

Grant eyed the three of us for a long moment. 'Okay, I'm happy with that.'

I turned to Cantrill. I figured he'd earned the right to have a say, now we had no QRF heading our way any time soon.

'Mate, you've really got nowhere else to go, other than staying with us lot. But you've earned a say. What d'you reckon?'

Cantrill managed a thin smile. 'All I know is I'm safer with you lot than I am on my own.'

'So, we're unanimous,' Grant concluded. 'We stay.'

Wag shared ammo stats. We could cross-deck ammo to H, Dolly and Nathe's positions, and even things up a little. But we were still on the cusp of being two-thirds down across the entire unit.

One more probing attack like the one we'd just suffered and the ammo would be exhausted, and we'd very likely get swamped.

But there was also a kind of logic to staying, warped though it might sound. We had great cover in the trenches. The rebels did not. Come sunup we'd be able to see properly to ensure one round made one kill. With a hundred-plus rounds per man, that still gave us a good 2000 potential kills. And in the next few hours we were sure to get some sense out of headquarters in terms of ammo resupply and reinforcements.

Tricky got on the radio and called in the patrol commanders. Apart from the crying and wailing from the direction of the village square, it was quiet as the grave out there. Even the moaning of the rebel wounded out in no man's land had died down to nothing. Either the RUF had pulled back taking their injured with them, or their injured were now very dead.

I told Tricky about the wounded on the village square, and he radioed for Bryan Budd, our lead medic, to get over there to see what he could do to help. The villagers' thin-walled huts would have offered no protection from small arms and machine gun fire, and for all we knew some of the RPGs unleashed by the rebels might have taken out entire buildings.

We got the patrol commanders in for prayers. They'd heard the Chinook come in, so they knew we'd got a helo down, but no QRF seemed to have materialised. We had to nip this in the bud, and get everyone's focus back on the task in hand.

'As you've probably realised, there hasn't been the response from Lungi that we expected,' Grant started. 'No QRF has come in. That being the case, we've got to make the best of a bad job. The decision here is that we stay: we stay and defend the village.'

There were grunts of agreement all around.

Nathe: 'Fucking right we stay.'

Dolly: 'Yeah, we stay.'

Ginge: 'I'm for staying.'

Taff: 'Yeah, bud, that's it.'

It was around 0600 hours, and the course of action had just been endorsed by all.

Decision made, I heard a yell from our front ringing through the half-light. 'Steve! Steve! Steve!'

It was the unmistakable voice of H. I ran forward in a low hunch until I reached his trench. H pointed north up the track. In the dim light I could just make out three bodies lying there, maybe forty yards away from us, with a fourth in the ditch beside the road. H had killed them with his first burst of fire. That was how close the rebels had got – crawling through the ditches that lined the roadway – before H had opened up on them.

The corpses were dressed in a mishmash of fluorescent shell-suits, plus combat fatigues. One had been armed with an RPG-launcher, plus there were AK47s, and a belt-fed RPK light machine gun. There was no movement from any of them and they looked very, very dead.

I gave H my SA80, and took charge of the GPMG, so I could give cover while he and Bucks pepper-potted forward to the bodies. With Bucks's SA80 aimed at the nearest rebel's head, H moved the fighter's weapon out of reach. He searched the body, spending twenty seconds doing so, before moving onto the next one.

H and Bucks returned, confirming four dead: the rebels were riddled with 7.62 mm and lying in huge pools of their own claret. The lads brought back one RPG, complete with two rockets, plus a couple of AK47s, each with a few mags of ammo. But best of all they had the RPK – a Soviet-era 7.62 mm machine gun, equivalent to the GPMG – with a full belt of ammo. We are trained to use just about any weapon money can buy. H grabbed the RPK and placed it by his side. The Death Dealer had just added significantly to his firepower.

I returned to the HQ ATAP and put out word to scavenge weapons and ammo off any dead rebels in the vicinity. With no QRF and no ammo resupply, it was time to get our hands on whatever we could retrieve off the enemy. At the same time I ordered the lads to keep scanning their arcs, and to be prepared to unleash hell if the rebels showed themselves.

We got a bit of a morale boost from the extra rebel weaponry. Every little helps. As the sun crept above the ragged tree line the village started to come to life. There was this weird, eerie calm about the place. After the chaotic insanity of the firefight, it was like a bizarre and unreal comedown.

Whenever a villager passed us by, they threw us this look like they could not believe we had given it to the rebels. But we knew the enemy were still out there somewhere. It was just a question of where and when they'd hit us next.

Time passed.

We cleaned our weapons. I took the opportunity to recharge any empty magazines, using the spare ammo from my bandolier. I was back up to six full mags now, and I was good to fight. We resupplied the patrols that had taken the heaviest fire with what ammo we could spare, and the lads settled down to watch and wait.

I did a short walkabout with Wag, checking on the village wounded. Bryan Budd was on the edge of the square, and one of the girls he had treated was cradled in her grateful mother's arms.

Bryan gave a smile. 'I've treated the girl. Took a through-and-through. She's fine now. She'll live.'

The girl was a teenager, and she'd taken a round in her left shoulder, but luckily it had passed clean through. Bri had managed to stop the bleeding and get her stabilised, and needless to say her mother was overjoyed. She wanted Bryan as her son-in-law.

As Wag and me walked around the place I could feel the villagers staring at us. They watched us pass, eyes glued to our every move. It was almost as if they were desperate just to get sight of us and believe we were for real – their great protectors. Their expressions said it all: *You fought the rebels; no one fights the rebels; you fought them and won; we're alive; we're alive.*

There was this feeling of total euphoria about the place. I didn't want to burst anyone's bubble. For now at least we were all still here and breathing – Pathfinders and the villagers of Lungi Lol. Operation Kill British hadn't quite succeeded as the rebel commanders had planned it. Not yet, anyway.

And right now, that was about as good as it got.

21

At 0830 hours Tricky took a call on the Thuraya. Apparently, finally, the QRF were inbound. Better late than never was our attitude. I headed out once more to guide the helo in, taking Grant with me for company. This time we made our way to the regular resupply LZ, to the south of the village. This was where the radio message had told us the Chinook would put down.

We grabbed a few lads, secured the LZ and settled into all-around defence. The wait went on and on. I told myself to have zero expectations, which meant zero disappointments. If the QRF arrived, so be it. If they didn't we'd scavenged just about enough weaponry and ammo to put up a good, solid fight.

Twenty-five minutes went by before I heard the Chinook. It was hours since the first rebel shots had been fired and our contact report had gone in to headquarters. They needed to rename this lot the SRF – the Slow Reaction Force. Well no, that wasn't fair. The 1 PARA lads had nothing to do with the delay. I had every faith they'd have jumped on the helo and ridden to our rescue with gusto. There had been confusion that night; delay and breakdown in the chain of command. Responsibility lay at the highest levels, not with the bayonets.

The Chinook came thundering in over the jungle. I wandered out so they could see me on the ground and know it wasn't a hot LZ. The helo came in low and fast, went down with the rear ramp open – and *bam*!

Almost before it touched the ground figures bomb-burst out to left and right. My feeling was one of massive relief and euphoria: *Great; at last they're here. We don't have to fight alone any more.*

The Chinook was on the ground for maybe sixty seconds before all thirty blokes were out and it was gone.

We now had a circle of guys from C Company, 1 PARA, ringing the LZ. The bayonets were decked out in webbing and daysacks with helmets on and ammo hanging off them everywhere. They'd come for a fight and they didn't care who they were up against. It was a great sight to see. Nothing beats thirty heavily armed PARAs spoiling for a punch-up – fire-pissers the lot of 'em.

To every side of the LZ guys were darting all over the place, hard targeting it from tree to tree, ready for the rounds to come from anywhere. In the midst of the melee was the distinctive figure of Major Bob Bryant, a guy I knew from Kosovo ops. Bob had his radio operator knelt beside him, plus his company sergeant major and platoon sergeant. Grant and me made our way over towards them.

Bob opened with this. 'Right, right! What's fucking happening? Where are we at?'

Grant held out a hand in greeting. 'Captain Grant Harris ...'

Bob waved him into silence. 'What's the sit on the ground and where are the enemy?'

Grant started to brief him, but Bob seemed to be only half-listening. The rest of him was itching to get on his way into the heart of the action, wherever it might be.

'Sir, this is it: during hours of darkness we were engaged by a large force of RUF. After a long and intense firefight we think the rebels are regrouping. We have no friendly force casualties; rebel deaths and casualties are unconfirmed at the moment, but there are four dead in the centre of the village.'

'Right, okay, take me to the village,' Bob announced.

With that he set off in the direction of the square at Olympic pace, leaving Grant and me floundering. We exchanged glances. The young PARAs were moving through the bush to either side of the major, darting from tree to tree and poised to unleash pure vengeance.

I broke into a half-jog as I tried to keep pace with the major, Grant doing likewise. We needed to brief him on the terrain and the positions, for the last thing we needed was a bunch of young PARAs charging about and stumbling into our punji fields.

'Sir, if you'll just look to your right we have two positions there, and the thrust of the attack came from the centre . . .'

Bob cut us off with a yell. 'Sergeant major, get the men spread out into cover! Get them digging shell-scrapes! I want the men in cover! Get them sparking! Get them going!'

'Yes, sir!' The sergeant major relayed the orders down the chain. 'Get the guys spread out. Take up arcs. Two-man shell-scrapes, and get the blokes down into the ground.'

Bob had come to a halt in the middle of the village track, his radio operator kneeling beside him. For a good five minutes he stayed where he was, barking orders. It reminded me of the scene from *Apocalypse Now*, when the American Marine Corps commander orders one of his men: 'See the way the waves break . . . Surf this beach!' The grunt replies: 'What about Charlie, sir?' – Charlie being the Vietcong enemy. 'Charlie don't surf!' the commander barks in reply.

Eventually, Grant managed to steer Bob towards the HQ ATAP. 'If you want to come this way, sir, this is the HQ. I can brief you fully in here.'

We got Bob in, whereupon Grant reached for the map, so he could properly talk him around our positions. Bob took up a stance in the centre of the depression, SA80 in one hand and the other jammed in his webbing.

'Right, tell me! What the fuck is going on? What happened?'

Grant gestured at the map. 'If you'll just close in I'll show you, plus talk you around . . .'

Bob gave a dismissive flick of the wrist. 'Never mind that! What's going on?'

Wag, Tricky and me inched away from the two of them. I got the strong impression that sparks were going to fly.

Grant stood up and put the map away. 'Well, sir, if you tell me how many men you've got we can start to look at bolstering our defences.'

Bob fixed Grant with a look. 'Right, Grant, let's be clear about one thing: I am the senior man on the ground here, so you now fall under my command.'

It was the first time Bob had addressed Grant by name.

Grant stiffened. 'I don't see it that way, sir. I am the commander of the ground force and until the CO of 1 PARA tells me otherwise, that's the way it stays.'

Bob turned to his signaller and barked. 'Get *Zero Alpha* on the net!'

Zero Alpha was the call-sign for Colonel Gibson.

Wag, Tricky and me were sat there thinking: *Well done, Grant, mate.* But I wondered what on earth Marine Captain Cantrill was making of it all. He'd just survived getting dragged into the teeth of a rebel onslaught only to be embroiled in this ... a scrap between the PARAs and the Pathfinders.

Bob was on the move again. 'Right, in the meantime, Grant – walk me around the positions.'

Grant and Bob disappeared in the direction of Dolly's trenches. Just then a message came in from headquarters. Our 'attached arm' – which had to mean Captain Richard Cantrill RM – was scheduled to get picked up by a helo at 1100 hours.

'Guess what, Rich, you're going home,' I told him.

Cantrill's face lit up like Christmas.

For a while we sat around chewing the fat and needling Cantrill about his getting out of here with the fight only half done. That got me thinking. Even now the rebels would be regrouping and trying to outflank us, so why not go out and hit them when they least expected it?

'What you thinking?' Wag prompted.

'I'm thinking we should take out a fighting patrol. They've been shot up, they've got injured, and they won't be moving very quickly, if at all. We have a chance to catch them on the hop, and that's the last thing they'll ever be expecting.'

Wag smiled. 'Yeah. Good one. Let's get after them.'

Grant was back some thirty minutes later, shaking his head in bemusement. I could still hear Bob's voice echoing through the trees, as he yelled out his orders. All around us PARAs were taking proper cover, using foldable spades to dig in. No doubt about it, as front line fighting troops these were about as good as it got.

Wag and me explained the idea to Grant – that we'd send out hunter patrols to track, follow and harass the rebels. 'We take everybody, push after them and try to pick up their trail.'

'Sounds like a plan,' Grant agreed. He smiled. 'Yeah, we'll all go.'

Wag shook his head. 'No, mate, not *all* all: you need to stay here and manage Bryant.'

Grant looked broken. 'But he's well and truly landed now, and the PARAs have a footprint on the ground . . .'

'No, mate,' Wag cut in, 'you need to stay here and manage this thing.'

'Well what about me?' Tricky piped up.

Wag shook his head again. 'No, mate, you need to stay here too.'

'You're fucking joking,' Tricky objected. 'What do I need to be here for? They've got a fucking signaller.'

'No, mate, you got to stay here and do our comms, relaying signals to HQ.'

Strictly speaking Wag was right. Our Clansman 349 radio only had about a 1.5-kilometre range. We'd need to be able to radio Tricky, so he could relay any urgent messages to Lungi Airport. Still, Tricky looked totally gutted and I couldn't say I blamed him.

Wag and I got the maps out and began to put flesh on the plan. We decided to push out two fighting patrols, one to the northern and one to the southern side of the main highway. The road would be each patrol's handrail – so helping lessen the risk of any blue on blue – friendly fire – incidents.

The ground from the village out to the fringe of the jungle

was ankle- or chest-high grass and bush. We'd change from open ground patrol mechanics to closed-forest drills once we entered the canopy. Each patrol would consist of twelve men, and we'd push out 1.2 kilometres from the village. That would be our agreed limit of exploitation (LOE). We'd follow the blood trails, track the enemy through the bush and hopefully put some rounds up their backsides.

With 1 PARA digging in all around our positions we were able to pull all the blokes back in, to brief them. Meanwhile, Grant was briefing Bob Bryant on what we were up to.

'We'll do it,' was Bob's reaction. 'We're the QRF. We're better suited to this. We're fresh on the ground . . .'

'That's the reason you can't go,' Grant argued, with infinite patience. 'We're tuned in to the environment. Your guys aren't. We've had blokes out doing clearance patrols for days on end. We know the ground intimately; we understand the terrain; and this is what we're trained to do . . .'

The argy-bargy went back and forth a bit, before Grant finished it.

'Look, it's a Pathfinder task and it'll be the Pathfinders that go.'

That decided, we sorted the orbat (order of battle) of the march. I'd lead one twelve-man stick, consisting of Dolly and Nathe's patrols. Wag would lead the other, made up of Ginge and Taff's lot. We'd go out with belt kit, weapons, ammo, medical kits and radios. We'd be light, agile and fast, which was key to the success of any hunter patrol – especially when the enemy was laden down with wounded.

The route march was simple. We'd move north through Dolly's position, then sweep east into the jungle, taking in Fern Gully as we went. From there we'd move ahead into the forest, then sweep south clearing as we went. Finally, we'd cross the main highway, sweep onto the railroad, and come back along that due west, which would bring us into Taff's position on the southern flank of the village.

When moving through close jungle the only way to navigate is with constant reference to a compass, and by counting footfalls – a process known as 'bearing and pacing'. You'd know that so many paces amounts to X distance covered, and that combined with a compass bearing meant progress could be plotted on a map. That's how we'd keep track of our position. If nothing else, this would be a proving patrol: by the end of it we would know where the rebels were located.

Most of the blokes had completed a Long Range Recce Patrol (LRRP) or a Jungle Tracker Course in the forests of Brunei, plus some of us had trained with the Kiwi SAS in Malaysia. The Kiwis are renowned for being the best bush-trackers in the world. They are even used by the New Zealand Government for tracking escapees from the nation's prisons, when they head for the mountains to try to evade recapture. The Kiwi SAS have unique skill-sets and are unbeatable.

Apart from the obvious – blood trails, dead rebels and discarded weaponry – we'd be searching for telltale signs of where the enemy were heading to regroup. We'd look for signs of ground disturbance, 'discardables', and 'transfer' – so where one piece of foliage might have caught on a rebel's clothing and been dropped in another location, betraying the direction of travel.

Before setting off, we agreed a set of verbal challenges and responses, should the 1 PARA lads see movement in the jungle and not know who it was. They would yell out 'Utrinque!' We would shout a response: 'Paratus'. 'Utrinque Paratus' is the Parachute Regiment's motto: it means 'ready for anything'. That way they'd know if it was us lot coming in, as opposed to the rebels ...

The last thing we needed to do before setting out was to bid farewell to Captain Cantrill. A Sea King was inbound from HMS *Ocean*, an amphibious assault ship steaming off Freetown, and Cantrill was going to be on it. He'd spent a night with a bunch of renegade lunatics, and been dragged into the rebels' maw by yours truly. He'd more than earned his stripes out here.

I shook the bloke's hand. 'Good effort last night. Well done. It's a shame to lose you, but it's far too grungy out here for the likes of you, eh, mate?'

He laughed. 'Yeah, it was good while it lasted.' He went around shaking everyone's hand. 'Fucking hell, guys, outstanding. You've done the business.'

Cantrill had come in on a four-hour recce, and ended up in the battle of his life, fighting shoulder to shoulder with a bunch of hairy, stinking, unwashed Pathfinders, ones that he'd never even met before. Respect.

'Get yourself a nice hot shower and sing a fucking song in it for us,' Wag told him.

There was similar banter from the rest of the blokes. Then we formed up in our fighting patrols and set out through the village. We were pushing towards Dolly's position, when there was a load of yelling and shouting from the direction of the dirt track. We paused to get eyes-on whatever was causing all the commotion.

From out of nowhere a battered, light blue pick-up had rumbled into the village. The 1 PARA lads sprang out of H's position and yelled out a challenge: 'Stop! Halt!'

They had their weapons very much in the aim and were yelling for those in the cab to dismount. Draped over the vehicle's bonnet I could see something; a shape; a person maybe. As the pick-up got closer I realised it was a corpse. A guy was hanging out of the passenger window holding onto the dead body, and in the rear were several blokes waving weapons about and grinning foolishly.

Seeing the PARAs spring into action the blokes waving the weapons stopped doing so very quickly. They also stopped smiling. The pick-up juddered to a halt, the head of the dead man banging on the bonnet. There was more rust than bodywork on the vehicle, and it was a miracle that it was still driveable. With the PARAs doing their stuff, the guys in the pick-up threw down their guns by the roadside.

The 1 PARA lads surrounded the wagon screaming for everyone to get out. As soon as the guy let go of the dead body it tumbled onto the ground. The corpse was dressed in the ubiquitous shell-suit 'uniform' of the rebels, so I figured it had to be one of the RUF fighters. Once out, the PARAs hustled the blokes around, lined them up at the rear and began to give them a good pat-down.

That done the PARAs dropped them onto their knees, hands over their heads, and kept them covered. I knew the village chief would vouch for these guys one way or another, and we had a job to be getting on with here.

We gathered to the rear of Dolly's position, all of us Pathfinders minus Grant and Tricky. Wag had done a fine job of redistributing the ammo, so every man amongst us was well bombed up. H was up to 400 rounds for the GPMG, which was top news.

I'd left the 51 mm mortar behind. It was heavy and cumbersome and of no use beneath the forest canopy, plus we only had illume rounds and it was daylight now. But we did have one 94 mm LAW per patrol, just in case we came across any rebel vehicles. It hadn't escaped our notice that last night's attack had been minus any of the rebels' captured armour, plus their heavy 12.7 mm DShK machine guns.

We had to presume they were saving those up for round two.

22

By now the sun was well up and it was burning hot. As we moved off from Dolly's position, giving a thumbs-up to the lead sentry from 1 PARA, I caught the faint sound of a Sea King, flying in to rescue Captain Cantrill.

I'd formed up my stick with Steve Brown – 'Steve B', a cracking bloke from Dolly's patrol – as my lead scout. Super-fit and immensely strong, Steve B always started his day with 200 press-ups. He was robust mentally, and hugely capable, which was why I put him on point. I took up position immediately behind him, the blokes forming up in line to the rear.

Whatever happened while we were on this fighting patrol, the golden rule was not to break the line of march. That way, each bloke would know where the other was at all times, which was key to ensuring we had everyone with us, and that the heaviest firepower – the 2 GPMGs and the one LAW – could be used to best effect.

We pushed into the waist-high vegetation, moving silently as one, coherent, animal fighting unit. This is what we had trained and trained and trained for, and for the first time ever the Path-finders were going out on an active seek-and-destroy mission. I could feel my heart pumping with the adrenaline. I knew with utter conviction that we would meet the enemy with deadly force.

This was no longer a peacekeeping mission, or OOTW. Each of us had our weapon in the aim scanning our arcs, and poised to unleash hell. The gun had become an extension of our head and shoulders: wherever the barrel moved our eyes were looking.

As lead scout, Stevie B's arc was 180 degrees to our front. Coming directly behind him, I covered an arc from his left shoulder ninety degrees to my rear, with the guy directly behind me covering the same arc but on the opposite side. This was replicated all down the snake, so that no part of the terrain we were moving through was missed. Steve B had no reason to look at me again now we were under way, and no one would make any verbal communications. It would all be done in silence, using hand signals.

We pushed ahead stealthily towards the canopy, moving through open terrain, with vegetation coming almost up to chin level, and at times head height. There were clumps of trees to skirt around, plus dips, depressions and small bushes to circumnavigate.

After ten minutes we came to the edge of a V-shaped ravine – the rear entrance into Fern Gully. Steve B went down on one knee covering the ground to his front, and I dropped to one knee covering my arc, the move cascading silently down the line. He placed his left hand on his head, the signal for me to close in on him, his right hand keeping a firm grasp of the pistol-grip of his weapon.

I moved up to Steve B's right shoulder. He indicated the footprints that criss-crossed the soft, loamy soil at his feet, leading into the gully bottom. Sure enough, scores of rebels had been through here. I could see by the direction of the footprints that they'd gone both ways – once as they tried to rush Dolly's position, the second when they were driven back under withering fire. In amongst the churned soil and crushed foliage were bright red strings of congealed goo: *blood trails*.

Further down the gully's length I presumed Wag's patrol was coming across more of the same, plus the rebel dead. I turned to Steve B, and indicated the bearing to push ahead towards the thick jungle. As we moved off I gave the bloke behind me a signal: two fingers into my eyes with one hand, then pointed at the gully. *Look in the ditch*. The signal was passed silently down the line, so everyone got to see the gruesome evidence.

We reached the edge of the trees, the shadows pooling thick and claustrophobic beneath the canopy. I glanced south, to check that Wag's patrol was entering the forest at about the same time as us. That confirmed, we nudged into the hot, musty interior, the smell of moist rot and decay heavy in our nostrils. The forest closed around us. Without the constant hum of the night-time insects, and the thwack of blundering basher-beetles, it was silent and foreboding.

Steve B paused again. He motioned to the ground at his feet. The leaves underfoot were thick with pools of congealed blood. No doubt about it, this was where the rebels had regrouped after we'd hit them in the gully. By the looks of things one hell of a lot of them had been seriously wounded and were bleeding heavily. Here and there a shaft of sunlight lanced through the canopy high above us, and where it hit the floor it formed a spotlight of bright, sickly red, like the hot point of a laser beam.

All we needed to do was track the blood trails, and we'd have them.

We pushed ahead, moving further into the ghostly silence. We moved due east for a good fifteen minutes, each footfall placed softly and with care, so as to cause minimum noise, or disturbance to the forest floor. When you're tracking an enemy in closed jungle you can't see very far, so you have to presume that an unseen force might be trying to hunt you. Or the enemy could be lying in wait, poised for you to move into their killing zone.

We'd lost sight of Wag's patrol as soon as we entered the jungle, but we knew where they were. Any movement to the north or east of us, and it was likely to be the enemy.

Steve B dropped to one knee again. Signalling the rest of the patrol to a halt, I closed up on his shoulder. He pointed ahead. About a hundred and fifty yards away I could just make out a group of small huts. There was smoke rising out of the centre of a cluster of buildings, from what had to be some kind of cooking fire.

I checked the map. I reckoned we were about 1.2 kilometres from the village, and via the Clansman 349 radios we had a range of 1.5 kilometres at best, less in thick jungle. We were on the limit of our comms, after which our only radio contact would be with Wag.

I lowered my mouth to my radio mic, which was strapped to my webbing. 'Wag, go firm. We've hit buildings.'

'So have we,' came back his hushed reply.

We remained where we were, totally motionless, for a good five minutes, studying the ground ahead. There were half a dozen mud and thatch huts grouped in a small clearing. Smoke hung beneath the trees like a haze of early morning mist, and I could smell its distinctive woodiness. I could see a huge cooking pot perched on the fire nearest to us, but not a soul could be seen.

This was the direction in which the blood trails – plus the scraps of vegetation ripped from the trees at the rebels' passing, – were leading us. We had to presume they had moved through this area, or maybe even used it as some kind of temporary base from which to launch their attack. More to the point, we had to work on the assumption that there were still rebels present, and very possibly this was where they were treating their wounded.

I radioed Wag: 'We've got six huts, no hostiles visible. But loads of blood trails leading in.'

'Three larger buildings,' Wag's voice came back at me. 'They look like kind of school halls.'

We agreed to go in and clear the areas simultaneously. Turning around so I was facing back down my patrol, I raised one hand showing two fingers. I closed it into a fist, before raising it to pat the top of my head. The fist was the signal that I needed the gun-group, the GPMG operators; two fingers indicated that I wanted both of them, and the hand on the head meant *on me*.

One of the GPMGs was positioned halfway down the patrol, to cover those forward. The other was second from last, to cover our rear. H and the other GPMG operator, Morgan Taff Hansen, a guy from Dolly's patrol, rose and came forward. I pointed out the buildings, speaking to them in a hurried whisper. We needed the short-barrelled weapons to go in and clear the huts – so the SA80s. I wanted the GPMGs positioned to provide cover, in case it all went noisy.

'You guys push forwards slightly left,' I whispered. 'Co-locate yourselves and cover us as we go in.'

They gave the briefest of nods, got to their feet and began flitting through the shadows. In a bent-over scurry they pushed 50 yards ahead, then got down into their fire positions, so we could move past them on their right.

I radioed Wag. 'Deployed a base of fire. Going in to clear buildings. H-hour fifteen.'

'Roger, out.'

Wag and I now had an agreed plan of attack. In fifteen minutes' time we'd each take our patrols in to clear the buildings, with a GPMG fire base set up to cover us.

I radioed Tricky: 'In canopy to north of village twelve hundred yards. Come across huts. Will move forward and clear. May go loud. Inform *Sunray*.'

'Roger. Out.'

Sunray was now Grant's call-sign, of course.

Poor Tricky. I could tell by the tone of his voice that he was sick to death with being joined at the hip to the radio. He was itching to get out here with us lot, taking the fight to the enemy. I spared a fleeting thought for what he was going through back there – with Major Bryant and Grant locking horns over command, and Colonel Gibson very likely inbound on a helo to bang heads together.

As I glanced forward at the smoke-enshrouded huts, I knew for sure where I'd rather be – out here on a hunter patrol.

I tapped Steve B on the shoulder and signalled for him to follow me. I moved back past each man, gesturing for him to converge on me. I dropped to one knee in the centre of the patrol. The others closed in so we formed a tight circle with our faces practically touching. It was another of the joys of working in a small outfit like ours: you grew so close to the blokes that you knew instinctively what each was about, and you weren't afraid of the intimacy.

I broke the patrol down into two-man assault teams, giving each a number to better facilitate my orders. Glancing at the faces ranged around me, I could see the excitement burning in the blokes' eyes.

A lifetime of training, leading up to this moment.

Let's not let it go to our heads, lads.

'Move silently into village,' I whispered. 'Assault Teams 1 and 2, move forwards under cover of fire base. AT 1, clear first building; once you're done go firm, signal to AT 2 it's clear; AT 2 move to clear second building. I'll move in with AT 3 and 4, and so on. We'll leapfrog across each other as we go, *but all on my orders.* Actions-on: SOP. Remember: weapons tight until we go loud.'

SOP stood for standard operating procedure.

I gave a final, searching look. 'Understood?'

I got nods of assent all around.

One of the greatest dangers now was of a blue on blue – one of the teams getting ahead of itself, and getting mistaken for the enemy. I needed to grip the lads, and keep it smooth, tight and controlled.

'Okay, AT 1 – go.'

It was deadly silent as the two blokes from AT 1 crept forward, threading their way between the trees. Two more blokes from AT 2 closed on their heels. We were now in Room Combat Mode, as opposed to Room Clearance Mode. Room Clearance is easy: you boot the door open, lob in the grenades, then open fire with max violence. You do that when you know for certain it is an enemy position.

But we couldn't be sure what this was, so we'd have to go in weapons at the ready and scanning the room for the bad guys. We'd go through the door with one weapon high moving right, and the other low sweeping left, to cover all angles. There could be women or children in there, or there could be rebel fighters or their injured. This was all about recognising the enemy before they got to open fire, and taking them out without killing any innocent bystanders.

I saw AT 1 scuttle across the sunlit clearing that stretched from the edge of the forest to the first of the huts. They reached the doorway, one behind the other tight against the wall. The forward guy stepped out and slammed a boot into the door, then both guys were piling inside, weapons at the ready.

Seconds later a head emerged. 'Clear!'

I signalled AT 2 forward to hit the next building. I moved forward at a low crouch, AT 3 and 4 at my heels, skirting by the GPMG gunners as we went. They had eyes-down their gun barrels and they didn't so much as nod at our passing. I heard a punching crunch as AT 2 went through the door of hut two, and an instant later there came a cry.

'Clear!' A pause. 'Ammunition! Blood!'

We'd found ammo already, plus blood trails. It looked like the rebels were here, or at least they had been very recently. I came up against the doorway of the first hut, joining the lads of AT 1. We were out in the open, the blinding sun burning hot above the forest clearing. The adrenaline was pumping, the sweat pouring into my eyes and trickling down my back in rivulets.

I glanced into hut one. It had a dark, damp, decaying feel to it. The roof was sagging with thatch that was semi-rotten. I didn't think anyone had been living here. Maybe this was just some sort of jungle camp, one where those gathering food or timber could temporarily shelter. It couldn't be a rebel base. That was inconceivable – not this close to the village. The chief of Lungi Lol would have known and he would have warned us.

Moving up to hut two I signalled to the next building: 'AT 3 – go!' I glanced through the doorway of hut two. Inside were several crates of what looked like AK47 rounds, plus belts of 7.62 mm ammo for their machine guns. Plus blood. Lots and lots and lots of it. In fact, it was like a charnel house in there.

I tried to get inside the rebels' heads; to imagine what sequence of events could have brought them here. From the blood trails in Fern Gully and the pools at the forest edge, I figured they'd retreated with their wounded that way, getting out of our line of fire. They'd moved through the forest heading east, and maybe paused at these huts to tend to their injured and take on water.

A lot of rebels had been bleeding profusely in this hut, so maybe they'd triaged their injured here – assessing who could be treated and saved, and who was beyond help. But if that was the case, where were the bodies of the dead? I searched with my eyes for any rebel fighters who had bled to death here, but there wasn't a single corpse.

It didn't make any sense.

Where were the rebels?

Where were their dead and their injured?

You didn't get blokes bleeding like this and surviving, especially not when you were in the jungle, presumably with no trained medics, no medical supplies and certainly no hospitals. So where were their dying and their dead? It was a total mystery. The only way to solve it was to keep going, and track them to wherever they had gone to ground.

They couldn't be far now.

Blokes bleeding profusely can't move far or fast, if at all.

As I moved on to the next hut, I reminded myself that an animal is at its most dangerous when it is injured. Human beings are basically animals – it's just that we have a thin veneer of civilisation laid over us. I urged the lads to remain ultra-alert, then sent them forward to hit the next building.

We pressed on through the clearing. In the very centre we came to a two-metre-wide fire-pit scooped out of the ground. The logs were still smoking and cooking pots were clustered all around it. There were tree stump seats to either side, plus a metal A-frame structure over the fire, for hanging pots. The smell of burning hung heavy in the air, with shafts of sunlight lancing through the lazy smoke.

Around the outskirts of the fire-pit was dark, hard-packed mud criss-crossed with footprints. Plus there was one massive, smoke-blackened cauldron lying on some hot coals. It was about three times the size of the one in which Nathe had brewed up his balti specials. In fact, it was so large you could have packed it with enough snails and fungi to feed the entire village of Lungi Lol.

Or you could have brewed up a dose of voodoo medicine large enough to 'treat' an entire rebel army. Back in Freetown we'd been briefed on how rebel fighters would bathe in a vat of voodoo medicine up to the neck prior to battle. It was via the total immersion method that you supposedly made yourself 'bulletproof'. Well, from all the blood I'd seen so far, they'd sure got the recipe wrong this time.

I placed my hand inside one of the smaller cooking pots and felt the remains of the food. It was still warm.

Where were the rebels?

Between the fire-pit and the far end of the settlement was eighty metres or so of open ground. I sent my teams pepper-potting across it. In the very centre was a huge pool of blood and body splatter, as if the wounded had been piled up there to die.

But where were the bodies?

We'd got all of the remaining huts cleared within ten minutes flat. More blood was found, plus piles of link ammo for the rebels' machine guns, and AK47 magazines. But still there were no wounded, nor any corpses – let alone any live enemy.

I sent my GPMG gunners east of the clearing to cover our onward movement. We formed up as a patrol and edged into the thick jungle again. As we went, I could hear the last of the cries from Wag's clearance operation filtering through the trees, as his team mirrored the actions of my own.

We exited the far end of the clearing, finding more blood and gore, plus piles of ammo, including bandoliers of AK47 rounds. There was a lot of freshly-crushed vegetation here, showing where a large body of men had moved through and very recently.

Via the damage to the foliage it was easy to trace the onward route they'd taken as they headed away from the village.

Having traced a wide arc north and east through the jungle, we were now around 1.5 kilometres north of Lungi Lol. This was further than we'd told Grant we were going to push. I spoke to Wag on the radio. He'd found similar signs of movement to us, and it was clear there had been wounded and dying rebels holed up in the larger buildings too.

So where the hell was everyone now?

We agreed to push east a further 1.2 kilometres, putting us a good 2.5 klicks or more out from the village. Hopefully, it would be far enough to catch the bad guys.

I informed Tricky over the radio. We crept ahead, hitting the densest terrain we'd yet encountered. It was approaching midday by now, so it had taken the twelve of us fit and very able blokes a good hour to reach this point. By the looks of what we'd discovered the rebels were laden down with scores of injured. They'd be moving at a fraction of our speed.

We should be right on top of them.

The terrain all around us was unerringly quiet. It was as if the very jungle itself was holding its breath, bracing itself for the next round of mayhem and carnage. I caught the odd animal and bird cry, but this time I was certain it was genuine jungle life, as opposed to rebel war cries. Occasionally, a fleck of sunlight filtered through the umbrella of leaves high above us, catching on a falling leaf or a speck of dust, but otherwise it was a network of shadow.

We moved silently across the jungle floor, pushing into a forest clearing. A giant tree had crashed to the ground sometime recently, bringing down a swathe of vegetation with it. After the musky dank of the forest interior the light in the open was blinding. I saw the glint of sun on something man-made. I bent to investigate. A crumpled cigarette packet had been dropped here. I retrieved it. It was smeared on the underside with dried blood.

Rebel wounded had been through this way, but how the hell were they managing to move so quickly?

We crept across the clearing, weapons in the aim, fingers on the trigger and safety catches very much in the 'off' position, scanning our arcs as we went. Every one of us was alert to the slightest movement or noise. The rebel dying and their wounded couldn't have gone much further.

Soon now.

23

I moved through the wall of vegetation on the far side, stepping back into darkness. Visibility fell to ten yards max with this level of light and the density of the surrounding greenery. This was close quarter battle (CQB) terrain par excellence, and we'd be on top of the enemy almost before we saw them.

When training for CQB in jungle as close as this you do so on a specially-designed Patrol Lane, and with your weapon held at the hip. Targets pop up from the undergrowth to either side, and the key is to hit them before they hit you. It's a given that you won't have the time in which to aim properly at such close quarters. Instead, you open fire from the hip instantly, working on instinct. The aim is to get the rounds down before the enemy has the chance to do so, in the hope of wounding them or at least putting them to ground – so giving you and your team the chance to pull back from the ambush.

That was exactly how we were patrolling now. Our aim was to move utterly silently and take the rebels by total surprise. By moving into the jungle to hunt them down, we were doing the completely unexpected. We were showing we had the battle skills to take them on in their own terrain, where they felt safest.

If we could smash them here from out of the blue – at a time and place very much not of their choosing – it would seriously deter them from launching a further attack on the village. Not only would they have got a bloody nose at Lungi Lol, they'd have got one when moving through the jungle – which they believed was their sanctuary.

We would instil total fear in their heads. Operation Kill British would start to look a lot less attractive. *If that's what twenty-odd British soldiers can do, what'll happen if we go up against 800 at Lungi Airport?*

As we moved ahead we kept picking up signs of the rebels' passing, but we reached the 2.5 kilometre mark still not having caught up with any. It didn't make the slightest bit of sense. Somehow, dead and injured rebels seemed able to keep moving through thick jungle . . . Maybe the voodoo medicine was working its dark magic, after all?

We went firm. I radioed Wag that we were there, no rebels seen.

'Roger, figures five,' Wag replied.

His patrol was five minutes behind us.

They arrived in the tree line on the opposite side of the dirt track. Wag and me linked up in one of the side ditches that lined the track and knelt for cover.

'Mate, lots of fucking blood in that village we cleared,' I whispered. 'Looks like they've been seriously shot up.'

'Yeah, maybe, but not so much on our side. We just patrolled up through, not really following anything much.'

'So, looks like they moved through my side after getting whacked at Dolly's position. But where the fuck are their wounded and their dead?'

Wag shrugged. 'Fucking search me.'

'Dead men walking?'

'Looks like.'

'Right, well, we've cleared to our front, mate. We've got to make the move back to complete a 360. Let's clear either side of the railroad as we go back through.'

By a '360' I meant a 360-degree clearance all around Lungi Lol – which was the ultimate aim of what we were doing now.

We crossed the highway, and with Wag's patrol on the far side of the railroad we started to move back towards the village, handrailing the metal tracks. Our pace quickened as we moved through more open terrain. We approached Taff's battle trenches,

Wag's lot stumbling upon more signs of rebel presence: a pile of hastily discarded weaponry and ammo.

We gathered up the hardware. There was enough here to start a small war, so it looked as if a serious number of rebels had tried to outflank us via the railway line. Following the tracks due west, we skirted by Taff's trenches, turned north to loop around the positions now manned by Mojo and his men, and finished off back at Dolly's position. That was it: 360-degree clearance patrol completed.

It had taken us two-and-a-half hours, and we'd collected up enough ammo and weaponry to arm a small insurgency. We'd also seen enough blood to sink a battleship, but the big mystery was – *where on earth were the rebel dead and injured*?

We made the village square and the guys filtered back into their patrol positions. Wag and me briefed Grant and Bob on what we'd found. That done we placed the captured weaponry in a pile on the main track, next to the growing heap of rebel corpses.

At 1430 hours – in an hour or so's time – we were scheduled to get a visit from Colonel Gibson. In the meantime, we noticed groups of villagers moving along the main highway into Lungi Lol. The expressions on their faces spoke volumes. They stopped and stared at the rebel bodies with these looks of sheer, unadulterated joy. *Finally, the rebels were getting their comeuppance.*

Mojo turned up looking inscrutable in his trademark immaculate dress. It was as if nothing much of any note had happened in the last few hours. How could he have been in his battle trenches alongside his men and have remained parade-ground smart? And how many bloody uniforms did the guy possess? Bob Bryant had no idea who Mojo was, of course, and I could see him staring at the Nigerian lieutenant suspiciously.

'Lots of people are now coming into Lungi Lol,' Mojo announced, speaking to Grant. 'They have come from outlying villages and they are going straight to the village chief. They have seen the rebels moving through, and they have come here in fear and seeking protection. Many villagers have been rounded up as work gangs and forced to carry the rebel wounded. And they are being forced to fetch them water and food.'

Right, so now we knew. That was how the rebels had managed to move their dead and their injured: they'd rounded up villagers to use as forced labour and stretcher-bearers. The riddle of their miraculous disappearance – the voodoo-dead-men-walking – had just been solved.

The new arrivals described how villagers had been forced to bury fourteen rebel dead here, ten there. They spoke of seeing strange wounds on the rebel bodies as if they had been *speared*. It looked as if the punji fields had done their work. Many villagers were still being held prisoner, and the fate of those so taken was an unknown. But at least we'd given the rebels a good pasting, and shattered the myth of their invincibility. And if this was the beginning of the end of their brutal rule here, then it had been something well worth fighting for.

Mojo gestured at the pile of rebel corpses out on the road. 'Those – I can take them? The dead? Take them to bury?'

Grant nodded. 'Yeah, get them in the ground, mate.'

Mojo scuttled away to his grisly task. It was a good idea to get the corpses buried, for they were attracting swarms of flies. I presumed Mojo would order his men to do it, for I couldn't imagine the man himself getting his hands – not to mention his uniform – dirty.

We used the opportunity of having the 1 PARA blokes on the ground to take a proper break. It felt fantastic not to have to be 100 per cent alert the entire time. Tricky was the brewmaster and since the girls had started their early morning water deliveries he'd been on permanent send on the brew front.

We'd ended up giving him all our brew kits so he could manage the catering. The Water Girls had got into the habit of collecting the empty containers at last light, and turning up just after first light with full ones. They'd deliver the water in silence, eyes downcast, as if they didn't want to be seen getting too familiar with the white men.

'Great, the Water Girls are here,' someone would announce. 'Thank you, girls. Biscuits? Sweets? Lancashire hotpot?'

The Water Girls had never taken a thing off us. They'd just smiled coyly and scurried away, delivery done. With a regular supply on hand we'd adopted a new water discipline. Tricky kept the brews coming from the Water Girls' supply, while each man kept one and a half litres of drinking water in his grab bag, plus two one-litre bottles in his belt kit. That was our E & E water, and we never made inroads into it.

But this morning after the battle there had been no sign of the Water Girls, so Tricky was forced to make the brews from our E & E supplies. He'd just got one going, when from out of the cloudless blue sky to the west of us a Chinook came thwooping in towards Lungi Lol.

We presumed it had to be Colonel Gibson, but it was taking a very odd approach route. It wasn't heading for the standard LZ. Instead, it hugged the length of the main track, swooping over the village square and going right over the top of us. By the time it reached the pile of rebel weaponry it was down to twenty feet, and spent bullet cases were getting blown all over the place in the downdraught.

The helo did a 180-degree about turn and put down on the track, practically on top of our forward trench position. The 1 PARA lads had to hold onto their helmets, as the downwash of the twin rotors practically tore them off their heads. The Chinook had come in with no warning, no one guiding it, no markers and no security. None of us could believe it. What the hell was going on?

Bob Bryant jumped up and hurried down the track, followed by his radio operator and sergeant major. I watched as the ramp went down, fully expecting Colonel Gibson and his retinue to be disgorged. Instead, out came the most ridiculous thing I have ever seen. Two gentlemen from the Royal Military Police (RMP) appeared, complete with spotless uniforms with knife-edge creases, gleaming pistols in their side holsters, and RMP berets clutched in their right hands.

As soon as they were off the helo took to the air again, banking south over Taff's position. The RMPs paused, put on their tomato-red berets and started marching up the track into the village. There is no other beret in the world like that worn by RMPs. You see one of those, you know immediately exactly who you're dealing with.

I turned to Wag. '*Fucking monkeys?* What the fuck are two monkeys doing here in Lungi Lol?'

Wag was speechless. He shook his head in silent disbelief.

It is a simple inalienable truth that all soldiers hate RMPs, and none more so than PARAs or ex-PARAs – hence the 'monkeys' nickname. Bob Bryant had got about halfway to the helo drop-off point, fully expecting it to be carrying Colonel Gibson. Now he was stopped dead in his tracks, staring in disbelief at the two RMPs.

They came to a halt beside the pile of rebel bodies – the ones that Mojo and his men were about to go and bury. The corpses had been blown half into the ditch at the side of the road by the Chinook's downdraught. The RMPs stood side by side, turning heads, nodding and pointing at the bodies, plus the ammo and the weaponry piled up beside them. Any second now I expected them to get out pens and notebooks.

Sure enough, one undid his shirt button, pulled out a pencil and paper and began making a note of the weaponry. Grant, Wag, Tricky and me exchanged these incredulous glances. If someone had asked me what had surprised me more – Tim Butcher of *The Daily Telegraph* pitching up in a white Lada taxi, or these two muppets dropping in – well, there was no contest. The monkeys had it, every time.

After five minutes' comparing notes over the flyblown corpses, they pushed on towards us. I could see by their shoulder flashes they were sergeants. They passed by the young PARA lads they'd just flattened with their rotor wash without the barest flicker of an acknowledgement. As they neared Bob Bryant, they 'bent and drove' in perfect unison – ramming feet down into the ground and sawing the right arm up in a parade-ground perfect salute.

Bob managed a fly swat towards his helmet in response. I couldn't hear what was said, but by the gestures Bob was making it was obvious: *Yeah, I'm the senior commander on the ground, but we didn't do this – they did.*

As Major Bryant handed the monkeys over to Grant – he was still the ground commander, after all – Tricky, Wag and me moved well out of the way. The RMPs came to a halt before *Sunray*, looking seriously nonplussed. They were staring at him with his long black hair, thick growth of straggly beard and unwashed, grungy combats, searching desperately for some indication of rank.

'Sergeant Blick and Sergeant Block, from 160 Provost Company,' one of them announced. 'We've been sent out here to investigate the incident . . . sir?'

We left Grant to brief them: the joys of command.

If anything could encapsulate the ludicrous, misguided priorities of Her Majesty's Armed Forces this was it. We were twenty-six blokes who'd been denied a QRF when we most needed it, and were yet to have a proper ammo resupply. We were here with no body armour, no grenades, no HE mortar rounds, not enough ammo in the first place, not enough water until the Water Girls had taken charge, dodgy rifles, dodgy night sights, dodgy rations – the list went on and on . . .

Yet at the same time someone, somewhere believed it was a good and proper use of Army time, money and resources to fly these two idiots out to Lungi Lol. It was beyond comprehension. It was mind-numbingly messed-up. But most of all, after what we had just fought through and survived, it made my blood boil.

It was a combination of luck, plus sheer bloody-minded good

soldiering that we hadn't lost a lot of lads when their SA80s jammed, or the GPMG ammo started to run dry during the long night's battle. Yet the fuel costs alone of flying those two wankers in would have covered the cost of each and every one of us getting M16s, with oodles of ammo to spare.

I could hear the CH-47 that had dropped the RMPs flying an orbit to the west of us. Presumably it was waiting for them to be done with whatever crap they were here for. It was scandalous. Lives were being put at risk due to the age-old excuse – 'lack of resources' – yet we could still fly two RMPs into Lungi Lol for a nice little jolly.

The RMPs had been on the ground for no more than fifteen minutes when they decided they were done. They saluted Major Bryant as smartly as before: 'Provost Company investigation complete, sir!' I had one thought going through my head: *as if anyone gives a damn, you self-important tossers.*

For a whole minute after their helo took off we just stared at it in stunned disbelief.

The silence was broken by Wag. 'Does anyone have the slightest fucking clue what just happened? Tell me I've been dreaming . . .'

'No, mate,' I told him, 'I saw them too. Two monkeys just rocked up, did whatever the fuck they do and now they're gone.'

Wag turned to Grant. 'So, are you going to jail or what?'

Grant rolled his eyes. 'No, mate, I think I'm all right on this one.'

I told Wag the obvious: it was time to get a feed and a brew on, plus clean our wanky SA80s.

The RMPs gone, Mojo came pottering down the track driving the same blue pick-up that had earlier carried the dead rebel into the village. He parked up by the corpses, and his men jumped down from the rear. Under Mojo's instructions they took hold of the rebel bodies, threw them into the back, and headed out west to bury them. Top news. At least now there were a few less rebel lunatics around to slice up Ibrahim, the Water Girls, Mojo, or Nathe's trench-digging boys.

Thirty minutes after the RMPs had left we heard another Chinook heading in. This one put down on the regular resupply LZ, and we had to presume it was Colonel Gibson. Bob Bryant and his head-shed went down to receive them. A few minutes later he was back at the HQ ATAP with the colonel, The White Rabbit, Jacko and a bevy of others in tow.

We got to our feet to welcome them. The tradition is that you do not salute a commanding officer if you're not wearing any form of headdress – a helmet, jungle hat or beret. We were all of us bareheaded, so Grant greeted the CO with a handshake.

Gibbo shot out his hand. 'Grant!'

Behind Gibbo were stood the others, and I got a few nods of greeting – but they couldn't come forward until the colonel and Grant were done with their meet and greet. At the same time Bob Bryant was bobbing about, anxious to be seen to be in control.

'Right, sir, this is what we need to do . . .' he began, but the colonel waved him into silence.

'Hold on, Bob, I want to hear from Grant.'

The two of them had a good old chinwag, and then Grant motioned for the CO to take a walk around the positions. As soon as they were gone the others moved in. Jacko was typical Jacko – a shock of wavy, bouncy, bouffant blond hair above an old Second World War leather shoulder holster, with his pistol slung inside. He was like Lawrence of Arabia – a throwback to an older, more innocent age. Everyone loved Jacko, and especially his hail-fellow-well-met attitude.

'Fucking hell, Jacko, you'd get where shite couldn't,' Wag greeted him – referring to his having taken over command of us lot, Donaldson being gone.

Jacko held out a hand for Wag to shake. 'Hah, hah, hah. Well done. Bloody incredible. Excellent. Bloody well done.'

Jacko tried really hard to swear like a 'proper' soldier. He'd start with bloody, damn and shit, escalating finally to a fuck, but even his 'fucks' sounded posh. We gathered in the HQ depression, passing a brew amongst us – sippers, naturally.

Jacko leant forward excitedly. 'The CO – he's fucking bubbling over! He's telling everyone – we gave those rebels a damn good shoeing. Right, tell me the story. What bloody happened here?'

For a good fifteen minutes or so we proceeded to relate most of it, and there was a real sense of decompressing here.

'How are the men?' Jacko asked me, once we were done. 'How are the men?'

'Mega,' I told him. 'They performed brilliantly. We couldn't have asked for more.'

Jacko nodded, vigorously. 'CO's bloody impressed. Bloody well impressed. Taught those rebels a thing or two.'

'Where did Captain Cantrill go?' I asked Jacko. 'Did he transit via Lungi?'

'Yes, and he looked as if he'd seen a bloody thing or two, I can tell you!'

After a good few minutes of us lot chewing the fat, Colonel Gibson, Bob Bryant, Grant and the rest returned from their walkabout.

Gibbo plonked himself down on the lip of the depression. 'Fucking Pathfinders . . . I knew I could count on you lot. I knew, I knew when I put you here it was a bloody good decision.'

We chatted for a while and then the colonel got up to go. But as he went to leave he turned back, and called over his shoulder: 'Steve, can I have a word?'

We walked out of the depression towards Wag's gym area. We stood there in the shade, out of anyone's hearing. The colonel pulled out his water bottle, took a good swig, then offered it to me.

'Nah, it's okay, sir, I've got some.'

'Tremendous action by the Pathfinders. Tremendous.'

'Thanks, sir. The blokes were fantastic. The right men for the right job.'

He fixed me with this look. 'Is that what you're telling me, Steve? The Pathfinders have got the right men on the ground now?'

I knew what he was driving at. 'Yeah. Absolutely, sir. Absolutely.'

'Good.' He screwed the top on his water bottle and slotted it into his belt kit. 'That's what I needed to hear.'

With that, we returned to the HQ ATAP. I made my way back into the depression, Colonel Gibson heading off to have words with Bob Bryant. The colonel signalled for Grant and Jacko to join him, and there was an animated discussion between the four of them – the CO, Bob Bryant, Jacko and Grant.

Everyone else was staring at me. 'So what was all that about, with Gibbo?'

I shrugged. 'He just said give the blokes a big chuck up. Well done. And he just wanted to check that we're the right men on the ground now. So I told him – yeah, we are.'

A few moments later Jacko rejoined us. He had a massive smile on his face.

'Bob was angling to stay,' he chortled. 'Said it was an ideal 1 PARA role, and they were fresh on the ground. The CO cut him short: "No, Bob, this is a Pathfinder tasking. Things can only get worse. I need soldiers on the ground who can look after themselves and move through and live in the jungle. Your force cannot do that. Bob, you will stay today, but I will withdraw you tomorrow morning. That's my decision – final." Bloody CO told it like it was!'

It made sense. By keeping the PARAs here for a day we'd get a twenty-four-hour break, before we were back in the hot seat.

It was also pretty clear that Gibbo was right when he'd said 'things could only get worse'. The White Rabbit had given us a heads-up on the flood of Intel they'd got in over the last few hours. The rebels had declared that 'the British troops at Lungi Lol will pay in blood for what they have done'. They had to take Lungi Lol and make good on Operation Kill British, or they'd lose all credibility.

And so the rebel commanders had declared an all-out onslaught.

24

We pulled the patrol commanders in so Grant could brief them. 'Right, guys, the decision's been taken that we stay. The CO's keeping us here. Period.'

'Good.'

'Great.'

'That's only right.'

'Fucking right, as well.'

'But there's a real chance now we're going to be facing an on-slaught,' Grant continued. 'The rebels have taken a beating and they're thirsting for revenge, so be prepared.'

'Yeah, fuck 'em.'

'Let 'em come.'

'I've been told 1 PARA will be staying the night and they'll be lifted out tomorrow morning. So take this oppo to get some serious rest, get some food inside you, and get personal kit squared away, 'cause tonight could be fun and games.'

All were good with that. We now had a platoon of 1 PARA lads in place, plus the twenty-six of us lot. That meant fifty-six all told, facing whatever the rebels intended to throw at us. Colonel Gibson had promised us all the weaponry and support we could wish for, so I sat with Wag drawing up our bucket list.

'Half a dozen Claymores,' I started. Wag noted it down. 'Grenades, if they're in-country, and 3500 rounds of 7.62 mm link for the guns; another two bandoliers of ammo each for the SA80s, plus 51 mm HE . . .'

Wag glanced up from his pen and paper. 'Tell you what, let's ask for a couple of 81 mm mortars.'

I grinned. 'Yeah, why not?'

We finished scribbling the list, then handed it to Jacko to get sorted. The CO and his retinue were flying out complete with the wounded girl – the one that Bri Budd had patched up – so she could be given some proper hospital treatment. The girl's mum was going with her, so it looked as if Bri wasn't going to be having a Lungi Lol wedding any time soon.

The colonel's retinue plus-some loaded up the Chinook and it took to the skies, which left us here for the duration.

With the 1 PARA lads manning our posts, we were looking forward to the first proper night's rest in eleven days – that's if the rebels didn't hit us tonight. We got fresh Intel in that evening, gleaned from intercepts of rebel mobile phone calls. They had taken a serious number of dead and injured. Their commanders were incandescent with rage: predictably, they were coming back at us with everything they'd got.

Just before last light Mojo rocked up.

'What, no bread tonight?' I joked.

He looked confused. 'No, no, not tonight – I do not think so.'

Mojo didn't really get the British sense of humour. He was incredibly formal and regimented, and wind-ups and piss-taking just weren't his thing.

'What happened to the bodies?' I asked.

'We took them into the jungle and we buried them.'

'Right, good work.'

Out on the darkening road a crowd of locals hurried past. I could sense their fear, and I knew instinctively they were headed for the village square. When I asked Mojo what was what, he confirmed what we'd suspected: all day long they'd had villagers turning up at Lungi Lol, reporting news of work parties being forced to bury the rebel dead and carry their injured.

Come nightfall, the inrush of villagers into Lungi Lol got the PARAs into a massive state of heightened alert. The tension was thick and greasy in the darkness – like you could cut it with a knife.

Bob was up and about, looking restless and twitchy. He jabbed an angry finger towards the villagers moving along the road. 'Right, we've got to fucking stop those people! They could be anyone!'

'How will you stop them, Bob?' Grant queried. 'They've been coming in for days now. Are you going to physically stop and search each one? They're women and children from outlying villages. They're coming here for sanctuary. That's why we're here.'

Bob snorted like a bull. 'Well, I'm not bloody happy there are people moving in and taking up residence in this village, and I don't know who they are.'

'What are you going to do about it then?' Grant repeated.

For a while longer Bob huffed, puffed and tried to blow the house down – before he gave up. The quiet descended over us again. It was so silent that I imagined I could hear a leaf falling in the forest. Even the insects seemed to have canned it for the night. We'd resumed our dark-hours sentry routine, because we didn't want to risk getting jumped by the rebels.

Wag and me took the first stag. 'You know what this is, don't you, mate?' I whispered to him.

'What what is?'

'This silence?'

'What, mate?'

'It's the quiet before the storm. They are out there at the moment, licking their wounds, and they are fucking mustering every man they can lay their hands on.'

Wag nodded. 'Yeah, I know.'

Silence.

By first light the feared onslaught hadn't materialised. We guessed it was taking a while to organise the kind of numbers they wanted to throw at us.

Meanwhile, we ripped the piss out of the PARAs, who were shortly going to be leaving. *They'll be back tonight; you can read about it in the newspapers.* Bob Bryant's face was as long as sin as he gathered his blokes to load up the incoming helo.

He had a few last words with Grant, then to everyone at the HQ ATAP: 'Good luck, Pathfinders.'

The Chinook came in at 0800 hours, ready to whisk the PARAs away. But first off the open ramp came these guys hefting the unmistakable forms of 81 mm mortars. The 81 mm is a seriously heavy piece of kit, and it comes in three lumps. First off the helo were what looked like three 81 mm tubes. Next came three base plates, like large steel dustbin lids, and finally the bipod legs.

Wag turned to me. 'Fuck me, we got the 81 mm mortars. Three of 'em!'

Next came the big green boxes of 81 mm mortar ammo – each round weighing some four kilograms. There were fifty illume rounds and fifty HE per tube. Even with the 1 PARA lads helping, it took a good fifteen minutes to unload all the ammo. *Shit.* With the mortars in position and this much ammo to hand, we really would have transformed this place into Sierra Leone's Alamo.

Mortars stacked up, we got our own ammo resupply off the helo. Once that was unloaded, we gave Bob the thumbs-up, the PARAs climbed aboard and the Chinook got airborne again. Wag and me were left surrounded by a massive pile of war *matériel*, plus eleven new guys – the 1 PARA mortar teams.

Each team consisted of three mortar men. They hailed from 1 PARA's Support Company, and their mortar teams are renowned throughout the British Army as being some of the best in the business. If we needed 81 mm HE rounds dropped down the rebels' throats, these were the guys to do it.

I knew the lead Mortar Fire Controller (MFC), ALPHA, a bloke called Mike 'Tommo' Thomson, plus his 2iC, Joe Caveney, from my 3 PARA days.

We shook hands. 'All right, Tommo? Joe?'

'Hear you was fucking mixing it up the other night?'

I nodded. 'Yeah, that's what you're here for.'

'Yeah, we're here to please.'

I did the intros with Wag. Then: 'Tell you what, you guys walk into the village with us, and leave a couple of blokes on stag, and we'll come back down with the Pinz for the ammo and the tubes.'

'Yeah, gleaming, mate, gleaming.'

As we made our way up the track towards the village square I briefed the guys. 'I'll leave it in your hands, Tommo, but what we need, mate, is a wall of protective fire – 81 mm rounds – all around village, and we'll talk you through a target list once we get you settled.'

'Okay, mate, okay.'

'Under your guidance, Tommo, let's look at the siting of the mortars and discuss marking and targeting.'

'You show me what you want, I'll site the tubes and we'll go from there.'

We got the resupply of ammo distributed around our patrols. By the time we were done, Tommo was already getting the mortars dug in. He was a total whirlwind of energy, and we could see him in the centre of the village getting his blokes wound up to speed. Mortar pit one was sited opposite the chief's house. Pit two was across from it, on the far side of the track, and pit three was staggered back from those two.

Tommo and his lads slotted together these collapsible shovels. They marked out each mortar pit, which would consist of a circular depression some seven feet across, and then they started to dig.

Wag nodded in their direction. 'Someone needs to tell them Ibrahim can get a work gang on that.'

We laughed.

Tommo struck me as being like the British Army's equivalent of Ibrahim, and he certainly drew the crowds. The villagers were keeping their distance as Tommo and his boys worked, for it all looked decidedly dangerous. But they were clearly thinking – *what are the British Army up to now?*

Wag grabbed one of the belts of 7.62 mm link that we'd been re-supplied with, and broke it down by snapping out the rounds. He piled the 200 loose bullets into an empty ammo box and handed it to Mojo, telling him to get his boys to properly bomb up their mags with the extra ammo.

'Make sure it's in their mags, not in their pockets loose,' Wag told him. 'Make sure it's loaded, okay?'

'Okay, okay,' Mojo confirmed. 'In the magazines for the rifles. Very useful for where we will go if there is a problem.'

By that Mojo had to mean the trenches to the rear of the village.

It took barely an hour for Tommo and his boys to dig the mortar pits. Then the mortar base plate went down in the centre of the pit, looking like a spoked wheel laid on its side. The tube went next, a ball-and-joint connection attaching it to the heavy plate. Finally, the bipod legs locked onto the barrel. An hour and a half in and we could see three large tubes poking skywards. Next, they stacked the ammo into the rear of the pits – one pile of illume and one of HE.

That done, they started filling these empty hessian sandbags with dirt, building up a two-foot-high, double-bagged wall all around the pit. It was 1200 hours by the time they were done, and they had never bloody stopped. We now had a fully operational mortar line. The three blokes in each pit would never leave their station, unless to piss or to shit. They cooked, ate, slept and fought from there.

After some rushed scoff, Tommo and Joe came to scope out some targets with us. We walked along the main track, passing the point where the rebel bodies had been piled up.

'Right, mate, you advise,' I started, 'but this is what we think the rebels did when they hit us, and what we reckon they'll do next time.'

Joe and Tommo got out notebooks and maps and held them at the ready.

I talked them around the maps. 'This, mate, is the point where we think they first broke cover and came across open ground to hit us. It's about 1.2 klicks out.'

Tommo nodded, vigorously. 'Where the track meets that feature, we'll mark that as the first target – Xray 1-1. Where else?'

'We think they broke out of the jungle there, mate.'

'Right – Xray 1-2.'

'Plus see where the train line drops into that dead ground there – that was another massing point.'

'Right – Xray 1-3.'

In this way we went around the maps and over the terrain, selecting all the obvious targets we could hit with mortar fire. We finished off with Fern Gully, the last point from where they'd tried to overrun us.

'Put one target at the far end of Fern Gully,' I told him, 'so we can bring fire down there, and one at the near end.'

'Right – Xray 1-7 and Xray 1-8,' Tommo confirmed. 'We'll give 'em all Xray numbers, to keep it simple-stupid. It needs to be so simple that under fire your guys can have a copy of this target list, and any one of them can call in the fire. All they need to say is: enemy movement Xray 1-5 . . .'

'Fantastic.' I paused, then glanced at Tommo. 'Mate, they got fucking close last time.'

'Yeah, mate, I 'eard.'

'So, we need an FPF.'

FPF stands for Final Protective Fire – in other words, calling in mortar rounds on top of your own position.

Tommo scrunched his face up. 'Right . . . You want an FPF?'

'Yeah, we do. What's the closest you can give us?'

Tommo scratched his shaven head. 'Officially, I can't come closer than 250 metres to friendly force troops. But you know how it is . . . The order to fire the FPF will have to come from Grant, though, mate, 'cause he's the senior man on the ground.'

I told him we were good with that.

'The mortar may get a drop-short, so you're pretty much dropping on your own men,' Tommo added. 'To be clear, mate, the FPF is pretty much only ever fired if we are about to get overrun: it's the last thing we can do. Once we've fired the FPF the mortars are pretty much useless. We'll have been overrun.'

'Okay, Tommo, yeah, I know . . . So we need to build you into our withdrawal plans. How about this: you fire the FPF, throw what you can on the back of the Pinz, then you and your blokes jump aboard and get the fuck out of Dodge.'

Tommo grinned. 'Okay, mate, got it.'

'One other thing,' I added. 'We've lived here with the villagers and become like a part of the place. Tell your blokes they have to shit down at the crappers, over near Taff's position. Plus we'll be getting you an early morning water delivery sorted, plus a delivery of bread rolls in the evenings . . .'

Tommo stared at me for a second. 'You serious?'

'I'm serious.'

'Right, bang on, mate, bang on.'

We ran through the plans in more detail, based on the fact that we expected a tidal wave of rebels. The eleven blokes in the mortar team were fit, robust PARAs, but they weren't trained to E & E or for jungle survival – hence the plan being that they'd take the Pinzgauer. In an ideal world they'd fire the FPF, collapse the mortar tubes and load them on the wagon, before hitting the road. That way we'd prevent the 81 mms from falling into rebel hands.

But Plan B involved blowing up the mortars, if they had to move real quickly. We used the last of the PE4 to make up three charges, each with a three-minute fuse.

'If we give you the signal to withdraw and there's no time to salvage the tubes, you simply light the end of the safety fuse,' I told them. 'Pile a dozen HE rounds around the mortar, for some extra umph, and you've got three minutes from the point of lighting the fuse to make your getaway.'

Tommo nodded. 'Got it.'

With the mortar positions and procedures sorted, Tommo and Joe moved up to co-locate with us in the HQ ATAP. That way they could get eyes-on the battlefront to better call in fire, plus they would be the relay between our patrols and the mortar pits. We'd just about got them settled in, when Mojo came to see us bearing an invitation to visit the village chief. We hadn't seen or spoken to him since the rebel attack, so a chinwag was long overdue.

'Yeah, we need to talk to him anyway,' I told Mojo. 'We need to tell him about the mortars. If they start firing it will be very loud and what we don't want is for the villagers to think they're getting hit. They need to know to stay in their huts and to expect some big explosions.'

We wandered over to the chief's place. Mojo rattled on for a while about the mortars, relaying what we'd just said, and then the chief spoke to Mojo at some length. He was about the most animated that I'd ever seen him.

Mojo turned to us to translate. 'The chief says he is very grateful to you British. You have saved his people and the village. And he says thank you for helping the girl who was badly injured and for taking her to safety.'

'We're here to help you and protect you,' Grant reassured him. 'That's what we're here for.'

'And we're here to stay,' I added.

The chief thanked us again, and with that we returned to our battle stations. We called the patrol commanders in and briefed them on all the Xray target co-ordinates that we'd sorted with the mortar teams. Pathfinders are trained to call in mortar fire anyway, so this was like second nature to us. I could see this light burning in the blokes' eyes. It was the extra sense of confidence that three 81 mm mortars, plus an extra bandolier or two of ammo each, brings.

If needed, we knew we could mallet the rebels with 81 mm HE

rounds. It's one thing being shot at by small arms, quite another being plastered with that kind of highly accurate and murderous heavy fire. The 81 mms would be a battle-changer, or so we fucking hoped.

'They're coming,' I warned the blokes, 'and the hammer will fall hardest here tonight. Any one of you, if you hear or see anything you can call for illume ... Be mindful HE will come if you call for it, but there are a lot of civvies out there trying to get in here to safety, so we need to be under rebel fire before we bring in HE. Last thing we need is to drop on the locals and destroy all the goodwill. So, we can't just call in HE on any movement. It's not ideal, but we need to be taking fire from a position before we can hit it. Put the call through, and Tommo and Joe will put up the illume, with HE to follow if and when it all goes noisy.'

That was it. Briefing done.

It was around mid-afternoon when Tricky got warning via the Thuraya to expect another set of visitors – only this time it was about as high-up as it could get. Brigadier Richards, the overall force commander, was flying in for a heads-up. I cast my mind back to the promise he'd made several days earlier, to Sierra Leone's embattled leader, President Kabbah – that the British military would end the war in Sierra Leone by knocking seven bales of shit out of the rebels.

Well, I guessed here in Lungi Lol we'd made a decent start.

Brigadier Richards flew in on a Special Forces Chinook, and Grant and me were there to do the meet and greet. He had with him his Military Assistant, Major Mark Mangham, plus his close protection (CP) team. He spent about an hour on the ground chatting with us, plus as many of the lads as he could get around. And he had a good natter to the locals, who couldn't have made it clearer how happy they were that we'd kicked the rebels' butts.

The Brigadier confided in us that it had been his ultimate decision to put us this far out and exposed in the jungle, and that he was mightily relieved we'd stood firm in the face of the onslaught.

In fact, he'd sited us here deliberately to lure the rebels out, know-ing how vital it was that British force gave them a right bloody nose early on – to establish our moral and fighting superiority from the start.

What we'd achieved here was crucial to the Brigadier's overall game plan in Sierra Leone, and making good on his promise to President Kabbah. It came as a bit of a surprise to learn that we'd been used as the bait in a trap to snare the RUF. Still, all's well that ends well – not that this was over yet. Far from it ...

The Brigadier's was of necessity a flying visit. With him and his team gone Mojo rocked up at the HQ ATAP. The same cardboard tray as always was balanced on his shoulder. His arrival was pre-announced by the whiff of ... freshly baked bread.

'I have the bread!' he announced. He glanced at Joe and Tommo. 'Also, I have for your friends.'

Tommo and Joe were staring at Mojo, like they couldn't quite believe it. I'd warned them about the bread and water deliveries, but maybe they'd thought it was a wind-up. Tommo was a typical chirpy cockney type, but right now he seemed lost for words.

'Don't worry about it, mate,' I told him, 'you're gonna be scoff-ing on some nice fresh bread.'

Wag loved getting around the blokes doing the bread delivery. The oldest man amongst us, he was like the father figure of the unit. *Dad's here with the bread rolls.* I could hear him counting them out in the background.

'Mate, can you manage up to thirty-seven?' I needled him.

'Fuck off, Smoggy ... Yeah,' he confirmed, once he was done counting, 'all your blokes got bread too.'

Tommo's grin split his face ear-to-ear. 'Fucking hell! Diamond geezer, that Mojo.'

Wag counted out the rolls for the mortar teams. ''Ere you go – take yours. Take your eleven.'

Tommo eyed the stack of bread. 'Where the fuck am I gonna put all that?'

'No idea,' said Wag.

'Tell you what, I'll open me daysack and fucking put it in there,' Tommo decided.

Leaving Tommo to make his bread delivery, Wag and me headed for Dolly's position.

'Yeah, I've got the bread,' Wag announced, as we neared their trenches.

Dolly chuckled. 'Oh, the bread's back. We thought the baker had done a runner.'

'Nope, he's still here.'

By the time we'd done the rounds of the battle trenches and got back to the HQ ATAP, Jacko had been on the radio with that evening's Sched. Grant made sure to read out the message to us all, Tommo and Joe included.

'Fucking standby, standby. Every, every source of info we have is that they're coming at you with everything they've got and most likely tonight.'

After Grant was finished there was a kind of collective rabbit-eyed stare from the blokes.

I broke the silence, doing my best impression of Michael Caine's accent in the movie *Zulu*: 'Zulus, sir.' 'How many?' 'Fucking thasands of 'em.'

Tommo chuckled. 'Yeah, fun and games tonight. Fucking going to get busy.'

As darkness descended on Lungi Lol we kept getting hourly updates from Jacko, via the Thuraya. With the rebels using mobile phones to co-ordinate their movements, and with our spooks having cracked the phone intercepts, I figured he was getting a live update on exactly what the RUF commanders were saying.

'They're advancing on your position and there are thousands,' Jacko relayed to us. 'They are coming to attack in great strength. Be ready for the onslaught.'

We figured every rebel and his dog would be in on this one, minus those we had already killed and wounded. As we stared down our rifle barrels into the gathering darkness, we were readying ourselves to get hit by a dark tidal wave.

All evening the tension rose, as villagers flooded in. It was like a mass influx of refugees now. But by around midnight the movement had died to nothing, and all went quiet. Then we started to hear the noises. It was a repeat performance of the night we were hit – unearthly, spectral screams and screeches echoing across to us. Amidst the ghostly cries we figured we could see fleeting movement, as shadows flickered back and forth across the tree line.

Dolly's patrol was the first to put out the call. 'Put up illume over Xray 1-4. Possible movement.'

Tommo and Joe relayed the radio message to their teams: 'Fire illume Xray 1-4.'

An instant later the first 81 mm mortar went up with a massive thump.

We waited the eight seconds or so it took to climb to the heavens and then: *fzzzztttttt!* It was like a giant party-popper being unleashed high above us.

The flare hung in the sky like a mini-sun. The cone of blinding light it cast was far wider than that of the puny 51 mm that Cantrill and I had been using. But despite its size and its brightness, we couldn't hear even the barest hint of the thing fizzing. It was utterly soundless as it drifted, sparked and burned. It struck me how eerie it was that so much light could fall upon us, but in total silence.

Everyone was awake now – those on stag and those not on stag. All of us were on a knife-edge as we waited for the first shots to ring out – signalling the onslaught was upon us. We'd agreed between us only to use '*maximise*' if we'd clearly seen armed rebels massing, or if we were under fire.

The silence lengthened as the flare floated earthwards, and still no shots hammered out from the tree line. Finally, the flare drifted behind the fringe of jungle and all went dark.

A short message came in from Dolly: 'Roger, out.'

In other words, nothing seen as yet to justify giving *maximise*.

The rebels had their own mortars, that we knew. We had to presume they'd brought them forward to hit our positions, plus their 12.7 mm DShKs and their 'United Nations' armoured personnel carriers (APCs). Each patrol had a LAW lying at the ready, in anticipation of seeing a rebel gun truck or one of those ex-UN APCs come lumbering out of the jungle.

Next up on the air was Ginge: '*33 Charlie*: put up illume over Xray 1-6.'

Tommo did a repeat relay, and the second 81 mm round went up. It too drifted into darkness with no shots having been fired.

Next, Nathe was on the air: 'That's not a fucking animal noise over at Xray 1-7. Get some illume up – let's have a look.'

Another 81 mm round lit up the heavens, this one to the front of *33 Alpha*'s battle trenches. Because the rebels had got so close in the first battle, we wanted to hit them and smash them as early and as far out from the village as we possibly could. We figured they were probing us again now, and testing our reaction times. Either way they seemed determined to keep us awake all night, allowing no one to get a wink of sleep.

Come first light, we'd fired a good twenty illume rounds all along our front. No one moved through the jungle between midnight and 0500 apart from the rebels. None of us had any doubts that they were out there in the cover of the trees, massing in serious strength, as their commanders put the final touches to their plan of attack. Still, sunrise brought a real sense of relief. We didn't figure they'd hit us during the daylight hours.

We'd had maybe a thousand extra villagers dossing down in Lungi Lol that night. They'd been terrified of what the darkness would bring. Well, tonight at least it had brought them no gunshot wounds, no horror of capture, nor the brutal torture and amputations that would follow. With the rebels' anger being such as it was, presumably they planned to wreak terrible vengeance. They would know by now how the villagers here were in league with us, and they would torture their very souls.

No ground assault had materialised that night, but it occurred to us that maybe we were being played by the rebels. In the Vietnam War the Vietcong had adopted a tactic designed to exhaust their American enemy: it was to probe and harass a position all night long, night after night after night. They had set up shifts to do so, making sure that the American soldiers got no sleep. Over successive nights the tension and the sleeplessness had proved exhausting, until finally the Vietcong had launched an attack from out of the darkness.

We figured the rebels were doing the same now, hoping that sooner or later they'd catch us napping.

There hadn't been the slightest hint of what was coming. It hit us like a bombshell.

For night after night now we'd been probed by the rebels, and night after night we'd put up the 81 mm rounds to deter them. We'd pushed out foot patrols during the day into the jungle, and found all the usual signs that the rebels had been there massing to attack, but still the expected onslaught hadn't come.

After so many sleepless nights we'd more or less lost track of how long we'd been here. We were counting out the days in bread and water deliveries. But of one thing we had been certain: *we were here for the duration.* No rebels were fucking us out of Lungi Lol, or wreaking havoc on this village.

Not our village.

Not on our watch.

Not while we still had ammo and men to fight.

We'd been expecting a normal evening's Sched: *rebels are poised to hit you; be ready; stand firm.* I could see Tricky beavering away with his notepad as he scribbled down an extra-long message, so I guessed we'd got some extra-juicy Intel in.

He stopped scribbling and stared hard at what he'd written for several seconds. Then he turned and handed it to Grant, his face like death.

'Fucking hell, mate,' he muttered, 'you'd better read that . . .'

This wasn't Tricky. He wasn't the melodramatic type. He was calm, cool, collected and laid-back to the point of horizontal. We were all sat up now, listening hard.

Grant ran his eye over the message: 'Fuuuuuck . . .'

Me and Wag both said it at once. 'Fucking hurry up and read it, then.'

Grant stared at us for a long moment. Then he flicked his eyes down, and started to read: 'PF withdrawal, plus 1 PARA, DTG 250800MAY00. Full stop. Resupply HLS. Full stop. No relief in place.'

'Read it again,' I rasped.

Grant repeated it word for word. Twice. Then he glanced up at me. 'Basically, from the resupply HLS at 0800 tomorrow we're all to withdraw. There will be no relief. Isn't that what it means?'

We sat there staring at each other.

For ages.

In utter silence.

Finally, Grant repeated the question: 'Isn't that what it means? Or am I missing something? So what are your thoughts on that?'

'I'll tell you what my thoughts are on that, Grant, mate: it means we're being pulled out, and no fucker's coming in to take our place.'

The reality of what this meant was just starting to hit us. 'But d'you really think . . . D'you really think they can just . . . ?' Grant's words petered into silence.

'Look at it this way, mate: for us to be relieved, some other blokes would have to come in to do a handover, like we half-did with Cantrill. They'd need to get boots on the ground and scope out our positions, and only once they were in would we pull out. That's how a RIP works. There's no way we're getting on a helo tomorrow and when we've left the village unoccupied a bunch of Marines will fly in and reoccupy. It just doesn't work that way.'

Grant was ashen-faced. 'But . . .'

'Steve's right,' Wag cut in. 'It looks like they're pulling us out and no fucker is coming in. We bail out. Village abandoned. End of.'

Grant shook his head, disbelievingly. 'No. No. They wouldn't just pull us out? After so many days manning these positions and with the threat still out there, surely they'd put someone back in?'

'Well, maybe all units are being pulled out of country,' I suggested. 'Op over. Endex. Or maybe we're being pulled out onto another task. You never know.'

'Yeah, but they wouldn't just pull us out and leave the village unoccupied,' Grant repeated. 'Surely they wouldn't do that?'

'Yeah, 'cause that's pretty much leaving the village unprotected. Undefended,' Tricky added.

Wag nodded. 'And especially now we've poked a stick into the hornet's nest big time.'

Grant glanced around at our faces. 'They wouldn't, would they? Surely?'

For twenty-odd minutes this went around and around and around. At the end we decided that based on the scanty information provided we had no option but to conclude the unthinkable: we were being pulled out of Lungi Lol, and no force was coming in our place.

We called the patrol commanders in to brief them. I didn't envy Grant's position as he stood up to face the blokes.

'Right, guys, we've just got orders over the net,' Grant began. 'Us lot and the 1 PARA mortar lads are being pulled out tomorrow morning at 0800. We're heading back to Lungi Airport.' Long, heavy pause. 'At the moment I have no more info on whether it's a retasking. All I do know is that right now there's no RIP by the Marines.'

Grant's words were met with utter silence.

It was broken finally by Nathe. 'So why aren't the fucking Marines coming?'

Grant shrugged. 'I don't know, Nathe. This is all we've got.'

'So who *is* coming, then?' Nathe probed.

'As I've said, Nathe, at the moment the message indicates that nobody is.'

A few seconds' silence for the words to sink in; a long, heavy beat.

'*Fucking nobody is?*' Nathe snorted, in disbelief. 'So who is going to protect the village, then? Who's gonna fucking look after them?'

'Well, I presume, Nathe, when we're gone the Nigerians will stay. So, it's over to them.'

'*The fucking Nigerians.* Get real. What the fuck're the Nigerians gonna do?'

'Look, Nathe, I am just telling you what we've got over radio, mate. Whatever decisions have been made, it's way above my pay grade. It's already been decided, mate.'

'Well, it's total fucking bollocks.' Nathe was so angry his two false front teeth had started to rattle about. 'It's utter bloody fucking bollocks that is.'

The other patrol commanders were murmuring their agreement. Nathe was right, of course. It *was* utter bloody fucking bollocks. But there was sod all we could do about it right now.

'Okay, okay, *guys*,' Wag tried to calm it. 'Fully understand emotions are running fucking high. We feel the same here, but the decision's been made, so we gotta get on with it. End of.'

There was a lot of angry muttering from the blokes. I tried to focus minds on what lay ahead – the logistics of organising the withdrawal – for none of us had had the slightest inkling this was coming.

'Right, guys, minds on admin, 'cause we've got a fuck load to do before now and 0800 tomorrow. Make sure shortly after first light you bring in and dismantle the Claymores. Do not leave anything one of the villagers could hurt themselves with. Plus make sure you do a hundred per cent kit check; when you get the order tomorrow, move direct from your positions to HLS. Any questions?'

Silence.

Nothing.

Angry, dark silence.

'Make sure you say your goodbyes before then,' I continued. I figured Nathe needed a tasking to take his mind off the shit sandwich that was being forced down everyone's throat right now.

'Nathe, there'll be no room on the Chinook for everyone plus the Pinz, so I want your team to drive it back pretty much after first light tomorrow.'

He grunted an acknowledgement.

I turned to the two mortar lads. 'Tommo, make sure you take care of your blokes and dismantle your mortars when you see fit to do so.'

'Okay,' Tommo confirmed, quietly.

'Right, guys, just before we wrap.' I glanced around the faces before me: Nathe, Dolly, Ginge, Taff and H. I'd never seen the lads like this before. There was bitter anger and defiance seething just below the surface. 'None of us wants this. None of us has asked for it. But, for better or worse, this is our last night. So, let's keep everything wired tight and let's get out of here in one piece.'

Without a word of acknowledgement the five of them turned and melted away. I knew what they faced now. They were returning to their patrols to brief their blokes that we were leaving Lungi Lol to its fate – and that meant leaving the villagers, plus the thousands more who'd come here seeking sanctuary. It wasn't exactly how I'd ever imagined us leaving this place ... or how I wanted us to go. Granted, we'd been here for days since the main attack, and still the rebels hadn't hit the village – but that didn't make it any easier on any of us.

No sooner were the blokes gone than the familiar figure of Mojo pitched up, tray-load of bread rolls perched on his shoulder. Grant glanced up at him, dejectedly.

'Mojo, mate, I need a word.'

Grant was sat on the lip of the depression with a face like death. Mojo was standing. He'd never once sat down with us all the time we'd been here. He was a stand-to-attention man through and through.

Grant gestured at a spot on the ground beside him. 'Mojo, take a seat.'

'No, no – I stand, I stand.'

'No, Mojo, sit down.'

Mojo sat down. He still had his Foster Grant shades on of course, but from behind them he was eyeing Grant nervously.

'Mojo, I've got some bad news,' Grant announced.

'Huh?'

'We have had a radio message this evening. We will all be leaving in the morning.'

'Leaving?'

'Yep.'

'All?'

'Yep.'

'And when will you come back?'

'We won't be coming back, Mojo.'

Mojo shook his head, confusedly. 'You won't come back?'

'We won't be coming back, no.'

Mojo tried a hopeful smile. 'And other British – they will come?'

Grant glanced at him. 'I honestly don't know – but I think not.'

'Nobody will come? Nobody?'

'Nobody will come. Mojo, you'll be here on your own until you have to leave.'

It was then that Mojo took his sunglasses off. For the first time in so many days we actually got sight of his eyes. He twisted the shades around in his hands, nervously, as he tried to take in all Grant had said.

'But what will happen now?'

'I don't know.' Grant's tone was very soft now. Wrapped in emotion. He shook his head. 'Mojo, I don't know.'

For several long moments we sat there, all of us enveloped in this heavy silence.

Then Grant said to Mojo: 'Will you take me to speak to the chief?'

'I will take you to speak to him,' Mojo confirmed.

He got up and put his sunglasses back on. I stood up and put my hand out. 'Mojo, thank you. And thank your men. Take care.'

As we shook hands I could tell he was still in shock. 'Thank you,' he replied. 'Thank you – for everything.'

Wag and Tricky likewise said their goodbyes.

As Grant and Mojo stepped away, Wag turned after them. 'I'll be coming with you, mate.'

Wag hurried after Grant, leaving Tricky and me alone in the HQ depression, staring at the tray of thirty-seven bread rolls, lying white and skull-like in the moonlight. I'd happily have faced another rebel onslaught, crawling forward with 51 mm mortar and SA80 in hand, than have to do what Grant and Wag were about to do now – tell the chief we were bailing out of his village.

Their willingness to do that – *to do the right thing* – was the real test of a soldier. Grant could have chosen the easy path – to sneak away quietly. The decision to withdraw wasn't his, and it would have been so much easier to melt away. But he displayed the mark of a real man and demonstrated incredible moral courage, when he chose to take the hardest road possible, and Wag had volunteered to stand with him.

They were back fifteen minutes later. I glanced up at them, guiltily. 'Fucking hell, guys, how did that go?'

Grant shrugged. 'Emotional.'

'What . . . What did he say?'

'Well . . . when we told him, it was pretty much a repeat of Mojo; "You will go and come back? You will go and new British will come?" I told him I didn't think so: most likely no. He didn't rant and rave. He just said; "So, no one will come?" I confirmed most likely no one. I thanked him for all that he and his people had done. Told him how we felt a part of the village . . . His people took us in . . . Grown close to them . . . Felt real close . . . At that point I had to pull away . . . Just leave it at that.'

'Fucking hell. Fuck me. Heavy.'

Grant turned away. 'Yeah, mate. A bit emotional.'

Last light was almost upon us by now, after which we slipped into our night routine. Only, tonight wasn't like any night that had gone before. All across our positions blokes were somehow having to get their heads around the fact that we were out of here come morning, leaving the village all but defenceless.

It lay across us all, dark and heavy like a death shroud.

Grant and Tricky took first stag. I lay on the I-bed, gazing up at the heavens. It was an absolutely crystal clear night. Directly above me were fingers of wispy tree branches, and above those a skein of stars so close I felt I could reach out and touch them. A thousand villagers were bedded down on the square tonight – as they had been for so many nights before – gazing up at that same sky, feeling ... secure. Secure because of us. And little did they know that tomorrow we would be gone.

I lay there with my senses on hyper-alert and praying for the rebels to hit us. If the onslaught came tonight, at least we could smash seven bales of shit out of the bastard rebels, and maybe deter them forever from trying to take this village. Or, we could use the attack to argue for a change of plan – to allow us to stay, or at least until a replacement force was flown in. But all I could hear from the forest was the rhythmic *breep-breep-breep* of the night-time insects and the odd animal cry.

Tonight, I couldn't detect the barest hint of the rebels' presence, and come daybreak no illume would have been fired. But as I lay there on the I-bed unable to sleep, I realised something. I couldn't seem to remember coming into this village – our arrival. It was weird, but I felt like I'd always been here. As if it had always been like this. Life before Lungi Lol felt like a whole universe away.

I couldn't seem to remember any other life before this, but tomorrow we would be gone.

At first light the Water Girls arrived. But this time it was us lot who had our eyes downcast as they made their delivery. We tried telling them we didn't need the water, but the girls just stared at us like it didn't compute. *This was our early morning water delivery. We got it every day. What were we saying?*

At around 0630 Nathe led his patrol up to the HQ ATAP. He was trying to act businesslike and soldierly, but I could tell he was having a difficult time keeping a lid on things.

'Right, Steve, that's us,' he announced, gruffly. 'That's everything accounted for. We're gonna head back...'

With that he led his guys over to the lone Pinzgauer, they loaded up their kit and he got the wagon under way. I could see the mortar teams dismantling their tubes, and emptying the sandbags into the pits they'd dug. By now Dolly and Ginge's teams had collapsed their positions, so I asked them to help lug the mortars down to the LZ.

The village was a hive of soldierly activity, and all around I could see the locals pausing to stare. They had to be wondering what the hell was happening. As the mortars were manhandled towards the LZ there was a lot of serious kit on the move, and it wouldn't take the brains of an archbishop to realise what was happening.

It came the time for the four of us to move out from the HQ ATAP. We headed onto the track. All around us people had stopped doing whatever they had been doing, and were staring at us. I paused for an instant, gazing back into our position: the I-beds, Wag's gym, the path I'd crawled with Cantrill the night of the main battle. I tried to commit those things to memory, and then the four of us joined on the end of the long line of blokes heading south to the LZ.

We were the last guys out. Word had clearly spread like the plague, for by now we had scores of villagers lining the track, silent and watchful. I felt as if we were marching through a corridor of staring, fearful eyes. Many of the faces we knew by sight if not by name. We'd sat with them, played with their kids, shared their food and water; they'd built our beds and dug our trenches, cleared our arcs of fire and planted our punji fields.

They'd stood firm with us in the face of overwhelming enemy numbers.

And now we were just walking out of here.

I'd half expected Mojo, or Ibrahim, or the village chief to come and see us off, but there was no one. Instead, there was just a crowd of confused and bewildered villagers.

At 0820 the Chinook came in and landed. The patrols moved up the open tail ramp in two files, and Wag and me were the last to board. We walked into the helo side by side and took a pew. The turbines started to scream to a fever pitch above us, as the ramp whined closed.

As the helo took off the top half of the ramp was open, and when we turned westwards towards Lungi Airport I could see down into the village, barely fifty feet below us. My eyes traced the track leading up to the village square, and I could make out this wide sea of faces, all turned skywards and staring at us.

I glanced at Wag, who was seated opposite. Our eyes met. I could tell he was feeling as shitty as I was. His eyes said it all: *this is not right.*

I glanced along the row of blokes. A couple returned the look. But most had their heads leant back against the helo's side, eyes wide shut in the comedown of it all, and the exhaustion.

As the helo levelled out for the flight to the airport, I had conflicting thoughts crashing through my head. *Why were we not getting RIP'd? Why were we getting withdrawn after stirring up such a hornet's nest? Why were we on this helo, leaving the entire village in the shit . . . ?* I felt some relief that we'd got all the blokes out alive, but that was buried under an avalanche of fear and guilt for those we were leaving behind us.

And leaving behind, I feared, to the mercy of the rebels.

EPILOGUE

The men of the Pathfinders were flown back to the UK some forty-eight hours after withdrawing from the village of Lungi Lol. Upon returning to the UK they sought out information on the welfare of the villagers, by searching through British military post-operational reports, Sierra Leone government bulletins, local and international media reports and other intelligence sources.

Thankfully, no further rebel push came through Lungi Lol after they were withdrawn, and there was no attack on Lungi Airport. Those twenty-six Pathfinders had held Lungi Lol for sixteen days. They were not replaced by the Royal Marines, or any other troops for that matter. In the final analysis the Marines had decided they did not have a unit capable of deploying to such an isolated, deep-jungle location, one bereft of escape routes, or means of relief or back-up. Accordingly, no unit took over the Pathfinders' positions.

The 1 PARA battle group was relieved by 42 Commando at Lungi Airport and in Freetown. The back-to-back deployments of two extremely capable fighting units had sealed the fate of the country, bringing an end to a horrific civil war that had lasted for over a decade and cost so many lives. Of course, a very large part of that success was due to a small force of Pathfinders and their extraordinary actions at Lungi Lol – the only significant military action fought against the rebels.

It was that action that broke the backbone of the rebel army in Sierra Leone. Having got the measure of the British forces at Lungi Lol, the rebels had lost the appetite for the fight. Even as the Pathfinders lasted out their final days in the besieged village, Foday Sankoh, the overall commander of the RUF, had been taken captive by British forces. He was captured in Freetown itself, and that, coupled with the crushing defeat of the rebels at Lungi Lol, left the remaining RUF commanders in hopeless disarray, and at loggerheads with each other.

The Pathfinders had been at the tip of the spear in Sierra Leone, and the action they fought at Lungi Lol was the decisive battle. In due course the mission received the recognition it deserved. Nathan Bell, the commander of *33 Alpha*, received a Mention in Dispatches, and amongst other honours Steve Heaney was awarded the Military Cross, in recognition of his role in taking the initiative during the heat of battle.

His citation reads: 'On hearing the first shots, Sgt Heaney immediately ran forward past the trenches, and against the axis of the attack, and under automatic tracer fire from the enemy machine guns. Armed with his personal weapon and 51 mm mortar, Sgt Heaney then proceeded to coordinate fire of the forward positions, while putting up illumination with the mortar, despite being out in the open and completely exposed to intense enemy fire . . .

'He continued to provide light across the frontage as the enemy conducted a fighting withdrawal, before mounting three subsequent assaults. Sgt Heaney's quick reactions and his part in winning the firefight were crucial to the successful repulsion of the enemy attacks. With complete disregard for his own safety he moved to a position from where he could put up accurate illumination for each enemy assault. His influence over the soldiers around him during the attack was considerable, displaying immense physical courage.'

In due course the Nigerian peacekeepers in Sierra Leone were replaced by an Indian contingent, but the RUF were by then already a broken force. They were never again to mount a significant operation in the country. The British military intervention had put a stop to them, and by the end of 2000 Sierra Leone was finally at peace.

The British military campaign in Sierra Leone was one of the most successful ever. A force of less than 1000 British soldiers brought to an end a decade-long conflict that 17,000 UN peace-keepers had failed to stop. It proved that interventions in war-torn Africa did not always have to end ignominiously – as had the 1993 US intervention in Mogadishu, Somalia.

Today Sierra Leone as a nation has known peace, democracy, development and progress – at least compared to the decade-long civil war that went before – for approaching fifteen years. The rebels have been disarmed and demobilised, and many of their leaders have stood trial for war crimes. Sadly, Foday Sankoh, the RUF's founder and overall leader, died in captivity before he could be put on trial to face his crimes.

Happily, Lungi Lol today is a peaceful, thriving village.

POSTSCRIPT: WHERE ARE THEY NOW?

Richard 'Rich' Cantrill OBE MC

Richard Cantrill is now a Lieutenant-Colonel in command of 42 Commando Royal Marines. In 2010 he was awarded the MC for his time as Company Commander in Afghanistan (HERRICK 9). He was appointed OBE in the 2014 New Year Honours list for two busy years spent in the Operations Directorate of the MOD. He lives in Devon with his wife and three rowdy children.

Eddie 'The White Rabbit' Newell MBE

Eddie Newell went on to replace Wag as the Ops Warrant Officer of the Pathfinders, a job in which he remained until he left the military in 2006. On completion of his 22 years' service he was awarded an MBE. His citation reads: 'For distinguished and exceptional service in five operational theatres, and unstinting dedication to the unit'. He currently lives in the UK with his wife and son.

Mark 'Jacko' Jackson

Mark Jackson left the military in 2003 and trained as a professional sculptor and painter. In 2012 his sculptures dedicated to the Airborne Forces were unveiled by HRH Prince Charles at the National Arboretum. The two sculptures represent a Standing Paratrooper in full jump equipment and Bellerophon astride the winged horse Pegasus. Mark has his own studio in France, where he presently resides.

Darren 'Taff' Saunders

Darren Saunders left the military in 2004 after being involved in a helicopter crash that left him with a broken neck. After making a full recovery he went on to become a private security consultant working in both the UK and abroad. He is presently employed as a consultant for a major UK oil company. He lives in the South of France.

Joe 'H' / 'Tackleberry' Harrison

Joe Harrison remained with the Pathfinders until he left the military in September 2002. He re-enlisted in the Pathfinders for the 2003 deployment to Iraq and again left the military in 2004. After a few years working in the private security industry he joined the reservists and deployed three times to Afghanistan. On one such deployment in 2010 he was awarded an MID (Mention in Dispatches). H lives in the UK where he grows his own fruit and vegetables. He is currently seeking employment, and is a self-confessed *war junkie*.

Neil 'Tricky' Dick

Neil Dick left the Pathfinders and the military in 2003 after operational deployments to both Iraq and Afghanistan. He was subsequently employed by a high-profile US communications company that produces military grade radios. Tricky currently travels the world providing both practical and technical assistance to countries that employ those communications systems. He lives in Scotland with his wife and two children.

Dale 'Ginge' Wilson

Dale Wilson returned to his parent unit after the deployment to Sierra Leone. He remained there and undertook several posts as a senior NCO. Then he returned to the Pathfinders in 2010 as the

Ops Warrant Officer. In 2012 he again returned to his parent unit to finish his military service. He and his family currently live in the UK.

Sam 'Dolly' Parton

Sam Parton remained with the Pathfinders until 2003, before moving on to another unit in the British military in order to receive promotion. Dolly is still serving in the military and lives in the UK with his wife and two children.

Nathan 'Nathe' Bell MC

Nathan Bell went on to replace Steve Heaney as the Pathfinders' Platoon Sergeant where he remained until June 2004. During the Pathfinders' deployment to Iraq in 2003 Nathe was awarded the MC for his actions during the Qalat Sikar operation (the story of which is related in David Blakeley's book, *Pathfinder*). Nathe also served as an instructor at the UK Land Warfare Centre at Warminster before returning to 1 PARA. He left the Army in December 2011 having completed 22 years' service. He currently lives in the UK with his wife and daughter.

Grant Harris

Grant Harris remained with the Pathfinders until 2003 as its Second-in-Command. He then returned to his parent unit in order to receive promotion. Grant is still serving in the British military elite and lives in the UK.

Graham 'Wag' Wardle

Graham Wardle remained as the Pathfinders' Ops Warrant Officer until May 2002, when he left the military having completed 22 years' service. From 2003 until 2007 he worked in Iraq on numerous Personal Security Details (PSDs), providing security for visiting businessmen and reconstruction companies. In 2008 he began working on a residential security team based in the Middle East, in which capacity he remains to this day. Wag and his wife live in the UK.

Stephen 'Steve' Heaney MC

Steve Heaney remained as the Pathfinders' Platoon Sergeant until February 2001. He then took the decision to leave the military and move into the private security industry. Having trained as a Close Protection Officer (CPO) he went to work for a very high-profile businessman in London from April 2001 until January 2002, providing security and personal protection to the principal and his immediate family. In February 2002 Steve moved to the Middle East to provide military advice and training solutions across the full spectrum of close combat operations. He currently resides in the Middle East with his wife and two children.

Bryan 'Bri' Budd VC

Bryan Budd remained with the Pathfinders until June 2006. He returned to 3 PARA in order to receive promotion and then deployed to Afghanistan in July 2006. On 20 August 2006, during a patrol in the Sangin district of Helmand province, his section was ambushed by Taliban fighters. Bri led his men forward to clear the enemy position, which resulted in the section sustaining three casualties. He was wounded but continued the attack on his own. Spurred on by his actions the remainder of his men cleared the position, forcing the enemy to withdraw. Bryan died from wounds sustained during that battle. When his body was recovered it was surrounded by three dead Taliban fighters. He was awarded a posthumous Victoria Cross.

ACKNOWLEDGEMENTS

A number of people have provided me with assistance in clarifying details for this book and to those brothers in arms, my thanks: to the men I have stood shoulder to shoulder with on countless occasions – you shall forever have my respect. To my mother and father who undoubtedly sat by the telephone whilst watching news reports for a decade and a half, I apologise for those sleepless nights and offer you my eternal gratitude for your unwavering love and support. To my brother Neil, my confidant and best friend – thanks, mate, for always being my release valve and drinking partner when I needed to unwind!

Thank you to my co-author Damien Lewis for his belief and steadying hand on this project and in helping me to articulate my experiences during those long days at his home (not to mention down the pub!). Thanks also to his wife and family for putting up with my dragging him away to work on this book. A special thank you to Alan Samson, Lucinda McNeile, Jamie Tanner, Helen Ewing, Hannah Cox, Jess Gulliver, and all the sales teams at publisher Orion who worked tirelessly to ensure this book was a success. Thanks to Andy Chittock, military photographer, for your help sourcing images for the photo plates herein. To my literary agent Annabel Merullo and her assistant Laura Williams – thanks for your unflagging enthusiasm throughout. Thanks also to film agent Luke Speed, for your belief in the story getting told. Fantastic work, the lot of you!

A very special thank you to General Sir David Richards GCB CBE DSO, for the Foreword to this book: suffice to say, no better commander could a soldier ever have wished for in the field.

Last but not least I wish to thank my wife Lisa whose unfaltering support and encouragement over the past twelve months has been incredible, and to my children Maisie and Miles who have wondered why their father has been locked away in a room for so long and unable to play as often as they would have liked.

Steve Heaney MC
April 2014,
the Middle East

PHOTOS, IMAGE AND QUOTE CREDITS:

The authors and publisher are grateful to the following for permission to reproduce photographs:

Andy Chittock, 1–6, 11–12, 16–21, 30–7, 44
Peter Russell, 7–10
Kadir van Lohuizen/Noor/eyevine, 28
David Rose/Panos, 29
AFP/Getty Images, 31, 40
Travis Lupick, 38
Pep Bonet/Noor/eyevine, 39, 42
Fredrik Naumann/Panos Pictures, 41
Francesco Zizola/Noor/eyevine, 43
Malcolm Fairman/Alamy, 45

INDEX

Lachlan's War

Lachlan's War

MICHAEL CANNON

VIKING
an imprint of
PENGUIN BOOKS

VIKING

Published by the Penguin Group

Penguin Books Ltd, 80 Strand, London WC2R ORL, England

Penguin Group (USA) Inc., 375 Hudson Street, New York, New York 10014, USA

Penguin Group (Canada), 90 Eglinton Avenue East, Suite 700, Toronto, Ontario, Canada M4P 2Y3
(a division of Pearson Penguin Canada Inc.)

Penguin Ireland, 25 St Stephen's Green, Dublin 2, Ireland
(a division of Penguin Books Ltd)

Penguin Group (Australia), 250 Camberwell Road, Camberwell, Victoria 3124, Australia
(a division of Pearson Australia Group Pty Ltd)

Penguin Books India Pvt Ltd, 11 Community Centre, Panchsheel Park, New Delhi – 110 017, India

Penguin Group (NZ), cnr Airborne and Rosedale Roads, Albany, Auckland 1310, New Zealand
(a division of Pearson New Zealand Ltd)

Penguin Books (South Africa) (Pty) Ltd, 24 Sturdee Avenue, Rosebank, Johannesburg 2196, South Africa

Penguin Books Ltd, Registered Offices: 80 Strand, London WC2R ORL, England

www.penguin.com

First published 2006

1

Set in 12/14.75 pt Monotype Dante
Typeset by Rowland Phototypesetting Ltd, Bury St Edmunds, Suffolk
Printed in Great Britain by Clays Ltd, St Ives plc

A CIP catalogue record for this book is available from the British Library

ISBN-13: 978–0–670–91632–3–0
ISBN-10: 0–670–91632–3

For Denise

I

During a freezing November sunset in 1941 Dr Lachlan McCready stands near the cliff edge contemplating his final house call of the day. In his gloved right hand he holds a cigar whose tip alternately glows and dulls with the gusts and lulls of wind coming up from the bluffs. Anyone looking out from the croft would see an ember in the growing gloom that seems to pulse in time with the soft concussions of the surf below. But the curtains are drawn against the elements and the occupants wait without curiosity.

To the informed observer Dr Lachlan McCready, sporting his cigar, beard, glasses and soft felt hat, bears more than a passing resemblance to a more illustrious colleague: the father of psychoanalysis. It is not a comparison the doctor would like to think he invites, for Lachlan has as little truck with the teachings of 'the Viennese witch doctor', as he refers to him, as he does with astrology or the theory of humours. Lachlan's dismissal of Freud is one of the many robust opinions that jostle for ascendancy in the fertile mind of the old man. By the age of ten Lachlan had formed views on many things, from the Aardvark to the Zygote, and, despite an eventful and sometimes traumatic life, found little cause for revision.

'Trust a Scot to build a house in a lightless gulley,' he says, throwing his cigar in the direction of the ruminating sheep and beginning his careful descent. Talking to himself is another of Lachlan's more obvious idiosyncrasies. For the past twenty-seven years most of Lachlan's meaningful conversations have been with himself, a habit broken by an event that the evening's proceedings are destined to unfold.

The afternoon snow has hardened in the Atlantic gusts to a hard crust. The fields appear crimson, colour leached from the sky as the submerging sun draws light towards the point of its disappearance.

He knocks. The door is opened almost instantaneously. The brightness of the interior belies the outside. Perhaps they are one of the few families paying attention to regulations. There is no hall. The door lets on to the parlour. The accumulated heat from the peat fire arrests Lachlan on the threshold. The younger Mrs Dougan is waiting. 'Isabel,' he says in recognition. She greets this with a wry downward smile and an easy movement that slides the coat from his arms. All her gestures are self-deprecating. He has remarked to himself before that she seems one of life's bit players, a character whose passing would not interrupt the momentum. The older Mrs Dougan calls him from the hearth. She is a large, handsome woman with masculine features and hands once more powerful than Lachlan's. Her son bears her imprint. The difference between the two women is striking.

'I cannot believe, Morag, that I have been summoned to visit you. You will outlive us all, if we outlive this war. I would more readily believe I have been asked to prescribe a hearty meal for that daughter of yours.' This is pitched at a volume the younger woman is intended to hear. It elicits a soft laugh from the next room. And there is an implied compliment of kinship. Isabel is not Morag's daughter but her daughter-in-law.

'I know, Doctor McCready. She is a good girl. I would not have called you. Nor would she, for herself.'

Lachlan makes a pretence of examining the older woman. Both know her only illness is age, the inevitable wear of heavy work over a long life in severe conditions. Her hip is porous. The large hands are deformed by arthritis. In good weather the croft glistens with sea-blown spray. He can only guess at the pain this woman endures without complaint.

'My bones are old,' he says. Both know he is talking about her. Both know there is nothing he can do and that the pretence of a consultation has been conducted for the benefit of Isabel. The misshapen hand takes one of his.

'See what you can do for her . . .' She is not a woman accustomed to talking sotto voce and has to stop as Isabel enters from the bedroom.

'Asleep,' she confirms of her children and, embarrassed by this single utterance, takes up position behind her mother-in-law's chair.

'And the other boy, the evacuee?'

'Frank.'

'And Frank?'

'No . . .' She hesitates. He is used to patients' perception of a social gulf between himself and them. But she is an extreme case. 'I was going to ask you to look at him too . . .'

'Can you fetch him then?' And when she goes, to Morag, 'Is Murdo not here then?'

'Is he ever here, doctor.'

'Fishing?'

'At night? He is . . . wherever he is . . .'

He senses a worried exasperation with her son and will not press. He neither expected nor wanted to see Murdo, but asked for the sake of form. Isabel has returned with the boy.

'This is Frank. He came with some papers . . . I seem to have lost them . . .'

'You will make the poor boy sound like something that came with instructions. And what does Frank have to say for himself?' While saying this Lachlan makes a further pretence

3

of examining the boy, looking at his nails and palms. Running his hands down the back of the legs, he feels the hollows behind the knees. His case is obvious. He is pitifully underweight. The eyes loom unnaturally large. Shadows smudge the sockets. Lachlan notices the rhythmic facial twitches the boy seems to be attempting to suppress. He assumes they are caused by their voices in the confined space until he realizes the spasms coincide with the bangs of the breaking surf below, barely audible to him. He has seen men in France subjected to days of bombardment react like this.

'That's just it, doctor.' Isabel is animated. 'He won't talk and he won't eat. I've tried everything. I'm worried. I'm more than worried . . .'

'We both are,' Morag adds.

Lachlan takes in the obvious profile of the boy.

'Show me what you have been giving him to eat.'

He is shown to the stove where a soup practically the consistency of stew stands on the heat. Stirring with the re-linquished spoon, he dredges up the lurking bone. Standing back, he makes three instantaneous diagnoses. It is his great strength, or weakness, never to be undecided and to act with complete conviction upon his judgement. He returns to the hearth and the audience of three.

'Isabel, I want you to give Morag two and a half teaspoons of whisky in warm water each evening half an hour before she goes to bed. No more than half a cup of water, warm not boiling.' When dispensing placebos he has always found that the more elaborate and precise the directions, the greater the advantage the patient, in this case Isabel, derives. 'For you, Isabel, I prescribe at least two bowls of that hearty soup next door every day and at least two meals beside. There is more than one patient in this house. With two children and Morag

4

the last thing we need is you coming down with something. And for the boy – get his things together. I'm taking him home with me.'

The speed with which Isabel complies with his last request suggests to Lachlan more than simply the obedience he is accustomed to. He knows that her circumstances, worse than they appear, are too much for her. One less responsibility can only be a relief. She stands in front of the boy and ridiculously mimes his impending departure, pointing alternately to him and to Lachlan, clasps her hands to illustrate their new compact and walks towards the door. Without acknowledgement to her that he understands the boy disappears and returns clutching a Gladstone bag he could practically sleep in.

'Won't go anywhere without it,' Isabel nervously explains.

At the door she touches Lachlan's arm. Before he can remonstrate she has forced two cabbages on him in lieu of the fee they both know he will not accept. The boy, waiting outside, is already stamping in the cold, blowing a plume of breath through the tunnelled fingers of an ungloved hand. Awkwardly Lachlan tucks a cabbage between each elbow and his ribcage, the bag now suspended a foot from his hip. Still standing inside, Isabel points to the boy, her gesture concealed from him by the half-closed door. 'We thought . . .' she has lowered her voice, obliging Lachlan to lean indoors to hear, '. . . perhaps he is . . .' With an extended forefinger she points horizontally to her temple and rotates her wrist, as if screwing, or unscrewing, something into her skull. He infers 'touched' from the aspiration too faint for him to hear.

'We'll see.' He disagrees. Embarrassed by the presumption of her own diagnosis, she closes the door without another word. The doctor labours uphill with the boy following.

He stops feet from the car. The immobile sheep are where

he left them, now pewter against the snow. He extends both arms to let the cabbages drop and places his bag on the ground. The boy does likewise.

'One thing I cannot abide is a cabbage. A strawberry, yes. A cabbage, no. We'll keep them if you want them. Do you?' He allows sufficient time for response. 'Thought not.' He picks up the first and throws it in the direction of the sheep. It hits the snow with a dull noise and rolls a few feet down the soft declivity with a protracted crunch, leaving a compressed furrow in its wake. 'Your turn,' Lachlan mimes, with, he fancies, more inspiration than Isabel. The boy grasps what is expected of him. His first attempt does not clear the fence. Parallel ropes of snow shudder from the wires. The second is better, matching Lachlan's own with the same pleasing noise. The sheep remain petrified.

'Come here.' He guides the boy to the front of the car. Leaving him, he reaches inside, starts the engine and turns on the headlights. Overlapping cones illuminate the boy starkly, the light dissipating over the dark Atlantic. Lachlan returns to the boy. 'Don't be afraid.' Cradling the nape, he tilts the boy's face to his own, rotating the head from side to side to study the depression of the temples, the lateral planes, the occipital curve which he traces with his hand, cupping the depth. He is not making any attempt to identify the boy's ethnic group; that was done infallibly on first sight. Lachlan has his own taxonomy that has nothing to do with racial prejudice. As he casts a last dispassionate look over the face his eyes meet the boy's. He sees a weary patience in the cast of features that has come with endurance of continued scrutiny, and worse. Because there has been no complaint, or resistance, Lachlan realizes the indignity of this ad hoc examination and drops his hands apologetically. But the eyes do not disengage, and in that brief moment there is a charged

6

intensity in the exchange of something understood and reciprocated, that startles the older man enough to make him take a step backwards. He exhales two tusks of freezing air from his nostrils. The boy is shivering. The ill-fitting trousers come half-way down his calves and his legs are so thin that the ankles hang like clappers, suspended from loose cuffs.

'Get in.' Lachlan turns on the heater to revive the boy and reverses over the crest of the hill. Headlights receded, the sheep make their slow way to the cabbages.

'Isabel's husband,' Lachlan says in the warm cab. 'You probably know enough to make up your own mind. Swine of a man. Every possibility he beats the poor woman. Rumours have it he has women up and down the coast. Even although it's common knowledge he doesn't seem to have any shortage of takers. Pulls them in like line mackerel it's said. There must be something about him that makes women suspend whatever judgement they might have while he's around. Can't say I understand it. He hasn't any scruples I've ever encountered to prevent him. When he can't have women it's said he anchors at random and lands to sodomize animals. I don't know about that. Too much of a womanizer I'd say. I'm not saying he wouldn't rob a bank. Women, larceny, embezzlement – if he wasn't so stupid, smuggling – yes. But animals – I doubt it.'

He continues in this vein till the headlights sweep in a crescent to illuminate the ashlar frontage of Lachlan's house. Lights are burning within. Agnes MacLeod, the housekeeper, awaits them in the hall.

'Dinner was served twenty minutes ago.'

Lachlan knows this is nonsense. There are only two of them in the house. She wastes nothing and would not serve to an empty chair.

'Dinner is somewhere simmering and will be the better for it. Agnes, this is Frank. He is going to stay with us.'

The old lady has taken in every detail of the boy's neglected appearance within a second of him crossing the threshold. She is accustomed to Lachlan's generous caprices and accepts the new arrangement without question. In her mind she has already run the child a hot bath and is making an inventory of clothes, discarded or altered, that could be used for him till they buy more. She shakes his hand formally. When she reaches for his bag he deflects her hand with a shy shoulder.

'Run him a bath.'

'I'm glad you thought of that for me, doctor. That medical training has not gone in vain.'

'Find him some clothes.'

'And where would clothes for a poor child be found at this time of night in a house like this?'

'Buy him some clothes. Until then you can . . . improvise.'

'I dare say I can.'

'But first we feed him.'

'We?'

'No bacon, pork, or anything to do with a pig. He's starved himself rather than eat the Dougans' ham broth. God only knows what else he has endured there. No shellfish either.' He indicates to Frank that he should put the bag down and takes both the boy's hands in his. 'You are welcome here as long as you wish. No one in this house is going to make you eat anything you do not want, but you must eat.' The intensity of this exchange surprises Agnes. This arrangement is not something Lachlan would customarily get involved in. He values his privacy too much. 'Go upstairs with this lady. She will make up a bed for you. Then we will find something you will eat.'

Lachlan passes one of the boy's hands to Agnes who takes it and begins to lead him to the stairs. She is alarmed when her fingers encompass his wrist. With an inarticulate grunt he strains backwards for the Gladstone bag he can barely lift.

'You are certainly fond of your bag,' she says, brushing the fringe out of his eyes with her free hand.

'If I'm right it's all he has. What's for dinner?'

'Mussel soup, then pork escalopes.'

2

Three months before Lachlan made his clifftop house call Gail Kemble sat in a farmhouse kitchen turning her ankle this way and that to admire the clumsy silhouette of her wellington boot. With an amused detachment she notices that moist earth and what she assumes to be cow dung have cleaved to the sole. She realizes that she should have left the boots outside and with an effort slides an ankle from each and carries the parallel boots to the door. She returns to the bench and sits down heavily. A month of voluntary labour has not accustomed her to the rigours of this life. Mrs Campbell puts a cup of tea in front of her. A cigarette is already burning in the upturned hubcap they use as an improvised ashtray. Gail watches parallel columns of rising steam and smoke, framed in the daylight. Her eyes are drifting in and out of focus with a sense of warm languor she knows she cannot allow to possess her at this stage in the day.

It is mid-morning. In her previous existence this meant she would have been teaching for just over an hour. She has been up since first light and now no longer needs the dawn inventory spoken aloud. Mr Campbell concluded she was a good worker from within an hour of her arrival, in clothes entirely unsuited to the tasks she had undertaken to perform. Like Lachlan, Hamish Campbell is a man of instantaneous judgements. He keeps his own counsel. His business acumen is suspect but his psychological marksmanship is unerring. Within three days of being told the same thing each dawn, Gail interrupted Hamish on the fourth repetition to recite the list and instructions verbatim.

'You're a quick learner.'

'It's not the instructions that are taxing. I got them the first day. The only reason I didn't interrupt before now was because I thought they would vary.'

'They will.'

'To save us both time, why don't I go ahead on the understanding that I'm doing the same thing until you tell me differently?'

'I'll teach you the tractor tomorrow, if you're game.'

'I'm game.'

He had anticipated some squeamish debutante being foisted on him and his wife, a girl who would stand high-heel-deep in slurry wincing at everything. His wife has passed on the rumours about other land girls on adjacent farms. Mrs Campbell does not keep her own counsel. Rumours have it that other girls sleep till noon, awaking only to paint themselves and fornicate. He has reminded Mrs Campbell that these rumours originate from a religious quarter so extreme that prudence must be exercised. Mrs Campbell does not believe these tales any more than her husband does. She has met the young ladies in question who seem to her nothing more than high-spirited girls unfortunate enough to be billeted on puritanical fanatics. Away from home for the first time, they are intent on extracting what fun they can from their new circumstances. But rumours are the currency of the village and she can no more help herself passing them on than can the source of the rumours themselves.

She turns round from the stove at the sound of an engine entering the yard. It is not erratic enough to belong to the farm. The only engine she has heard that runs that smoothly is Dr McCready's, and no one has called him. She hears a muted exchange, tantalizingly too far out of range for her to distinguish the actual words.

'Did you hear?'

Gail, abstracted by the smoke, looks round. She had not noticed anything. Before she can answer Hamish comes in.

'There's a man from the Ministry here.'

'Tell him that if they dropped as much paperwork on the Germans they'd have surrendered by now.' The man, in a trenchcoat and shoes as unsuitable for a farmyard as those Gail first turned up in, stands behind Hamish. Eileen Campbell's comment was intended to be heard.

'He's here to talk to Gail.'

'What does she know about livestock?'

And stepping aside to allow the man access: 'I don't think he's from agriculture.'

This does indeed turn out to be the case as David Anderson introduces himself to everyone. Standing up to shake his hand, the first thing Gail notices is the perfect clarity of his accent, Inverness, she believes, eschewing the singsong cadences of the locals here. The second thing she notices is slurry on his shoes, and the third the toe protruding from the hole in her sock. He also contemplates both their feet. In mutual embarrassment they sit down and tuck their feet underneath their respective chairs. Once the obligatory tea has been offered and delivered, Hamish invites his wife to join him outside to allow the others privacy. She loiters in the hall, out of sight and within earshot. At his peremptory cough she joins him.

The man from the Ministry seems discomfited by the sudden privacy. Gail decides to help him.

'Agriculture?'

'Education.' And in a rush, to pre-empt the objection, he anticipates, 'I know you may have come here to get away from all that, get your hands dirty, make a difference . . .' He falters after his good start.

'Actually, I came here for a change.' She notices her nails are filthy and wonders if this is what he was alluding to. Dirty nails would apoplex her mother. Somehow this thought comforts her. She thinks of the forms she filled in to come here and wonders where he has unearthed the information to locate her.

'Have you carried out some kind of skills audit to find local people with experience?'

'As a matter of fact I'd never heard of you till last night in the pub. The thing is, we have a bit of a situation here.'

3

In most parts of the British Isles the prospect of conflict has involved subordinating prejudices for the common weal. The interchangeable men from the Ministry concern themselves more with quotas and national defences than the basic education of children marooned on a wind-blown promontory on the West Coast of Scotland. More urgent matters are afoot. Make do and mend is the order of the day. Here in the village of Rassaig, however, things are different.

Since anyone can remember there has been a primary school in Rassaig and another some ten miles up the coast run by Catholics. The Catholic school roll is made up from all the villages in the district that arrange transportation for the children. The segregation ends at the onset of secondary. Everyone is obliged to send their children to the same secondary school.

Mobilization stopped these arrangements. There was not the transportation or the teachers. In the cities, retired teachers were brought out of mothballs. In Glasgow and Newcastle and London old men, gaping like fish, were tormented by children they no longer had either the inclination or stamina to discipline. Myopic elderly lesbians had obscenities chalked on the back of their tweed jackets as they peered at textbooks whose font had inexplicably shrunk. In Rassaig a compromise arrangement was organized by yet another man from the Ministry. All primary pupils were lumped together in the local school. In the commandeered village hall three 'teachers' turned up every day at the ad hoc secondary school. It had a catchment area of five miles, encompassing Rassaig and two satellite villages.

The youngest of these unfortunate instructors was a fifty-five-year-old woman. The two others were men, one five years her senior, the other indescribably older than that. Each had an eclectic portfolio: the old man taught mathematics, science and all technical ramifications thereof, including wood-work; the woman taught domestic science, to perpetuate the same bondage to sink and cooker which had held her in thrall; the ancient man taught everything else, including humanities, geography, 'rhetoric' (his advertised specialty) and Scottish country dancing.

The affair was a sorry catalogue. These good people's good intentions were misconstrued, deliberately or otherwise. Word percolated back to Gavin Bone, Elder of the Free Presbyterian congregation in Rassaig, that dancing was to be taught. A strongly worded letter arrived at the 'school' suggesting that the 'unregenerate' might like to practise this 'impiety' in the privacy of their own homes. The ancient man, a God-fearing Methodist, penned a response explaining that the joyousness of dance was a celebration of God, not a denial. He went on to explain that private Scottish country dancing was in fact a contradiction in terms as a minimum of eight was normally required for a reel. His rhetorical subtleties served no purpose. Mr Bone threatened a boycott at the first sound of an accordion.

Round two consisted of the younger of the old men attempting to teach the mechanics of pollination. This was a rural community. The working population comprised mainly fishermen with a plot or farmers with a boat. No one could legitimately object. Gavin Bone loitered after hours peering suspiciously through the windows. There was something indecent in the lovingly chalked depictions of pistil and stamen.

When the old man guilelessly drew the practical analogy between the fertilization of plants and that of livestock, the Free Presbyterian community took note. The next logical progression was from the coupling of beasts to that of humans. They interrogated their children, gathering evidence. The last straw came one Friday afternoon when the ancient man, intoxicated by the prospect of two days without the drudgery of this ghastly and thankless work, gave way to his artistic bent in an attempt to raise their minds above the quotidian and intoned a 'filthy' poem by John Donne, 'combining', as was subsequently reported by a parent following interrogation of a hapless schoolboy, 'sex and geography'. A third of the class fell off the roll instantaneously. The school closed. The three teachers returned to wherever they came from. Old arrangements were restored for secondary pupils. The bus ran fifteen miles inland. The reinstated curriculum did not include rhetoric.

Against her better judgement Gail allowed herself to be persuaded into returning to the primary school classroom. She knew nothing of its new ecumenical constitution, or the tensions this entailed. Her assurances as to her shortcomings had been airily waved away. Mr Anderson seemed equally cavalier when she broached the subject of checking her credentials. Her references were never taken up. In retrospect she would realize that this should have given her a clue as to how desperate the authorities were. She reasoned to herself that there was little danger of anyone in Rassaig emerging as a prodigy. If she could shed some light on these children before war closed in still further, then so much the better. At her insistence this was to be a probationary arrangement. Mr Anderson said he would talk to the Campbells who, he was sure, would be happy to allow her to stay here. The stipend that came with the job would more than cover accommodation. There was enough space if they wanted to get more help. He was no expert, but he imagined that with the approach of winter work around the farm was probably tailing off. The Campbells would understand her services were more urgently required elsewhere. Without explaining the context, or what her duties fully entailed, he left the house telling Gail he had no doubt she would 'go down a storm'.

4

Lachlan and Frank have had a jolly day. Frank, Gladstone bag at his side, sat in the car or was invited to sit in the parlour while Lachlan attended to the prosaic round of flu, bunions and one case of particularly bad piles. Refusing to subscribe to the public assumption of Frank's imbecility, Lachlan has proceeded on the theory that treated normally, with nothing demanded of him until he shows the inclination to volunteer it, the boy will come out the end of the tunnel. He has explained his theory to Agnes, who is quick to point out that children do not *normally* accompany doctors on house calls. Nor are they privy to the kind of uncensored opinions she has overheard him pass on to the boy. For a reason he will not and cannot explain, Lachlan believes his candour is part of his compact with Frank, silently sealed during their clifftop exchange.

When Frank has gone to bed, Lachlan and Agnes have speculated as to his age. They think he is around twelve years old. He is tall enough but still underweight, although making progress. Lachlan believes the boy to be naturally slim and tells Agnes not to expect to plump him up too much. At lunchtime Lachlan took Frank to the Drovers for a pub lunch, introduced him to the locals, who expected no more from the boy than the shy stares they received, and sat with him sharing bread, Orcadian cheese and local chutney. After warming himself with a single malt Lachlan strolled back to the surgery, the warm spirit and the presence of the silent boy suffusing him with a quiet, rare happiness. He was particularly charming to his afternoon patients, especially the ladies, many of whom left thinking the old man a card and wasn't it strange he never married?

Washing his hands for the final time, Lachlan leaves the surgery and goes to find Frank in the lounge.

'Get your coat on.'

Being modest, Lachlan's domestic needs demand no more than a tidy house, clean clothes and a good dinner. Consequently Agnes has no one on whom to lavish the attention brimming in her surfeit heart. Her husband is long dead. She has two adult children. Her son has been in the merchant navy since the close of the last war. In her mind he is floating somewhere in a dark expanse that, in sleep, she cannot disassociate from purgatory. Restrictions being what they are, letters carrying exotic postmarks arrive erratically, like wind-blown spores. Her daughter 'emigrated' to Leeds fifteen years ago and is engrossed, the way Agnes was at her age, holding a family together. So Agnes has been prodigal in her attentions to Frank. When Lachlan tells him to get his coat on the boy, for the first time in a long while, is presented with the dilemma of choice. Within a week of his arrival at Lachlan's he is fully equipped. All his clothes are comfortable and expensive. Missing nothing, Lachlan notices the ease with which he wears these, seemingly accustomed to the best.

Taking his stick, Lachlan strides out the front door and points up the hill. They walk together in the gathering dark, Frank lumbering with the inevitable Gladstone bag, the lights of the village winking on around them. It takes half an hour to reach the summit, a wind-blown ridge that gives a prospect of the crescent bay they have just left. To the right there is a small harbour, illuminated at this distance by a dim necklace of lights. To the extreme left a barely visible jetty is being absorbed into the dark sea.

'People here don't pay much attention to the restrictions.

I've yet to see a warden around these parts. Rationing doesn't bite either. Not so as you'd notice.' Holding his stick horizontally, he bisects their view of the village. 'If you were to take a line from the point of this stick to the sea you'd notice there is a little corridor of darkness. It's not that there are no houses that have put on their lights, it's that there are no houses. That's because what we call one village has been two settlements that have grown towards each other but can't consummate the marriage.' Lachlan laughs at his own little joke. Frank stares at the scene before him.

'Moses must have felt like this separating the waves. From here to the harbour lives everyone not of the same persuasion as those from here to the jetty. It's not an absolute division but it's a good enough generalization. The harbour lot comprise a large proportion of Catholics who, as far as I can see, seem to think they have a monopoly on guilt. From here to the jetty are our Free Presbyterians. They sit in their buttoned-up Sundays frowning across the abyss. They live with the abiding fear that somebody, somewhere, is having a good time. As far as I can tell their only consolation is in the fact that those who are not the elect get their eternal comeuppance. They can sit upstairs and see everyone else cook. It's a bit like watching the Sunday roast, except it goes on for ever. It's a grim theology. I've never yet managed to find whether all of them think themselves the elect. If you're not, why bother?' By this time Lachlan is thinking aloud. Taking stock, he turns to the boy. 'The rest of the world is on fire and this lot from the jetty sit stoking a dislike for their neighbours just because they commit the cardinal sin of trying to enjoy themselves. The other mob has people just as bad. People are dying all over Europe to defend the freedom most locals here take for granted, and look what they do with their liberty. Honest to God . . .'

5

Lucy Vernon and Harriet Pearsall are getting ready for a night out. They are the other two land girls in Rassaig. The Campbells, who accommodate Gail, are people of firm convictions, the strongest of which is tolerance. Gail has never fully appreciated how fortunate she is, having never seen the adopted domestic circumstances of the other two. Lucy and Harriet are not permitted visitors.

Lucy and Harriet have had the misfortune to be billeted on the McHargs, Ewan and his wife Elsbeth. It is from the McHargs that Gavin Bone receives much of his intelligence, generating the rumours of slovenly 'foreign' girls of easy virtue.

Lucy's behaviour does little to scotch these rumours. It is Saturday and she is adamant she is going out. Harriet, weary, would be happy with a good book and an early night. She has been persuaded by her friend to make the effort. Ewan McHarg is standing just outside the gloomy room the girls have been given. Lucy is confronting him, arms akimbo.

'You want a bath *again?*' He succeeds in sounding both incredulous and aggrieved.

'Again.'

'Both?'

'We're not livestock. We need more than a bath a week.'

'There are restrictions, you know.'

'I'm from London, dearie. You don't have to talk to me about restrictions. I haven't noticed you and the missus practise them.'

Somehow he feels there is something indecent in her mentioning anything to do with him and Mrs McHarg as a couple, although, as God and the long, long nights are his witness, there is nothing indecent in Mrs McHarg.

'It is right to be frugal.'

'Cleanliness is next to godliness. Isn't that what your mob say?'

He dislikes mention of God from her mouth even more than mention of himself and his wife.

'You'll have to share then,' and quickly, as an afterthought, 'one at a time!' He does not want rumours of impropriety although he has often furtively wondered what two naked young women would look like together. Even if they stood immobile with no part of one touching any part of the other, Ewan believes that two naked women would be more than twice as alluring, and therefore pernicious, as a single naked woman. There is an erotic synergy here that can only be the work of the Devil.

'Fair enough,' Lucy concedes, and turning to Harriet without closing the door, 'first or second?'

'First, if you don't mind.'

'All the same to me.'

Ten minutes later, lying back in the shallow bath, Harriet coils her hair and secures it above her head, thinking how it could never be all the same to her. She cannot imagine consenting to use someone else's bath water. From her brief acquaintance she has come to like Lucy but recognizes something blowsy in her.

Five minutes after that, the evening feed distributed, Ewan McHarg sits in his room adjacent to the bathroom, clenched fists trembling. From the soft lapping he can imagine the larger, darker of the two girls, not the mock blonde tart from London, soaping herself in the next room. She has legs as long as a horse's. He has washed a horse's legs before. And applied a poultice. The little blonde is blonder than she was two days ago. Before that a dark crevice outlined her centre parting. Does this mean she would have a dark cleft? No doubting the colour of the taller girl. That brunette delta is probably being soaped at this very minute. It is true; the Devil is in the detail. 'Begone!' he pants and forces himself to think of Mrs McHarg.

An hour later the girls have left, lily of the valley wafting from their room. He can hear their voices recede as they walk towards the Drovers. Locking the bathroom door behind him, his minute examination of the soap can only disclose one pubic hair, a corrugated grey follicle whose provenance, by elimination, can only be traced to Mrs McHarg.

Lucy has arranged for them to meet Gail in the Drovers. It is this that has prompted Harriet to go. She feels an affinity with the quieter girl. With Lucy it is the demand of their daily rota, of having always a task to hand, that keeps them companionable. She thinks three unchaperoned hours of Lucy would be too much. Feeling guilty at entertaining such a thought, she slips her arm through the younger woman's and they walk on, Lucy singing softly in the dark. They reach a junction in the main street. The Drovers is a hundred yards up the hill.

'I'll catch you up.'

Thinking Lucy has to pull her stocking up or somehow put herself to rights to make an entrance, Harriet says she will wait.

'No. Honestly. I'll catch you up.'

'What? You expect me to go into the pub on my own?'

'You won't be on your own. Gail will be there.'

'How do you know?'

'I asked her to be there half an hour ago.'

'So she's on her own?'

'I don't see what the problem is, being on your own in a pub.'

'Because we're comparative strangers here. Some women don't like sitting on their own in a bar. I don't. It invites comment.'

'Who gives a fuck about comment? If you're that worried you'd better not leave Gail alone.' Harriet is too angry to answer. Failing to notice, Lucy stretches up and kisses her, leaving a smudge. Laughing, she licks her hanky and wipes off the offending mark. She turns and disappears in the direction of the harbour, heels clicking into the dark. Harriet turns and walks up the hill.

Gail is smoking a cigarette and talking animatedly to Lachlan, who stands to admit the other girl to their company and goes to the bar to fetch them all a drink.

'Lucy left me at the junction.'

'I wonder why?' Both girls laugh.

Lucy clicks her way down the hill to the harbour. Douglas Leckie is waiting for her near the stairs. Laughing, she touches him.

'Not here.'

'Where then?'

He guides her down the steps. The oars plash softly towards his fishing boat.

'I wish they'd observe the restrictions and keep these lights down.'

'Worried about a U-boat, or your wife?'

He rows determinedly on. She laughs at his silence. He clambers aboard the small fishing boat and helps her on deck. He gestures her down the stairs. She expected an overpowering smell of fish but the cramped space smells of tobacco and engine oil. In one corner is a rumpled bunk. She is aroused at the lack of anything remotely feminine. Having been silently purposeful in bringing her here he looks hesitatingly around, as if thinking of a suitable preamble. She pre-empts him by lifting her dress over her head and stepping out of her pants.

As Gail returns the favour by overriding Lachlan and standing the next round, Lucy lies, eyes closed, cupped palms beneath her crooked knees, pulling her thighs progressively wider. Soft eddies radiate from the gently heaving craft and she too is carried out in accumulating spasms. Experience having taught her to keep quiet, she exhales a whistling climax, eyes suddenly opening to her vicarious partner. Douglas, transfixed in mid-thrust, feels she is surprised to find him at the other end of his member.

'Go on, lover,' she encourages. But the damage is done. He withdraws. She smokes a cigarette to give him time to collect himself. She lets him know she is prepared to go again, but by this time he is already climbing the three steps to the deck. As they row back he tries to keep the urgency from his voice.

'When can I see you again?'

'Anytime. Pop over. Those miserable bastards won't have you in the house but you can find me knee-deep in shit any day of the week.' They both know it is not what he meant but she is already preoccupied, thinking ahead to the next thing as she always is: the bar, the faces, her friends.

6

Lachlan's first emergency call out at Rassaig, twenty years previously, exemplified the philosophy he had formulated on life and death and the professional manner in which he would conduct himself thereafter. It was a breezy September afternoon. He saw the two vehicles clearly on the metalled road that bisected an expanse of gorse receding on either side into the autumnal distance. The police car sat squarely on the road, the other vehicle at a tangent, half askew in the ditch. One policeman, the more senior of the two, was leaning into the vehicle through the passenger window, talking to the prostrate figure behind the wheel. His younger colleague stood in the middle of the road looking completely redundant. As Lachlan approached he saw the younger man vomit. Lachlan drove round the hunched policeman and sticky pool and came to a halt beside the damaged vehicle. As he reached across for his bag he noticed the truncated telegraph pole, like a large exclamation mark, tilting from the impact, push up and out from the number plate of the other car.

He took two careful minutes before coming to a decision. From the smashed window on the driver's side he could see across the seat to the policeman, stroking the driver's shoulder, speaking soft, reassuring nonsense. The snapped portion of the telegraph pole radiated out from the smashed pelvis like some grotesque erection, through the mutilated steering wheel and out the space where the windscreen had been. The pulse was weak and erratic but unmistakably there. Infinitesimal noddings of the drooping head suggested a man who had fallen asleep over his newspaper. With a sure movement Lachlan took out a large syringe and a bottle of morphine.

'What are you doing?'

'Killing him. For some reason, God in His boundless mercy, having seen fit to allow this man to become impaled, has decided to revive him long enough to let him appreciate that the rest of his short life will be spent in excruciating pain.'

The policeman looked as if he was about to remonstrate and thought better of it. He watched as Lachlan administered as much fluid as he had only seen injected into a cow before. The nodding stopped. Lachlan continued to feel the pulse till it failed. Reaching deftly into the inside breast pocket Lachlan retrieved a wallet. He flicked it open on the dented bonnet, inspecting the card that first disclosed itself. The man is some kind of agricultural salesman, animal feed and fertilizers Lachlan expects. That would explain the samples strewn on the back seat. Rifling further, he discovered cash and what he suspected would be there and hoped not to find: a photograph. The salesman is standing with his hands on the shoulders of the woman seated before him, presumably his wife. His hair looks as if it has been painted on and reflects light. His suit is formal, the collar restrictive. They both wear unnatural smiles, poised erectly like a Victorian couple in contrived arrange-ment, held by unseen struts for the long exposure. On the woman's lap is an infant, the head outlined by a ghostly second image, recording the child's movement before the closing shutter froze them.

Lachlan McCready was born in Morningside, Edinburgh, on 14 December 1877. A late and only child of conscientious and loving parents, he was given every advantage their reasonable means could provide. His father, an insurance loss adjuster who rose through the ranks by means of diligence and a reputation for integrity, wanted to ensure that his son enjoyed the professional standing he felt his own indeterminate status lacked. Lachlan was christened, both parents being regular if not devout worshippers. He was educated at one of the private merchants' schools, the fees requiring of his parents sacrifices both were happy to make. Happy, confident and precocious, Lachlan found little to tax him academically. His father wanted him to read law but didn't demur at his son's preferred option. Lachlan matriculated at Edinburgh University Medical School in 1895, graduating some seven years later. During his studies he lived in rented accommodation, the darling of a species of genteel elderly Edinburgh landladies who rented to 'proper' young people. Unbeknown to him his parents, on a dwindling income, retained the house they could no longer afford in anticipation of his possible return. They entertained expectations of him as a young intern, with a younger wife and child who would stay with them while their son worked every hour God sent, as young interns do. They would help with the grandchildren till Lachlan achieved the status when he could delegate and take over the responsibility they had gladly adopted.

His easygoing manner concealed a naturally introspective side to Lachlan's nature. His ready wit ensured he made friends easily and he had a reputation for gregariousness he neither deserved nor sought.

A few of his University friends with artistic leanings tore from themselves angst-ridden poetry of the worst sort. He observed everything and said little about what mattered most. While members of the gregarious circle he moved in discussed politics, female emancipation, sex, religion, Madame Blavatsky and anything else that exercised their young minds, he wondered why it was that they failed completely to discuss something that occupied his.

It took some time for Lachlan to realize that not everyone

saw things in the same way he did. He had been born with the visual equivalent of perfect pitch, a facility to recognize beauty in the most obscure configurations. Clutter could be exquisite. He experienced the same sensation observing recesses disclosed by the scalpel on the dissecting table as he did watching the mist clear from the Forth. Where others saw in terms of function he viewed from an additional perspective. The striae of separated muscle fibres, his landlady's blue jug glimpsed through the half-open door on his way out, the skittish intelligence in the horse's liquid eye as it strained in the traces all afforded him the same joy. He became accustomed to but not complacent about this faculty, and once he realized it existed in many others only to a diluted extent, or not at all, he never spoke about it.

His father fell ill. The prognosis did not require a medical degree. Lachlan was grateful his father remained alive long enough to see him graduate. His mother died within a year. He never knew the fantasy he failed to fulfil. Settling his parents' affairs, he did come to appreciate the financial sacrifices they had made. The day he buried his mother he came to appreciate emotionally what he had apprehended, if at all, only as a fact: that in the natural order of things we are born to be orphaned. He thought himself stupid to have arrived at such an obvious conclusion so late.

His sense of calm was infectious, his tranquil manner pacifying those he came in contact with. He thrived on the constant duress of instantaneous decision-making that agitated others to the point of stupefaction. He preferred the succession of often mortal dilemmas to plotting the prognosis of slow recuperation or gradual decline. His exposure to women had been limited to chaperoned visits in their genteel lodgings, or faculty parties he attended to humour friends. He had few female acquaintances. He spent two years doing relief work in Africa and the next eight years working in the hospitals of Edinburgh and its environs, steadily scaling the ladder. He was not ambitious; this seemed a logical progression given his expertise and a natural gravitas he had acquired. Contemporaries married off and consigned him to the category of confirmed bachelor. He drank in moderation most evenings, read voraciously and socialized when the mood took him.

During an early autumn evening in 1912 Lachlan walked the length of the New Town terrace, flowers in one hand, a bottle of Chablis in the other. The flowers are for the two hostesses, the Misses Crawford. The wine is for him, to make the evening more palatable. He is fulfilling his duty as a past tenant, an obligation he is called upon to dispatch once every few years. The Misses Crawford have a new quota of 'guests'. In order to break the ice, and set the tone, they invite selected past tenants to an evening buffet to meet the latest intake. Turning round at the door, he takes in the concertinaed perspective of the terrace, a succession of oriel windows giving back the light in receding increments, the short walk eliciting a catalogue of memories.

He is roused from his thoughts by the door being opened. He has not even rung the bell. The Misses Crawford beam from the threshold. They have been awaiting his arrival. At thirty-five he realizes he is the elder statesman. The demands of children have excused the contemporaries he used to meet here. He remembers a previous incumbent who occupied this role, an awkward bachelor who obviously couldn't say no, who failed to hide chronic shyness behind the paraphernalia of his pipe, who sucked and puffed and spluttered and was terrified by the twenty-year abyss that separated him from the ranks of the young. Lachlan walked into the lounge prepared to outdo this uninspiring prototype, to be pleasant and bored. Among the petrified bric-a-brac he has unconsciously committed to memory he sees younger incarnations of himself and, to his astonishment, women.

He teases the Misses Crawford about their moral erosion. 'Women guests! If only in my time.' They exchange a look with each other and laugh in unison, 'That Doctor McCready!' They enjoy being scandalized. He knows they will police the sleeping arrangements with Prussian ruthlessness. He is introduced to some of the young ladies. He hadn't expected suffragettes and he wasn't disappointed. Most of them struck him as female equivalents of all the male guests the Misses Crawford had ever entertained. They are young and clean and wholesome women destined, in five years, to partner the same kind of young and clean and wholesome men they are currently rubbing shoulders with. One woman stands slightly apart. She is the only woman smoking. She looks only slightly less young than the others but this, and her air of rueful tolerance towards the young man at her side, stammering through a long anecdote, marks her out.

'Our Kate,' says Miss Crawford, seeing him observe her. This is said at a volume intended to introduce the two. The woman looks up. Lachlan smiles and, obliged by the introduction, crosses the gap. The young man is now caught in a dilemma: should he limply abandon the anecdote or go for the quick conclusion? He knows no better than to try and finish. The presence of the composed-looking older man at his side aggravates the stammer. Lachlan finds himself contemplating the carpet, knowing from experience that the more attention is focused on the poor boy, the worse things will become. He casts around looking for a diversion but the room has grown quiet. The boy, now aware that he has become the centre of attention, is paralysed. A succession of consonants escapes him. There is an elaborate little stand at Lachlan's side supporting a grotesque vase. Calculating that it can withstand the concussion on the carpet, Lachlan decides to put the boy out of his misery and kick the stand. His foot collides with hers as she beats him to it. The ensuing confusion releases the boy. The stand is put to rights, her apologies waved away, general conversation restored.

'You left the vase intact,' Lachlan says to her.

'I'll get it next time. Are you a relative?' He cannot place her accent.

'Why would you assume that?'

'You're younger than Jean and Doris and older than everyone else.'

'Kate smokes,' says one of the Misses Crawford, interrupting with the tiered sandwich plate. 'That's London for you.'

'Kate thought I was related to you. I could be your son, or Doris's.'

Doris, circulating with an identical plate, is waved across by Jean to share the joke. 'That Doctor McCready!' they say, and separate.

'Previous lodger. I've been asked back for tonight to keep the tone. You seem to have your feet under the table: it took me two years to be on first-name terms.'

'If you were here for two years why didn't you get rid of the vase?'

'You should have seen the place when I arrived.' He feels her cigarette is a prop. She seems to advertise a confidence he is sure she does not feel. But then, he reflects, he cannot know how composed he appeared at her age. 'Do you have a second name, Kate?'

'Roddick. Do you have a first name, doctor?'

'Lachlan.' The preliminaries dispensed with, an uneasy silence falls. He fails to understand why this happens and is irritated. He is a socially adroit man in his mid-thirties who delivers traumatic news daily. She looks like a composed young woman. Then he realizes what bothers him. He likes her; more, he is attracted to her, and her face is beginning to adopt the same expression of rueful tolerance she directed at the stuttering boy. On point of principle he determines to stay until he breaks the ice, but immediately he is called away.

'Duty calls . . .' Even saying it he is aware it sounds limp.

'Don't let me detain you.' Her smile seems genuine. He wonders if she is being ironic.

He is shuffled by the Misses Crawford to meet a series of young people and finds himself saying the kind of thing he might have ascribed to the pipe-smoking predecessor. It was never this difficult before. He is aware she is watching him from the other side of the room and puts his woeful performance down to this. When she leaves the room he is relieved. When she fails to return within half an hour he is piqued. He eats a desultory sandwich and when he turns back for another finds the students have devoured everything.

Within another hour the soirée is breaking up. The food is gone, the night is young, the students are hungry. The Misses Crawford hand him back his unopened wine at the door. They brook no denial. 'House rules. No alcohol. Surely you remember, Doctor McCready?'

'There were no women here either at one time. Perhaps you're introducing vices gradually.'

'That Doctor McCready!'

Kate is standing on the raised step on the other side of the front door, unlit cigarette in hand. He is hesitant to hope she is waiting for him.

'Can you stand here for a minute?'

'Of course.' He is perplexed by a sense of pleasant apprehension.

'If you stand there they can't see me smoke from the hall.'

'They don't mind you smoking in the house.'

'They think smoking in the street is common. I must say,' she lights the cigarette and extinguishes the match in one of the potted plants, 'I agree.'

He laughs and finds he has nothing to say to this vital, smiling young woman.

'I was told you were a catch,' she says.

'I think of a catch as something that breathes its last on the ground.'

She exhales the next question with the smoke while studying the half-buried match. 'Are you still hungry?' He can see from her false preoccupation that she is nervous and is heartened by this.

'I didn't think about it. Yes, I suppose I am.'

'Would you like to take me to dinner?'

'Yes.'

'I'll get my shawl.'

'No, allow me.' There is no need. The door opens and a disembodied arm belonging to one of the Misses Crawford hands the shawl out. He turns to Kate, suspecting collusion, but there is no mistaking the surprise on her face. As the door gently closes they both laugh. He offers his arm.

She is a nurse, working in Edinburgh to avoid the pitfall of growing up and dying in the same postal district. He walks her back home after dinner. The door is locked. She has not been given a key and is obliged to ring. Both Misses Crawford beam from the other side of the open door at the fruition of their scheme. He is obliged to say goodbye more quickly and formally than he intended, his airy 'Good evening' incorporating all three. Only later, walking away, does he realize he has made no arrangements for their next meeting.

He equivocates for two days and finally telephones. He is surprised when she answers and is caught flat-footed by her response.

34

'Why did you wait so long?'

'I . . . I wasn't entirely sure you wanted to hear from me.'

'I asked you out last time.'

'Strictly speaking, that's not true. You asked me if I wanted to take you out.'

'You should be a solicitor, or a Jesuit.'

She is armed with a key when he next walks her home. They have the luxury of the hall to themselves for two minutes before one of the Misses Crawford walks the diagonal length from lounge to back stairs and nods gentle encouragement to the doctor as she disappears. He would not presume to test the security. If they wanted complete privacy they have his flat. He knows from Kate's behaviour that she will not be constrained by social rules she considers absurd, but, despite her sometimes flip manner, there is a seriousness to her that touches a similar chord in him and precludes him from making any suggestion that they sleep together.

She stops smoking. Unoccupied, her hands flutter. Something of this nervousness communicates itself to him. Walking in the Botanic Gardens, he kisses her on impulse and only succeeds in restraining himself from telling her he loves her. That night, alone, he analyses his feelings. He is of the opinion that 'love' must be the most abused word in the language, debased by common coinage. He will never use it inappropriately. The following afternoon he tells her he loves her.

They marry that winter. She is ten years his junior but looks younger. Both are virgins, brought together, as he puts it, by the well-intentioned connivance of older virgins still. It was a kind calculation. The first time he saw her naked was their wedding night. She stood, her clothes on the floor around her, inviting assessment. He took in the flare of her pelvis and, kneeling, pressed his face to her stomach.

They conceived quickly. It was part of their plan to start a

35

family as soon as they could. Coming home, late and tired, he would nightly run his hands over the protuberance of her belly, inventing features of their baby he claimed his clairvoyant examination revealed. He marvelled at her green-veined breasts, the beauty of her gravid movements.

As her time approached her desire to be near her mother outlived her fear of parochialism. They moved to London. He met her family, visiting as often as his punishing hours would allow. They held a doctor of his seniority in some awe.

He is urgently summoned home. She has had a discharge. She sits in the lounge looking stricken. He draws the curtains. When his clairvoyant hands fail to detect any movement he adopts a professional manner. She had anticipated a consolatory smile and hopeful news. She starts to cry. She is vomiting before the ambulance arrives, her pulse shallow, her respiration quick. Their baby died before it saw the light of day. She developed septicaemia before the dead foetus would abort. From being the provider of a family he overnight became a widower of considerable means. It was 1914. The looming conflict seemed somehow pertinent to the context of his life. His sense of beauty abandoned him.

In 1916 Lachlan stands at the tent entrance watching the stretchered ranks being laid out. 'You're only allowed to die in straight lines around here.' He is musing aloud to himself but within earshot of the orderly. The man makes no response. Looking across at him, Lachlan recognizes in the almost granular complexion a weariness that surpasses even his own. He hands the orderly his flask. Those of Lachlan's rank do not like this fraternizing. They see it as bad for morale. Whatever idea Lachlan has had of his place in any hierarchy disappeared with Kate's death. Noises have been made. He has been told that one of his seniority need not attend, personally, to all the wounded. The cover is so makeshift, the conditions so brutally inadequate that he has wondered if they are being ironic. What do they know? So he has shrugged at their hints. If they persist he is prepared to be bullish. 'What else would I do?' he has astonished his senior officer by saying, and, nodding towards the tents, 'I will stay here.'

He has a reputation for macabre humour. He has seen some terrible things, but nothing that he considered worse than the sight of his dead wife with their dead baby inside her. He will not explain his motives for refusing to leave, that he is not here to help forget but to honour her memory by occupying himself and not giving way to despair. What strikes him at the field hospitals is not the severity of the injuries, or the number of casualties, but the sheer arbitrariness of death. Fortune does not favour the brave. To be first is to be foolhardy. Reticence is no guarantee of safety either. And among the battalions of dead and mutilated he formulates the philosophy that is to inform his professional behaviour for the rest of his life: not the preservation of life but the annihilation of pain.

He had not inherited his parents' comfortable and modest leanings towards religion. Nor was he convinced to the contrary. In a thicket of otherwise fixed opinions Lachlan was prepared to be guided by a healthy scepticism and convinced by convincing arguments of either persuasion. It was not his personal tragedy, but the sheer aggregate of human suffering he witnessed that convinced him. Pain as a warning, a deterrent, he could understand. But motiveless pain that did not warn, did not aid recuperation and was presented to him daily in all its various guises, dispelled any thought he had had of a benevolent overseer. He lost patience with the chaplains.

'Are you a Catholic?'

'Anglican, sir.'

'Are there any other denominations here?'

'You mean among the men?'

'Of course I don't.'

'There are Baptist chaplains, but none that I know of assigned here.'

'So what happens if you're a dying Baptist?'

'We all worship the same God.'

'But not in the same way. It seems to me that although you say that, you all think the other has got it slightly wrong. If they haven't, then why are you different?'

'I don't quite see it that way, sir.'

'And the more extreme, the more exclusive.'

He waits for an answer that does not come and realizes he is being unfair. Even if the chaplain has an answer, he cannot give it. Lachlan has rank on his side.

His restraint didn't last. Three days later the inadequacies of the field hospital were made manifest when the dead and dying began to arrive in numbers he hadn't seen before and no one had planned for. The first arrived in ambulances and continued to come in vans, horse-drawn carts and any form of transportation commandeered for the purpose. Lachlan took charge. The logistics of the situation demanded a brutal assessment. The most severe and those certain to die stayed. The rest he ordered moved on, knowing many might not survive the juddering ride. The field hospital was now wildly beyond capacity. Further casualties would have to be diverted elsewhere. The dying were given as much relief as he could administer. The most severe cases were treated as best they could. At the sound of commotion he left the makeshift theatre to find chaos outside the tent. Trucks had continued to arrive. Either his orders had not been carried out or the drivers had refused to go on. The whole compound was littered with wounded. A junior doctor was shouting at a driver. Lachlan strode across. Both fell silent at his approach. The driver's eyes seemed unnaturally bright against the grime of his face.

Looking at him, Lachlan recognized the symptoms. The man seemed capable of shooting anyone.

'Are there any more wounded coming?'

'How the fuck should I know? Ask the Kaiser.'

The other doctor interrupted. 'We're told this is all we are going to get.'

'We were told that after the first arrivals. Get on the telephone. Find out what you can,' Lachlan said, and, turning to the driver, 'sit down somewhere. Have a drink.'

'No time.' The man swung himself back into the seat and drove out of the compound.

More casualties continued to arrive until drivers, seeing the hopeless confusion, took the initiative and drove on. Medical supplies ran out. They were reduced to carrying round water and applying primitive first aid to those lying on the ground. They worked through the night, carrying lights. Dawn disclosed figures, like Lachlan, moving between the injured with the same sense of numbing fatigue. In this half-light everybody seemed to be shading into death.

Among the medical staff he noticed a Catholic chaplain, administering extreme unction. The soldier the chaplain now kneels over is no more than ten feet away. He is obviously dead, his young face contorted in a rictus of pain. Laying his bag on the ground, the priest removes a small bottle, sketches a cross over the dead soldier's forehead and anoints the eyes, ears, lips, nostrils and hands.

'I thought you only did that when they were dying, not dead.'

The chaplain looks across. He looks scarcely older than the soldier. Lachlan is perplexed. He had expected someone older to assume such responsibility.

'Don't you realize that five miles that way German priests are doing the same thing over their dead?'

'I certainly hope so, sir.'

For the first time in his adult life Lachlan shouts, pointing at the corpse.

'Dear God! What kind of an expression is that to face annihilation with?'

'Sir, if you'd like we can step inside the tent.'

'Don't patronize me! Not only do you say the same words when they're dying, you invoke the same God as those others over there to justify them killing one another.'

The chaplain's expression infuriates him. He realizes he is being treated with the same circumspection as the insubordinate driver, on the verge of snapping. He turns away. The chaplain kneels over the soldier again and resumes his prayer.

The war ended. He returned to London. He still had accommodation with all his effects there. But there were no ties to renew. Kate's relatives treated him with renewed respect. He was now also a veteran. He and they only succeeded in reminding one another of the woman who wasn't there. He packed up on a whim, left instructions to the estate agent to sell up, and took the overnight train to Edinburgh. He realized his mistake as he walked out the grimy cavern of Waverley. His friends had changed, but not as much as him. He looked for a bolt hole and found the vacancy in Rassaig for which he was ludicrously overqualified. He told the few taken into his limited confidence that this was a temporary arrangement till he decided what to do. He bought a car and left a forwarding address.

He drove north-west, from one coastline towards another. Consulting the map, he found no distinguishable landmarks. This was reflected in the view of nothing beyond the circumference of moorland that moved with him through the mist. As late-morning sun began to penetrate, the air seemed to grow luminous. For no reason he could explain he stopped. Beside the cooling engine the silence was complete, the space within visible radius charged. He waited, not knowing why. The mist quickly lifted. Overnight pools had gathered. The earth was tawny and purple with gorse and heather. With no reason for deviation the road disappeared into vanishing point. As the last wreath drew up to evaporation Lachlan found himself standing on a metalled strip like a placed ribbon across a mosaic of flashing groundwater. His sense of beauty returned in a cascade of sensations and he was lacerated with the thought that she was not there to share it with him.

The temporary arrangement, that had lasted for twenty years when Lachlan made his clifftop house call, was a period that only established its full continuity in retrospect. For the first few years he still contemplated moving, but the alternatives that presented themselves paled beside Rassaig. He became addicted to its austere beauty. The work was not difficult. Most of the locals were appreciative and accepting. He was assimilated before he knew it. Without making any attempt to socialize he had a vacant place held for him most nights in the Drovers, that he came willingly to occupy more often than not. His friends were mostly fishermen and farm labourers, the local postman and, after a wary probation, Brendan Keenan, the Catholic priest.

His first half-dozen meetings with Brendan consisted of tersely polite exchanges in the Drovers. The ice was broken by their first professional exchange. Nagged to make an appointment, he sat across from Lachlan in the surgery watching the doctor contemplate his blood pressure.

'I could tell you to drink less.'

'You could. And I could tell you to make a novena. And which of us is more likely to follow the advice? We only ever meet in the Drovers. If I do what you say we're never likely to see one another again. Do you ever take your own blood pressure?'

'I'm not the one who made an appointment.'

'Do you know the one about pots and kettles, Lachlan?'

'If you don't pray for me, I won't nag you.'

'Done.'

He knew that most of his medical school contemporaries would have thought he had sold himself short, a man of his talents languishing in a village prey to the vagaries of the Atlantic, discussing mackerel quotas and the purity of breeding strains, but he did not care. In the quiet of this backwater he came to a slow and private reconciliation with himself.

Every evening he avidly read the newspaper, his reading accompanied by a running commentary Agnes learned quickly to ignore. He watched Nazi predations with a sense of dread, and regretfully acknowledged that on this topic he agreed with Churchill. His occasional sortie to the cinema served only to fuel his indignation. It was here, in the Pathé News reports, that he saw footage of Chamberlain waving his pathetic slip of paper. It was here that he listened to the strident propaganda of Dunkirk and wondered if he was the only one in the audience, or nation, to understand what the euphemisms presaged. The day he sat beside the radio and listened to Chamberlain announce a state of war he looked out of the window and wondered if any of the poor bastards around here had the faintest idea what this really meant.

Staring into the fire, he did some thinking. Coming back from France he had passed through some of those sad English shires. The devastation of a generation of young men coming to grief was bad enough in the cities; it had utterly destroyed some of the rural communities. Looking around, he took inventory and realized what conscription would entail for Rassaig. If he was correct, the conflagration that was about to burst over Europe could swallow a thousand times over the complement of men this village could provide and their sacrifice would not matter one iota in the general scheme of things. He knew that if everyone thought likewise the darkness would spread, unopposed. He decided that short of falsifying medical records and telling outright lies he would do what he could for the men of this village, especially the younger fathers. The country needed food, now more than ever. Many already worked in reserved occupations and he used what patronage he had to have others similarly employed. The more adamant refused his help. Some did not wait for conscription. He had seen this patriotic fervour before and saw them off with an outward smile, shaking their hands, wishing them well, advising caution, taking silent inventory of their health and strength, the proportion of their intact limbs, and all the while remembering the stretchered ranks, skin bags of excrement and viscera, slipping away before he or the chaplains could get to them.

Nightly he read. Kristallnacht. Czechoslovakia falls. Poland is carved up. Hints of euthanasia in Germany. News of rationing introduced. Scapa Flow bombed. Denmark, Norway, France, Belgium, Luxembourg and the Netherlands all capitulate or fall. Something filthy has been spilled that darkly blots the map as it spreads. U-boats sink merchant shipping. Families atomized by blitzkrieg while men flail in freezing water.

And nightly he would go to his eyrie, the vantage point he had taken Frank to, and he would look at the scene before him and wonder how long this fragile tranquillity would last.

7

'And this is Miss Kemble. She has come a long way to help. Can we show our appreciation as we practised?'

'Good morning, Miss Kemble.' It is a ragged salvo. She thinks they cannot have practised much. Having dispensed with the introductions, the man from the Ministry rubs his hands redundantly and departs on the pretext of leaving her to it.

'Leaving me to it,' she repeats to herself. To what? She has been taken aback by this denuded, makeshift classroom. She cannot remember what she expected but she knows it wasn't this. She also knows this is not the time to equivocate: this vital first hour is crucial to obtain their confidence and respect.

'We won't start with the register. We'll start with each of you introducing yourself, since I've already been introduced to you.'

'Miss, why do you talk funny?'

'I don't find it funny. My accent is different because I come from another part of the country. Another country in fact.'

'Miss, are you a filthy Hun?'

'Miss, he talks funny and he's from here.'

'You can talk.'

'Yes, I can.'

'Your big sister's the town bike.'

It is a little boy and girl who are arguing. It is the girl's sister who has been insulted. She thinks they are both too young to understand what they are saying.

'Quiet, both of you.' But the dialogue continues and threatens to bring in those on the periphery. She claps her hands, the sound louder than she had anticipated, reverberating in this empty space. All the children immediately fall silent, some alarmed, the gesture more potent than she expected.

'We won't use the word "Hun" in here. We'll use "German" and we won't call them filthy. Not all Germans can be held responsible for what some of them are doing.' And to the boy, 'Your behaviour was ungentlemanly.' They giggle at her choice of words. 'Apologize for what you said.'

'Your sister's not the town bike. She was but my dad says it's that English girl now.'

Gail turns away, frowning. They do not understand what they are saying and order has been restored. How upset would Lucy be knowing her reputation is common currency? She spends the rest of the morning getting them to talk about themselves. From this brief assessment she believes that she has here the same mixture of abilities she has encountered in half a dozen classes. Some of the children are very poorly dressed. She guesses their means are as various as their abilities. Many are very reticent. It is almost as if they believe this invitation is a trap.

At lunchtime most of the children disperse to their homes. The majority live within walking distance. Three stay behind. One has a packed lunch in greaseproof paper. The other two, brother and sister, have some woeful-looking sandwich between them. Gail thinks that even if rationing bit here, and it doesn't, there would be no excuse for this. Eileen Campbell has been lavish packing Gail's lunch. She shares this with her reluctant pupils, thinking how much more enjoyable it would be to go to the Drovers. During the remainder of the lunch break she looks at the supplies. The textbooks are tattered and too few in number. In the course of the afternoon reading lesson pupils have to double up, and in some cases share three to a book. Coaxing answers from them, she gets the inescapable impression that they are paying more attention to the cupboard behind her.

She disbands the class early, remaining behind with the intention of writing out for David Anderson a list of what she needs. This shortage of textbooks means that it is impossible to stream the children into groups. Unless they are segregated she knows the inevitable result: learning progresses at the pace of the lowest common denominator, leaving the more gifted bored. And the bored become insubordinate. David Anderson did not make clear the conditions she would be expected to work under. She feels she has been conned. If she had known she might not have accepted. But she is here now and it is not in her nature to do anything half-heartedly, especially when children are at stake.

She does not stint in her list. If he expects her to make sacrifices he can strain every official sinew to get what it needs to make a go of this. The austerity of this classroom is terrible. How can children be encouraged in such a severe place? Thinking this, her eyes turn curiously towards the cupboard behind her that seemed to be the object of so much nervous attention.

8

An extract from Gavin Bone's journal, November 1940.

We are all dead in trespass and in sin. We are all spiritual corpses.
The best that we can do is to tremble at the threatenings, embrace
the promises and yield obedience to Him through whom we are
saved.

Gavin usually prefaces his writings with formulaic paragraphs discussing man's unworthiness and inclination to evil,
culled from printed sermons he has pored over. It is when he
wanders from dogma or memorized phrases that his prose
begins to degenerate.

He pauses, pen above paper, hesitant how to continue
till he remembers the previous night's conversation. He had
returned surprised to find Ewan McHarg alone in his parlour,
Mrs Bone nowhere to be seen. On seeing him, Ewan immediately launched into a tirade against the lodgers, growing
increasingly vociferous till Mrs Bone entered, presumably
from the bathroom, still putting herself to rights.

Exercising their duty, the McHargs have told me yet again of the
doings of those foreign women. All women are skittish creatures.
This one has the morals of a hot bitch, as do others who don't do
something about it and by that I mean stopping themselves. This
latest piece of intelligence I have of the blonde one exceeds even
my worst expectations.

And she was seen rowing out to a boat with that papish oaf no doubt for her carnal pleasurings to wallow in sin lying on the nets or if that was a bit wet his bunk. And after that going into that hellish den for drink and an alleged game of dominoes. Ewan has been diligent. I see the fervour of righteous excitement when he tells me about her.

He recalls the tirade stopping and the additional details, delivered in private, as Mrs Bone retired to the kitchen.

But I don't understand the thing he is saying about the soap.

9

The same week Gail receives her visit from the man from the Ministry, Frank sits perched in a high-backed chair in the corner of the Dougans' parlour on a blustery Tuesday afternoon. He is practising remaining absolutely still. This has become his strategy. His unforeseen reprieve at Lachlan's hands is three months hence. Most children are at school. The grandmother is resting. Even from his brief sojourn here he has noticed that she sleeps more and more frequently, as if rehearsing for the perpetual sleep that will soon engulf her. Evaluated by Murdo and considered unfit for learning, Frank sits, ignored. His hearing has become attuned to something the other inhabitants of the house fail to notice. Soft as it is, the noise of incessant battering from the waves below causes him to twitch at each collision. Maintaining a semblance of composure, even when alone, has become a sustained act of concentration.

Gradually he becomes aware of a second rhythm superimposing itself on the first. It began quietly but is getting louder and more frequent. It sounds like a soft impact followed by the noise of escaping air, as if a punctured football is being repeatedly stamped on. Intrigued, the boy climbs softly from the chair and leans from one side to another in an attempt to find the source.

It is coming from the direction of the couple's room. He does not know if they are in, having returned with the grandmother to what both assumed was an empty house. The periods she can spend with him are shortening as the demands of her illness punctuate her day with sleep.

There is a sudden violent increase in the noise, like a spasm, and a sound he can only think of as a drowning man coming up for air. Astonished, he crosses to the bedroom door and pushes it noiselessly ajar.

Isabel Dougan is kneeling across the bed, her head towards the doorway he stands in. The upper half of her body that he can see is fully clothed. He cannot see her face as it has been pushed into the mattress. In the tangle of her hair he can see Murdo's sinewy hand. The grip suggests relentless leverage. From the shudders as she pushes against it, straining for air, he can see the force used. Murdo stands behind her. From the height of the bed and his perspective Frank can see the man's corduroy trousers, rumpled like an accordion around his ankles. Braces trail on the planking. There is a puddle of dripped seawater beneath one scarcely visible boot. From the trousers to the underside of the bed Frank can glimpse the upper part of calves, knees and lower thighs, contoured cylinders of wiry black hair. The enormous latent power terrifies the boy. The legs flex rhythmically in time with the concussions as he pushes against her. Isabel's skirt has been bundled up in corrugated folds on the small of her back. Murdo's other hand loops round her waist, pulling the lower half of her body upwards as he pushes her head down.

Murdo's visible torso is also fully dressed. He does not see Frank. He does not see anything. His head is straining back and upwards as his pelvis pushes in, his eyelids fluttering. Frank can see the workings of his huge neck, the fleshy throat swallowing. This is an organism totally preoccupied with its own sensations.

With another spasm Isabel wrenches her head to one side. The sound is almost like a scream, as she draws in air, followed by a sob. The sight of the boy standing in front of her registers. She looks as if she is about to cry out again when the hand rotates her head, face downwards, and pushes it again into the mattress. This has been achieved by him without looking down. She wrenches in either direction. This seems to afford him more pleasure as he arcs into her with a hoarse grunt. At his climax she kicks backwards and squirms. He looks down to find a hank of hair in his hand and the terrified boy standing opposite.

She is sobbing between draughts of gulped air, now lying the length of the bed, trying desperately to pull down her skirt. He is slowly hoisting up his trousers. The boy notices with growing fear the attenuating thread of glistening sperm from the still tumid glans. The man tucks the strange thing away with more care than the boy has seen him exhibit with anything. He is aware he has witnessed some adult collision he should not have. Instinct tells him to run but he is too frightened to move.

Murdo adjusts his braces and walks round the bed towards the door, paying no attention to his huddled wife. His next action is almost as an afterthought, as he draws abreast of the boy.

'Did no one in idiot land ever teach you to knock?' He slaps the boy in a sharp chopping motion, the hand encompassing the area from ear to jawline. The boy falls, his head ricocheting off the doorjamb, causing him to slump against the bed. Without further comment the man walks slowly out, the bedroom door left ajar behind him, the house resounding to the habitual bang as he slams the front door.

The boy gets unsteadily to his feet. He does not look at Isabel, knowing somehow that she does not want to be seen. In the corner of the room one of the floorboards has been disturbed and for no reason he can divine he walks over and looks into the space. Startled at what he sees, he turns back to Isabel. She is now sitting on the bed dabbing the gap between her legs, the handkerchief disappearing up the bell of her skirt. Again he looks into the space, taking note. He turns away, keeping his eyes to the wall furthest from Isabel, and walks out of the room, closing the door softly behind him. He returns to his chair, ear and cheek still throbbing from the slap, and sits as still as he can, twitching at the incessant surf.

IO

Impervious to the winter sunburst that sank into the Atlantic in arresting splendour, Gavin Bone is making his way back from the jetty. It is early Saturday evening. He is muttering disgust at the sallies of noise from the distant village hall.

As the light fades the noise increases. He can see the winking doorway as an interrupted beam as people come and go from rehearsal. An accordion wheezes and he can hear the stutter of a drum.

There is a ceilidh on tonight. Locals from neighbouring villages will shortly be pouring in. Gavin knows that in the fullness of time these transgressors will be brought to book, but occasionally he wishes that He would make His dictates more palpable, indulge in some Old Testament severity, perhaps launch a discriminating tidal wave on the stroke of midnight publicly to chastise those who profane the sanctity of the Sabbath. Walking on, he contemplates this evening's entry in his journal.

Within an hour all light has faded. Various vehicles have arrived and the proceedings are well underway. Drink is flowing under the harsh lights. Drawn by curiosity, Harriet and Gail arrive together, trying to make as unobtrusive an entrance as possible. Short of wearing their land girl uniforms, both are conservatively dressed. This is strange to them. Gail expected something like the Drovers, scaled up. She is pleased by the sight of children. Despite the drink it is more of a family affair than the girls anticipated. She is also glad to see the fair proportion of other young women present. For her and Harriet there is always an initial awkwardness walking into the Drovers, comprising as they do most of the young female contingent.

Their arrival has passed off as uneventfully as they hoped. Both look round for Lachlan. He is not here. This is altogether too noisy for Lachlan's tastes.

Lucy is running late. Working up for an effect, she grew as impatient with Harriet as Harriet was with her, urging her to hurry. She told her to go on. Harriet needed no second bidding, catching Gail at the village cross. Neither has mentioned it to the other but neither wants Lucy's notoriety to rub off.

She arrives colourful and smiling. She brings with her the unmistakable feel of an infusion of oxygen into the place. Both the other girls have been persuaded to take part in a reel, laughing at their own ineptitude and allowing themselves to be good-naturedly nudged into position. The proceedings do not stop when Lucy arrives but everyone in the place knows simultaneously that she is there.

At the end of the dance Gail is happy to bow out. She stands apart, changes the monstrous measure of gin she has been presented with for a beer, and studies the faces. Lucy has thrown herself into the proceedings with predictable verve, enjoying being manhandled. As the main door continues to open and close Gail sees a figure standing outside, arrested in a series of tableaux each time he is framed in the light. Puzzled, she dismisses this until she realizes she has seen him somewhere before, in the same context, hovering on the periphery of the schoolroom gazing in. He is too old for primary, too old for secondary. She assumed he was there as some kind of janitor. His face is illuminated again, framed by the light in an aspect of childish longing. She feels suddenly compelled, puts down her drink, refuses the offer of making up a set and walks outside. After the warmth of the interior and without a coat the cold is bracing. When she speaks her breath hangs momentarily suspended before dispersing into the dark.

'Alan, isn't it?'

He swallows, nervously summoning a reply. 'Angus.'

'Of course. Angus. Sorry.' A mutually uncomfortable pause falls. 'Isn't it cold just standing here? Why don't you come in?'

'Not allowed.'

'Not to drink.' She is puzzled by his age. Does he come under the legal age? Even if he did, would it be enforced here? 'There are . . . young people in there too.'

'Not allowed.' He looks acutely embarrassed but dogged. She sees from the intermittent glimpses they get of the interior that he is fascinated by Lucy. She recalls now something she had heard about him, mentioned in passing, that he was 'slow'.

'I'm too cold to stay here. Are you sure you won't join us?'

'I'll stay.' For the first time he directs his attention at her. She estimates he must be in his late teens or very early twenties, but he looks like a beautiful child. 'Thank you, miss.' His face breaks into an artless smile and she feels suddenly saddened at such gratitude for such scant attention.

The door opens. Lucy comes out. The light behind her disappears with the closing door. Her face is suddenly illuminated, an oval sheen of sweat, as she strikes a match.

'I'm not interrupting anything?' Gail introduces them. After staring unaffectedly at her for the past twenty minutes Angus is now unable to make eye contact and stares fixedly at the ground. 'Cat got your tongue, handsome?' Lucy spends the remainder of her cigarette being kind to the boy, despite his inability to reply. Finishing with a long exhalation of blue smoke, she throws the butt on the ground, makes a half-hearted attempt to tread on it, smiles goodbye and has gone as suddenly as she arrived.

'Are you all right?'

'I'm happy here.' With Lucy gone he can speak again. He cannot expect the night's quota of happiness to be any more fulfilled. When the door closes on Gail he looks at the cigarette end till the smouldering tip extinguishes.

She returns feeling somehow that the night has been thrown out of kilter by her meeting with Angus. She dances again, then takes her beer over to a table where she settles with Harriet and a few others. She is irritated by the scrutiny of a big man across the room who has been staring unashamedly at their table for ten minutes. She steels herself to return his look until he smiles, then she looks away.

'Don't let him get to you.'

'Is it me, or us?'

'I didn't notice him staring till you arrived.'

'Arrogant bastard.'

'Yes,' Harriet concedes, laughing. 'But he is rather splendid.'

'He certainly thinks so.'

'He's the first person I've seen who's managed to make you swear.'

'It's this beer.' They both laugh. The night wears on. As they collect their coats Lucy says she has arranged a lift for all three of them. Make that five, no, twenty minutes' grace and meet her out back. After twenty minutes they are left with dispersing cigarette smoke in a jaded hall.

There is a single vehicle at the back, a dilapidated Vauxhall rocking on protesting springs. The windows are partially obscured with condensation. The girls look at each other and back towards the door they have just come out of. Before they can go back in, the large man who has been staring insolently comes out. He seems amused at the spectacle of the car and the girls' embarrassment at their friend's behaviour. Douglas Leckie, searching for Lucy among the departing throng, comes round from the outside of the building. He is transfixed by the rocking car.

'She's keeping up the war effort,' Murdo says, to anyone. There is a sudden strangeness to the lines around Douglas's mouth. He leaves through the hall without speaking or looking at any of them.

'Would you ladies like a lift?' He purposely looks at each of them in turn. There is nothing sardonic in this scrutiny and Gail wonders if Harriet feels the same sensation she experiences, a kind of pleasing discomfort she knows she could not adequately explain to her friend. They arrived in Rassaig to confront many preconceptions, few of which were flattering. And Lucy's behaviour hasn't helped. She is frequently looked at by the local men, a flicked glance that takes inventory of her breasts and thighs and ricochets off when confronted by her own gaze. Aside from Lachlan few look directly into her face, and she is flattered by the directness of this man's manner.

'No thanks,' Gail responds for them both.

'No charge, of any kind.' His stress is on the second last word.

'No thanks.'

'Tell me, does your friend accept coupons?' And, as they turn away without answering, 'Does she hand them out?'

They begin walking, linking arms and matching each other, stride for stride, slowing as the lights recede behind them.

'That man . . .' says Harriet. The pause hangs.

'Yes?'

'I can't explain.'

'I can't explain it exactly the same way.'

'And Lucy . . .'

'I know.'

'Maybe he wasn't so far off the mark saying those things about coupons. Maybe he's got a sense of humour to go with that look.'

'That'll be the look you can't explain.'

'And us standing there as if we're at a bus stop and Lucy in that car for anyone to pass by . . .'

'I know.'

'Some day I'll see the humour in this,' Harriet says, and for no reason they both begin laughing, leaning against each other, snorting condensation, covering their mouths with their gloved hands. They are young and healthy. The night is cold and beautiful.

II

Frank's arrival in Lachlan's household has prompted something of a dilemma. Lachlan has long since given up asking Agnes to use his first name, despite the fact that he uses hers. The desire to maintain the distinction of employer and employee is entirely hers. Both speak to Frank with equal unaffected concern, which begs the question of what terminology he will adopt for the doctor if he emerges from his silence.

And then there is the additional problem of dinner. Each night Agnes serves dinner to the doctor before disappearing back to her own modest parlour. She knows everything about his domestic arrangements, given she supervises them. He knows almost nothing of hers. She lives in apartments whose furnishings and dimensions he can only guess at. He showed her round ten years ago when she applied for the position and left her to 'cheer them up' at her discretion and his expense. Short of being deprived of a salary and accommodation, she would manage if he left, which is not to say her self-sufficiency is any reflection of her feelings for him. If anything were to happen to her then, in the domestic sphere, he would be utterly lost. Both know this and both know the other knows.

Her ability to cook is matched by the discrimination of his palate. Every evening she delivers a simple, impeccable dinner to him in his front room and disappears for the remainder of the evening. They may bump into each other in the top hall as she turns down his bed or offers supper on colder evenings, but generally their last exchange is a 'goodnight' spoken loudly by the first to go up the stairs to bed. His meal is eaten the way he prefers, in silence. When eating he gives himself over entirely to concentration on the activity, because her food and his wine deserve no less. There is a dining room he uses half a dozen times a year for the more formal occasions he is sometimes called upon to host. But his parlour table, scarcely larger than two tea trays, suffices for his solo meals.

It is unthinkable to Lachlan to relegate Frank to the kitchen, or Agnes's parlour, for his meals. He is not an employee. But to eat with him alone somehow seems to Lachlan insulting to Agnes. Despite the distance she has sought to maintain, and which he suspects does not feel, he is unwilling to reinforce domestic apartheid by having her act as Frank's servant too. So the good doctor ruminated for ten minutes and came up with a decision.

'Agnes, I'll have dinner from now on in the dining room, with Frank.'

'Very good, doctor.'

'And you too.'

She raises fewer objections than he anticipated, perhaps guessing at his dilemma, perhaps looking forward to spending more time with the boy.

'Call someone in to check the hearth and flu.'

'That will be the sweep, doctor.'

'We'll burn a fire. Get rid of the mustiness. There's no need to pull a face like that, I'm not calling your competence into question. Body parts atrophy if not used. Must be the same with a house.'

'You'll want to amputate the attic then, doctor.'

'A through draught for a couple of days should do it. Do something with the furniture, will you? Let's make it less like a morgue. Those curtains, who chose them?'

'You did, doctor.'

'Are you sure? Well, anyway, make them more like . . . your curtains.'

'And what are my curtains like, doctor?'

'How on earth would I know? Cheerful, I expect. And by the way, just because his beliefs might restrict his diet, there's no need for them to restrict mine.' She raises her eyebrow sufficiently to make him realize he may have overstepped the mark. With a gruff apology of sorts he dons coat and scarf for last orders at the Drovers.

They settle into a routine. He comes home of an evening to the room she has somehow cheered up. A fire burns from late afternoon every day. She has imported his favourite chair. He sits reading the paper as she busies herself in the kitchen. Frank usually sits on the hearthrug, endlessly reassembling a child's jigsaw he has been given. A hatch links the two rooms and they can hear her cheerful clatter as she cooks. If feeling gregarious Lachlan will talk about his day, making the kind of disclosures that brings a tut of disapproval from the other side of the wall. At Agnes's instructions, Frank sets the table. Within a week he is entrusted with carrying the hot dishes. The trio sit down, the boy eating silently, missing nothing of the exchanges. It is not lost on Lachlan that this is the nearest he, and perhaps the boy, have come to a family meal. He avoids the introspection this thought gives rise to by talking. He has taken it upon himself to educate Agnes's palate.

'It defeats me, Agnes, how a woman who can cook the way you do can drink tea with everything.'

'I drink tea after a meal, doctor. I think the food stands for itself. I do not understand how you, being, I have heard, an educated man, need to drown the flavour in grape juice.'

'Wine does not drown. Caffeine drowns. Wine enhances. And you do not even have the excuse of your religion.' Agnes is a devout Catholic. 'One thing that can be said about your mob compared to some of the others is that they aren't abstemious when it comes to the bottle.'

'I believe you will find that more people here drink tea than wine.'

'There are more people here read comics than serious newspapers.'

'We are fortunate to have you to enlighten us from our quaint ways.' She clears away the dishes. He lights a cigar. Frank, after a nod from Lachlan, retires to the hearthrug to stir puerile jigsaw pieces in an attitude of boredom. Agnes returns with a deliberate cup of tea. Pleasantly tired, Lachlan pours himself another drink. He is willing to let the matter rest. It is she who reopens the conversation.

'I'm sorry you find it regrettable I drink tea.'

'Think nothing of it.' But it is obvious that she does. 'I apologize if I've offended you, Agnes.'

'You haven't offended me, doctor. We can't all share all your enthusiasms.'

'Any time you want a drink, feel free.'

'I'll bear it in mind.'

Her asperity hasn't escaped the boy, who looks up from the hearth at one then the other, as if following a rally.

Lachlan gestures in the direction of the lounge. 'And if you want to read . . .'

'I only dust your books and files, I don't open them.' She takes a thoughtful sip. Her next comment is made with the cup still raised, half concealing the lower half of her face. 'Although I've never dusted that book in your surgery.'

The steady stream of smoke he is placidly blowing terminates with an abrupt puff as he coughs.

She has identified Lachlan's major idiosyncrasy. The close examination of Frank's skull by the car headlights, on the night of the boy's reprieve, is not an isolated incident. Lachlan makes his mind up about people within seconds of meeting them. Since childhood he has looked at the shape of heads to corroborate his instantaneous opinions, a conviction the rigours of his medical training have not rid him of. In his surgery, beside the usual apparatus including a height chart and scales, Lachlan has pencilled two faint horizontal lines at right angles on the walls behind the patient's chair. By means of this obscure scale, whose gradations are sensible only to Lachlan, he can squint at whoever he is examining and infer the size of their skull from two dimensions. Beside the haphazard medical notes he is obliged to keep and never refers to, the book Agnes referred to, kept in the locked bottom drawer, contains crude pencil drawings of skulls with cryptic notes linking characteristics to topography. Patients' names are not even disguised as anagrams. The purpose of this is not to produce Lachlan's magnum opus. It is not intended for dissemination. He does this merely to satisfy his own curiosity.

He contemplates her, surprised, hand suspended half-way to his mouth as the ash silently accumulates.

'I'd no idea you were so interested in my work.'

'Work? Do you get paid for it then?'

'I get paid for dispensing my professional opinion and . . . various things help inform that opinion.'

'Your fascination with the shape of folk's heads isn't the complete secret you seem to think it is, doctor.'

She has him at a disadvantage. He is avid to know who else knows.

'It might not be the perceived wisdom today to take the same interest in the shape of skulls as I do, but this wasn't always the case. Tell me, are there many others aware of my interest?'

'Are you reviving many other practices, doctor? Isn't it the case that a lot of what doctors in the past believed in is now discredited?'

'Yes, Agnes, it is. No one believes in the theory of humours or bleeding people any more. But it isn't all discredited, and there's no point in throwing out the baby with the bath water. Oscar Wilde said that only shallow people do not judge by appearances.'

'Oscar Wilde. Wasn't he one of those ... theatrical gentlemen?'

'His tastes don't invalidate his point. Is this discussed at the Drovers?'

'I'm only saying he was theatrical because it seems strange you mentioning what a theatrical gentleman said when you want to prove a medical point. And it seems to me that people who go about quoting what other folk said are only employing their memory, not their intelligence.' She gives him an opportunity to respond but he is momentarily silenced by her argument. 'And as for things being discussed in the Drovers, I'm not really qualified to say, having set foot in the place scarce half a dozen times in my life. I've seen you look at folks' heads and scribble whatever it is in your book but it's no concern of mine what you write and if anyone in the Drovers heard anything about it, it wasn't from me.'

He begins to laugh gently. Unlike many of the older women in the village she has a reputation for discretion. No one else, beside himself, has the access to the surgery that she has. He is surprised that anyone apprehended him making notes and is fairly sure that no one else has seen him do so. It will remain another of their confidences. He is partly relieved, partly piqued that she bested him so convincingly when he set out with the intention of educating her.

'It's not rubbish, you know. There's a name for this line of enquiry.' He knows the fact that something may have a name is no guarantee of its authenticity, but he wants to go some way towards redeeming his reputation with this piece of arcana.

'Surprise me, doctor.' Her tone is flat, tolerant.

They are both distracted by a preparatory cough from the hearthrug.

'Phrenology,' says Franz.

12

Shortly after her pupils dispersed on her first day of school Gail sought out Lachlan to ask advice. She found him in the surgery waiting room, the paper hoist in front of him. 'Everyone is healthy – or dead,' he explains. It is obvious from her manner that she would like some privacy. To avoid interruption he takes her to his surgery and sits her opposite him.

'I'm not here about my health, so there is no need to make notes.' He has inexplicably retrieved a large hardback notebook from a bottom drawer and seems to be squinting at something behind her. 'I'm here about the school, or, more accurately, the children.'

'What about the children?' From the seriousness of her tone he has abandoned whatever he was doing.

'Their manner. It was . . . subdued. I don't think there's any point in asking Mr Anderson anything.'

'Who's he?'

'The man from the Ministry.'

'He's a functionary. He might do better under Comrade Stalin. There's a shallowness to his cranial arch I associate with blind obedience. It's common enough around here.'

'Can't say I've noticed.'

'Stand outside either of the churches as they empty and look closely. Anyway, about the children.'

'What was my predecessor like?'

'A mindless sadist who would have made an even better apparatchik than the other one. I thought he had a crew cut. Turns out his head was completely flat. Beat learning into the children. Terrorized them into remembering facts and probably put a fair proportion off ever learning anything again. I'm sure he'll do well in the army. I'd be surprised if he hasn't made sergeant by now. That poor boy, Angus, isn't the cleverest boy in the village, but he deserves to be better educated than he is. He preferred to be considered a moron than go back to the class and face the teacher.'

The following morning, while the children were still in the playground, she had searched the cupboard, an airless alcove the size of a small room, racked on one wall with dilapidated shelves. Among the stubs of chalk and stacked slates of past pupils she found a large leather belt. She was intimidated by its density as she weighed it in her hands. She could surmise its purpose. The sheen of the receiving end testified to exuberant use. The dark stain where it had been held suggested enthusiastic handling. She could sense something of his relish. She was revolted.

The belt was on display on her desk as the pupils filed in. A frightened silence descended. Realizing they had mistaken her motives, she marched them in a ragged crocodile to the jetty. On the way they came across Angus, who, as ever, had been hanging around on the periphery. She asked him to come with them. Although bitterly cold it was a beautiful day. They remained cowed. At the end of the jetty she handed the belt to Angus and told him to throw it as far out as he could. It convulsed in its arched trajectory. She expected laughter or some cathartic outburst at the splash but turned only towards a row of questioning faces.

'You will never again be beaten as long as I am here. Not understanding something is nothing to be ashamed of.'

This produced a cheer and they walked back in a nebulous group. Her hat blew off with a boisterous gust. Angus set off in pursuit and shyly presented it to her. The children laughed at the spectacle of her trying to tuck away the flying abundance of her hair in a high wind. She laughed and spontaneously threw her hat in the air, which Angus, spontaneously, set off in pursuit of again.

By the time they returned to the schoolroom Angus had allowed his pace to drop and lagged behind. She made a point of speaking to him. His employment seemed to consist of whatever odd jobs he could find. 'Folk always need something doing,' he explained. There seemed to be no supervision. Judging from his appearance his income was as irregular as his hours.

'I don't want you to stay outside the schoolroom. I want you to come in. You don't have to join in if you don't want to. You can just listen.'

And that's how she came to recruit her new pupil. He felt hulking among the children and scaled-down furniture, and wanted to leave at the first amused titters he elicited. She sent him to the village hall to find one of the old adult's desks used during the aborted teaching experiment. He sat at the back, making himself as unobtrusive as possible, and the children, as children do, came to accept him as part of the furnishings.

13

Miklos Cherny moves to the drawing-room window to look out on the street below. Behind him he can hear his wife, Ida, give final instructions to the caterers. The window he looks from is on the first floor of their terraced house. The narrow street slopes down towards the river. A frost has descended with the night. The air looks brittle. A passing dray horse snorts a vivid plume and he sees a momentary spark in the darkness struck from its shoe against the frozen cobbles.

The room is not yet lit. Passersby in the street looking up would see a silhouetted figure, dark in his evening suit, his shadow projected by streetlight against the coffered ceiling.

'Come away from the window,' his wife instructs, lighting the room. He enjoys staring down into the street. He has always enjoyed the spectacle of passing life, but not the prospect of being observed. Nothing acts normal knowing it is under scrutiny. And now that the room is lit that is what he would be, a watched observer. Ida thinks staring out of a window is common but he has never had her preoccupation with social norms. He was born into this house, this money. His father had the same attenuated sense of social discrimination his wife possesses. He thinks it must be to do with poverty. His father made enough money to get out of Josefov and move his family to the grandeur of this Mala Strana house. And then he died and went back to the Jewish cemetery of his birthplace. All that striving to cross the river and climb the hill, only to go back again, like the Grand Old Duke of York in the nursery rhyme the English governess taught them.

Now in his late fifties, he has grown plump, not with the protuberance of a gross stomach but with a gradual spreading that has widened him, splayed his pelvis and ribcage, inflated his hands and chin and cushioned his eyes. He feels his centre of gravity is lowering. Perhaps eventually, he will be like one of those toys it is almost impossible to knock over. He has no personal vanity about his appearance. It is the penalty he gladly pays for his sedentary life and the relish of food. His lack of concern is obvious: he carries his weight majestically.

Ida is also thickening. Unlike him, she has a regimen that fails to combat the inevitable. They are both aware that they are becoming more alike. He is pleased. The children are grown, and gone. They are becoming old together. Beneath her social aspirations and failing attempts to keep her figure she shares almost all his opinions.

It is a cold December night in Prague, 1923. Miklos cheerfully awaits the arrival of his guests, having left the arrangements to Ida. As long as the food is good he is happy to take care of the rest. His amiable manner usually predominates most gatherings. He is a man who would make the best of whatever he has, with the wit to see that what he has been given is more than could reasonably be expected.

Natasha has told him he has 'a genius for happiness'. The expression pleased him so much he spent the remainder of the week repeating it to anyone who was vaguely interested. He repeats it to himself again as he awaits her arrival. It is not only the appositeness of the words that pleases him but the fact that it implies he possesses a quality he knows he has no right to claim. He has spent his life among competent men and women and even kept company with the exceptionally intelligent, such as Natasha. But he has never rubbed shoulders with genius, and even if he had, suspected it would not rub off.

He likes to think of Natasha as his protégée. Ida has told

him, without rancour, that the influence travels in the other direction, that his mind is pedestrian in comparison to the younger woman's. Ida is as fond of Natasha as he is. Intellectually the two women are poles apart. Ida staked her claim in the domestic sphere.

'She's here,' she says.

'Come away from the window,' he replies, 'it's common.'

He can hear the door being opened below, her coat taken in the hall. She comes up the stairs looking around curiously. She has dressed in her usual subdued manner, simple and elegant. She is what he would describe as a handsome woman, her jaw too determined to be pretty, her features mobile, her expression alert. Her looks will only improve. She exchanges a kiss with Ida and turning to him asks, without preamble, 'Who's coming?'

'Friends. Do me this courtesy, Natasha – be nice.'

'I'm always nice.'

He groans. A large part of his social repertoire is histrionic, pretending to be upset, astonished, hurt, drowsy. He enjoys being an overgrown child. Natasha has chided him for it. Life is not a trivial matter. Given her history, he can see why she thinks so.

'If people say something wrong, please don't point it out.'

'I'll try not to.'

'People don't change, you know. They don't alter their point of view just because you point out a flaw in their thinking.'

'They might.'

'It might surprise you to know that most people don't have arguments to back up what they think. They have opinions because they just do.'

'If that's a description of the friends you have coming I can see it's going to be a long night.'

71

He turns to Ida for corroboration. 'See, she's doing it again.' But his wife has gone to irritate the caterers by reviewing the arrangements she has reviewed twice already this evening.

Among his many concerns Miklos runs a small publishing house. Knowing little about the industry, he had an image of modest print runs of exquisitely produced books for distribution among the Prague literati. He even attempted to design the colophon himself, eventually handing over his attempts to a professional for completion. In envisioning the enterprise it was more appearance than content he thought about.

His finances did not depend upon the business, but it began to be such a drain on his other resources that he seriously considered abandoning the whole enterprise. At this point Natasha arrived as a part-time proofreader and incrementally assumed complete editorial control without resistance when she realized no one else was up to the task. With Miklos's blessing she also took on the job of translation.

She hailed originally from the Ukraine, one of three daughters. Her far-sighted father had had all three educated as well as his considerable means allowed. This was done in a small-town community that viewed an educated woman as an anomaly. The family was forced to uproot, during yet another of the habitual anti-Semitic pogroms, leaving with what they could carry. Natasha could argue cogently in several European languages. Their impoverishment bothered her less than it did her sisters. She was happy to forfeit past luxuries for the opportunity of being part of the intellectual life of this capital. Provincial indolence would have killed her.

The guests begin to arrive, individually and in couples. Miklos greets each new arrival from the head of the stair, his broad face creasing into an easy smile, introducing them to the guests already present with easy aplomb. They begin to arrive thick and fast and he is obliged simply to wave the latest additions into the company with an expansive gesture.

Natasha is having difficulty making small talk. There is an intensity to her that deters. The caterers are circulating with cocktails. She drinks two martinis in quick succession. She does not normally need the stimulus of alcohol to talk, but Miklos's remark about opinions generally being groundless has given her pause.

Miklos makes an exception for the next guest and brings him across.

'Natasha, you are abandoned.' His face adopts an expression of bottomless woe.

'I've been standing alone for a minute enjoying watching the proceedings.'

Miklos raises his eyebrows. 'Well, if that's all . . . I too enjoy watching proceedings, usually out the window. Ida says it's common. What do you think, Gregor?'

'I'm sorry. I don't understand.'

'Looking out the window. Is it common? Is it normal?' He turns to Natasha. 'Gregor is a doctor. He'll know. Gregor, are common and normal the same thing?'

Gregor is unable to judge if the older man is being serious. 'Pushed at short notice for a distinction I'd say "common" has social connotations that "normal" doesn't.'

'No wonder they pay you so much, or if they don't, they should do. I think "normal" is an abstraction. Personally I don't know anyone who is normal and don't aspire to either. But tell me, what about the common cold? It doesn't confine its attentions to people with no taste. But I see you're looking perplexed. I'm only joking. Natasha disapproves of triviality.'

'You have too much money, Miklos,' she says.

'And you will help me earn more, in the worthy cause of

educating us further.' He turns to Gregor. 'Natasha is the translator I told you about.'

Having set the tone that neither of the others will maintain in his absence, he excuses himself with the obligation to circulate. Gregor has as little time for triviality as Natasha does.

'What did Miklos tell you?' She knows that on a one-to-one basis Miklos is far more serious than his public persona would have people believe. She is certain he would not trivialize the circumstances that brought her here.

'He told me about your family's unfortunate deportation.' She raises her eyebrows at the euphemism. He fails to notice. She begins to ask him a series of questions, her manner almost forensic. She draws him on the question of religion. He is as cynical as Lachlan.

'I think it's institutionalized superstition. I think it's responsible for a great number of evils by perpetuating ignorance. Dependence on myths keeps people from thinking for themselves. What we call "evil" is a result of moral ignorance. Enlighten people and they will stop behaving badly. Take your deportation, that was the result of a collision of spurious theologies. I think that if only—'

But she has listened enough.

'Do you know what I think, I think it might do you the world of good to run away from a burning house in the middle of the night with only the clothes on your back. I think it's astonishing that an intellectual fop, who has never faced a crisis greater than a broken collar stud, feels he has the right to pontificate on others' actions.'

Seeing the telltale signs, Miklos has begun to make his way across the room towards them. She catches sight of him from the corner of her eye and holds up her hand in the universal gesture, causing him to halt. He turns to his guests, wiping mock perspiration from his forehead.

'Miklos might have told you about our "unfortunate deportation". He told me something about you too. I know you were brought up as a Jew the way I was. I know you have chosen to give up your faith. That is your right. Perhaps if you had been unfortunately deported for your religion you might not have shrugged it off so easily as an intellectual exercise. I don't know, your motives are your own, but a consequence of your decision is that you have no idea of the worth of what you abandoned. I've seen you at many of the concerts and Miklos tells me you read everything that we produce and more. He also tells me you're eminent in your field, so you're obviously a cultivated man. I don't decry your learning, but that's not what elevates us. What does is our contemplation of the divine. I feel sorry for you that you feel compelled to deny that portion of yourself that participates in eternity.'

They are by now the centre of a small, circumspect vacuum.

'Dinner is served,' shouts Miklos. He is premature. Seeing the heat of the exchange, Ida is in the process of changing the seating arrangements when the door is opened by her husband and she is caught in the act. Natasha and Gregor are compelled to sit opposite each other.

The noise of the cutlery seems very loud to Natasha during the meal and she can hear her own chewing. Gregor confines his conversation to those at his side. Afterwards she seeks him out.

'Perhaps I shouldn't have been so forthright. But really, it had to be said.'

'I take it that's the nearest thing I will get to an apology.' This is so far from the truth she is nonplussed. He offers his hand. It would be churlish not to accept.

As she shakes it she says, 'I don't think that if we tried for three hours we could find a single thing we agree on.'

They share a departing taxi.

Miklos says, 'It's a match made in heaven.'

Ida says, 'I give them a month.'

General opinion agreed with Ida. Neither Gregor nor Natasha altered their opinions one iota. The only concession she would make to herself, in secret, was that she had done him a disservice. But really, what could he have expected, introducing himself like that?

Unlike Lachlan, Gregor Brod did not cavalierly dismiss the teachings of 'the Viennese witch doctor'. He kept an open mind to advancements of any kind, believing development to be another incremental progression in human improvement. He was a meliorist, and although he did not believe in human perfectibility, he did believe that if we all tried a little harder to be nicer to one another the world would improve by orders of magnitude.

He was a neurophysiologist. In politics he was, predictably, a liberal. He reminded Natasha of one of those tireless men, prominent in the Victorian era, who combined large families with boundless zeal for espousing good causes. It took her the month that Ida had allocated to find these things out, because he was an unassuming man.

They adored each other. When it became obvious to them both that neither would change they saw little point in deferring things further. They married the following autumn.

Within ten months of marrying they had their first child, a boy. Two more boys followed at eighteen-month intervals, Franz the youngest. Gregor, ever the rationalist, had said that their children should be born in a manageable cluster. This would both make best use of the nursery resources and would mean that they were both sufficiently young to enjoy a shared and active retirement when the children were grown.

Seven years after Franz a girl, Nina, arrived. The active retirement would have to be deferred. Their daughter compounded the happiness both parents already thought complete. Natasha spoke only Russian to the children at home. Gregor would return from work feeling he lodged at a club he was not a member of.

The only argument they ever had, and it was ferocious on her side, was over the issue of the children's faith. She refused to have the rigours of existentialism foisted on them.

'You believe in nothing. Nothing isn't something that can be taught. It's an absence. You arrived at a point of scepticism. You chose to give something up. If they choose to do the same then that's their decision, but they have to have something to abandon first. They should at least be afforded the same opportunity you were. I shouldn't have to tell you this.'

He conceded, not just because of her vehemence but because he believed the weight of argument favoured her. His habits of decency had been formed before doubt assailed him. Even if she had not prevailed she would have brought them up in the faith clandestinely. Their mother was a Jew. They were Jews. It was that simple.

The concession Gregor won, by giving in to her on this issue, was his supervision of the children's secular education. The children showed as much promise as any child brought up in a polyglot household with the run of an extensive library and two keenly intelligent parents would. Even so, Franz exceeded expectations.

Money was not an issue. The boys were educated at home until the age of eight. Gregor devised the curriculum. An ardent advocate of the League of Nations, he took upon himself the task of teaching history. Scientific objectivity was left in the hall. His selection of events chosen to illustrate a preconceived view was worthy of Gavin Bone. According to Gregor, the past was littered with dictators who temporarily assumed control before history prevailed. Despots were becoming fewer in number as monarchies fell. Governance of nations on rational principles and in harmony with one another was simply a matter of time. And we were to take example from the larger sphere in our everyday conduct: 'The first man to throw a punch is the first man to run out of ideas.'

By the age of eight, and half a dozen playground encounters later, Franz realized how utopian his father's views were. His mother predicted it all. She had contemplated getting the boys secret boxing lessons but resisted the temptation. She had won the more important battle. She reasoned that a few weeks among their contemporaries, a few skinned knees and they would acclimatize. And she was right.

But the stain was spreading. As Lachlan watched from a distance, with a growing sense of dread, Gregor, from a more immediate perspective, was incredulous. This could not be happening. News of the treatment meted out to German Jews arrived by hearsay, then via more formal channels. He abandoned his medical duties to pitch himself with almost frenzied desperation into political activities. And like Benes, his President, and the other Czechoslovakian diplomats, he listened in stunned disbelief to the news that Chamberlain and Daladier had gone to Munich to surrender a portion of his country to the Germans at a conference to which they had not even been invited.

The scientific endeavour that Gregor so fervently believed in as a means of curing the world's ills had gone into the production of weapons. Fragmentation of order was dragging Europe into another dark age of warring fiefdoms and carnage that would pass unnoticed in the scheme of larger atrocities. Gregor thought his disillusion complete. He had no idea how far he had to go.

Natasha had. She had seen this before. She began making arrangements before German troops marched into the

Sudetenland. The diaspora that had deposited her family in Prague had spread others across Europe. She had relatives she could call upon. When Gregor returned dumbfounded with news of their country's betrayal he found half the furniture gone and most of the family's belongings in three trunks. The boys stood in the hall, each holding a Gladstone bag which seemed to grow larger as their heights diminished.

Although well travelled, Gregor had never lived anywhere else. To leave now seemed another betrayal. He climbed the stairs and found his wife dressing Nina for the journey. From the curve of her back he could only guess at her exhaustion and realized immediately that she had been right, about this and practically everything else.

Farewell letters were stacked on the mantelpiece, stamped and addressed. He asked for two hours' grace to put his affairs in order. She gave him one and called him down to the eldest boy's bedroom. The sore throat the boy had been complaining of since waking, and to which Gregor had paid cursory attention that morning on his way out of the house, had worsened. Fearing the worst, Natasha had been praying since early afternoon, hesitating to bring this to her husband's attention because she knew the conclusion he would draw: that the health of the state had monopolized his concern at the expense of the health of his family. When she told him what she had been doing he pushed back the bedclothes silently to conclude that her prayers had been as effective as his political activities. The confluent rash ran down his cheeks, neck and shoulders to dissipate across the chest. The diagnosis corroborated what she already knew: it was scarlet fever.

Suspecting the damage was already done, he ordered no one to leave the house and for the boy to be kept separate until they could establish whether or not the others had been infected. The other two boys presented early symptoms by the following morning. Nina seemed immune. Natasha paced the downstairs rooms. She had no doubt about her husband's skill. It was delay, not disease, that could prove fatal.

By the time the illness had abated Gregor knew it was too late. He emerged from their self-imposed quarantine to get food when the first vehicles rolled in. He stood in the recess of a shop doorway, his scarf round his mouth, listening to the rumble of half tracks and troop carriers. He could feel tremors through the soles of his shoes. The citizens looked on, silent, resentful.

Within two days there were machine guns posted at every bridgehead. The number of armed men seemed disproportionate to the population they had come to subdue. The first evidence that reached them was anecdotal. A Jewish cemetery had been desecrated and a restaurant they frequented burned; what was presumed to be the Jewish owner found in the smouldering ruins.

Miklos visited. Natasha answered the door.

'If I let you in you risk infection.'

'The atmosphere's better in there than out here. I'll take my chances.'

She was surprised at his appearance. He had lost weight and dropped his histrionic repertoire. Nothing was trivial any more. He sat down warily.

'What times we live in, Natasha. My genius for happiness is being put to the test.' She watched him work up to something. 'They smashed the press.' She absorbed this in silence. Like him and Gregor she knew they had left it too late. News of suicides spread before official pronouncements.

There was a sense of contained panic. Funds were seized. The Prague Bar Council, members of which had been guests in their house, ordered all non-Aryan members to stop practising. More ominous still, the organization for Jewish emigration was closed. People clustered outside the British Consulate shouting that they wanted to get away. Gregor thought it a bitter irony to appeal to the nation that had sanctioned his country's dismemberment.

While they could still be had he took the English newspapers. When these became scarce he became one of those to whom week-old copies were clandestinely circulated. The German Foreign Office in Berlin was prepared to admit to the British press that 'some people opened their mouths too wide. Some neglected to get out in time.' Prague was condemned as 'a breeding place of opposition to National Socialism'. The head of the Gestapo in Prague was happy to be more definite to foreign journalists: 'We have ten thousand arrests to carry out.'

They had been living out of half-disgorged trunks in the desperate hope of a quick exit. When the children were in bed the couple sat leaning towards each other across the kitchen table, preparing themselves for the unthinkable conversation they had deferred as long as possible and knew they must now have. For the first time they acknowledged to each other what both of them knew the other had already apprehended. He was the one who said it.

'We won't be able to leave as a family.' She nods, staring at her knuckles. His hand covers hers. 'We will send the boys ahead.'

She had a series of destinations westward already plotted out. The persecution that had driven her from the Ukraine had spread extended family members across the continent. They had all been diligent in communicating, keeping the heritage of their extended family alive. She shows him the list, pointing.

'They can go there first.'

'No, Natasha. They cannot all go there.'

'What do you mean?'

'No one honestly believes it will stop here. Not us and not the British and French who allowed this to happen to us so it wouldn't happen to them. The Germans will move west. The boys look . . . the way they do. To look the way we do is a liability. The people you want to send our sons to will soon have to look to their own future. We can't, in all conscience, ask one family to look after three children who look like us.'

'But to separate them . . . They have never been apart . . .'

'We are going to have to smuggle them. They stand a better chance of getting out if we smuggle them individually. We can pass one of them off as a family member of whoever we get to take them, but not three. Whatever else the Germans are they're not stupid.'

There was one final argument for the boys' separation that logic dictated but that he could not bring himself to enunciate: if scattered, the chance of at least one of them surviving was greater.

'Each of the boys should carry money and a letter of introduction. In all probability these relatives will be risking their lives on behalf of children who aren't theirs.' His hand still covers hers. She cannot bring herself to reply. She fetches writing materials and leaves him to the task.

An effortlessly verbal man, Gregor normally found the translation from thought to word instantaneous. But he stared at this paper and found himself unequal to the task. He was writing to his wife's relatives, people he had never met, his appeal based on ties of blood and a common faith he did not share. But that was not his problem. He had already accepted his wife's arguments: the children were Jews because their mother was a Jew. He was unequal to the task because he was entrusting half his heart to the unknown.

By the early hours he had produced a terse communication that he laboriously copied out two more times. Coming upon this the following morning, his wife again copied it in English, Russian and French, adding a postscript of her own in each of these languages. Each document was sealed in a vellum envelope that was then placed inside a larger one.

Franz does not remember either of his brothers' departures. All he recalls is the lack of playmates in an increasingly empty house and parents who had stopped speaking. He remembers being roused in the middle of the night and being taken in complete darkness to the lane at the back of the house. The local baker's van idled. He was handed his Gladstone bag, a thick envelope and a bound cylinder of banknotes to conceal in the waistband of his trousers. He remembers the exchange among spluttering exhaust fumes. Till the day he died the smell of carbon monoxide evoked for him this leave-taking. Both parents kissed him in a silence broken only by the coughing engine.

Nina was too young to send away. Even if she hadn't been, neither parent could send her. The plan, although neither of them could bring themselves to call it a plan, was for mother and daughter to leave at the first opportunity, with Gregor following when he could. Three addresses in encrypted form were sewn into the lining of their luggage. The boys would be collected on the way. The family would unite in Paris before seeking passage to New York. The thought that sustained Natasha was a nurtured image, improbably cinematic although she knew it to be, of Liberty's torch being disclosed through the mist to her family, huddled but intact on the forward deck.

Franz remembers leaving with the smell of fresh bread. The journey from then on is a confused memory, a series of tableaux that blurred and ran into one another with the light-headedness of recuperation. He remembers transferring to a number of different vehicles, usually at night. In one he hid under a tarpaulin. No one ever asked him for money. After the border he travelled unaccompanied on a train, bemusedly watching fields pass by, his ticket stamped by a puzzled-looking official. By then his sense of dislocation was such that he would not have been surprised had the train come to the end of the world and plummeted off. At a rural station outside Paris he heard his name being called and a shouted general enquiry in Russian. He knocked on the window. A friendly-looking man boarded the train and took him off. Had he not been so traumatized he might have recognized a family likeness. The man took the envelope and slid it into his breast pocket. His offer to carry the bag was politely refused.

They drove in the direction of the disappearing train. Franz spent the remainder of the year in a tidy Parisian suburb. The family was kindly. In the spring he sensed something of the same unease he had felt at home towards the end of his illness. Almost on the anniversary of his departure from Prague he was sent to a small village in Brittany. The new people did not have the same family resemblance and spoke only French. They dressed him in different clothes and sent him to the local school. He felt the same way he had hiding under the tarpaulin.

Every evening the father listened ever more anxiously to the radio, a habit he had seen his own father adopt. Talk at school was all of the Germans. He sensed a feeling of growing circumspection towards him. The people he stayed with tried to disguise it but he knew they felt the same. What Gregor had feared most was happening. Franz, so obviously Jewish, was a liability. The more tenuous the links became to the successive families that fostered him, the less the likelihood of him being concealed to put at risk the same families his presence endangered.

In May he was shipped across the Channel. Three days later the Germans rolled into France.

His cylinder of cash was still intact. His letter had been read by his successive hosts and handed back. He was told he would be met off the boat at Plymouth. He was given a telephone number and name if for some reason his contact did not arrive. He disembarked with the departing throng feeling everyone in the world had a destination except him.

The link was now indeed tenuous. He was met at the quayside by David Munroe, brother-in-law to Leon, the man who had seen him off from France. David had married Leon's sister. She died on her thirtieth birthday. Working as a buyer, David had met Irene Dougan, Isabel's sister, on a trip to Scotland to look at cottage textile industries. The loss of his French wife had left him more emotionally redundant than genuinely bereaved. His work involved travelling. By disposition he could not stay at home, but intermittently craved a home to return to. He was based in the south of England. Irene saw him as a ticket out of Rassaig. There was no pretence of great love on either side. She knew he would be an indifferent husband and a good provider.

They married in Rassaig and settled in Chelsea. He stayed at home for a week before resuming his itinerant life, leaving Irene lonely and pregnant. She suffered the nausea alone, suspecting a man of his vitality must have other women. She never asked. Over the next couple of years he seemed to be home only long enough on each occasion to impregnate her. They had three children. His reaction to her exhaustion was to employ a home help. It never occurred to him to stay longer.

A man of considerable acumen, he foresaw the coming war and realized the opportunity for someone in his line of business. War meant a demand for uniforms. He established a small clothing factory. It was a risky enterprise that survived at subsistence level until, calling in every favour his limited patronage allowed, he won the company's first order. The workforce was comprised almost entirely of women. He demanded a great deal from them and paid extravagant bonuses. It was a winning strategy. A second order meant expansion of staff and premises. He established a track record of delivering on time. He regarded the growing threat as a licence to print money.

He moved his family to a bigger house. He employed more domestic help, a woman who turned up without forewarning looking for instruction from a mystified Irene. By this time Irene's children were her family. She neither knew nor cared about her husband's suspected affairs.

Communication between the brothers-in-law had been intermittent and finally stopped, not because of a growing coolness but because each recognized the other's commitments. David's first wife had returned to France to die. He had a keen sense of obligation to his brother-in-law. Both knew there was no chance of Leon's appeal being refused.

At each change in location Franz spoke less and less, like a slowing locomotive. He came to a standstill on the French side of the Channel. This cheerful, immaculately dressed man chatted amiably all the way to a large house in Chelsea. He handed the boy over to his wife who by now had ceased to be mystified by her husband's caprices. 'Refugee I said we'd keep. Doesn't say much,' was his only comment. Undaunted by the prospect of her sleeping back that night, he was up and out before the family stirred.

Somewhere in this inadequate transition Franz became Frank. Two days after his arrival he solemnly handed his envelope to Irene. Baffled by the Cyrillic script of the first two paragraphs, she folded the document and handed it back. 'You keep it safe for me, dear.' She never demanded anything of him. She could see premature marks of care in his young face. Had she had more information she might have been able to treat him more like one of her own, but like so many of David's surprises he had come unannounced, with no history and no indication of how long he was staying. David might reward her efforts by taking him away tomorrow. The boy never spoke. She thought him incapable of education, or at least the kind of rudimentary education on offer now there was a war on.

He hung around the house for a few months, eating with the family, surreptitiously reading the newspapers David left around following his infrequent visits. With the mother, children and domestic help he practised evacuation to the Anderson shelter. Nothing surprised him any more. These rehearsals did nothing to reinforce in Irene's simple mind the reality of the situation. But she panicked at the first genuine siren and moved everyone to hastily rented accommodation in Somerset. The first raid on London, late in August 1940, incinerated their factory.

David arrived at work to find a doused hole, bewildered relatives of the vaporized security man having been forced back from its smoking periphery by the firemen. Suddenly redundant, he returned to his childless house. Irene had no idea of the extent to which they lived beyond their means. The extravagance of their domestic arrangements was a fraction of their extravagance.

The first thing to go was the domestic help. He had the good grace to turn up in Somerset with news of the debacle for Irene and an envelope, with as generous a settlement as their drastic means allowed, for each of the helps. The indefinite upkeep of the country accommodation went next. They were released from the terms of their lease when David made it quite clear to their landlord that there was no point ruining an already ruined man. With a sense of foreboding they all returned to a darkened London. The house in Chelsea was beyond his means to maintain, and her energies to clean, but he could not unload it in the middle of a crisis. He was an energetic man. It was a matter of time and continued health till he revived their fortunes. In the meantime Irene closed up the rooms they did not need and went back to cooking with thrift learned of necessity in Rassaig.

They found a family camaraderie in retrenchment. Adversity drew them together. The forced economies he saw as a personal indictment cheered her. She had grown up in a place characterized by vegetation that clung and she found reserves even she did not know she possessed. He saw the value in her he had been too preoccupied or obtuse to notice. She was happier than she had ever been.

The national evacuation programme was in full swing. When the children were asleep he sat her down.

'If we are to send them away we have to decide now.'

'No. I can't. I won't send them away. It might be selfish but I've never been separated from them yet and I couldn't bear it now.'

He was prepared to defer to her. Up till now all he had invested was money.

'I can't imagine the thought of life without them any more than I can the thought of them being brought up by strangers and not knowing me.' And having said this she thought of Franz and for the first time realized the appalling sacrifice he represented.

'All right. We'll stay. We'll see it through . . . or not, as a family. I'm happy to go along with you on this but I don't think either of us can take the decision to expose Frank. He's not blood. It's not fair.'

'What do you think we should do?'

'Most of my contacts are in the south. Most are no safer than this. I'll telephone Isabel.'

'No. It should come from me. I'll telephone Isabel.'

The following afternoon a drinking companion of Murdo's turned up at the croft to say someone had called the local pub last night hoping to leave a message for Isabel. Her sister was looking for her. She was to call the number he had written down. She could reverse the charges. Leaving her mother-in-law in charge of the children, she went to the only public phone box, situated ludicrously on the exposed wharf. The concrete floor was intermittently swamped by higher tides. The noise of the sea made for halting exchanges. She had to wait her turn and shout into the concavity of the next approaching wave.

Franz found himself on yet another night-bound train. Perhaps it was his imagination but when he changed at Glasgow the rural darkness seemed to deepen the further north he travelled. He did not know what his parents had intended for him but he knew it was not this.

The station he found himself finally deposited on comprised two concrete platforms linked by an overhead walkway. The ticket booth was closed. The departing train wavered along parallel moonlit streaks until it, like them, disappeared into moorland. The man who emerged from the otherwise empty waiting room was not cheerful, immaculate or talkative. He made no effort to take the Gladstone bag. Later that night, when Franz was getting undressed in the Dougans' house, the same man entered unannounced in time to see the cylinder of notes fall from the waistband. Murdo picked it up, flicked through the unfamiliar currency and pocketed it. 'It's our secret,' he said.

Until then Franz had not considered his plight captivity, but he did so now. And one day, a month after his arrival, a large envelope arrived. It was from London, and contained within it a short note from David clipped to a smaller envelope.

The smaller envelope was for Franz, its frayed discoloration testifying to much handling and the delay of its transit. The lack of other official stamps suggested it had travelled by the same surreptitious route he had. He opened it in private and in silence, poring over the same Cyrillic script in the same handwriting that had dissuaded Irene from examining his credentials. And he knew, with precocious certainty, that this was the last chink of light that had escaped from a room whose door was now closed for ever. As his contemporaries in the village school, a walk distant and under Gail's tutelage, familiarized themselves with long multiplication and the dates of Magna Carta, he slowly absorbed the fact of his family's dissolution.

So Franz listened to the surf and waited. By now he saw himself as a harbinger, preceding annihilation. He had come a long way. Rassaig was remote. By entirely different reasoning he had come to the same conclusion as Lachlan: the tranquillity of this place was fragile. Whatever followed him might take longer to get here, but its progress was inevitable. Sooner or later it would come.

14

The day after Franz dropped his four-syllable bombshell, Lachlan went back to see Isabel Dougan. His pretext was a follow-up visit to the mother-in-law. His real intention was to find out if Franz's silence had been total during his stay with the Dougans. He was looking for any kind of clue to the boy's antecedents and intended asking for the papers Isabel referred to so absently, that might be the only link to his past. But his intention and the pretext for his call escaped his memory when Isabel opened the door. If she had ever worn makeup he had not noticed, but even heavy cosmetics wouldn't disguise the mark on her face. The previous night she had interrupted Murdo in the bedroom raking his hand into the space created by floorboards he had just pulled up. Standing, he had shouted, 'Where the fuck is it?' She didn't know if he addressed the question to her or discovered her behind him as he spun round shouting. She credited the next second to instinct. She explained to his mother that it was not his fault: he had been taken unawares. The arc of his hand followed the line of sight as she hove into his peripheral vision. His hand was only half closed as it made contact with the side of her face, otherwise it would have dislocated her jaw. She slammed into the bed. The look she cast him was more accusatory than her subsequent accounts. The look he cast at her was bewildered, not apologetic. He kicked the boards back into position and left the room.

She tries to refuse Lachlan's examination. There is no structural damage and the swelling will subside. He orders a cold compress and leaves her something for the pain. The mother is asleep and he does not disturb her. Murdo is nowhere to be seen. Lachlan is glad. The only thing that would have forced him to hold his tongue is the knowledge that the victim of any public recrimination would be the same one who is suffering now. Against her objection he leaves with a promise to return.

Despite running late he makes a point of finding Michael Murray, the constable. The exchange occurs in the Drovers. The younger man seems preoccupied with the blemishes of the table as Lachlan speaks. They have spoken enough times for Lachlan to know he is listening. Michael, nodding, hears him out.

'I know. It's not the first time. You're not the first person to mention it either.'

'Nor the last, from what you say. How bad would it have to be before we can do anything about it?'

Michael is heartened by this 'we'. Lachlan is renowned for being opinionated and ploughing a lonely furrow. He has never been a member of a team. This is not empty rhetoric.

'Bad enough for her to press charges or someone who witnesses it to come forward.'

If Lachlan needed further proof of inequity this is it: as long as he continues to do so in private Murdo can beat his wife with impunity, and the fact that this constitutes nary an atom of the suffering being experienced elsewhere does not lessen the misery of a woman being punched behind closed doors. But Lachlan does not need further proof. The tragedy, from his perspective, is that Murdo has a legitimate excuse for not fighting. He suffered some kind of accident as a child, falling into a freezing sea and perforating an eardrum. He lives now with tinnitus in one ear. Bouts of disorientation are infrequent but unpredictable. When he feels them approach he can do no more than navigate home and lie in a darkened room till the nausea subsides. Tragically, it is at such times when he despises his own weakness that Isabel likes him best. She will minister to him tirelessly. He will ask for nothing and dislike her for witnessing his humiliation. When he recovers she is exhausted and he is colder.

He was avid to enlist, first in the queue when recruitment was announced. The prognosis of his condition was such that he could not be entrusted with any responsibility. His humiliation was compounded when he was referred for a second examination with the lame, the twisted, the flat-footed and the stutterers. He sat in a waiting room with these untouchables breathing deeply to quell his anger at being similarly classified. The regret of the recruiting officers at losing one of his build was nothing in comparison to the smouldering resentment with which he heard the news. He was, by disposition and physique, a natural warrior. And from experience Lachlan knew that such men were not good survivors. The temperament that would have propelled him into the fray would have earned him an early bullet. Murdo's tragedy, from Lachlan's perspective, was that he remained intact when decent men were being blown to fragments.

Thanking God for his intervention, Isabel tried to console Murdo as best she could: people need to be fed even when there's a war on, especially if there's a war on; it requires more courage to face a gale than an enemy. These attempts simply stoked Murdo's simmering anger. At such moments he despised her. Irrespective of the consequence to his family he would have been glad if an advance invasion force had landed on the coast. He knew nothing about Nazis, but he would happily have hunted down and killed as many Germans as he could until they killed him.

He temporarily assuaged his anger by pitting himself against ludicrously superior forces. He would listen to the shipping forecast in anticipation of putting to sea in the teeth of a weather front that sent everyone else scuttling to harbour. On a pretext of business he went to Glasgow and haunted the bars, looking for someone sufficiently sinister to challenge him about his civilian clothes. He had nothing but contempt for conscientious objectors, and when someone referred to him as one he spun round in anticipation. But the man was drunk and too small. On the way out, and almost as an afterthought, he slapped him off his barstool.

Two hours and six pints later he found what he wanted in a bar off the Trongate: three uniformed soldiers, the biggest as big as him, kit bags at the ready. He made a point of unceremoniously kicking their luggage out the way as he bawled above the throng for his drink. The smallest of the three was the most sinister and his reaction was instantaneous. There was no verbal escalation that resulted in a punch being thrown. The soldier snatched up a cane from an old man at his side and brought it down with enough force partially to detach Murdo's ear. Galvanized by pain, Murdo ducked down and ran the soldier into a pillar, breaking his jaw from an upward butt delivered by the back of his head. The competition was so unequal there was no pretence of one-on-one. They had not come this far together to lose their comrade to a bar-room psychopath. The fight spilled into the street. They left him there twenty-five minutes later. Murdo had kicked one of them so hard in the side of the head that the eyeball burst. With one eye, he was confined to logistical tasks while his comrades went to Burma. Neither came back. The man who had unwittingly done him a favour lay in the street spitting. The fight had concluded with Murdo face down while the only soldier still capable jumped up and down on the back of his head. The soldier staggered off with his comrades, strands of hair attached to his hobnailed soles. Murdo's skull was perforated. His nose, jaw and ribs were broken. An outstretched hand, fingers curled underneath, had been repeatedly stamped on.

They went to the Royal Infirmary. He lay in the Victoria for three weeks. He returned to Rassaig more taciturn than ever. Rumours of his association with the Glasgow criminal fraternity spread. He continued to go out in calamitous weather, pull the larger dogfish from the net and beat the still palpitating ones to death against the bulwarks.

Lachlan reflected that if he could have somehow falsified Murdo's medical record to qualify him for active service, he would have done so.

15

The schoolroom has undergone a transformation. With an ultimatum to the man from the Ministry to requisition the list of goods handed across, or find himself another supply teacher, Gail has managed to prettify the place. She has even written to her parents to have some things salvaged from past teaching positions sent on. Charts of various kinds now bedizen the walls. She has had Angus screw up in pride of place her favourite artefact, a shallow glass case containing several crucified butterflies who, when unpacked, continued to coruscate through the dusty glass.

Within a short time she believes she has managed to create an atmosphere whereby most of the children are happy to come to school, and those who are not are not afraid to. She has separated the children into sections for reading and arithmetic. Everything else, as she predicted, goes at the pace of the slowest. She is a slender resource and has done as much as could be reasonably expected. During the last part of the day she reads to them a child's edition of *Huckleberry Finn*, simplified into manageable chunks. They are into the second week of instalments when Gavin Bone walks unannounced into the schoolroom.

'This is not work.'

Several of the children automatically stand at his entrance. Initially stunned by his rudeness, Gail takes stock. She has a vague notion that the parents of the standing children are members of the same congregation as this arrogant bastard. She is further incensed by the fact that they will not sit despite her gesture to do so, seemingly awaiting his permission.

'I have no idea who you are and what credentials you presume to possess that you think entitle you to criticize my methods, but do not ever walk uninvited into my classroom again and speak to me in this manner.'

It is his turn to be stunned. He physically steps back.

'I am not accustomed to be spoken to by women who —'

'The limitation of your experience is of as little interest to me as your opinion of my teaching. I am sure the sheer tonnage of what you are unaccustomed to would sink a liner.'

She is so angry her eyes are smarting. The silence is complete. The standing children are aghast, anticipating some Old Testament apocalypse. He is so astonished he turns away, as if temporarily dispelling the sight of her will confirm the fact that this is an hallucination. But when he turns back she is still there. A woman, a young woman, has not only spoken back to him but has seen fit to upbraid him in front of children, some of whom have parents in his congregation. His eyes wander over the classroom till they settle on Angus. Of all those at a desk he is the only one not observing the exchange. His eyes are fixed on the ground in his overwhelming desire to remain inconspicuous. Gavin addresses himself to the boy.

'Angus. A young man of your years in this . . . place. It is indecent. Step outside.'

'Angus, you are not officially a pupil of mine, so I can't order you to stay. You don't have to go if you don't want to, which is more than I can say for this man.'

Gavin turns to her. He has a public voice of sudden fortissimo, perfected in the barn on startled livestock in imitation of denunciatory sermons from pulpit belters it has been his privilege to hear. He is about to direct this like a lighthouse beam at Gail when she pre-empts him.

'Paul, please run and fetch your father. Say we have an intruder in the school.'

Eager to fulfil the commission, the boy scrapes back his chair. His father is the constable, and a Catholic. Gavin envisages the uniform, the boots, the Catholic relish as he is escorted off the premises, the official reprimand, the unofficial glee. He walks out with as little forewarning as he arrived, heading in the direction of his journal, there to give full expression to the denunciation he was prevented from voicing in the schoolroom.

News of the exchange spreads like wildfire through both sections of the community. For the first time in Agnes's experience she hears Lachlan cackle. Gail's stock has risen, certainly with the contingent who live nearer the harbour. To reassert his standing among his own, Gavin has been more publicly severe than ever in his observance of Church discipline.

Unaware of her notoriety, Gail continues to do her best. She persuades Angus not to let the prejudice of the older man dissuade him from trying to learn. His reading has progressed to the halting narrative of a precocious seven-year-old. He has confessed to her his longing to be able to sit in front of the *Oban Times* without dissembling. The paucity of this ambition saddens and shocks her. She has spent half an hour, three nights out of five, staying back to help him. He now haunts the schoolroom. She half suspects he has nowhere else to go. Anticipating that Gavin Bone will do what he can to discredit her, she feels these solitary lessons will provide ammunition. But she will be damned if she will abandon this boy because some warped old man doesn't like being talked back to by a woman.

Reading aloud to her after four o'clock, Angus was stopped short by a new arrival. Gail's back was to the door. From the consternation on Angus's face she expected to turn around and find Gavin. Instead she saw Lucy, who managed to get as much innuendo into 'Late lessons?' as she suspected Gavin would. It was clear from the effect of Lucy's arrival that they would get no more work done. Gail finished the lesson off. The three left the schoolroom together, walking to the junction that separated the girls.

'Going my way?' Lucy asked Angus. He fell in behind her without comment.

'You didn't say why you'd come,' Gail said to her, mildly anxious at the turn of events.

'Fancy going out later?'

'I can't tonight.'

'There you are then.'

And the exchange stopped at that. Gail could hear Lucy's voice and their footfalls till they disappeared in the direction of the McHargs' farm.

The following afternoon, having accustomed the children to expect something beyond the syllabus, Gail diversified.

'You all know what this is.' She handed it round, allowing each child in turn to examine the texture. When the piece of coal was returned to her she held it aloft. 'Did you also know this was part of a forest, long, long before anyone else was here?'

16

Having heard the first word Franz uttered in Scotland, Agnes expected a torrent of reminiscences, and asked him a number of questions till Lachlan told her to stop. His expectations were more realistic. 'Who knows how much that one cost him?' he said, once the boy had gone to bed. His instruction was that the order of the day should be the same as before: talk to him in the expectation of being listened but not replied to.

'There is at least one thing we can now be sure of, doctor. We know that he can understand.'

'I always knew he understood.'

'It must be a marvellous skill to have, doctor, the ability to predict things after they happen.'

But she knew that he was right; he had always known. And she went to bed piqued that on this occasion his insight had been keener than hers.

Lachlan has plans for Franz's education. But he will not force the issue till the boy is forthcoming. He continues to take him on house calls, to lunches at the Drovers and on evening walks. The dinner conversation is still confined to the table-top exchanges of the doctor and his housekeeper with Franz unashamedly listening to the proceedings, as if preparing to adjudicate. He no longer has the absurd jigsaw and childish toys Agnes provided him with. Against her advice Lachlan has given him the run of his library, and Agnes, who will casually decapitate a chicken, looks over Franz's shoulder as the boy pores over *Gray's Anatomy*, and considers it ghoulish.

Confirmation of the boy's understanding has not led to any

circumspection on Lachlan's part. Finding Franz reading about the lymphatic system, Lachlan is happy to hold forth on patients, past and present, whose ailments are pertinent to this field of study.

'Don't you at least think you should try and disguise certain names?' Agnes asks.

'Nonsense. Look how long it took him to say a word. He's not going to blurt it out. And even if he spoke as much as you do, he is obviously intelligent. I trust to his discretion.'

'I would not say, doctor, that intelligence is any guarantee of discretion. You must have passed exams and look at the way you talk to him.'

'And I would add,' he continues, ignoring her comment, 'that the shape of Franz's head corroborates my theory. It would be impossible for the boy not to be intelligent with a head shaped like that.'

She returns to her cooking, exasperated. He raises the newspaper, satisfied. Franz, taking up a pencil, makes a note in the margin of the anatomy textbook, unnoticed.

Having corroborated his theory in his own mind if not Agnes's, Lachlan is curious to know just what level of intelligence the boy has. Poring over *Gray's* is no guarantee of anything. He could be simply exhibiting the same macabre curiosity that would prompt a schoolboy to poke a dead cat with a stick. Lachlan is content to wait. He feels life has dealt him enough surprises. Unlike Agnes, he has an abundance of patience.

The following week he is sitting in the surgery making another of his haphazard notes on the record of the last patient, when there is a soft knock on the surgery door. He tuts with impatience. It has been a long day. He believed his last patient was his last patient. He is looking forward to asking Franz to play chess with him.

'Come in.'

The door opens. Franz stands on the threshold. The boy has never knocked before. He either enters a room or reads elsewhere until called upon. There ensues a charged pause. Lachlan is about to fill this.

'There is a woman here.'

The voice is soft. Lachlan cannot place the accent. He is anxious to hear more.

'Does she have an appointment?'

Franz disappears from the frame of the door. Lachlan hears a murmur. The boy returns.

'No, she does not.'

'What did she say?'

'She moved her head, like this.'

'What is her name?'

Again the boy disappears. This time Lachlan hears the reply. From her voice he knows the identity of the patient.

'Mrs . . . she told me but I cannot say it.'

'Urquhart.'

'Yes.'

'Tell her I will be with her in a moment.'

The boy gently closes the door. On this occasion Lachlan would have preferred if he had left it ajar. He hears the murmur of Franz's voice again and a response, followed by the boy's voice. This seems to be a muted dialogue. Of all the people to whom he should start talking, Rhoda Urquhart is the worst, or best. She will not demand anything of him by way of a response. She does not conduct conversations, she sustains a running monologue as a continuous commentary of her experiences and fictitious ailments. She is old. In the past few years Lachlan has watched her slip from idiosyncrasy to near lunacy. She is a single woman, as rare a specimen here as he is himself. What family she had she has outlived. She lives on a farm, too old to manage, the land leased on. She no longer has the distraction of a punishing regime to occupy her. Lachlan thinks her condition symptomatic of chronic loneliness. It is strange, he thinks, that some people are born into a remote landscape that ill befits them for town existence and still succeeds in unhinging them by the resonance of its solitude. She used to shop once a week but now makes daily forays into Rassaig and has become something of a diversion in the village. Previously abstemious, she will now command the hearth of the Drovers with a pint in her hand and pontificate at the ceiling. People are kind. She has become something of a sacred cow.

Lachlan wonders if he will hear better if he puts his stethoscope to the door. This fails. Risking observation, he opens it a crack. She is in mid-flow.

'You're not from around here.'

'No.'

'It's my hysterical lung, y'see, sonny. Lot of them won't believe. Doctor McCready believes. Good man. Most of the others are spies.'

'What are they spying on?'

'Hysteria of the lung runs in the family. Lots of my ancestors went to Canada after the clearances. Spread the condition through Saskatchewan. I'm thinking of going there.'

'Will that be possible? Will the war not mean that you have to stay here?'

'What war?'

Although he would love to hear the boy being drawn out, Lachlan thinks it advisable to intercede.

'Rhoda, please come in.' She precedes him into the surgery. 'I will join you in a moment.' Closing the door behind her, he turns to the boy. 'Would you be good enough to tell Agnes I will be ten minutes late. One other thing before you go – do you play chess?'

'Yes.'

'Perhaps we can play a game after dinner.'

'That would be good.'

Fifteen minutes later, having sent Rhoda off with a placebo for her hysterical lung, he finds the boy in the dining room reading the newspaper whose formal prose daunts Agnes. She is staring through the communicating hatch, waiting to catch his eye and nod meaningfully towards the small reading figure.

'Any news?' Lachlan asks casually.

'I think there are lots of things happening that this newspaper says nothing about.'

'Did you read a lot at home?'

'Always.'

'And is your name really Frank?'

'Franz. Franz Brod.'

17

The guilt of sin is imputed from our first parents. The corruption of their nature is ours, conveyed to all posterity. Sinfulness proceedeth from the sinner, not from Him. Being perfect He cannot be the approver of sin, which is a transgression of His righteous law and will bring upon its author His wrath, with all its attendant miseries. It is the privilege of His immutable will to leave His iniquitous creatures to pursue temptations, to wallow in corruption so that they be chastised and humbled and come to realize their dependence on Him.

That a teacher should be a woman and not appreciate her place is receiving instructions and not giving them is bad enough. That woman who usurps her betters place . . .

Here Gavin stopped, temporarily defeated by the positioning of the possessive apostrophe. Reflecting that punctuation should not impede the afflatus when it is upon him, he draws a large red mark through the previous sentence. 'That woman who occupies a place that any man would be better suited to hold . . .' Even the blinkers of Gavin's fanatically restricted vision could not prevent him from realizing that this was not true. Some of the farmers and fishermen of his acquaintance are semi-literate. Put them in a schoolroom and the sense of displacement would be as great as that of some primitive monster transported to the teacher's desk. This last inadvertent reflection is pertinent to his train of thought. Summoning himself, he cancels the last attempt and begins yet again:

To put a woman in a man's job is a perversion of the natural order and look what happens, I am spoken back to in public and threatened with the law. She will be made to learn that there are larger laws, His laws. And now I hear she is holding up pieces of coal. Coal was made by Him for us to burn to keep warm. And here she is talking about creatures stuck there since before our first parents arrived . . .

18

If Lachlan was expecting a prodigy whose tactical insight would confound him from the outset, then he was disappointed. The truth is that he did not expect a prodigy, and he was a little disappointed by the ease with which he beat Franz in their first game of chess. Reflecting later that night, he realized he had beaten the boy with the same ease with which he defeats the harbour master, who is a fifty-year-old man of solid but not scintillating intelligence.

The second game Lachlan won with equal ease, although he noticed that the boy seemed to pay more attention to Lachlan's moves than his own. The following evening, a Wednesday, was chess night in the Drovers. Chess night consisted of eight or ten sufficiently competent people playing at several boards while darts were conducted in the corner. Against Agnes's strictures about the effect that smoke and such company might have, Lachlan had Franz wrap himself against the cold and took him to the pub, ordering him half a Guinness for medicinal reasons. Amid general laughter Lachlan offered to write a prescription should the barman prove unwilling to pour it. The drink arrived and the boy took it, settling himself near Lachlan avidly to watch. Having proved his speaking credentials only to Lachlan, Agnes and Rhoda of the hysterical lung, Franz was treated with a certain good-natured condescension. One player being left redundant without an opponent, Lachlan was asked to perform what was considered locally as the prodigious feat of playing two simultaneous matches. He reluctantly complied. Lachlan played for his own stimulation, not public esteem. So he played his two opponents, defeated one and achieved a stalemate with a second he would have beaten had his attention been monopolized by the game. There followed several games of speed chess, the tactics growing sloppier as the evening progressed. Having dispatched several more opponents, Lachlan ordered Franz to drink up, downed his own whisky against the night and walked back to the house chatting to the boy who seemed to have stored what conversation the night's activities provoked until they were alone.

The following night the doctor was uncharacteristically dyspeptic. Agnes's dinner had not improved the world. Franz had set the chess pieces up in readiness. Rather than upset the boy, Lachlan sat opposite him, moving uncomfortably in his chair, contemplating a vindictive bubble of trapped wind. The doctor's attention is desultory and at one point he excuses himself to stand by the back door and raise his leg to break the seal on a blissful fart.

'That will be the Drovers' lunches, not my cooking.' Agnes has startled him in flagrante. The doctor is stoical, not embarrassed.

'It is age, Agnes. It comes to us all, women included. The days of definitive and predictable bowel movements have gone. I compare my intestines now to the bilges of some decrepit old scow, disgracing the flag of convenience.'

It is the exaggeration of poetic licence. Feeling considerably better, Lachlan returns to the game to find himself in trouble. It takes what concentration he can muster to summon a stalemate. The following night his undivided attention barely produces a win. Several harsh realizations simultaneously dawn upon him. He has been playing the same game for the past fifteen years. A winning strategy that needed no revisiting has left him strategically flat-footed when faced with someone capable of predicting his next move. Indulging all his idiosyncratic interests is all very well, but he has lost whatever mental flexibility he once possessed. Ever since he can remember, at University and beyond, nothing presented him with any great difficulty; he is accustomed to being cleverer than his contemporaries, and sequestering himself in Rassaig he has been the only fish in the smallest of pools – until now.

The boy proves more talkative over subsequent games. From the brief answers to deliberate questions Lachlan begins to build up an intelligible picture of Franz's background. The following nights produce three consecutive stalemates. On the next of these Lachlan knows Franz has conceded a stalemate in deference to himself.

'I think our games are finished.'

'I have not won.'

'I think we both know you could. You have watched my only game and beaten it. I will not get better. You will only improve and you are better than I am already. Tell me, did you play at home?'

'Always.'

'With your father?'

'Yes.'

Lachlan appreciates the need for caution. In their brief exchanges they have studiously avoided talk of the fate of Franz's family.

'And did you beat him?'

'Never.'

This is doubly humbling, coming as it does on the night of his first reversal in Rassaig.

'He was a doctor?'

'Yes. Like you. But he did not visit people in their houses. They visited him. In hospital. He looked at brains. He knew about phrenology also, although I do not think he gave it much . . . credit.'

It is the first time he has spoken about his family in the past tense. They both gaze for a few moments in silence at the dormant pieces till Franz begins carefully to replace them in their box.

The following afternoon Gail returns from school to a note from Lachlan asking her to come and see him at her convenience. Glad of the air and the chance for conversation other than Eileen Campbell's, she walks to the house. Lachlan is in the lounge. At his insistence she agrees to stay for dinner. His invitation accepted, Lachlan disappears into the hall. She hears him tap on one of the doors, presumably leading to the back of the house, and when it is opened say, 'One more for dinner.'

'And what evening will that be, doctor?'

'This evening.'

'Unlike Our Lord I cannot stretch a fish. Perhaps you could find out if the young lady is partial to mackerel portions.'

'I'm sure anything will be fine.' And to Gail, once the lounge door is closed on them, 'We're having fish.' Never one for preamble when preoccupied with the matter in hand, Lachlan begins, 'I've brought you here to talk about the boy.'

'Frank?'

'What do you know about him?'

'I've heard he's an evacuee. I've heard he hasn't spoken and that he's considered to be . . . well, slow is I suppose the kindest way to put it. Although it strikes me that any child uprooted from everything he knows may have reasons of his own not to speak. And from my experience, limited though it is, if someone is silent it doesn't necessarily mean their understanding is impaired.'

Lachlan strikes a match with a sulphurous burst, nodding

to himself as he does so. She believes he is agreeing with her. He is congratulating himself on the judiciousness of his choice in selecting her. She watches the ceremony as he rolls the cigar end, slowly lighting it in the flame.

'Angus is slow. Frank does not exist. Franz is a well. I threw down a stone when I first met him and I've not heard it hit the bottom yet.' He talks intensely for fifteen minutes as a cylinder of ash accumulates. She listens without interruption. Concluding, he waits for a response.

'Well, frankly, if you can't beat him at chess I don't think that academically there's much I can teach him.'

'To be quite brutal, I don't think you can either. But if not you, who else? He's too small for the High School. In any normal environment he would be moved up a few years as soon as he was properly assessed, but with his accent and size I think there's a fair chance he'd be bullied and I don't know if they could teach him either. I imagine you're more competent than the teachers there. He needs some kind of normal routine and to be near other children. There is more he needs to learn than lessons. Most things he'll pick up through osmosis. Just keep him around.'

19

Angus is stacking creels on the jetty. It is mid-afternoon, December, and he is working against the fading light. He works quickly. It will not do to be still for any length of time in this cold. He is young, and supple. He can carry out with grace tasks the older men grunt over. As he is stooping he feels a hand follow the curve of his spine down past the waistband of his trousers. He straightens in a sharp movement and spins round. Lucy is there. The wind is coming off the sea and he has not heard her approach. She is wearing her bib-and-brace overall and green pullover.

'Cold.' He does not respond but continues to stare at her. Having now met her on several occasions he is no longer completely mesmerized. As he looks at her now he appraises, the way she is used to being looked at and is comfortable with. 'Cold,' she repeats, as if not speaking but voicing her thoughts aloud.

'Cold,' he agrees, although he does not feel it. The response snaps her out of her train of thought.

'The thing I hate about this place is that there's no place to go.'

'What do you mean?'

'What do you think I mean? I mean there's no place to GO!'

'Are you working?'

'Whatever gave you that idea? I've been working since . . . dawn.' Dawn these mornings is eight o'clock. 'I gave myself a few hours off and came to see you.' He is dumbfounded. She guesses. 'What, never had no visitors before? Have you got anywhere to go? I live with those miserable bastards who would shoot a man within ten yards of our room. Do you have a place to go?'

'I have a room above the shop.'

'What shop?'

Any of the locals would have known. 'The shop' sells the kind of miscellany small places with a near-monopoly do. He tries to explain by giving examples. She interrupts.

'You don't get it. I'm not interested in what it sells but where it is.'

'Near the harbour.'

'That's fucking miles.' She looks at her feet and between the planking to the recess below. 'What's down there?'

'The sea – at high tide.'

'Well, it isn't high tide now. C'mon. At least it's out the wind.'

The rocks are slippery with flaccid seaweed that pops beneath their feet as the small bladders burst in tiny spumes of brine. She leans against one of the stanchions nearer the beach, the high-water mark coming to just below her shoulder blade.

'Come here.'

He moves towards her, his step steadier on the rocks than hers. In the failing light the two figures seem to merge and disappear into the upright she has her back to.

The observer moves from the lee of the wind-blown oak, sure of being unseen by the couple preoccupied with each other. Turning its back on the sea, it begins to make its way inland across the dull fields.

20

Giving time to Franz is not as difficult as she first thought it would be. Angus's attendance, always intermittent and dependent on the haphazard work schedule of whatever odd jobs he can pick up, has now fallen off almost completely. He turned up at the Campbells' the previous Sunday morning, without forewarning, standing in the middle of the kitchen floor, and needlessly apologized in a rehearsed explanation that degenerated into a torrent of stammers, prompted by the audience of the elderly couple he had not anticipated being there. Taking pity, she had silenced him by explaining that his attendance was optional and to come only when he felt he could. He left looking chastened.

She wonders if he was so simple as not to have foreseen the possibility of the Campbells being in their own kitchen. 'God forgive me,' she thinks, 'but there will be more stimulation in teaching someone who may not need me than in nursing that poor boy.'

The time she had set aside for Angus is used to accommodate Franz. She waits until the class disperses before inviting him to come up and sit across from her at her desk. He walks between the rows of children's desks, lugging the Gladstone bag. His arrival with it the first morning prompted laughter in the class. She had diverted their attention elsewhere. At the first break he seemed disinclined to join the children outside.

'You shouldn't be here, Franz. You should be out there, with them.'

Taking this as an instruction, he climbed out of his chair

without a word and walked out to stand in the middle of the playground, bag in hand, listing slightly with the weight of its mysterious contents. He stood like a stone in the midst of the flux around him. Several games were being played simultaneously. She watched him anxiously, her breath misting the cold pane. A ball ricocheted off his shin. A ragged circle formed round him, the bag being the object of curiosity. She could see questions being addressed. He mouthed responses. Attention spans being momentary, curiosity faded. Spectators moved on. Another ball hit him on the back. He was in the middle of two impromptu football games. One of the boys said something to him, pointing to a specific spot on the playground, currently occupied by the jumper of the pointing boy. He was being asked to put his bag down to mark one of the goalposts. The pointing boy was cold and wanted his jumper on again. She saw him agree and replace the goalie, their concession to let him be near the bag they needed as a marker.

When she sounded the bell he came in. For the first time since leaving home he looked like someone his age should, flushed and if not happy then animated. She looked forward to telling Lachlan.

'To be frank . . .' No pun is intended. She starts again. 'To be honest, from what Lachlan tells me, I don't know what I can do for you. You can have access to any of the textbooks we have here, but Lachlan tells me you read whatever of his books you want to. And I think the books you find at home will do you more good than anything here. What I thought would be a start would be if we introduced ourselves to one another. I tell you about me and you tell me about you. Do you think this is a good idea?'

'Yes.'

'Would you like to go first or would you like me to?'

'You go first.'

'Right . . . Having suggested it, it would probably have been advisable if I had thought what I was going to say. There's really not much to tell. I imagine your story is much more interesting. I was a teacher back home.'

'Where's that?'

'Winchester. When my fiancé enlisted I thought somehow I should be making a greater sacrifice than I was.'

'Why?'

'It seemed too easy, just comfortably staying at home doing the same things I had been doing when everyone else was doing so much more. A lot of the children I taught moved to more remote places.'

'Like this?'

'Perhaps not as remote. I thought working on the land would be a good idea. I looked forward to working with my hands, probably because my mother hadn't.' She laughs. 'It seems strange but I looked forward to getting dirty.' From his reaction he does not find her aspiration strange. She stops laughing, realizing they probably have no common experience to allow him to gauge the incongruity of this. If what Lachlan guesses is true, Franz has been through enough in the past year to relegate everything she has experienced to the commonplace. 'And here I am, clean hands, sitting in a classroom again.'

'You could always pick up some mud on the way home.'

'Yes. Somehow it wouldn't be the same.' They fall silent. She is under no obligation to justify herself to the boy but somehow feels she has done herself an injustice. The reduction of her life to this summary makes it sound banal; yet to embroider it with irrelevant facts to infuse interest would be worse. It would be pathetic. She comforts herself that she is much more than a summation of details.

'Your turn.'

'English, French or Russian?'

'. . . English,' she answers, perplexed. He slides from his seat and lifts the bag to an adjacent child's desk, set at a convenient height for his investigation. Opening the bag, he delves into it, like an entertainer into a beast's maw, his back concealing the proceedings. He straightens, holding some kind of packet, which he opens and methodically goes through till he finds the appropriate document. He turns, extending his arm towards her, holding the papers like a relay baton.

21

Angus's simple mind is in a blissful whirl. For the past two weeks now he has been seeing Lucy intermittently. She arrives when it suits, finding him wherever he happens to be working, or here. He cannot predict her arrival and lives in a state of anguished anticipation. When she is not with him he has no knowledge of her whereabouts. His movements are more predictable. She has a reputation for doing as little as possible on the farm. The times they are not together cannot occupy her with work and sleep. She seems to find him when she wants him. He has taken to reconnoitring around the Drovers in the hope of seeing her, without working up the courage actually to enter. But this evening she has told him she will be here.

His preparations have been frantic and ineffectual. He has spread the bed, left unmade since she last lay there, unwilling to erase her cherished imprint. He has cleaned his one-ring gas burner. The toilet off the narrow stairwell is shared with other desultory tenants. Having no cleaning materials, he has gone to 'the shop' for bleach and cloths and cleaned that.

Besides the bed and the gas ring the room has a small fire and is furnished with a deal table and two collapsible chairs. Linoleum that does nothing to cheer the prospect or conserve the heat had been laid on top of a previous layer and is now worn through in patches to reveal strata. The curtain covers half the window. There is nothing between the pane and the Atlantic; he has no need for privacy.

He was sure she said something about five o'clock and sits

perched on the edge of the bed from darkness onwards. She arrives around seven. He can hear her pant as she makes her way up. She is smoking a cigarette as she enters.

'Y'know, if you were on the game it wouldn't be the work but the stairs that would kill you.' He doesn't understand. He is prepared to take her coat. 'Not just yet, dearie. Wait till I heat up. What's to drink?'

'Tea.'

'No gin? Beer?' She is touched by his confusion. Fishing in her purse, she pulls out notes. She is as lavish with her money as with her body. 'Here, nip down to the Drovers and get half a dozen bottles of stout.' He is nonplussed. 'What're you waiting for?'

'The Drovers. It's not allowed.'

'And I am? I've been on my feet all day. My back's killing me . . .' His confusion deepens. Seeing this she stands, stiffly.

'No. It's all right. I'll do it.' He leaves her stoking the fire, one hand massaging the small of her back.

His entrance provokes a ragged chorus of greetings and good-natured jokes. Looking round, he cannot see the obvious iniquity of the place. He has carried out casual work for almost everyone here except Graham MacKenzie, the landlord, who leans on the other side of the counter with a quizzical smile.

'Seen the light, Angus?'

'Six bottles of stout please.' He proffers the money in a single crumpled handful. Graham takes what he needs, handing the bottles across with the change.

'Having a party, Angus?'

'Something for the weekend, Angus?'

'She'll eat you raw, Angus.'

Douglas Leckie and any of the other half dozen men Lucy has worked her way through would have made a show of accepting this banter in the spirit of randy camaraderie with which it is intended. Angus begins to reverse out, looking as if he expects to be shot if he turns his back. His head bangs against the doorjamb and he drops a bottle, eliciting a titter that runs round the room. In his confusion to retrieve the bottle he drops another, which bursts open in a foamy plume, provoking a guffaw. Help comes from an unexpected quarter. Murdo, dart poised, stoops down and picks up both bottles in his hand. He speaks at a volume to be overheard. 'Never mind them, Angus. They're just jealous. At least you've got something warm to go home to that doesn't look like a farmyard animal in curlers. Not many of us here can say the same.' The deflection is adroitly done, too subtle for Angus to notice. Murdo turns to the bar. 'It's been so long for most of you bastards that you'd come off quicker than the stout.' There is a general shout of laughter that has nothing now to do with Angus. Murdo lays the open bottle on the bar. 'Graham, give him another. Put it on my slate. I'll drink this.' Angus accepts the replacement wordlessly, exits staring fixedly at the floor and runs up the stairs, bottles clinking. When he goes in she has lit another cigarette. She sees on his face more than confusion.

'What's the matter, love?'

'They made fun. Of me. Of us . . .' He cannot explain. Despite all the things he has been told about innate evil and our predisposition to sin, this is the only sacrosanct thing he has ever had and it is held up for public ridicule.

'Fuck them. They're just jealous.'

'That's what Murdo said.'

'The big bloke?'

'Yes.'

'Well, he's right. Forget them.' But she sees this casual dismissal will not do. 'Come here.'

She has never yet met a man who is not consoled by sex

and she has met many men. This is earlier than she intended. She wanted a sit-down and a drink first. Not much chance of anything to eat from the look of this dump. She has never come across anyone so pathetically grateful for the smallest of intimacies. There is something touching in his gratitude, his eagerness to learn and to please, the embarrassment of his almost instantaneous climaxes, the stamina of his youth, the persistence of his desire again and again till she really must go. She abandons her cigarette to the hearth and stands.

'You must be upset.'

She is surprised at not being presented with the automatic erection she is usually confronted with when sliding her hand down his trousers. She coaxes the blood easily in rhythmic clenches. It was well practised before she came to Rassaig. She laughed at the ease with which she milked her first cow. Watching from the shadow of the barn, Ewan McHarg overheard her make the comparison to Harriet. He intended coughing to make his presence felt but somehow forbore, and stood in aroused silence, listening to the drum of milk on tin.

She undresses and kneels in front of the fire. The room is cold. Glowing coals warm her nearest side. There is a narrow strip of rug. One knee rests on the flattened pile. She can feel the grit of coal dust beneath the other knee on the linoleum. Obediently he kneels behind her. The first time she told him to do this he told her it must be wrong because it was 'like the beasts'. On the occasions they have been together she lets him enter her quickly, getting his first orgasm out the way so that she can enjoy him at her leisure, controlling his position and speed at their next coupling. She anticipates the same now, but his upset causes some delay. He remains erect, rhythmically pumping. His explosive climax deferred, she feels herself float. Her hanging breasts bob slackly, rocking with expanding waves that radiate out from between her legs. She climaxes before he does, the snort from her nostrils dispersing grit. He continues. With surprise she climaxes again, and moments later feels herself rising once more on the upward slope. Young men are better, this one better still. His pubes and thighs are slick with her juice, she, his marvellous ripe, ripe fruit. She pants, exhaling words between thrusts, 'Don't . . . stop . . . let's go . . . for the . . . hat-trick,' and gives a strangled laugh at her own humour. He leans forward, turning his face sideways to rest his cheek in the hollow between her shoulder blades. Both are sweating. She is too preoccupied to feel the tears trickle on her spine. Adoringly he kisses the mole on her back – his beloved has a blemish that complements her perfection – and reaches round to cup her dangling breasts. As he squeezes she spasms, pushing back to force him in, and contracts. Moistly socketed, he comes in a surge that clouds his vision and prompts a scream from her. She rests her forehead on the dirty rug till her breathing subsides.

'Angus. What a talent. What a waste till I got here. Aren't I lucky?'

'I love you.'

22

Since reading the letter Gail has had to restrain herself from putting her arms around Franz each time she sees him. Most mornings he is hunched attentively over his desk reading whatever absorbs him as she claps her hands for general attention and the register. No matter how preoccupied he is, he does not need telling twice. The large book disappears into the larger bag. He brings his full focus to bear on problems she knows he must find puerile. If he is bored by the simplicity of the lessons, no trace escapes him. She is grateful for this courtesy, knowing from experience how unruly bored children can be, particularly boys.

Despite the isolation of this community his idiosyncrasies haven't marked him out. His accent, the care Agnes has taken with his clothes, his notorious bag, his reserve in lessons, only ever volunteering the answer when it is apparent no one else will and she is getting exasperated by the general uncomprehending silence, all the traits that could have identified him for victimization go unremarked by the motley assortment of his schoolfellows. She is relieved. Children will adapt to anything. She thinks the parents could learn something from this.

Just as they have accepted his clothes, accent and bag, they have accepted that he stays when they leave. It occasions no comment. He is different, and staying behind is simply part of his difference.

The limited experience she has had teaching precocious children is of little help to her here. Previous experiments have involved finding out how much the children know, gauging their advancement on the curriculum and taking it from there. With Franz she finds herself at a loss. The curriculum is of little help in calibrating the intelligence of a boy who presented a letter in three languages, all of which he no doubt understood. In private she will not insult him with the rudimentary arithmetic sufficient to teach the sons of fishermen and farmers not to be short-changed at market. So mostly their lessons begin with something he effortlessly absorbs and become conversations. Given what she knows, she thinks the best thing she can do is to befriend him.

His father encouraged all the children to question and to speak. He would have been prepared to discuss almost any topic with them. Her faith taught Natasha greater circumspection, but she too encouraged conversation. Of all the children Franz availed himself most of this advantage, and it was he who felt it most when the privilege was withdrawn. He never spoke about anything personal after he left Prague, and eventually he never spoke about anything at all. Natasha had been careful to write to male relatives, reasoning that the battle would more easily be won if she could persuade them. The women Franz has had any experience of since leaving home have been limited to the wives of the men who took him. They had their own commitments. And he was astute enough to know that nice as these women might be, they saw him as someone who could come to jeopardize their families. Irene was the exception. She had only seen him as an encumbrance. Confronted by his impenetrable silence, she had drawn her own conclusions. She was not a bright woman and Franz had ascribed to her the limited intelligence she thought his silence betokened.

And now here he was, his slow recuperation being fostered by Lachlan and his library of facts up the hill, and this attractive and attentive young woman in the schoolroom, people who do not see him as a liability or an imposition.

It did not take Gail long to notice that he said almost nothing in public, besides putting her out of her misery when the correct answer refused to come from the class. He was more forthcoming in private. She was in a quandary, wondering how much of a professional distance to try to maintain. But then, she reasoned, there is little she could actually teach him. She could not envisage circumstances where he might exploit a friendship and become rowdy in the classroom. So she asked him if, Lachlan's agreement permitting, he would like to come with her the following Saturday to Oban.

Lachlan didn't object. There was nothing remarkable in the outing. Franz followed in tow while she window-shopped. They walked up to McCaig's Tower, the Coliseum-like folly overlooking the bay. The sea was membranous under the low cloud base. From their vantage point they saw columns of light puncture the canopy, daubing luminous spots on the shifting water.

'Those shafts of light. We called them Jacob's ladders when I was a girl, from Jacob's dream in the Bible when he sees angels climbing to heaven. I don't know if the expression translates.'

He did not reply but looked from her face back out towards the spectacle she was pointing to, beyond the island of Kerrera, out towards the Inner Hebrides, where the weather front was congealing. They could see opaque curtains of rain or snow being driven landwards. And all this, the Victorian solidity of the uncompleted folly, the brindled sea, the approaching storm, her at his side leaning into the wind, traffic in the harbour below, raucous cries of the gulls circling the returning smacks, all poured in to be indelibly committed to his memory.

'We should go down, beat the weather.'

They make the tea room with seconds to spare, the first pattering of hail on the awning driving pedestrians off the street. Others have had the same idea. They stand together waiting for a table while she reads selectively from the menu. Finally seated at a window table he is allowed to choose, he uses his cuff to rub out a circle of condensation from the misted pane and from this blurred porthole watches pedestrians emerge as the weather lifts. She presses her face against his to share the view. He wonders if she can also hear his heart.

'Look at the harbour. The water is churned into peaks. I'm sure my mother would think of meringues if she saw that.'

A three-tiered cake stand, complete with tongs, arrives with the tea.

'Posh,' she comments.

Hostile as Lachlan is to the teachings of the Viennese witch doctor, he understands the concept of transference, tacitly subscribing to it by the use of layman's terminology to describe the same thing. When they return from their jaunt to Oban, Gail comes to the house to deliver the book Lachlan asked her to buy. By prior arrangement they all eat together. Talking to her across the table, Lachlan observes Franz throughout the meal. He watches him formally thank Gail in the hall as she takes her leave. He watches him in the lounge afterwards, toying distractedly with the pieces of a model Lachlan has given him to assemble. Brief as his acquaintance with the boy is, Lachlan believes this to be out of character. And he watches him as he says goodnight and takes his leave early to read in his room.

Tomorrow is Sunday. Franz imagines the schoolroom in the darkness, the inert furniture, like him, awaiting her arrival. For the first time Sunday will be as long for him as it is for the Presbyterians.

23

My dearest Arkadi,

If this letter goes no further than you then there is really no need of it. You do not need me to ask you to care for my boy. I know you will treat him as one of your own, and bring him up in the faith we share and which I have been careful to have him instructed in.

Having denied to himself the seriousness of our position, my husband, now accepting it, has given himself over entirely to doing what he can to better our circumstances. And having accepted this state of affairs he has, as with most things he turns his attention to, seen more clearly than I have what the outcome might be. And he has concluded that it may not be possible for Franz to stay with Arkadi.

So this letter is to you, whoever you may be, who now have the care of my dear, dear boy in your hands. This letter is so very difficult to write, and I have left myself so little time to write it. Were it longer it could not begin to do justice to my feelings or those of my husband.

Franz is an extremely intelligent child. I am aware that this may sound like listing one of the advantages of a piece of merchandise I am trying to sell. I am writing this only to explain that he has the kind of sensitive nature that normally accompanies one of his gifts. He is reserved at home. If he has found his way to your care by who knows what path, he may be more reserved than ever. Please do not mistake this for coldness. He is a very loving boy and for all his intelligence he is just that, a boy.

Please care for him. Be kind. I cannot begin to guess what he *must have been through if this letter is being read by someone who is strange to me, and I cannot begin to express the gratitude that I and my husband feel towards you, this unknown person to whom we have entrusted the most precious thing we have.*

My life now is a constant prayer. I pray for my boy and I pray that you, whoever you may be, will have the decency and fortitude to bring him up to become the kind of man he would have been, had circumstances allowed him to stay with us. And I pray that somehow, somewhere, his father and I will be given the opportunity to thank you in a way that this inadequate letter cannot.

Please do this thing for me. You cannot know how terrible it is to consign your child to the unknown, and to depend on the kindness of people you have never met.

My greatest hope is that this letter remains unread. If you are reading this, if you have my boy, if you are doing what you can to keep him safe, you have more than my thanks. You have my love.

Natasha Brod. Prague. 20 March, 1939.

It is very late. The rest of the house is in darkness, the rest of the world asleep. The only illumination in the study is provided by the glow of dying embers from the hearth and the desk light. The curtains have been carelessly drawn, casting a vertical bar of orange over the short expanse of garden. Snow is falling again. Within the visible slit large flakes loom out of the heavy sky to drift down, disappearing noiselessly into the white carpet. Lachlan removes his glasses, squeezes his eyes closed and massages the bridge of his nose, pinching the red crevices that years of wear have eroded. Replacing the glasses he reads the letter once more and places it, face down, within the luminous pool of his desk. Gail handed it to him this afternoon without comment, asking only that he return it to Franz once he had read it.

If possible this has drawn him closer to the boy. We are all born to be orphans but now he knows that he and Franz have something additional in common: they stand at the bow-wave of the present with nothing remaining in their wake. Franz cannot fail to know that the author of this letter, her husband and daughter are obliterated. Aside from the tragedy of the situation, what strikes Lachlan most forcibly is the irony of the fact that this is an indirect appeal to faith, the faith that earmarked Natasha and her family to be consumed by the inferno aimed at them, and of all the people to whom an appeal of faith could be addressed he feels the least qualified.

He made a silent pact with the boy that first freezing night on the clifftop. Irrational though he knows it to be, he now makes another with the dead woman.

From the garden the curtain chink is a narrow column of light. From a distance this is a tiny strip in the immensity of the surrounding darkness, as snow continues to fall softly into the void.

24

School has finished for Christmas. As Gail dismissed the children, chairs scraped back and the class was cleared with an exuberant rush. Her desk is dotted with presents, mostly home baking, which she feels her short tenure has not entitled her to. She lists the names with the intention of writing thanks to the parents. Looking up, she finds that Franz has waited behind.

'Lachlan's celebrating Christmas,' he says.

'So I hear.'

'Agnes says it's a miracle. Do you believe in miracles?'

'I don't think Agnes means it literally. I think she just means she's surprised.'

Previous Christmases have involved Agnes demanding money from Lachlan that he hands across with a histrionic groan, reminding her that 25 December was a pagan festival whose date has been arrogated by 'her mob'. The truth is that he allows her to cajole from him the virtues he would otherwise practise in secret. She would order the tree and buy presents on his behalf for whatever members of his small clique she believed deserved it. This usually comprised those who bought for him. His only concession was to make a secret foray to Glasgow or Edinburgh and walk mystified among the Christmas lights until something sufficiently garish seized his attention, that he would then buy for her. The standard routine comprised her attending midnight mass on Christmas Eve, returning to find him still up. They have a drink, exchange presents, with her invariably thanking him and asking for the receipt. On Christmas Day his small circle of intimates from the Drovers come round for a late-afternoon dinner. He pays lip service to helping and stands redundant in the kitchen until dismissed. Despite being the only atheist present he is a magnanimous host, and enjoys reading labels, dispensing parcels whose contents are a mystery to him and receiving thanks for presents he has only paid for.

Last week he astonished Agnes, pre-empting her arrangements by turning up with an enormous tree he had had Angus drag up to the house.

'I've already ordered a tree from Kyle.'

'I bought this from Kyle.'

'It's too big.'

'You've no sense of style.'

'It won't fit.'

She is correct. Help is summoned. After two abortive attempts Angus, in the middle of the lawn, saws four feet off the top. The truncated version now dominates the lounge. Each slammed door dislodges a green halo. Viewed from the garden, a tree appears to be growing through the interrupting ceiling into Lachlan's bedroom. Agnes is obliged to buy more ornaments. Adorned, the thing looks even more monstrous.

'Any more surprises?'

Unasked, he passes her a wedge of notes. This is far more than she would have demanded. 'The usual and . . . be good to the boy.'

'Does he celebrate Christmas? Being Jewish, I mean.'

'Would you have him excluded?'

'Of course not. What a thing to say, Doctor McCready.'

'I believe in Yahweh no more than I do the Holy Ghost or the tooth fairy, and I celebrate Christmas. I'll support anything that promotes good will, no matter how specious. And anyway, show me a boy who doesn't enjoy getting presents. And by the way, before you try and convert him, there's a Jewish gentleman will be coming over from Oban from time to time. I've asked him to come and talk to Franz. I said we'd be happy to put him up here if it's more convenient for him to stay the odd night.'

'You've traced a relative!'

'Not exactly . . .' She has not read the letter. Lachlan complied with Gail's request and handed it back to Franz with as little commentary as he received it. 'I'm having him instructed in his faith.' He has confounded her. She absorbs this in total silence and goes away to consider its repercussions.

Gail has been invited to Christmas dinner at Lachlan's and been obliged to turn this down due to other commitments. Gracious as ever, Lachlan has told her that Agnes cooks for a battalion and that the cold remnants will be available for days. 'So if you come back earlier than you intend, don't be a stranger.' As ignorant of his history as everyone else, she cannot know that the invitation comes from personal experience.

So she packs. It is an embarrassing departure. Now that she no longer works on the farm she feels she occupies her accommodation on sufferance. The Campbells have been kind enough and now give her a departing gift. Having nothing to return the unexpected courtesy, she kisses them both, unexpected tears welling. She tries to cover her confusion by lifting her bags and abruptly walking out to the waiting van. Lucy has called in favours, or bestowed more, to have Douglas Leckie agree to drive her to the station.

On the swaying trains south she has time to contemplate her situation. Her tears were not just caused by the Campbells' generosity. She is apprehensive about meeting Clive. Her anxiety is not lessened by the journey. Rural darkness is replaced by the muffled lights of cities. Here restrictions are imposed. She is moving towards the war. The plan is to spend Christmas and a few days afterwards with her parents before going up to London to meet Clive.

Her mother is delighted that she has abandoned the farm for the classroom. She has never understood her daughter's motives. To move to manual labour seems to her a retrograde step. Dirt is degrading. If she had to do it, why not somewhere more accessible, why Scotland?

Of her parents Gail more closely resembles her father. She has his intelligence, if not his complete reticence. She knows her mother feels excluded by the intimacy she enjoys with him. What her mother fails to appreciate is that she excluded herself. Gail's respect for her father's judgement is tempered only by her failure to understand why he chose to marry a snob. But ironically, if Rassaig has taught her anything it has taught her tolerance. The determination that ordered Gavin Bone from her classroom was not her father's. She now knows that. She also observes that even in the brief interval of her absence, both parents have noticeably aged.

She is solicitous towards them both. Something has happened to them that she has noticed happen to others: adversity, or perhaps simply acceptance of compromise that age brings, has reconciled them to each other. Foibles do not seem to grate. They are kinder towards each other. This kindness puts an end to her role as go-between, a position she reluctantly adopted from her late teens.

For the first time she encounters powdered egg, interminable queues and the national loaf. Her parents are proud of procuring half of a turkey. She makes a mental note to try to be more diligent in sending food parcels south.

She goes to London two days before the New Year. Clive held on to the flat in Bayswater. Before leaving home she used to apoplex her mother by coming up to stay with him for the weekend. She arrives before he does. It is late afternoon. Slanting lemon sunlight drenches the dormant furniture, awaiting her arrival to bear witness. The silence is eerie. She sits in a familiar cane chair and is startled by the fusillade of cracking. She opens all the windows: cold is preferable to stagnation. The place is a corridor of air for ten minutes. She closes them, prematurely draws the blackout blinds and sets the fire. The queues here are worse than in Winchester. She does not want to shop. The cupboards yield unexpected dividends, the residue of purchases before rationing bit. There is beer and tea. There are tins of chopped pork, each with the key attached. She breaks a nail prising a key off, unwinds a metallic spiral and upends the tin over a plate. The meat is mottled, like a cold thigh, and emerges with a sucking sound, surrounding jelly retaining the internal contours of the tin. The rattle of the key in the lock startles her and she stands erect, her heart hammering, as if caught in the act of stealing.

The conversation is stilted. Perhaps, she thinks, he is as apprehensive as she is. They have written to each other so diligently, anticipating the meeting, that the moment has been invested with a significance that kills any spontaneity. On previous meetings, after a period of separation, they have simply undressed and had sex where they stood. She has lain, or sat, or crouched on every appropriate surface. The flat is fraught with mementos of their importunate lovemaking. Now, when he enters, he sees the makeshift meal and a desultory conversation circulates round dinner. They drink warm beer. He eats voraciously. Not hungry, she hands him hers.

Despite the awkwardness neither is willing to suggest going out. Their correspondence has hinted at satiation, to be together all night. There has never before been a question of taking the initiative, it had always been a mutual urgency that dictated the pattern of behaviour. Knowing somehow that he will not begin, she goes into the bedroom and takes her clothes off, calling him through, reflecting, as she does so, that her mother may have done the same to her father. He walks briskly into the room and begins to undress. He has not looked at her. Previously he has always watched her undress. The motions of his hands are violent and precise, as if dismantling a weapon under drill inspection. It is obvious from the first instant that there is something different about the two of them. She wonders if the weight of this change is due to either or both. She lies down, putting a pillow just below the small of her back to raise her buttocks. Despite the lack of preamble she is moist and anxious for him. They have made love many times before in this position, him kneeling above her with her calves resting on his shoulders. It is not until he kneels between her parted thighs that he fully looks at her for the first time since entering the flat. His gaze wavers. There is something dreadfully different that she cannot place. Has he been with someone else? Before she can conjecture further he enters her in one progressive, slow thrust, pushing her legs from his shoulders to lie on top of her, his face buried in the rope of her hair looped on the pillow.

The action of his tilting pelvis seems independent from the rest of him, which clings. She realizes what is wrong: he is frightened. He is going to war and he is terrified he will die. His fear is palpable. She kisses his neck and whispers to him that it will be all right, that she is here. His grasp tightens. His fear is more real to him now that he has silently admitted it to her. She knows she will not come and strokes his back till she feels the muscles spasm with his soft outpouring.

In their present mood it is too early to stay in bed. They return to the lounge to drink more beer and listen to the radio. Suddenly hungry, she opens a second tin of meat and begins to gorge, both relieved and guilty that it is he who has changed more than her. She tells him it is nothing to be ashamed of, that everyone must be terrified and not admit it, that she would be paralysed by the prospect of seeing action, that it is so much easier for her and she can only imagine what he is going through, that it is more laudable to go if you are frightened. Having unburdened himself he feels like a school-boy who has voluntarily admitted to shoplifting, his guilt alleviated by confession. At the first sound of news on the radio he grabs for the dial, warbling through static till he locates some more music. She touches his hand.

They spend the next three days and nights almost exclusively in the flat. She goes out to shop and stays in the fresh air as long as she can, for the first time feeling no irritation with the queues. To listen to the complaints and conversation of others is a form of communion. Any contact is welcome. They both know he is not relaxing but hiding. He rouses himself only when the sirens sound the second night. Fascinated, she stands in the street, loath to exchange the flat for the confines of the Anderson shelter. He insists. At the first sound of the all-clear he scuttles up the stairs as quickly as he can.

They hear in the bells of the New Year over the radio. She is stifled. After their first encounter they make love frequently at his insistence. There is something frenzied in his performance. It is as if he is trying to wring an epiphany out of every sensation, greedily manufacturing memories, ballast for stability against a turbulent future. Previously he had always been a considerate lover. For her this has degenerated into a kind of captivity of intermittent sex, with him totally preoccupied, keeping fear at bay with stimulation. She climaxes despite his disregard of her reaction.

He sees her off at Euston. He is rejoining his regiment a

day early to allow them to leave together. She suspects he needs the impetus of her departure to make him move; if he did not leave with her he would not leave until fetched. She tells him not to wait till the last moment, till the receding platform separates them. He nods wordlessly in agreement and despite the absence of blowing whistles and slamming doors kisses her with an intensity that anticipates the train drawing them apart. She can feel the desperation in the embrace. She doesn't know what to say. Anything sounds trite. Perhaps this is a time for unspoken promises to be articulated, but neither succeeds in saying anything. He lets go. Manufacturing a jaunty air to lighten the moment, he sets his hat at a rakish angle and walks off the platform. The parody only distresses her. It has not been a good parting.

She is numb, swaying north, up into colder, darker, welcome Rassaig. If their time has convinced her of anything it is that she loves, without being in love, with him. He has been in love with her now for two years. There has been no declaration but both know this. She has been waiting to feel the same way and has managed never to exploit the advantage which the discrepancy in their feelings for each other conferred. Part of him has resented her tact.

They became engaged in preparation for her making the leap of faith. Her mother hoped the war would accelerate their plans. Instead it succeeded in deferring things indefinitely. She refused to be a war bride, at home with an absent husband, coerced into a marriage she might otherwise fight shy of in civilian life. So they settled for cohabitation and recreational sex till his call-up papers arrived and she enlisted in the Women's Land Army.

She watches the darkling landscape slide past till the train is shuttered against the Luftwaffe. She feels she has failed him. Emotionally she has kept him at arm's length and in the past few days her only response to his fear was to lend him the use of her loins. Given on these limited terms, who can blame him for his preoccupation?

She spends the night in the Central Hotel in Glasgow. The following morning she has two hours to kill before her train. She shops, enjoying the flux of people and her sense of distance from them. She buys Lachlan a half Corona, Franz a fountain pen and Agnes a scarf. She is in Rassaig by late afternoon. The thought of going directly to the Campbells' depresses her. She goes to Lachlan's house to take up his offer. Agnes and Franz are in, Lachlan out, probably at the Drovers. With luck Lucy and Harriet might be there too. She stops long enough to deliver the presents and makes her way down the hill into town. Someone is leaving just as she is about to enter. Spilling out with the light flows a wave of sound: the thud of a dart and a genial hubbub. Her heart lifts for the first time since she left the village.

The departing customer has held the door open for her. His enormous shadow blends with the dark recess. It is not until she gets closer that she can see it is Murdo.

'Nice to see you back.'

She had no idea he knew she had gone. She is not sure whether or not he is being sarcastic. She thanks him and stoops under the outstretched arm holding the door open. He exudes a smell of clean cotton and fresh sweat. Evidently changing his mind, he follows her inside. Without even looking back she can feel the full vitality of him, the sheer animal health he radiates like heat on her thighs and buttocks and back and neck. Telling herself not to, she glances round. He is waiting for this and levelly meets her gaze. It is glaringly obvious he isn't frightened of anything.

In the privacy of his room Franz is still staring intently at the fountain pen, as if trying to distil some meaning from its darkly lacquered surface. He has other pens he can write with. Finally he wraps this in a handkerchief that is then wrapped within another and placed with other cherished paraphernalia in his Gladstone bag.

25

While Gail sat half naked with her fiancé, eating from tins, listening for Big Ben to chime in the New Year over the radio, Lachlan stood at his hearth, glass in hand. Hogmanay at the magnanimous doctor's house has become something of a recent institution. Half the clientele left the Drovers at early closing to climb the hill and avail themselves of Lachlan's alcohol. It is the one time of year he extends his hospitality beyond his own small circle. The crowd is always boisterous and good-natured. Agnes is vigilant against burns and spillages. He finds her armed with a cloth and empty ashtrays, confiscates them and orders her to enjoy herself. Franz, having satisfied himself that his bag is safe in his room, threads his way through the adults, enjoying the novelty of the scene. He will only instigate a conversation with Lachlan, Agnes and Gail, but will now talk back to others if addressed.

Lachlan has been watching him keenly all night. The boy has metamorphosed from the traumatized, underweight child he brought home. The letter comes back to Lachlan at every unoccupied moment. He thinks frequently of his pact with the dead woman. He also thinks of the odds of Franz being here, now, and believes the variables defy calculation.

Since the death of his wife Lachlan has ceased to look for equity or signs of benevolent purpose. But somehow the sight of the boy and the thought of the concatenation of unknown circumstances that delivered him here, to Lachlan's hearth as opposed to all the others in Europe, stirs something long dormant in him. Why has Franz, of all children, been preserved from the obliteration to which an unknown proportion of his race have been consigned? He has heard of Comrade Stalin asking how many divisions the Pope has, deriding God's proxy warriors, and of Mussolini's calculatingly profane ultimatum, slapping his watch on the podium and giving divine providence a minute to intervene. But the God who has presided over a race with a history of atrocities to its credit is not likely to be goaded into revealing Himself by the predictable antics of a demagogue. Lachlan has read enough to comprehend the meaning, if not imbibe the message, of the leap of faith. The incremental progression of logic stops at the abyss. Such a leap is an emotional, not an intellectual jump. Why should faith require a plunge into the unknown when love and every other crucial transaction of the heart do not? Does everyone in this room know something he does not? He has always considered the gift of faith a lack of healthy scepticism by any other name. It is a long time since Lachlan was assailed by any doubts. Perhaps he left himself open to the possibility. He is not asking for much, not an apocalypse, perhaps a billowing of the curtains, something private, cryptic, unobtrusive but inter-pretable.

He waits, perhaps five minutes, perhaps ten, smiling at the hubbub, to all appearances pleasantly abstracted, his large mind at intense full stretch. Finally giving up, he smiles, rebuking himself for his private folly. Franz, concerned at the old man standing alone, looking at nothing, comes across. 'My intelligence has gone porous,' Lachlan explains, taking his hand. 'Old age. It comes to us all.'

'No. It does not.'

'No. I'm sorry. You're right, it doesn't.'

'Are you enjoying your party?'

'Very much. But I don't think I'll get to Damascus tonight.'

26

This time he has awaited the dismissal of the class and Franz's tardy departure before making an appearance. She is arranging the books for marking. She does not hear him enter. His shadow across the page is the first indication she has of him and she starts back, the chair scraping loudly in the echoing space.

'Get out!'

'Not before I have a word with you.'

'Get out!'

'There is no one to send for the constable.'

'I will go myself.'

'Not before I have a word with you.'

She is already on her feet. The position of her desk in the top corner of the classroom is such that one side is against the wall. He is directly across from her. When she moves to the open end he moves in parallel. For the first time she is frightened.

'Are you threatening me?'

'I understand that there are certain things you are teaching the pupils.' It is not a question, although he pauses for a response. She is unwilling to engage in a discussion about anything. She feels her only protection is the desk between them. He is prepared to go on without a reply. 'There are certain things that you may believe to be true but that I, and the congregation I am a member of, do not. Nor do I want them presented to the children of our Church as accepted fact. Let the papists have their children's minds filled with what they will. There will be a reckoning and they and you and everyone else will find out how old the world is and how hot hell is. I do not want discussions about pieces of coal and animals older than the world of His creation.'

'Don't presume to tell me what to teach. If you do not move out of the way I will throw this chair out that window and begin to scream.'

'I will have said what I have to before anyone arrives. I have not touched you. I have committed no crime.'

'I will tell the constable you detained me.'

'Angus detained you every night for weeks.'

'Don't be absurd.'

'But he does not detain you any more, does he?' She refuses to answer. 'That is because your friend detains him. That hot bitch spoiled him under the jetty. She copulates like an animal in the fresh air. Perhaps she thinks her actions go unnoticed. Perhaps she does not care. I don't care about her. She is hellbound anyway. I don't want her polluting anyone else. Tell her—'

'Tell her yourself.'

She has not moved but he is now circling the desk towards her. 'You come here with your whorish friends and your filthy theories. One more word about men standing up from four legs and I'll have our children taken away. It is almost believable that that blonde harlot came out of a beast. She certainly takes it like one. And meanwhile you presume to teach. You don't teach, you contaminate.'

She has lifted the pointer. She wishes she had kept the belt. She can imagine the dull slapping sound it would make on his face. The front door opens. Murdo walks in. He takes in the scene at a glance and walks slowly between the desks towards them. Gavin seems unconcerned till he sees the look of relief on her face. He is trying to remember the other man's affiliation. He is not of any Church as far as Gavin is aware.

143

Murdo looks at Gavin only long enough to take a grip on the other man's jacket. Turning his attention to Gail, he rotates his grip until the material corkscrews round his fist. The jacket now too tight to shed, Gavin is held.

'I saw a light.'

'Mr Bone here objects to the teaching of evolution.' She is both relieved and frightened. There is something even more alarming in Murdo's stillness than there is in the older man's fanaticism. Gavin can feel it too. Despite his sense of righteousness he suddenly wants to urinate. The unfair odds would be of no more account to Murdo than they would if he was confronted simultaneously with all the men of Gavin's congregation. If he deems it appropriate he will beat Gavin with as little compunction as he dispatches palpitating fish. Turning away from Gail, he focuses his full attention on the older man.

'I've never made a threat. I don't see the point in telling someone what I'll do. This isn't a threat but I'll make an exception and tell you what I'll do.' He clamps his free hand on the top of Gavin's head and rotates this until he is forced to face Gail. As Murdo speaks his voice gets quieter. 'If you come here again . . . No. Start again. If you come near her again, wherever she is, I'll club you like a lame dog. It doesn't matter if you're wherever it happens to be first. If she arrives, you leave. I won't ask you if you understand because there's nothing not to understand. If you want to go and fetch the constable, go now. Once he's taken statements and gone to bed I'll come and find you.' He releases the head and unwinds the fist almost gingerly. His voice now is almost a whisper. 'Get out.'

Gavin automatically straightens his clothes before turning and walking out. There is a list to his stride and he totters slightly, as if light-headed. With a genial nod to her Murdo follows. For a moment she thinks he has gone to check on

Gavin's departure. A minute elapses and Murdo has not come back. She realizes that he too has gone and that no force this side of hell would coax Gavin to return. She is still standing, holding the pointer defensively before her in a raised diagonal shielding her body. She drops it on the desk and sits limply in the chair.

27

Gavin has been as good as his word. When in the course of the next free period she took down the butterfly case from its mounted bracket, several raised hands confronted her as she turned to face the class.

'Morag?'

'Miss. My father says if you say anything to us about animals I'm to leave.' From the other hands still raised and the homes she sees them depart to she knows they have received the same instructions. She finds herself in a quandary: continue for their own good and find her lessons boycotted by a substantial fraction of the class, or abandon this theme altogether. She replaces the case on the wall and goes back to *Alice in Wonderland*.

That night she sits in front of the fire, gratefully accepting Hamish Campbell's offer of a drink, and gives herself over to thinking about the options of the situation. She is under no obligation to teach the rudiments of science. To stop doing so deprives everyone. Besides which, what might Gavin object to tomorrow? A fanatic cannot be allowed to determine the curriculum. When she considers the children under his tutelage she thinks it is a shame that those most in need of learning are denied it. But she cannot allow them to be taken away to rot in complete ignorance. The compromise she reaches with herself is announced next day.

'Anyone who wants to stay after hours on Tuesdays and Thursdays to talk about the coal and the butterflies and the lizards and all the other things we've been talking about during the recreation period should ask permission from their parents. If your parents don't want you to talk about these things you can go home at the normal time. Can you make sure your parents know we won't be talking about them at all during normal school hours. If any of your parents are unclear about any of this tell them to come and see me and I'll be happy to talk to them.' The last sentence is a lie. She has no desire to defend herself to more of Gavin's ilk, if they exist.

A gratifying complement stay back the first Tuesday. This means more work for her, which she is happy to accept. Theoretically it also bites into the time she has privately to tutor Franz, but he needs company more than tuition, and he can get it if he stays behind too. Lachlan's predecessor, who sold him the house, bought books by the yard, not to satisfy intellectual curiosity but to fill the shelves of a study and give the impression of learning he had no right to. Lachlan has dipped into these books, morocco-bound editions of the Waverley novels, Dickens, Hansard, the King James Bible and a motley assortment of others. He has told her that the boy started with *Little Dorrit* and is inexorably working his way forward. Gail has consistently to remind herself what that poor woman said in her letter: for all his intelligence he is just a boy. She wants him to continue to attend school because she feels the best thing she can give him is the comfort of a routine and the company of his contemporaries. She has explained all this to Lachlan, who agrees.

She has also given Lachlan an edited version of Gavin's visit. She told him what Gavin said without relating the menacing way in which he said it, because to explain this more fully she would have also to explain how the threat was removed, and for reasons she cannot explain to herself she wants her brief interaction with Murdo kept out of it.

In Lachlan's view there is no stigma to being congenitally

stupid. But for a person deliberately to restrict the scope of their own natural intelligence is, to him, blameworthy, and to curb the potential of young minds by forcing on them a blinkered theology is infinitely worse.

It was with some satisfaction then that Lachlan emerged from his surgery to see Gavin next in the waiting room. Lachlan held the door open. Gavin preceded him to sit in the chair and look suspiciously around.

'What can you give me for a persistent cough?' His manner is aggressive enough to suggest Lachlan gave him the cough. One of the reasons Lachlan let Gavin in first was to get a side view of the head against the scale on the wall behind, as he passed. Sitting down, he views the head from another angle and reaches down to unlock his bottom drawer.

'I imagine you will have exhausted every other remedy you could find before placing yourself in my hands.'

'I am not here for a discussion.'

'No. You are here for the help of medical science to alleviate a cough that old wives' remedies could not.'

'Give me a pill.'

'That would be a pill produced after extensive tests on animals then?'

'You're the doctor.'

Squinting at his cranium, 'Tested on animals whose physiology is sufficiently similar to ours to allow us to infer that if it does them good it might help us too.'

'What language are you speaking, doctor?'

'The language of common sense. It would appear to me, Mr Bone, that you seem to believe in the proofs of science when it suits and deny them when it does not.'

'If you're going to talk about that heretical mumbo-jumbo that so-called teacher spouts, then save your breath. Do I get a pill?'

Lachlan momentarily toys with the idea of a volcanic laxative. But the linkage of cause and effect would be too direct. 'Yes. You get a pill. And by taking it you admit, whether you like it, or not, your common ancestry with the animals who tested it for you.'

'Keep it!' He stands abruptly and walks out, slamming the door behind him.

'Always glad to be of assistance,' Lachlan calls after him.

The same evening of Gavin's visit to the doctor, Gail makes an unscheduled visit to Lucy and Harriet. She has only visited them once before at the McHargs' house. The atmosphere was so strained she did not return. Ewan answers. He takes an inordinate amount of time looking at her on the doorstep before shouting over his shoulder in the direction of the girls' room. Harriet comes into the hall and gestures Gail in. Ewan stands grudgingly to one side. The doorway is wide enough but he has positioned himself in such a way that she is obliged to rub past him. She walks straight past them both into the room. Harriet follows and closes the door behind them.

Despite a low ceiling, the room is surprisingly spacious. The curtain looks small, covering, she supposes, a smaller window. She suspects that this place would require artificial light even in the height of summer. A fire burns in the small grate. There are two beds, a plain bureau and an old leather suite. The girls have tried to soften the austerity with various ornaments and a swathe of material over the battered sofa. Lucy is lying on this, smoking a cigarette. Harriet has obviously been reading, her seat angled near the standing light. At the sight of Gail, Lucy claps her hands.

'A visitor! I'll get tea.'

'No. I'll get it.' Harriet can guess that Gail would not come here without a purpose. She infers it has not been to visit her. She goes to brave Mrs McHarg in the kitchen.

'Can we be overheard here?'

'This place is medieval. Like the McHargs. The walls are two feet thick.'

Gail takes off her coat and settles herself on the seat Harriet vacated. 'Gavin Bone came into the schoolroom the other afternoon.'

'I didn't know he had kids.'

'I don't think he has.'

'I heard there's a Mrs Bone. Can you imagine that old grunter climbing on, puffing away between prayers?'

'He mentioned Angus to me.'

'What about Angus?'

'Bone is doing everything he can to make things difficult for me at the school. And when he wants to score points he mentions you and Angus.'

'The boy is gifted. I'll say that for him.'

In her frustration Gail has an impulse to reach across and slap Lucy. 'You're missing the point.'

'To tell the truth, dearie, I'm not really that interested in Gavin Bone's opinion.'

'It's not just his opinion. If he makes it his business he can make it the opinion of lots of other people too.'

'There's a war on.' She stabs the cigarette out prematurely in a little incandescent collision, a look of irritation clouding her usually cheerful face. 'You have to find your fun where you can. Who cares if it upsets some dreary bible-thumpers?'

'It's not just about fun.'

'You're beginning to sound like one of them.'

'And it's not just Gavin Bone.' She thinks of her first day in the classroom, of how the boy referred to Lucy. 'Your reputation extends wider than one congregation around here.'

'So I'm well known for having fun. It was the same back home.'

'If it was just your fun I wouldn't be here to talk to you. But your . . . behaviour rubs off on the rest of us, me and Harriet I mean. We're all being tarred with the same brush.'

'You want to get out a bit more then, have some fun yourself to justify the label.' Harriet enters with the tea tray. Her manner is almost apologetic. She has guessed Gail wants privacy if Lucy does not, but short of standing in the freezing barn there is nowhere else for her to go. From her prone position Lucy launches her next remark across the room. 'Hey, Harriet, Gail here says that the two of you are being tarred with the same brush as me. It seems that you two get some of the reputation and I get all the fun. What do you think?'

'I think that you should keep your voice down.'

'The walls are two feet thick.'

'The door isn't.'

Gail makes the point again, as much for Harriet's sake as in the hope that repetition might cause it to sink in. 'It's not the reputation rubbing off, it's the fact that your behaviour is making my position teaching here more difficult than it already is. Gavin Bone objects to me being in the classroom and he's using you and Angus against me.'

'I'm not a fucking nun, you know. I always thought that was why they were called nuns: they get none.'

'And it's not just additional difficulties in the classroom. It's Angus.'

'I saw him first.'

As a matter of fact she didn't, and Gail has to prevent herself from dragging the conversation down by saying so. 'Lucy, he's a child.'

'Well, he certainly doesn't perform like one.'

'He doesn't know anything.'

'He didn't know anything. At least after meeting me he knows a lot about one thing.'

'Lucy . . .' She is at a loss. It occurs to her that Lucy's moral development is as retarded as Angus's literacy. 'You can't just take up with him because it suits . . .'

'Why not?'

'What will you do afterwards?'

Lucy tilts her head slightly as if trying to rid her ear of bath water. Her normally animated face is momentarily vacant, as if being presented with a mathematical problem wildly beyond her capabilities. 'I don't know . . . Something else. Who knows? We might get invaded tomorrow.'

Gail leans over. Her voice drops. 'To be honest, it's not you I'm worrying about. You'll always get by. It's him.'

Lucy's expression immediately brightens. The solution was obvious all the time. 'You're just jealous because he chose me,' she says without rancour.

'Lucy, he didn't choose anyone. He isn't capable of choosing anyone. You chose him.'

'All right, I chose him before you got the chance to. No hard feelings. Let's have the tea before it stews.'

28

The Day of Judgement is unknown to us so that we must desist all carnal activities and be perpetually vigilant. In anticipation of that day we must purge the leaven that might affect the whole lump.

There is an attack of iniquity in Rassaig. For years now we have had the misfortune to have one of the unregenerate as a doctor, a man dead in spiritual faculties. He is now abetted by these foreign women, one who defiles young men in the fresh air and another who attempts to teach impious nonsense to children who are not at an age to know better.

These three have executed a pincer movement—

Gavin stops. Can a pincer movement come from three sides? Isn't the whole point of pincers that they are two-sided? He scores through the last line and is now irritated. In his heart of hearts he would have to admit that this journal is being kept for posterity and now the whole effect of the page is spoiled. These heretics: they sow doubt with their spurious medicine, pollute the minds of our children with their profane theories, despoil our young men with their bodies and now ruin the effect of the pages of our journal. No detail is too inconsequential for the hellish machinations of the dark forces. Always in a state of simmering rage that he intermittently stokes to feel the pleasure of righteous anger, Gavin is determined he will not let this blemish stop him.

These three have executed a three-pronged attack. I have warned the parents. Angus is another matter.

29

Since his intervention in the schoolroom Murdo haunts Gail's thoughts. He arrives unbidden in the slacker moments, when the corrections have become too tedious to persevere with, when falling snow compels introspection, when the wobbling oval of her bath is punctured with an exploratory foot, when she lies alone in her farmhouse bed, a conscious speck in the cavernous silence of the Glen. She has thought back and does not remember the same preoccupation in her earlier days with Clive, and catching herself having given space to the comparison feels a stab of self-reproach that dispels the image of Murdo till his next interruption.

He has not come back to the schoolroom. Aside from the evenings she stays back with the children, she is accustomed to remaining two other evenings. These are usually spent alone while she plans future activities, reduces the stack of corrections or contemplates how it will all end. A letter from Clive arrives, tersely circumventing an apology. What has he to be sorry for? Without the immediate absolution of her presence and her loins he is too embarrassed to admit to fear. She knows him well enough to know that his former candour now embarrasses him and now, again, he will resent her tact. Instead, by a cautious vocabulary that escapes the censor's pen, he hints at future activities and foreign travel.

It is while reading this letter in the deserted schoolroom that she hears the door click open and her hope rises. But it is only Paul, the constable's son, and she is shocked at the infidelity of her trapped heart, that it could be so unsettled by a forgotten muffler and a returning child.

She has the courage to force herself to face the possibility that she may not be as good as she thought she was. Her imagination, she knows, she has almost no control over. Her actions are a different matter.

When he comes to her in her dreams, or daydreams, there is no dialogue. Nor is there any marked transition from the initial meeting to his penetration of her. Her imagination requires no context for this coupling, just an urgency that transports them instantaneously from wherever they happen to be to this bedroom, undressing them en route. Perhaps she credits him with no dialogue because there is nothing he could say that would augment his function. A week after he evicted Gavin Bone she woke from a dream disturbed by the fact that the thought of Murdo has succeeded in arousing her more than the presence of Clive ever did. This gives more cause for self-reproach. She thinks that perhaps she has credited Murdo with erotic qualities he does not possess. She still has the good sense to be frightened of him.

For two weeks, again to possess herself, she forgoes any outings to the Drovers or elsewhere, with the exception of a dinner invitation to Lachlan's, one of the few places she can be assured of not meeting Murdo. Every night, after she finally leaves the abandoned schoolroom, she walks to the little harbour and stands at the extremity of the sea wall, gulping down lungfuls of freezing air. She stands till the wind has numbed her face, listening to the suck of the backwash, watching seaweed flail in the moonlit swells, the reverberation of ceaseless pounding shuddering up through her boots. She stands till she feels purged and coldly vacant, till the Campbells' kitchen will feel like a welcome reprieve, not a bolt hole she has retreated to straight from work.

This becomes her favourite part of the day. By the end of the first week she is aware of him watching her from the door of the Drovers. It was foolish not to foresee that they would meet here. This sea is his living. But she is unwilling to forgo her exposure at the promontory. There is something in her willed isolation that deters. He has the tact not to approach as she stands alone and for this she is glad. But she is obliged to walk past the pub on her way back to the farm and he has begun to notice the predictability of her timetable. When not out in his boat he has taken to abandoning his drink at the bar to stand within the shadow of the doorway to watch her pass. He says nothing but has begun to follow her a hundred feet behind as she threads her way through the few brief, half-lit streets into the surrounding gloom as she finds her way to the farm.

Without looking back she is aware of his presence. Besides the vague fear she feels something else. She is aware of his reputation, but then he had her alone after evicting Gavin Bone, and he left without touching her. All the sinister rumours can't be all the truth. She knows he helped to extricate Angus from his only foray into the Drovers. None of the gossip she has heard about Murdo ever hinted at compassion. He still carries obvious marks of the beating he received at the Trongate and she has come to believe that this is an indication of some inner mutilation. She asks herself if she is inventing extenuating circumstances and then reflects that she does not know what there is to excuse. He is just the focal point of rumours, as is she, and they may be as groundless in his case too. She cannot imagine he has been so badly maimed, both inside and out, without imagining a role for herself in his recuperation. Illogical though she knows it to be, the more damaged he appears the more attractive he becomes.

She carries a torch that she turns on intermittently, in the five-minute dark expanse between the edge of the village and the farm. She has never turned round and directed the beam back. Just as she can sense his presence she knows he stops at the end of the village, within the little island of light. Paradoxically, it is in the dark that she feels safest.

She is not the only one to notice his intermittent presence behind her. Having kept Lachlan company on an evening house call, Franz, sitting in the passenger seat, sees a figure, swathed against the cold, glide past the side window. Within the fraction it takes him to deduce who it was the headlights illuminated they have also picked out Murdo, walking in her wake. Suddenly animated, Franz persuades Lachlan to turn round and pick Gail up. As they pass Murdo the second time Franz notices him peel away, looping backwards in the direction he has come from. Nevertheless, Franz is gently insistent to Gail that they take her home. From behind the wheel, looking from one to the other, Lachlan gently nods, and from this she infers he wants her to humour the boy.

Lachlan's house commands a view downhill of most of the village, a prospect of steeply tiled roofs receding to the surging expanse of sea. A stunted beech obscures the view from all but a disused and unheated room on the top floor. It is here that the boy goes each night after class, climbing the stairs without taking off his coat. Stamping to keep warm, he alerted Agnes to a presence in the uninhabited room. She found him in his outdoor clothes, standing on an upturned tea chest, straining to look at something down towards the village. Noting her presence, he returned to his task without further acknowledgement. Something intense in his vigilance caused her to retreat. She thinks it may be some imagined horror of his past come to haunt him. Lachlan had given her a summary of the details he has gleaned of Franz's recent history. In Agnes's mind Europe is simply a confused morass of foreign countries whose current disagreement is threatening to spill over into England. All she has taken from the résumé is that Franz's arrival here is a merciful escape. Perhaps he is staring down the hill in anticipation of imagined persecutors eventually arriving in Rassaig. She has not yet told Lachlan of the boy's evening vigil, thinking it may be best to allow the thing a chance to work itself out.

Between the descending tiers of white roofs Franz can just make out the chink of the crossroads that will allow him to mark her passing. On three consecutive days her swathed figure, leaning into the wind, has galvanized his already strained attention to intense pitch as he awaits her accompanying shadow. He appears on the fourth. Pre-armed with his written slip, and noting the time of his descent, Franz runs downstairs and frantically awaits the estimated period of her return. The Campbells are among the privileged few in the village to have a private telephone installed. Clumsily dialling Franz asks to speak to Gail, and at the sound of her puzzled voice relaxes sufficiently to make the pretext of the call not quite as ludicrous as it appears on the written sheet before him. These conversations occur three times in two weeks. Only in retrospect does she make the connection between Franz's calls and the attentions of her shadowy admirer.

30

For the first time in his conscious memory Lachlan calibrates the passage of time differently. This is no longer the daily rote, extending into the cyclical transition of seasons with him and Agnes winding down in tandem like old clocks. Since he and Agnes and all the older people of their acquaintance age at the same pace, no one notices.

But now, time, for Lachlan, is calibrated by the boy's progress, his reserved but growing confidence, his independence and the still closed books of his past and full intelligence. Lachlan has become absorbed with the child he never had, trying to familiarize himself with the boy's history, as if mentally making marks on the doorjamb calibrating heights Franz has grown beyond to occupy his present proportions.

January slips into February. The cold does not abate. Although the novelty of teaching him has paled, Lucy continues to visit Angus, although she now admits to herself she is bored with him when not joined in the act. She has begun to realize that nature is relentless and all the tasks she was forced to carry out on the farm will become necessary again when spring finally approaches. What, she asks herself, is the point in that?

Murdo continued intermittently to shadow Gail. From his eyrie Franz saw the two figures finally meet at the chink of the crossroads. Superimposed, two became one, became two, who continued in the direction of the farm separated by a sliver of streetlight that suggested neither surveillance nor strife but companionability, until absorbed by the diagonal white blanket of the foreground roof. Her exuberant response to Franz's call that night did nothing to allay his fears.

The 'Jewish gentleman' Lachlan alluded to in his conversation with Agnes has paid two visits, admitting his provenance by carrying under his arm a copy of the *Oban Times* Angus aspires to read without dissembling. For the first time Lachlan finds himself on the other side of the exchange, anxiously awaiting a prognosis of a kind. His instructions to Agnes about the food to be prepared have been precise. Having unhelpfully described Franz as a 'delightful boy', Mr Levine surprised the doctor and his housekeeper by donning his coat and picking up his portmanteau again to brave the elements. It seems he is staying with an elderly couple on the other side of the village who keep themselves to themselves, who most people believed suffer the same unfortunate scepticism as the doctor because they belonged to neither indigenous congregation but who now, after years of apparently languishing in a spiritual vacuum, cynically turn out to be Jewish. Having discovered the persuasion of this couple, Lachlan wonders aloud in front of Mr Levine if there would be any point in Franz visiting them. Mr Levine opines aloud at equal volume that he doubts it, that the couple are very elderly, that in a village of this size they must know of a Jewish boy in the environs and that if they have not already volunteered their services they must have their reasons. Lachlan helps Mr Levine on with his coat and expresses his regret that the other cannot stay to sample the food 'specifically prepared in expectation of his accepting their hospitality'. Mr Levine expresses regret with sufficient grace to charm Agnes and irritate Lachlan. He does however return the following morning to apologize for the misunderstanding with a promise to stay on the next occasion. Agnes warns Lachlan not to indulge in the same gentle goading with Mr Levine as he does with 'Father Keenan'.

'Brendan is not my father, Agnes. But you are right. I would have to know Mr Levine better before I know what liberties would not give offence.'

Mr Levine, 'Morris' at his amiable insistence, is as good as his word. At his next visit two weeks later the dinner is a genial affair. Breakfast the following morning is as protracted as Morris's timetable allows. Lachlan has cleared his diary and Franz is at school. In response to further questions from Lachlan, Morris suggests it would be to the boy's advantage to visit a Rabbi in Glasgow. He hopes he does not mind but he has taken the liberty of mentioning him, nodding downhill in the direction of the school, to the Rabbi, nodding in the direction of Glasgow, a personal friend. Lachlan is far from minding. He needs all the help he can get if he is to keep his pact with the dead woman.

Another handshake on the doorstep, another donning of the coat and picking up of the portmanteau, a promise of telephoning to finalize arrangements once he has spoken to his friend, a blast of outdoor air as the door opens and closes, and Lachlan, a man not easily impressed, has been as charmed with Mr Levine during his second visit as Agnes was by his first. And asking himself why, he realizes that the man captivated him the more complimentary he became about Franz. Now he knows he has a blind spot to add to his bald spot. 'Old age,' he says aloud to the airy lobby, 'it comes to us all.' And remembering Franz's correction, tells himself to keep his platitudes to himself.

That night he knocks gently on the boy's door. Lying on top of the covers in his pyjamas, Franz is poring over yet another of the doctor's anatomical textbooks.

'Lachlan, don't you find the body interesting?'

Lachlan considers. Agnes would never ask the same question, being too old and too conscious of impropriety. If she did Lachlan would say that the body is a fragile bag, easily punctured, and that the novelty of investigating its machinations eventually palls. But for Lachlan one of the wonders of the boy is his lack of cynicism, given exposure to circumstances that Lachlan can only begin to guess at. And in looking at him Lachlan remembers his own curiosity and naive optimism. It is this that is too fragile to puncture.

'Fascinating.'

'Is it true women have all their eggs inside them when they are born?'

'Even before they are born.' Déjà vu. He remembers the sense of wonder this realization gave rise to in him: unborn people containing potential offspring, progeny accommodating their successors like Russian dolls. 'Put down the book a moment, please.' The boy does so and looks at him gravely. 'How did you get on with Mr Levine?'

He smiles. 'As well as can be expected.' It is a euphemism Lachlan has told him he dispenses like placebos, their little joke. 'He is a nice man but I do not think he can tell me anything about my faith my mother has not already told me.'

This is the first time he has ever made mention of his mother without being prompted by a direct question. Lachlan suspects Mr Levine finds himself as unequal to the task of teaching Franz as Gail does.

'He has suggested that you visit a Rabbi in Glasgow. Would you like that?'

'I am always happy to learn.'

'I know you are.' Touching Franz's cheek, Lachlan stands stiffly to go. The preparatory cough as he turns away reminds him of something: the preamble to Franz's first word in this house. He turns back. The boy's mouth hangs open, but having drawn attention to himself he seems uninclined to speak.

'Is there anything you want to say to me?'

'No. Yes. Gail. We cannot leave her alone with him.'

It is not difficult to guess who he is talking about. Franz is not the only one who has noticed him catching her up after her evening detour to the sea. 'If she wants to be alone with him there is little we can do about it.'

Having delayed the doctor's departure the boy now appears to ignore him. He is engrossed in the counterpane, picking with increasing agitation at some invisible flaw, the hand moving faster like a pecking bird gorging before the others arrive. Eventually Lachlan stays Franz's hand with gentle pressure of his own. He is patient. His bedside manner is infallible. They sit in this tableau, the old man's hand resting on the boy's, almost unconsciously registering the pulse, until Franz is prompted to speak.

'She does not know him.'

'And you do? Is there something about him you want to tell me?'

The boy takes a moment to consider his response and blinks several times in preparation. 'Only that she should not be with him.'

Another closed chapter in a closed book. Knowing that at this stage there is nothing more the boy will say, Lachlan leaves it at that.

The following week Mr Levine telephones. The week after that Lachlan drives Franz to the station for the southbound trip. The written instructions are precise, laboriously set out by Lachlan in block capitals given the obscurity of his handwriting. He presents this to the boy in an envelope also containing a number of new banknotes. He cannot know that this only serves to remind Franz of previous paperwork in a previous parting. Standing on the platform, Lachlan hands Franz the inevitable Gladstone bag. The boy refuses to have it on the rack out of reach. The carriage is otherwise unoccupied. There will be no problem. Tapping the window that separates them, Lachlan watches Franz pull it down and hands him a handful of change.

'Just in case . . . Now, you've got your instructions, your sandwiches, money, the address . . .'

'Yes.'

'Our telephone number?'

'Written inside my hat.'

'It's only two nights!' Lachlan blurts. Having said all there is to say, he is thinking aloud now. Franz seems to be accepting the separation with disarming aplomb. Lachlan realizes why: young as he is, Franz is the more accustomed of the two to leaving familiarity behind. He wants to assure the boy that it is all right, that he will come back, that everything will be as it was – better, since Franz will have continued on the path that his mother intended for him and will know more about the subject she considered more important than anything else. But he doesn't say a thing. He just stands there, clapping his hands in the cold like solitary reluctant applause. At the first judder of movement the boy closes the window, takes an improbably large medical textbook from the bag and sits with this still closed like a shelf on his lap. He raises his hand to Lachlan to mirror the other's gesture as the old man begins to accelerate backwards.

Lachlan is frozen in an attitude of farewell till the train turns out of sight. As he drops his arm his old heart seems to be caught in a prolonged systolic squeeze, and he realizes, with apocalyptic certainty, that nothing in the world matters so much to him as the fate of that departing child.

31

Snow melts. Morning frosts persist. The gusts of late February presage a blustery March. If anything, Gail enjoys this turbulent weather more. In daylight, spume overarches the sea wall, forming transient rainbows for the benefit of anyone fortunate enough to see. Several times he has walked her home now. She has never invited him in. He has no expectation of being asked. She knows this is childish, like deliberately dropped schoolbooks to instigate a meeting. On the last occasion he walked with her Mrs Campbell was looking anxiously out the kitchen window, awaiting her arrival in the yard. He saw her before she did and retreated back into the dark with a muttered goodbye. She knows that if Eileen Campbell saw them walking home together the news will be common knowledge by tomorrow, but believes that they have got away with it this time. And she knows her relief makes her complicit.

His conversation is terse and sardonic, usually at someone else's expense, and almost always funny. She did not anticipate a sense of humour. Every instinct tells her she should disapprove of this man, but it is almost impossible to dislike someone who makes you laugh. At his first request to accompany her she told him it was a free country. She tried to placate her conscience later by telling herself that she could not stop him. But she knows that is not true. She knows she encouraged by not actively discouraging. Her reproach prompts her to write frequently to Clive, as if the thought of him is an antidote to the thought of the other, inane rambling letters that touch only on the superficial. She is too apprehensive to venture into the morass of their reciprocal feelings. Although guilt prompts her to write, she feels even more guilty sending these letters off, envoys entrusted with worthless trivia, destined to wander in search of a lost recipient.

The presages of February were correct. The beginning of March blows keen and dry. There is a sense of reawakening, an airy vigour few can fail to notice. The war, unable to stop the inexorable approach of spring, seems another world away. The sunsets are still early. Lucy arrives later and later at Angus's room, reluctantly keeping an appointment to assuage an appetite that was keener when the arrangement was made. There is a listlessness to her now and then. He is at a loss to understand and construes every one of her increasingly pronounced mood swings as an indication of their bond. His gift for misinterpretation is such that there is almost nothing she could do that would fail to corroborate for him what he desperately believes to be true, because the alternative is too awful to contemplate. The truth is that she is even more careless of his feelings when she is not in the mood for what she considers the only thing they have in common.

'I'm late.'

'It doesn't matter.'

She snorts. She could have predicted the exchange verbatim. She knew the misinterpretation he would put on the words. She lights a cigarette from his fire and tries to explain in words of one syllable what 'late' means. His gaze is so vacantly placid that in sheer exasperation she grabs her coat, pushes her way out into the narrow passage and clicks her way down the stairs. He stands bereft in the middle of the floor, conflicting emotions struggling as the full import of her words finally registers. Finally sitting, he is quietly exuberant. His least suspected solution has presented itself.

32

'You can put your clothes back on now.' She adjusts herself quickly. Lachlan believes this to be a matter of practice. Local folklore would have it she has had lots, getting in and out of clothes like a cormorant diving and surfacing. Looking at her, he knows she knows the result.

'I'm sorry, I can only confirm what you already suspected.'

'That's not all you can do.'

'Yes it is. You can't continue to do the heavy work that's been expected of you. You might want to consider going home.'

'For all I know home's a fucking crater by now!' She bursts into tears and huddles herself, her back rising and falling with the sobs. His hand hovers indecisively over her head till he finally sighs and strokes her hair. At the feel of his touch she believes she has sensed a concession and sits upright, almost cheerful.

'You'll help me then?'

He knows why she has come to him. Since his first emergency call out at Rassaig all those years before he has helped dozens of people prematurely conclude the remainder of a life consigned to pain. He has been as discreet as he could about this, but despite his silence word obviously got around. People from outwith the village came to consult, looking for the help they knew their own doctor would not provide. He has only ever aided a natural deterioration. He thinks it is one thing to ease someone out of this world, helping them to retain what faculties or dignity corrosive pain has left them with, but quite another to deny a human being the opportunity of ever arriving.

'I'll help you with your pregnancy. I won't help you end it.'

'What kind of life will it have?'

'The best you can give it, if you try.'

'Can you imagine me with a baby!'

'What did you imagine would happen if you persisted in having sex without using anything.' It is not a question. She makes no attempt to answer.

'For God's sake, there's a war on. Who can bring a child into this?'

This has occurred to him. Were he to follow his credo to its logical conclusion he might give her argument more thought. But he knows she is citing this as a convenience. The fact that there is a war on did not cause her to minimize the risk. And truth be told, awful as the circumstances are, life being held so cheap elsewhere simply makes what comes within his compass that much more precious to him. When he thinks of Franz's family that stayed to be consumed, and the fraction that they represent, he cannot bring himself to add to the aggregate of abbreviated lives. And Lachlan believes there is another reason, if one is needed, that he cannot even begin to explain to her. Unlike the war he saw active service in, he feels this war needs to be fought. If they do not prevail then all the humane values he believes in will perish with the dead. And to terminate a life for convenience insults the sacrifice.

'God knows there are enough orphans, but if you stay I will do what I can to find you accommodation and help you have the child adopted.'

'I'm not like one of these women you have around here who keeps digging up turnips or whatever and takes ten minutes off to have a baby in a field.'

'I will not help you end this pregnancy.'

33

He has stopped her, in the dark between the village and the farm. He has laid a hand on her and spun her round. Placing his flattened hand in the small of her back he has grasped a fistful of her coat, the way he did with Gavin. The latent strength she can feel is almost pneumatic. With the one encompassing arm, she feels he could lift her towards his mouth. But he does not. Her heart is hammering.

'I can't just go on walking you back.'

'You don't have to. I never asked you to.'

'That's not what I mean. You know that.'

'Yes.'

'I want more.'

'I have no more to give.'

'That's a lie. You have more and you want to give it.'

She looks towards the dark, fluid expanse. At this distance its sighs and swells are reduced to an ebbing murmur. How awful to think men are out there, crouched in steel cylinders hunting one another in the blackness of its depths.

'Whether I want to give it or not does not matter. I will not give. I should not have encouraged you this far.'

'But you did.' And letting her go, he turns away and in the darkness the two figures go their opposite ways.

34

Half a mile away from the separating figures Lucy stands on the jetty, listening to the slap of the water Gail heard from a distance. She has assembled what she needs. Looking at the water Gail contemplated, she experiences a similar sense of dread, but for an entirely different reason. It is not in her makeup to consider the fates of the unknown out there who seek to invade or defend, who perish while she equivocates.

There is a horror at the dark mass that swells up towards the planking. She feels she is tottering, and it is the platform she stands on that rises and falls towards this seething abyss. And staring down into the dark water she feels a dreadful sense of vertigo while her mind rehearses the sequence of events: twisting in the darkness as she is pulled further down, flying tendrils of hair as the final blurt from her lungs erupts in a postponed bubble, then seawater surging into her lungs. She knows that people who do this do not rehearse such consequences, do not dwell on scenarios of their absence. And she knows not only that she loves life, but that she loves herself more than the life inside her.

35

A tread on the stairwell. Angus is all attention, hoping it will proceed beyond the entrance of the other tenants. He is at the end of the narrow passage. The tread continues, but is too slow, too heavy and measured to be hers. He has only ever locked the door when she is here with him. No one here steals. Even if they did, he has nothing worth taking. The door is pushed slowly ajar. Gavin Bone admits himself and softly closes the door at his back. Sitting near the fire, Angus does not speak. Gavin stays where he is, seemingly happy to conduct this interview from the threshold.

'Is she here?' Everything is visible, from the bed to the open tins beside the gas burner. The question is facetious. Failing to realize this, Angus shakes his head. 'Has she left you?'

'No.'

'I have felt for you, Angus. I have thought that perhaps it is not all your fault. Since you were a child your mind was open to confusion. I think perhaps it always will be. It is like earth awaiting a seed. I thought it had been planted with a good seed.' Contemplating the tangle of the bed sheets, 'I see I was wrong. I do not consider myself blameless. I should have stopped that schoolteacher earlier. I should have known when she had you chasing her hat like a dog. To allow a woman like that to poison your mind—'

'She didn't do anything wrong.' Angus has never interrupted anyone before.

'To allow a woman like that to poison your mind was one thing. When I found out I took the necessary precautions. But the next choice you made yourself. It was not something you passively took in just because you sat in a class and listened. You acted. Oh, Angus, Angus . . .' his tone has dropped an octave and is almost tender, 'to go with that whore —'

'Not!' He has shouted. He has interrupted and now he has shouted. This explosive syllable has shocked him. He stood to shout, jerking upright as the sound erupted out. Conscious in the startled aftermath, he sits slowly down again looking towards the fire, his voice collapsing in on itself. 'Not . . . No . . . She is not what you said. We love one another. We are to be married.'

'Your marriage bed is stained before you get into it. Tell me, Angus, is this your idea or hers?'

'It is ours.'

'And why would she want to marry when she has had what she wants without it?'

'We are to have a child. We will be married and she will have our child.' He repeats this twice more in a kind of litany.

'I don't think so. She will leave.'

'No she won't.'

'And one bastard begets another. It is the way of things.' Angus looks up from his preoccupation with the fire. 'Where did you think you came from, Angus? Your mother was like her. She came with a story of a dead husband, taken by the sea. We might have believed her if she had not behaved the way she did. And now you and your trollop. It is the cycle of sin. You will meet your bastard in hell, Angus.'

36

Of all the places she might be Angus finally finds her on the jetty, their first trysting place, the bolt hole of his childhood. It was here he would run to in all weathers, after the arguments between his mother and the succession of men who drifted through their house, after persecution at school. Larger stones revealed by the low tide give way to shingle in the steep upper part of the beach. Even at high tide there is a sheltered alcove beneath the jetty above the watermark, the shingle floor rising to meet the level roof of the planking in a constructed cave he always thought of as his. He has lived his life with the constant tidal ebb and flow, with the incessant hissing of dissipating waves. Here he has lain curled on dried seaweed finding comfort in the rhythm, a foetus mesmerized by a larger heartbeat.

At the sound of footsteps she kicks sacking over the pieces in front of her, embarrassed by the evidence of an intention not followed through. When she turns to see that it is him, a flicker of something moves across her face. She turns back to face the sea. He puts his arms around her, alarmed at her proximity to the dark water, standing as she is on the extremity.

'Gavin Bone came to my room.' She says nothing but accepts his embrace like a coat, her mind still sucked down beneath the swell to where her imagined histrionic self twirls at the end of the rope. 'I told him you were going to have a baby.'

'That's marvellous.' She is still too listless to be angry.

'It's all right. I've worked it out.'

'More than I have.'

He struggles to articulate what he has worked out. He was prepared to believe the two of them together, enjoying one another, was wrong. He has grown up with a theology that penalizes pleasure. Anything carnal carries a debt. But he cannot believe that what they now feel for one another can be wrong, or that the baby they will have will be wrong. He is prepared to gamble everything he has been taught against the realization that has dawned on him. Everything will be all right: they are redeemed by love.

But he doesn't articulate this. A collision of confused thoughts distils the sum of his reasoning to a single statement: 'We will go away.'

'Away where?'

'Anywhere. They won't know we were not married before you were expecting. We will get married somewhere and then go somewhere else.' He has never been inland. He has in his mind some rural pasture with an idyllic cottage awaiting their occupancy. 'To the new people we will just be like anyone else – married people having a baby.'

She no longer finds any comfort in his embrace. She realizes how far this fantasy has been allowed to run and slowly disentangles herself from his arms.

'Look, Angus, we've had some fun . . .'

'We can have more fun.'

'No, dearie, I don't think we can. People get just so much fun out of one another and that's it. I know. I think our fun is all used up. The only fun either of us is going to have now is with someone else.'

He blinks several times in quick succession, perplexed. 'But we love one another.' His eyes remind her of a cow's.

'No we don't.' She is irritated at the look of wounded imbecility as the gulf of their feelings and expectations begins to dawn on him. He begins to breathe rapidly.

'We . . . you could learn, when we go somewhere else.'

'You've never been anywhere else. What do you know? What would you do? How would you survive anywhere else?' She has been manufacturing anger to overcome her feelings towards herself. She knows herself just well enough to know that she is behaving badly. At the look on his face she begins to cry. 'Oh, Angus. You haven't a clue. This place keeps you. You get odd jobs from people here to help you. If you went somewhere else you'd be lost. You can barely read. I have trouble managing myself at the best of times, and they aren't now. I can't manage us both . . .'

'. . . the baby.'

She flares up in genuine anger. 'The baby! The baby! Everyone keeps talking about the fucking baby. No one talks about me!'

He feels a physical pain in the centre of his body. His legs slowly fold like a collapsing chair and he sits, cross-legged on the planks, trying to make sense of the water below. There must be a purpose to divine in this lapping against the piles, this ceaseless Morse. He had imagined wrapping her in his coat as he explained and her relief as the plan unfolded. He had imagined escorting her to the McHargs', standing vigilant at the bedroom door, deterring questions as she packed. Her case, his meagre bag, the morning bus, a convenient mist to obscure their destination from enquirers and the specifics he cannot envisage for a real departure.

She looks down at him. His disillusionment is another burden she cannot carry. Have some fun and look at the baggage. He is young. He will get over it, find someone more suited, some stupid farm girl who doesn't mind being ankle-deep in shit. And at least she's taught him how to please a girl. Not like some around here: boots off, dick out. His wife should thank her. They'll have a brood like themselves. Snowbound in delivery. Midwife arriving in a tractor. Placenta in the pig swill. Baby bathed in the front room. Three of them by the fire, just what the doctor ordered.

At least he enjoyed a taste of the exotic while it lasted.

Without looking down she tousles his head as she passes, already looking on to the next thing.

37

By the time Gail arrived at school that morning she had decided to go straight home after lessons. If the end of the day leaves her with additional work to do she will take it with her, at least for the next week or so. They can spare her a corner of the kitchen table to spread her paperwork out on. She does not want to repeat the encounter from last night. He was right in saying that she wanted to give more.

Since the only exercise she will get will be walking the brief distance between school and farmhouse, she walks out at lunchtime. Normally she sits in the class, keeping watch over her charge in the small playground. The paved area is fenced. She expected to walk out to interrupt the usual melee of different games. But the children are all arranged round the periphery of the fence, standing on the lower rungs for a better view. Some balance precariously on the top. She shouts to them to get down. At her approach they break a gap in their ranks to let her through. There is a crowd of adults gathered at the sea and several figures can be seen hurrying across from the harbour end.

There is something ominous in the scene, in the stillness of the observers. She orders the protesting children back into the class. Paul, picking out the uniformed form of his father in the distance, clambers over into the field and begins running. She calls him back, but, like her, he has sensed the authority of a larger event. Telling the children not to leave the playground, she hitches her skirt and climbs over after him. She resists the impulse to run, knowing that if she does they will follow, irrespective of her instructions.

Lachlan had not been telephoned. David Crawford, sent by Paul's father, walked through the waiting room. Authorized by the constable, he tapped on the doctor's door to interrupt the consultation. Observers were rewarded with a subdued exchange at the surgery door and then the sight of Lachlan snatching up bag and coat to follow the man out to the waiting car.

By the time Gail gets close there is a semicircle of backs Paul is trying to penetrate. At the sound of her voice shouting the boy's name his father emerges from the midst of the group looking grim. He picks the boy up.

'I'm sorry, Michael. He ran away. I'll take him back.'

'Don't bother. He's going home.' He puts the boy down, and on an impulse picks him up again and kisses him. He puts him down again. The look of his father coupled with this unprecedented display of public affection is enough to convince the boy of the gravity of the situation. Without looking for any further concession he turns in the direction of home. Drawn by macabre curiosity, Gail moves between the figures toward the nucleus of the group. Angus is lying on the pier. Lachlan has covered his face with sacking he found lying here, hiding the spectacle from public display as he tries to sever the cord that has been tied in a running knot around the neck. Low tide discovered him. By the pallor Lachlan estimates he has been in the water since last night. Any longer and the soft flesh would have begun to be eaten. The tongue is swollen and protrudes obscenely. The rope is deeply imbedded in the congested purple flesh of the neck which bears the indentations of Lachlan's fingers attempting to tug some slack. He turns to David. Since fetching him he has shadowed the doctor.

'Do you have a knife?'

'What for?'

'To cut the cord.'

'Don't you carry a scalpel or something in your bag?'

'Why would I? I'm not a surgeon. If you don't have a knife can you ask?' He nods grimly towards the assembled crowd, held back by the two or three Michael has deputized to throw up a cordon. 'They're fishermen. One's bound to have a knife.' He sees Gail looking askance at him from the other side of the impromptu barrier. She has shown more compassion and understanding towards Angus than anyone else of late. He gestures her forward. Witnessing the exchange, Michael orders her to be admitted.

She has already guessed as she approaches. David returns with a clasp-knife and stands a few paces back. Lachlan pulls back the sacking. She stands.

'Are you all right?'

'Yes.'

'Hold this up so they don't see.' He has to cut into the flesh of the neck to sever the embedded cord. She is surprised at the lack of blood, and is in turn surprised at the impartiality of her reaction. He puts the sacking back. Someone comes through with a blanket. They cover Angus. From his kneeling position Lachlan extends his arm towards Gail. She helps him to his feet, his knees cracking as he hoists himself erect. He takes off his glasses and pinches the bridge of his nose, a gesture normally confined to late evening after a day of reading. The canopy of clouds is lit by an unseen sun, suffusing the dome beneath in a metallic glare. In the harsh light she suddenly notices how old he is, the cross-hatching of creased skin on his neck, the network of broken veins ramifying like a rash.

The cord runs from under the blanket to two large rectangular blocks, tethered together at the other end. With his foot Lachlan nudges some random-looking piece of smaller machinery. He cannot know this is the only remaining evidence of Lucy's aborted attempt, besides the rope that Angus put to the use she pretended to contemplate.

'I don't know why he would bring this. Insufficient ballast.' Nodding towards the rectangular blocks, 'Car batteries. Didn't make any mistake there. Michael says he got one of them from the harbour. Thrown out. No one took the trouble to get rid of it – until now. We don't know where the other one came from. He was always tinkering with things. I don't know why. He never got things to work. As much mechanical aptitude as I have. I suppose you're in a better position than anyone to say what aptitude he did have. Either you or your girlfriend, the bottled blonde.' They are at the extremity of the pier, where Angus found Lucy last night. Lachlan turns in the direction of the sea and inhales sharply half a dozen times, as if intending to dive.

'I got him to throw the belt off here only months ago.'

'What?'

'The belt. My predecessor's. The man you described for me. I got Angus to throw his belt into the sea from here.' To cover his head adequately the blanket has been pulled up short, exposing his feet. Looking down, she sees that one shoe has been somehow lost. The sock is threadbare. She thinks this the most forlorn thing she has ever seen.

Lachlan takes one last sharp breath for the plunge. 'The thing is – the thing is . . .' He stops and speaks each word separately. 'The. Thing. Is – he had to make two trips to get them here. From here to the harbour and back twice. Can you imagine what must have gone through his mind walking that distance, with that weight, knowing its purpose . . . ?'

A stretcher arrives. The road ends two hundred yards from the jetty. They will be obliged to carry him the distance to the waiting vehicle. The crowd separates for his departure.

Lachlan is about to follow. One of Michael's deputies crosses to the tethered batteries and attempts to lift them. Grunting, he manages to straighten with the load and puts it back down. David returns with the knife and cuts the rope binding them. They lift one each, staggering through the ragged gap left by the departing stretcher. 'Evidence,' the other one needlessly explains to whoever will listen. Aside from the strain of lifting he looks quite cheerful at the novelty of the situation.

Turning round and looking at her before he leaves, Lachlan takes Gail's hand. He calls Michael across.

'Can you have someone go across and dismiss the class.' It is not a question.

'I'll be fine.'

'You're the same colour as him.'

Michael nods. The stretcher is half-way there, the crowd beginning to disperse.

'Walk with me as far as the van.' They link arms. Who is supporting whom? Having asked for her company, he seems unwilling to talk. And suddenly, with barely suppressed anger he says, 'No doubt they'll have a ceremony of some kind for him.'

She helps him clamber into the improvised ambulance. She sees him perch his buttocks on some kind of welded ledge, contemplating the prone figure, seemingly immune to discomfort in his preoccupation. The doors close on this tableau.

She watches the van's slow progress across the rutted surface till the proper road begins. She imagines Angus, without the suspension of conscious restraint, juddering, the threadbare foot lolling. She looks around for something to lean on, a fence post, anything. The nearest upright is the playground fence. It is too far. At the realization of his absence she sits down on the ground, the way he did when Lucy left him on the jetty.

38

She has no desire to see Ewan McHarg. She has even less desire to be alone and another woman nearer her age seems more suitable company than Eileen Campbell just now. When she gets to the girls' farm she is admitted by Harriet. There is no sign of Ewan or his wife. Harriet simply says, 'She's in there,' as if having guessed the purpose of the visit. News travels faster than Gail anticipated. Lucy is sitting in the same position as on the last occasion but this time crying instead of smoking.

'Would you like tea?' Harriet asks.

'I . . . I don't think so. I can't think at the moment.'

'Why does everyone think tea fixes everything?' Lucy says. Her voice is nasal. She looks as if she has been crying for days. She moves her legs to make space for Gail. Harriet sits in her reading chair.

'I don't know that either. I've just come from there. I thought he'd just been found when I arrived. How did you know?'

'Know what?'

'That Angus is dead.'

The other two exchange a blank glance. In the prolonged silence the fire seems loud. Gail stares at the embers. She is only now understanding in instalments and only because she has seen for herself. Lucy's mouth hangs open. With her swollen eyes and red nose she looks momentarily imbecilic. Harriet is the first to rally.

'How?'

'He . . . he . . .' Gail is experiencing the same difficulty as

Lachlan explaining the logistics of the act. Someone is going to have to do this for the relatives. Are there relatives? 'He drowned himself.'

'Dear God . . .' It is Harriet who speaks. Lucy is still dumbly staring. She is so abstracted it does not seem rude to speak about her in the third person.

'What's she crying for then?'

'She's pregnant. She's been to see Doctor McCready. She says he refused to help.'

'There's been some misunderstanding. I don't believe Lachlan would have said he wouldn't help.'

'He said he wouldn't help me get rid of it.' Lucy has revived. She has dealt with the news the way she deals with most things. She understands that she understands this as much as she is going to, at this time, and she has put it to one side to concentrate on something else. She compensates herself with the thought that she might revisit this fact when the time is more opportune. But the truth is that she will not. The time is never more opportune. This thought will languish among the miscellany of other things she temporarily shelves till they disintegrate: forgotten fruit. Sometimes a bad memory is occasioned by something someone says, a smell, a fragment of music, but mainly there is only the flux of her immediate present. And talk of Lachlan has brought her back.

It is Gail's turn to look dumbly startled. She recalls Lachlan's remark about herself and Lucy being best placed to understand Angus's aptitudes.

'Is it Angus's baby?'

'Probably.'

'Did he think it was?'

'Probably.'

There is another long pause as she tries to digest the implications of this.

'Did you tell him it was?'

'What is this, twenty questions? I told him I was pregnant. I don't think he liked the thought of me with anyone else.'

'What did he say about the baby?'

'I didn't take notes. He was happier than I was.'

'If he was happier why did he drown himself?'

'I don't know! I'm not his fucking guardian angel!'

The anger is disproportionate. Gail realizes the other woman is prepared to allow herself a fit of temper to submerge what the conversation might otherwise disclose.

'You were happy to let that boy think the baby was his when the truth is that you don't know whether it is or not. And he was happy about it. What I want to know is, what happened after he was happy that caused him to make two trips to the harbour to find car batteries to tie round his neck and throw himself off the jetty?'

At the description Harriet turns her face away. Lucy, faced with the image of Angus twisting at the end of the rope that snared her fictitious self, the last bubble bursting from his lips, lets loose a wrenching sob.

'He wanted us to get married. Can you imagine? Me and Angus and a baby! He wanted to go away with me. He's . . . he was . . . not bright. Can you imagine him in a city? I told him . . .' As she slows her voice shrinks. She concludes almost in a whisper, staring at the ground, 'That we . . . he couldn't.'

Full realization of what occurred dawns simultaneously on the other two. Harriet turns back to exchange a look with Gail. Both read their own thought in the expression of the other. Between them there has always been an unspoken reciprocity. Lucy's lip is hanging down imbecilically again. A large thread of saliva droops towards the floor. She bursts out in a series of sobs, each preceded by a sharp inhalation. There is something histrionic and purging in these, as if everything will be all right by the time they have run their course. Gail does not believe them. She is too busy. A summation of Angus's life plays itself out in her imagination: ignored, bullied, brainwashed with an ideology that taught him he was in all likelihood damned; then he had the misfortune to meet Lucy.

'That boy . . . You chose him. He didn't choose you. He was willing to give up everything for you. Do you realize what that meant? For him to leave the familiar? For someone who's never been anywhere else? Not just a job or a room. Everything. He was taught to believe that going with you was going to hell, and he was prepared to do it for you and the baby. Everything. And I bet you didn't even thank him.'

The sobs have subsided sufficiently for Lucy to look up with a ready reply.

'How do you know he didn't just see me as a ticket out of here?'

Gail stands. 'You're not the first selfish person I've ever met, but I think you're the first one I've known who is incapable of understanding that people act from motives different from yours. And I don't want to meet another like you, if there are any.' She moves towards the door and speaks without looking back. 'I won't come here again. God help your baby.'

39

Angus is buried, his room let, his possessions disposed of, the few friends that attended to this last obligation struck by the meagre accumulation of a curtailed life. Nothing is left to mark his passing but individual recollections and a growing seed. After Gail's departure Lucy has turned remarkably discreet. Her condition is not common knowledge. Gail and Harriet keep their confidences to each other. Lachlan, the repository of countless secrets, is bearing up under the burden of yet another. Gavin's machinations are known only to Gavin. Lucy would be pleased had she known he kept his revelations for the posterity of the written word.

Gail has been subdued for the week. Franz's attempt at comfort after Thursday's lesson draws from her a rueful smile. What right does she have to indulge when he has gone through so much more? On his way home he runs into Murdo. He looks quickly back at the school. His inclination is to run back to her and stay to see out whatever happens. As Murdo bears down on him he finds himself unable to move.

'I'm not looking for her. I'm looking for you. I hear you're no longer a moron. I hear you don't talk much. Let's keep it that way. I wouldn't want talk circulating about anything you might have seen when you were our guest. Even more important, I'm looking for something that's gone missing. From my bedroom. You wouldn't happen to know anything about that, would you?' The boy is rigid with fear. This seems to mollify Murdo, confirm the boy's ability to keep a secret.

'I can't make up my mind whether or not it went missing at the same time as you left. If I think you've got something of mine and you're not giving it back, I'll come and see you. Do you understand?' Franz stands mute till Murdo, satisfied with the effect he has had, turns back in the direction of the Drovers.

The following day Lachlan again drives the boy to the station, for his second arranged visit to the Rabbi. Franz is silent in the car, debating whether or not to tell him of his encounter with Murdo. Eventually he decides not to. To mention the encounter would tease out other facts about his stay with the Dougans he prefers not to revisit. His main concern is Gail, but Murdo admitted he had been waiting for him, not her. Her evening visits to the harbour have stopped. And as Lachlan said to him on his last trip south, it's only two nights.

Again he sits with the Gladstone bag at his feet. Two other passengers already occupy the carriage, an old man half asleep from the journey's beginning, yet further north, and an anonymous woman who has precluded conversation by hoisting a magazine before her. Again Lachlan slides backwards on the platform, hand raised. This time Franz abandons his book to push down the window and shout into the watery midday sunshine, 'Watch Gail.'

The trip is uneventful. But arriving at Glasgow Central he already feels a sense of something more pronounced than on his previous visit a few weeks ago. The Rabbi smilingly awaits him at the barrier. When he hands his ticket across the old man gestures him to step aside to let someone behind pass. As he does so he sees Lucy stride past. There is no one else similarly dressed. She must have been the anonymous woman. She cannot have failed to notice him, especially since he shouted Gail's name out the window. It is clear from her speed and preoccupation that she does not want to talk. He shakes the old man's hand, politely refuses offer of help with the bag, and fascinated by the cacophony in this riveted space, walks companionably with his teacher out to the taxi rank.

40

That evening Lachlan stops while passing Gail to give her a lift. He tells her that Franz called to confirm his safe arrival. The boy also thought it curious that he saw Lucy coming off the same train. He said she couldn't have failed to see him but didn't make herself known. Confronted with these premises, Lachlan has drawn his own conclusion but adds nothing beyond what the boy has said.

With a sense of trepidation she cannot give reason for Gail breaks her promise and goes back to the McHargs'. Harriet is out. At the risk of running into Murdo she makes her way to the Drovers. He isn't there but she is.

It takes them several days to trace Lucy's movements. By the time they discover her destination the address has adopted a significance all its own.

41

Lucy's preoccupation when she strides past Franz at the barrier is genuine. Her speed is not. She stops at a paper stand till she sees the boy and whoever the old man is disappear into the departing throng. He was right in his assumption that she has no inclination to talk. After Rassaig the novelty of commerce and people on the move would normally buoy her naturally exuberant spirits. Crowds stimulate. Change of any kind excites her. But she is subdued, bent to a purpose that will not allow diversion. She stops at a tea room, flattening the piece of paper she has had as a crib note in her magazine, reading it yet again to commit to memory the arrangements she already knows by heart. She had not planned on the accents. She has no trouble with the slow musical cadences of Rassaig. Her first few encounters there made her realize the harshness of her own speech. Her accent is common currency. They hear it even north of Rassaig, listening to the music-hall comedies broadcast by the BBC to bolster the nation's spirits. No one has any difficulty understanding her, including the waitress who took her order and replied in an accent so thick Lucy has had to ask twice to understand, and nodded, still uncomprehending. She is not sure if what she gets is due to misunderstanding or rationing. She knows she has to understand, if she is to conduct the transaction she came here for.

It is dark by the time she leaves the station, lights all subdued in compliance with the regulations. She knows the name of the tram and the place to catch it, but the whole enterprise seems more difficult conducted in the dark when the street signs have been inexplicably removed. She swears softly. Do they really think they will daunt the Nazis by disguising the whereabouts of Sauchiehall Street?

She stops at a closed shop front in Union Street and in exchange for a light asks directions. The young man cups his hands, cradling the brief flare, smiling in that small illumination as he leans over to let the tip catch a glow. He blows out the match with a snort of smoke. His cigarette describes arcs in the gloom as he explains and she, inexplicably, begins to cry. Without a further word he takes her arm and begins walking. At the stop, while they wait, he offers to take her there. She says no, she must go alone. When the tram arrives he helps her up and says above her head to the conductor, 'She's looking for Ellinger Terrace. According to her directions it's just off Dumbarton Road.'

'It's next to the terminus at Dalmuir West. I'll keep her right.'

She understands most of this and turns back to thank the young man who, with a cavalier wave, has melted anonymously back. She thinks: 'Two weeks ago he would have been an opportunity.'

The windows are darkened. Headlights are blackened over, leaving only a slit to navigate by. She wonders about accidents. Unlike London, no one here has been bombed. By the time this is all over the darkness will have killed more people than the Germans manage to. Blacked-out tenements rise on either side. They seem to be passing down a gloomy canyon. She is cold. Passengers are laughing. How can people be happy? She falls into a reverie till she realizes the conductor is calling to her, 'Dalmuir West, dear.' As she shuffles off he points in the direction of Ellinger Terrace.

There is still a surprising amount of foot traffic, given the darkness. She supposes you can get used to anything, or, given her reasons for coming, perhaps not anything. The numbers above the tenement entrances are obscured by baffle walls, built to shield the closes from the blast of street explosions. In the gloom she is obliged to cross the street twice to work out the run of numbers and calculate the address. She knows she is there when she sees the number, but somehow she is compelled again to fish out the piece of paper and corroborate. The close is dull. Windows on the landings have been blackened out. Lights burn at minimum wattage. In this twilight the Victorian tiling gives off an eerie ceramic sheen. Uprights of the banister are carved with delicate spiralling flutes. Repeated polishing has rendered the wood the colour of jet. Despite everything else she stops briefly to admire the craftsmanship. People who built this chose to care.

Top-right flat. There is no need to corroborate the name on the brass plate: she committed this to memory the first time she heard it. The bell seems to sound from a deep inner recess. She hears no sound of approaching footsteps, just the mechanical jangle of dangling keys. The inner door is noisily unlocked, as are the solid storm doors she is facing, one of which swings inward.

'I'm—'

She is interrupted by a figure that brushes past her on the way out. It is a woman. There is a pantomime subterfuge in the combination of high-turned coat collar and low hat. She gasps the syllable of an apology. Holding the banister, the woman begins to make her way down the stairs as if they are covered in ice. Lucy feels a sense of shock when she realizes the movements are caused not by caution but pain.

A pleasant-looking middle-aged woman in carpet slippers and housecoat waits patiently in the hall. Prompted by her smile, Lucy walks in. Both sets of doors are locked behind her. The place is clean and well lit, the high ceiling creating an airy space which dilutes the unmistakable tang of disinfectant. No explanation seems necessary: anonymous women obviously only come here for one reason. The woman takes her coat. Several others women's coats hang on the peg. The sight of this somehow alarms Lucy. Her coat has established her place in the queue. The woman's dress suggests she is some kind of charlady but from the informality of her manner Lucy guesses she lives here.

She is shown into a room. The furniture looks almost municipal, the waiting room of an impoverished dentist. Everything is clean. A girl who looks no older than mid-teens sits on one end of a sofa with a middle-aged woman at her side. They are obviously mother and daughter. Although the mother wears a severe expression, she is sitting very close to the younger woman and from her perspective, as she takes her seat across the occasional table, Lucy can see they are holding hands. The otherwise sparse room is dominated by an enormous fish tank standing on a table against one wall, opposite the fire. It is backlit, diffusing a dim liquid glow. In front of it, and with his back to Lucy, a schoolboy still in uniform taps the glass to agitate the fish. The door opens again. The woman in the housecoat says something to the boy, a single-syllable reprimand Lucy cannot make out. He turns. His similarity to his mother is as striking as that of the wretched girl to hers. Lucy realizes that this boy lives here. It seems inconceivable that a family could live in this place. Perhaps for the first time she appreciates how little she understands.

The door is closed. The boy returns to his diversion. Lucy looks dumbly at the carpet. In the silence the incessant tapping of the boy's fingernail against the glass grates. At the first sound of keys approaching he jumps back from the tank. The door opens. The woman with the housecoat gestures to the girl, who stands. The mother also stands.

'I'm sorry. Only her.'

The mother sits. The girl goes through. The door is closed behind her.

The boy takes a ruler from his bag. Dragging a chair across, he stands and dips the ruler into the water. Lucy's eyes flick from the spectacle of the mother's wringing hands to the boy. The line of the ruler is distorted by refraction. Balancing on the chair, the boy looks at this from various angles.

'Looks bent but it's no,' he announces to the room, turning. Only Lucy has looked up. By default she is his audience.

'What?'

'Looks bent but it's no. Cannae huv a bent ruler. Wouldnae be a ruler if it was bent. Couldnae measure nothin'.'

'No, I suppose not.'

Having exhausted the novelty of the illusion, he diverts himself by stirring the water into a small whirlpool. Debris from the bottom drifts up. The water is becoming opaque. It seems he can continue this indefinitely. She watches, mesmerized. Any distraction is welcome. She does not know how long passes. The keys again approach. The boy jumps from the chair. Two desultory fish rotate in the roiled water. The door opens. The girl is leaning against the woman with the housecoat. Her face is drained of colour. She is crying. The mother runs forward and puts her arms around the girl. They stand in this pose for perhaps a minute, rocking slightly. The boy's mother stands patiently to one side till they compose themselves.

'She can wait here.'

'We'd rather go.' It is the girl's mother who responds. The daughter nods in agreement. She is dabbing her nose. The handkerchief can absorb no more. Six inches from her face a string of catarrh attenuates from her nose to the sodden bundle. The mother takes this from her and hands across her own handkerchief. The three make their way out of sight. In the rustling delay Lucy can hear the girl gasp. They must be putting their coats on. Then follows the elaborate opening and locking procedure. The woman in the housecoat reappears almost immediately. The turbid water is slowly settling. Without taking her eyes from the tank she expertly slaps the boy on the back of the head. As she moves towards the door Lucy stands.

'He's no ready yet. Cleanin' up.'

An image of a foetus in a bucket is conjured. A top-floor flat, a string of women: how do they dispose of ... of ... everything? Another image: smuggled with garbage, bloody linen, a confused heap of tissue. Left alone with the boy, she turns to him desperately for further distraction. He has taken the routine slap without complaint but obviously thinks better of stirring again. He has improvised a game of pressing his face as close as possible to the tank and mouthing in time with the larger fish. She wonders if he is in some way retarded. This last thought recalls Angus. Someone needs to speak to fill this gap.

'Why are there only two?'

'Used tae be mare.'

'Did they die?'

'Bigger ones ate'm.'

'That's awful.'

''at's whit fish dae.'

'That's brutal.' And having said this the immensity of her decision strikes her. Life is relentless. Life devours to perpetuate. She is here to extinguish a life and has just been horrified by the fate of goldfish. For the first time ever she experiences a sense of displacement. Had this occurred an hour ago she would not have climbed the stairs.

The woman opens the door. Motivated by a sense of being

caught in something larger that she has put in motion, Lucy follows her out. They cross the hall. She stops at the open door.

'This is a kitchen.'

'Whit did y'expect?' Aside from a kitchen table with improvised stirrups Lucy can see the paraphernalia of ordinary family life. There is a grotesque incongruity. This is all wrong. The table has been scrubbed down. She wonders if they eat off this afterwards. Among the strata of other odours she detects caustic soda. A large pot on the range is maintained at a rolling boil. The single blacked-out window drips condensation. The man who has had his back to her, administering to the pot, now turns. He is ceramically bald. His head reminds her of the eerie sheen in the close. He wears glasses which he removes intermittently to wipe free of steam. Beads of sweat stand out on his head and forehead. He wears a sleeveless V-neck jumper. The rolled-up shirt cuffs are bloodstained, although his hands and forearms seem clean. He looks like some kind of tradesman. She can imagine him helping fit out a Cunard stateroom as a liner takes shape on the Clyde.

She moves to take off her dress.

'We always settle in advance.' His voice is smaller than she expected, an academic drone. Perhaps not a tradesman. Some kind of inventory clerk? She hands out the exact sum, counted in advance. He laboriously recounts and hands the folded notes to his wife.

'Take off your shoes, pants and stockings. Lie down and lift your skirt up.'

A towel is laid across the table, more, she guesses, to protect its surface than to cushion her. She has to lie back exposed and lift her legs into the stirrups. Looking down the line of her belly, across her rucked skirt, she can see him between her thighs. He turns away from her to wash his hands and attend to the pot. With a pair of kitchen tongs he is lifting items from the boiling water, running each under the cold tap before leaving it on the wooden draining board. They seem rudimentary: an ordinary table knife with rounded tip bent at right angles to the remainder of the blade; some kind of skewer or perhaps a trussing needle; kitchen scissors. In her growing sense of dread she does not hear the distant droning.

He does. His back tenses. He exchanges a look with his wife. She taps the pocket containing the notes he just passed her. He nods back in agreement.

'Should I take the boy doon?'

'We should be all right here. If they're looking for anything it'll be the yards. This won't take long.'

He looks at the implements, taking inventory, selects one and turns to her. She has just noticed an open packet of tea on an adjacent shelf, spilled leaves radiating in a charcoal fan. Perhaps minutiae yield something. Perhaps purpose is divined in observation. Perhaps the world is just a vast accumulation of meaningless trivialities. Beneath the shelf is an oval galvanized tub, the size of a hip bath, covered with a cloth, large enough to brew hooch in, large enough to duck for apples as they did in her mother's house when she was a kid, large enough to . . .

The remaining moments of his life are a confusion of cause and effect. Her scream, her repeated. 'No!'s climax with a collapse of the ceiling. A portion of the floor, bigger than the table she lies on, disappears in the gap that separates them. Her vehemence has conjured a shaft through the flat. The air is full of swirling dust welling up from another collapsed floor below. He has just realized that something has fallen through the building when a bomb detonates in the street outside. The kitchen faces the communal back court. The blackened lounge windows explode inwards. The force of the blast catapults the boy through the glass tank. Perforated, he falls senseless on the floor with dripping glass fragments and two suffocating fish. In the kitchen his father is leaning over the hole. A dangling joist in the attic, freed by vibration of the street explosion, tilts to vertical as it falls to drive his bald head into his shoulders. He is already dead as he falls into the shaft. His trajectory is interrupted by the detonation of the dilatory bomb, embedded in the ground-floor kitchen. The last sight Lucy ever witnesses is framed by her parted thighs as a molten globe erupts through the shaft to expand in annihilating brightness.

42

The morning after Franz's departure to Glasgow Lachlan sits alone at the breakfast table. He breaks open his egg with unaccustomed violence, causing the yolk to explode on the slope of his waistcoat. This will require a cloth. This brings the number of things that have disrupted his usual composure to three: the boy, the paper and the egg. He missed the boy last night and now he misses their inconsequential exchange over breakfast. Given the brief time they have had together, he realizes the disproportionate attention directed at Franz. Even if he could have things otherwise, he would not. He misses his paper. Agnes always gets up at an ungodly hour, a habit of her farming upbringing she has never shaken off. She gets the paper before he does, scans this for human interest and disguises her perusal by ironing the broadsheet flat. As long as his paper awaits him at breakfast he pretends not to notice. It is a charade they have played daily for years. His quick reading of the paper is augmented by a longer examination before dinner, when he will read the editorials or look at a late edition. But his paper, ironed or crumpled, is not here.

And now this egg.

He crosses to the hall. The kitchen door is ajar. 'Agnes, a cloth, please.' It is not a shout. He has not raised his voice since an incident with a Catholic chaplain outside a field hospital in France twenty-six years ago. The rest of his remark is made over his shoulder as he returns to the table, as much to himself as her: 'I don't think it unreasonable to expect my paper with breakfast. I could even endure powdered egg, like those poor souls down south, as long as I have my paper. How am I expected to keep a grip on things without a morning read? Just because we live here doesn't mean—'

But he is interrupted by the sight of her entering. The paper is crumpled, her face ashen. Wordlessly she puts the paper in front of him and points to the headline. He never shouts. He never runs. But he runs to the telephone now.

43

As Lucy is on her tram, abortion bound, Franz is saying his goodnights. It has been a long day for them both. He has agreed with his teacher that they will spend most of tomorrow together. He will sleep here tomorrow night. This is sufficient excuse, if one is needed, for an early night. But one is not needed. He says goodnight to each of the family in turn and goes to the room set aside for him.

A few weeks earlier Agnes took him into her confidence and told him of her evening prayers, their intention if not their content. Now, in his mind he runs through an inventory of those he wants preserved, and prays for the repose of those lost to him. He always begins with the latter: mother, father and Nina. Next come his brothers. In praying for the boys he is shading into the living, his prayer an entreaty that they are among them. Then follows the mental list of those deserving who have sheltered him. Towards the end of this he prays for Isabel and Morag, but not Murdo. He concludes with a prayer for Agnes, Lachlan and Gail. In this last prayer his fervour is lately tinged with a sense of guilt because he now can conjure Agnes, Lachlan and Gail more vividly than he can his own family. He has discovered that to those who remain behind, death is not a state but a gradation. The dead become deader. The images of Lachlan and Gail are colourful, while his family is gradually sinking into historical sepia, fading to some indiscriminate eternal radiance.

As Franz lies down to his three blankets and his medical textbook, Lucy lies down to her fatal curettage. But he is in no danger. His bed is on the south side of the river, as far from Clydebank as city boundaries permit. He sleeps the healthy sleep of his years and awakes, momentarily disoriented by the unfamiliar wallpaper. The family breakfast is interrupted by the shrill ring of the hall telephone. And so it is that news of obliteration on the other side of the city comes to them from Rassaig. And despite his assurances and remonstrances Franz is prematurely summoned back that day. And on the other end of the line, Lachlan, having employed sterner tones than the boy's recall demanded, returns the receiver to its cradle and leans, suddenly weary, on the hall table.

'He's safe.'

'Thank God. My prayers are remembered.'

'What about the prayers of the people of Clydebank?'

'I'll get a cloth for your waistcoat.'

Having assured Lachlan that the city is safe, Franz's visit to the centre, to catch the train north, gives him the lie. There is the movement of the displaced, hordes of people appearing both tragic and confused, carrying bundles, ridiculous miscellanies picked at random from warm rubble. And overall, in the faces of those around, he senses an air of determined embattlement. His train is delayed. He has no way of getting in touch. When, in darkness, the train draws into the rural station Murdo met him at a lifetime ago, he sees two figures, petrified with cold, levitating in smoke, anxiously scanning the carriages. For the first time he abandons his Gladstone bag to chance, drops it on the platform and runs towards the old couple.

Lachlan's caution proves well advised. The night of Franz's return, 14 March 1941, the bombers return to Clydebank. The night after that, Lachlan, sadly vindicated, paraphrases aloud from the late edition, expurgating as he sees fit.

'They used Dorniers and Junkers . . . Dropped landmines the first time. Landmines! On civilians. How do they sleep?'

'Is it a quiz?'

'Don't be absurd, woman. It says here there was still a distillery burning the second night to guide them back . . . Dropped incendiaries the second night and burned what remained . . . You'd think with all that fire they might have been more accurate. Didn't get a single shipyard, or the Singer factory.'

'Were they looking to blow up sewing machines then?'

'Apparently it has been converted to make sten guns.'

'Who makes the sewing machines then?'

He momentarily folds down the top half of his paper to stare at her in exasperation.

'What has that got to do with incendiary bombs dropped on Clydebank?'

'Folk need things sewed. Even if there is a war on. Especially if there is a war on, all those uniforms and badges.'

'We managed well enough before sewing machines were invented. We'll do so again.'

'We?'

He flicks the paper vertical and resumes.

'One theory for their inaccuracy is that the German navigators saw Great Western Road in the moonlight and mistook it for the Clyde. Personally I don't see it. I can see a moonlit road being mistaken for a canal, but not a river. If they can afford all that ordnance to drop on innocent people you'd think they could afford decent maps and a compass. And they can't even get it right when the place is lit up like a roman candle. So much for the Luftwaffe.'

'Their airforce isn't much good either.'

'For once, Agnes, we find ourselves in agreement.'

'Has Lucy come back?' says Franz.

44

It is a question Gail and Harriet have been asking with increasing urgency for two days now. With his concern for the boy, Lachlan has forgotten all about Lucy. The girls haven't. Risking welcome interruption from her, Harriet looks through Lucy's things. Almost all her life is up for public scrutiny. She is not the kind of girl to keep a diary. Introspection is not in her nature. There is no address book. The only lead Harriet can find is a piece of scrap paper with a London telephone number written on it.

The McHargs don't have a telephone. The Campbells do. Both girls agree they don't want to make the call from the Drovers or the public telephone on the promontory. Gail makes the call, prepared for sarcasm or to be rebuffed – given the tenor of their last exchange. She anticipates a relative, not a London pub. It sounds as if she has interrupted some perpetual party, contrived to affront the Luftwaffe. There is ragged singing in the background. A man takes the call. No, he's not her father, he's the publican. No, he doesn't know her personally but some of the girls who work here might. Can she hold? Without waiting for a response he goes to fetch someone else. Gail reflects that everything about this is in keeping with Lucy: the capricious departure without letting anyone know, the contact being a pub. She will probably arrive back momentarily irate that they have gone through her things, and then offer good-naturedly to forgive them when it is she who should seek forgiveness. A girl comes on. There is a suppressed hilarity in everything she says. She sounds like Lucy. Yes, she knows her. They both worked here till she decided to go to some Godforsaken place to pitchfork shit. Oh, that's where the call's from. No, no one's seen her since Christmas. Yes, she'll ask. Lucy's brother comes in here. And Gail's number?

She returns from school the following day to Eileen Campbell's news that a young man called and would call back at eight o'clock. This is said with the rising intonation of a question. Hamish makes sure she has the hall to herself when the call comes through. It comes from the same pub. The perpetual beano is still in full swing. The caller is Lucy's younger brother. Either he is drunk or has been given a garbled interpretation of her last call. He expects to speak to Lucy and is under the impression she lives there. No, he hasn't seen her, has she? No? Why did she call? Gail gives a patient reiteration of her last telephone conversation. He interrupts to add his order to the list being circulated. She finishes to a vacant silence.

'Well?' she is finally obliged to ask.

'Well what?'

'Do you think there are any grounds for concern?'

'Well, I'm not concerned.'

But the mother is. She calls at some unconscionable hour from a public box. She gets out the news that no one down here has seen either hide or hair of her before a siren goes off in the background.

'How did she seem before she left?'

'I . . . I didn't see her just before she left.'

'She's a good girl. There's no harm in her.'

'Shouldn't you take shelter?'

'Suppose. She hasn't done this before. Get her to telephone me. If I hear, I'll telephone you.'

'I will. Please go.'

Something of the older woman's panic has communicated itself. She looks out the window towards the sleeping village and feels guilt in her seclusion, imagining people huddled in Anderson shelters and on tube platforms. The following day Douglas Leckie sheepishly gives Harriet the same name he gave to Lucy, someone who knows someone who can help. Gail again makes the call. She speaks to a woman in Inverness.

'I'm only looking for my friend. I don't want to resort to threats.'

A snort of laughter at the other end of the line. 'Take my advice, dear, don't try. You don't have the accent.' And without further prompting, 'Ellinger Terrace. There's no point in looking. It's not there any more.'

'Why.'

'It's in Clydebank. You know where that used to be?'

45

A telegram has arrived in Rassaig. No one recalls this having occurred before, which would make the event portentous enough. But a war and a telegram draw the inevitable conclusion. The messenger has collected a retinue of schoolchildren, who run following his bicycle. Opening the door, Liz McKinnon almost faints at the sight and rallies against the cool of the doorjamb when he explains he is only looking for directions. She looks at the address and points in the direction of the other poor bastard. The children have only been able to keep up as he hesitated from street to street. Confident of his way, he stands on the pedals to accelerate and leaves the breathless group hovering on the edge of the village.

Following the discovery of Lucy's destination, Gail and Harriet have spent the night at the Campbells'. This was done at Eileen's insistence. Lucy's silence has grown eloquent. Both women draw the same conclusion. Harriet offers to call the number Lucy left them with. Difficult as the news is to pass on, it is going to be more difficult still to take. Gail reasons that scant as her association with Lucy's mother is, it would be better if she heard this from her and not yet another stranger.

The tiresome singing has abated to a hubbub. She leaves a message for Lucy's mother to call back and two hours later walks to the ringing hall telephone with a sense of dread. She can't explain why they think Lucy was in Clydebank without revealing the reason. Rather than have this teased out in instalments, she has prepared a mental script which she recites.

She gets to the end of this without faltering, her purpose deterring interruption, and is confronted with a dreadful silence followed by sobbing. This is cut short by the line going dead.

Numbly she walks back to her room. There is only one mental topic. She imagines Lucy, sitting in a tawdry waiting room, or worse, recuperating alone, frightened and in pain, perhaps half-way down a stairwell when everything is reduced to constituent atoms. In a way the sight of Angus is preferable to this. To have nothing to dispose of leaves a hole the same shape as the person missed. And the way they parted leaves the gap ragged.

There is a pile of corrections in the corner. She can concentrate on nothing. There is a gentle tap on the door. Harriet, yet a shade paler than sleeplessness has left them both, noiselessly crosses the room.

'There's a telegram . . .'

46

Eileen telephones Agnes. For once she is not motivated by the compulsion to circulate information she has the thrill of knowing first. There is no pleasure in this at all. She calls Agnes to ask her to send Lachlan across when he comes back.

Lachlan, weary, returns not to the anticipated aroma of dinner in the making but to news that Gail's fiancé is lying dead in Tobruk and that, according to Eileen, she is in 'a bit of a state'. He pulls back on the coat he had just shrugged to his elbows, picks up the bag and goes. He is prepared for the worst. Of all people Gail is the one he would least like to see discomposed. Eileen's vicarious description suggests melodrama. He suspects this has more to do with Eileen than Gail. Hamish Campbell meets him in the darkened yard.

'How is she?'

'She's a good one, her.'

The house is in silence as he is shown into the hall. Eileen hovers nervously outside the bedroom door. Lachlan nods as he passes. Eileen looks through the door as he enters, only to find it gently closed upon her. She doesn't know what she expected but finds she is holding the doctor's hat.

Gail is sitting in the only armchair. Harriet stands behind, stroking Gail's hair. Gail does not appear to be in a bit of a state. She is merely pensive, staring abstractedly at the floor. Lachlan sits wearily on the bed, older than him. The springs protest as much as his knees.

'Do you want me to go?' Harriet asks.

'No. How long has she been like this?'

'There's no need to talk about me in the third person.'

'Perhaps a cup of tea,' Lachlan concedes, wanting his dinner. Harriet goes.

'Who sent for you?'

'Eileen called Agnes. She said you were in a bit of a state. I doubted it. I think she thought you might be in the kind of state she would be in if she had had this much bad news one after the other.'

'I parted with both of them badly, you know.'

'I didn't know. A last parting will always be inadequate, unless you recognize it for what it is, and how many times does that happen? You can't go around making farewells assuming they will be the last.'

'There was a fair chance with Clive it was the last. I knew. I think he did too. He was frightened and I didn't have it in me to give him what might have helped.' She begins to cry almost silently. He sighs, shifts his weight to the accompaniment of groaning springs, leans across to take her hand.

'Perhaps it wasn't in you to give.'

'And I fell out with Lucy. Perhaps I'm the common denominator.'

'That girl would try the patience of a saint. Underneath my best professional manner I fell out with Lucy. I think even she realized, which shows how professional my professional manner is.'

'Why are you here, Lachlan?'

'Because I want to help you any way I can. If you want, I can give you a sedative at least to help you sleep.'

'Why would I want a sedative? Why postpone things?' He does not say, but he knows from personal experience that delay can be a merciful safety net to allow the impetus of death to intrude gradually. 'I don't want medicine, I want an explanation.'

'I'm sorry, but that's the one thing I find myself uniquely unqualified to provide.'

47

Ewan McHarg is standing in front of a seated Lachlan. The patient is staring doggedly at the ceiling, the sight chart, the colourful cross-section of the respiratory system, at anything that will distract from the embarrassment of the moment. This contrived preoccupation is not working.

On his arrival Lachlan cordially invited him to sit. Ewan coughed in preparation for his memorized delivery. The doctor appeared not to notice his patient's paralysed embarrassment as he squinted in a rather peculiar manner at Ewan from the other side of his desk, and then again from another perspective as he swivelled his chair around to the side. Returning to his original position, Lachlan proceeded to pull a large book from the bottom drawer and scribble mysteriously for a few minutes before closing the tome with a satisfied thump and cheerfully asking, 'Well, what can I do for you?'

There follows a period of prolonged swallowing on Ewan's part before the apparatus, sufficiently lubricated, will recite the script he has prepared. Even if the symptoms are harmless, which Ewan doubts, the nidus is a sign from God, a mark of His disapproval of his recalcitrance. Why would it appear there unless it was a sign of his transgression?

It seems that description alone is not sufficient. He had hoped to conclude his recital and be given something, a powder, a pill, a balm, but it seems not. He reflects, bitterly, how easy it is for others: the Catholics would get a prescription from the doctor, three Hail Marys and an Act of Contrition from the priest, and that would be that. But then, they're all damned anyway. And so, following instruction, Ewan stands, excruciated, trousers and underpants down, his stingy penis exposed to the curious gaze of this godless old man whose understanding of the situation stops at pathology.

As a matter of fact, Lachlan, thoroughly enjoying himself, is fully appreciative of both the physical and metaphysical aspects of Ewan's condition. He may not share the theology but he understands both what he is looking at and what it signifies to Ewan. To Lachlan it is a hard, insensitive lesion that is the first manifestation of syphilis. To Ewan it is the first infinitesimal indication of the limitless and eternal torment that awaits those who come by these symptoms.

'That, Mr McHarg, is what we in medical circles refer to as a chancre . . .'

48

Gail's next appearance at the Drovers is two weeks after she has received her telegram. In the interim she has given herself over entirely to work, devoting more time to this than the task merits. Her social circle at this time has shrunk to Harriet, events drawing the two girls closer, the Campbells and the occupants of Lachlan's house. Her after-hour lessons with Franz are now invariably talks across her desk on topics which seldom wander near the arbitrary curriculum. With him she never mentions Lucy or Clive or her sense of loss. He has lost far more than she has. She feels admiration tinged with shame because she thinks he has coped better than her. In the very inconsequence of their talks she is aware of a reversal: she is taking instruction. Nothing is demanded of her at the Campbells'. She can sit in companionable silence. When she wants to talk she visits Lachlan.

It is Lachlan who tells her to go to the Drovers. He tells her he enjoys her company, but that at her age she shouldn't limit her exchanges to the narrow rote of school, the Campbells and his house. He knows it is inevitable she'll run into Murdo, but in his mind the risk this presents is less than the consequence of entrenching herself into a routine whose comfort becomes a trap. He tells her he admires the way she has immersed herself in work.

'What else am I to do?'

'Others wallow.'

'If I don't occupy myself I'll go insane.'

There is an element of truth in this statement. She is not

being melodramatic. She feels that if she gives herself time for introspection she will go under. Apart from correcting school work she does not read. She avoids the news. Her insistence on being constantly occupied even involves volunteering to Hamish what help she can give after hours.

'There's not much you can do after dark. Go to the Drovers like Doctor McCready says.'

She feels this is some kind of public prescription. She tells herself she will prepare for this first drink, imagining the embarrassment of being confronted with a deferential silence. She thinks the village's opinion classifies her as some kind of emotional invalid.

The following night she has arranged to go to Lachlan's for dinner. He awaits her in the hall, coat already on.

'I've told Agnes we'll eat in the Drovers.'

'I'm – I'm . . . not sure.'

Ignoring this, he takes her arm. 'The food's inferior but at least we don't have to sit through grace.'

'I heard that.'

Putting his hand in the small of her back, he propels Gail back out the door she just came in by. He takes her arm, talking cheerfully as they walk down the hill. She stiffens as they approach the lights. Sensing the tension, he momentarily stops and turns to face her.

'Indulge an old man.'

And so she comes back. Harriet is there. There is no damp-ening of noise at her entrance. The only comments that come her way wouldn't have been out of place a month ago. If anything, she is diplomatically ignored. She feels the whole thing has been stage-managed by Lachlan. She watches him order at the bar. There is respect in the space automatically made for him. When she first saw him and how he was treated she did not understand the reason for deference. It was more than just age and a rural doctor's status. She understands now. Turning, he finds her watching and speaks across the gap.

'Stovies?'

'Stovies,' she agrees, with an upwelling of feeling towards him. She knows he knows. Perhaps he has seen the symptoms before. To give her time he consults with Harriet who has been waiting for them to arrive before she eats. The plates arrive at the table a moment after he has seated them with drinks. For a reason she cannot explain Gail blurts a laugh and takes her face in her hands. Looking out between splayed fingers, like a child, she sees Lachlan waiting to say something.

'Was I right?' His manner is almost mischievous.

'Yes, Lachlan. You were right. The food's inferior.'

And so she comes back.

She views the letters sent to Clive since New Year as a rambling apology that was never properly made and now cannot be. When he was alive she felt guilty at not loving him enough. Now the obligation has been removed she cannot work out whether it is him she misses or, perversely, the burden of failing to requite. If nothing else, a sense of guilt gave her emotional ballast. It held her down. It held her back. Angus is dead, and Lucy, and Clive, and Franz's family, and thousands upon thousands of others she will never know. The world is on fire. Perhaps Lucy had the right idea. What's wrong with fun? Lucy ignored the consequences, ran up a tariff and paid the compound debt in one fatal instalment. Not everyone does. Some live at a pace that outstrips consequences their whole life. Some never pay anything. And who's to say that everything we enjoy carries with it a debt? Continue thinking that way and she might as well throw in her lot with Gavin Bone. Some end up the same way Lucy did without having had any enjoyment. There is no equity. Who knows how much time is left? Perhaps it's time to stop counting costs.

She always thought of Lucy as childlike in the assumption that she deserved to have something simply because she wanted it. All Gail's better instincts, what she had learned at home and seen brutally corroborated here, tell her that if there is a purpose to anything, it's not just getting what you want. Happiness is ancillary. It is earned. It occurs, it is not invoked, and not at someone else's expense. At any other time she would pay attention to the dictates of conscience. To find him now is to do violence to her nature, to consent to be the beneficiary of someone else's misery. But the cumulative effect of all the deaths she has apprehended, either indirectly through Franz or directly in the sudden removal of Angus and Lucy and Clive, has left her morally concussed. Distinctions normally clear to her seem less so. She feels that her loss gives her some kind of dispensation. And in this blunted state she is prepared to grasp happiness, or if not happiness, anything that might temporarily pass for it, any way she can.

She begins to revisit the harbour after school hours. Blustery March turns to blustery April, scudding clouds and bloody sunsets. Green walls of water shudder the promontory in repeated explosions of foam. Observing this behaviour, Franz contrives to detain her, but she will not be deterred. It has become necessary to her, this lustral exposure. The more severe the weather, the greater her enjoyment and sense of being cleansed. She knows the interpretation Murdo will put upon this. She tells herself she cannot help what he thinks, but she knows she can, and she knows her exposure is not only for the sensation of feeling clean.

He does not approach her while she is out there. As before, her willed isolation deters. As before, he stands at the doorway and watches her pass on the way back. As before, she sees him watching.

From his eyrie at the top of the house Franz sees her

standing alone at the crossroads. She is waiting. There can be no mistake. She waits till he comes. From his window Franz sees the figures meet and begin walking together till the roofs intervene. In agitation he jumps off the table. She has cut short their after-hours lesson to go there and meet him on the way back. There is nothing accidental in this. She has chosen, perhaps without realizing what he is. But she has chosen. He does not know what to do.

While she stood waiting for Murdo her mind ran through the possible alternatives of what he or she might say. Who would speak first? There is no reason for her to be there besides the obvious one. She feels cheap, but the feeling does not deter her. As he turns the corner she feels her heart grow hot at his approach. All her speculations about what might be said are wrong.

'Where?' he says simply. His assurance is arrogant.

'I . . . I don't know.' She did not expect it to be reduced to this brutal simplicity, but she does not disagree either.

'My boat.'

'No.'

'Are you frightened of water or are you thinking of your friend and Douglas Leckie?'

'I didn't know it was common knowledge.'

''Course you did. He was so worked up he couldn't scull without trembling.'

She imagines Murdo's boat: some masculine space, tackle, no adornments, no concessions to comfort he probably considers effeminate.

'I don't want to become public knowledge the way she was.'

'At least you're honest. Where then? We can't go to mine. What about your room?'

'No. They go to bed early but not that early. And there are

dogs.' She does not want him in her room. She does not want the Campbells' hospitality abused. She wants him immediately, piercing her, and she wants him kept at arm's length.

'The schoolroom,' he says by process of elimination, and taking her hand begins walking.

Nothing in Rassaig is ever locked. He crosses the brief hallway racked at her waist height with pegs for children's coats. There is only one classroom. An intermittent street-light just beyond the short playground casts a sodium glare, throwing rhomboids of light on the opposite wall. By now he is pulling her. This place, the hanging drawings and pressed leaves, the clumsy mounted projects, a place for children, somehow it is wrong.

'No,' she says. But, like Lucy, she feels she has set in motion a train of actions she cannot now stop, only guide. She points towards the shelved store cupboard at the back of the class, still stacked with old slates and the detritus of itinerant teachers and successive years. He drags her in, kicking the door behind them so hard it ricochets open again. By this time he does not care. He pushes her against the unshelved wall, pulls open her blouse, takes her left breast in his huge hand and squeezes so hard the nipple bursts though the gap of encircling forefinger and thumb. Bending down, he takes this in his mouth. She can feel the rasp of a day's growth on the areola. She grasps his hair, pulls his mouth from the bursting nipple, tilts his head and bites his lip. Released, he takes two steps back and pulls at his clothes. She makes no move to undress but watches. In the aquarial gloom his body is a section of overlapping angular planes. Looking up, he sees her watching and momentarily stops. She marvels at the prominence of his collarbones, ribs, corrugated stomach, the density of his thighs and his penis, heavy with blood but still pendulous. He is breathing like the Minator, the sound immense in the close space. Without stepping forward he reaches across for her, pulling her so hard that both her feet leave the floor. She struggles to undress lest he tear her clothes.

'Put your arms round my neck.' It is not a request. Bending, he takes the crook of a knee in each hand. She is lifted and splayed, held in a moment of exposure that brings with it an intensity of anticipation she feels cannot be appeased till he pushes into her with an explosion of force that triggers her ferocious release. He continues to gore her, snorting. She spasms again and feels him arch till finally he leans against her, shoulders heaving, shuffling forward till she is sandwiched against the wall, her breasts pressed, her back indented against the exposed masonry.

'Poor Clive,' she thinks. Like Franz she has just made the discovery that the dead become deader.

49

It seems to Lachlan that beyond Rassaig the world continues to tear itself to pieces at a furious pace. Tobruk, a place no one had ever heard of, continues to dominate the headlines as others die, to line up statistically with Clive and generate posthumous telegrams. His reading of the evening newspaper is as thorough as ever, he understands the words in front of him, but somehow the outside has lately come to be less real to him. Since the arrival of Franz, the completion of his own world has relegated what lies beyond this domestic sphere. His greatest concern is not for the outside world but for its intrusion on this one. He is not thinking of himself.

He begins to tally the passing of the weeks not by the ebb and flow of hostilities, the campaigns he monitored so diligently and still abstractly follows, but by his weekly visit to the cinema in Oban with Franz that has become a staple of their routine. They drive there for Saturday matinee showings. Agnes goes with them only once. Make-believe of any kind entails for her an anticlimax. Why drive all that distance to see people dress up, walk about and say a lot of memorized words? Lachlan, with conscious irony, tells her she has no soul. But there is another reason she doesn't go. She knows Lachlan treasures time alone with Franz and she thinks the boy also enjoys it more if she stays behind. The cinema has given them a shared appreciation of something that eludes her and she is happy to leave them to it.

To Franz's embarrassment and the irritation of those in surrounding darkness, Lachlan keeps up a whispered commentary over the Pathé News reports, translating the euphemisms of war reportage. But when the main feature comes on he sits in rapt attention. Franz has never seen him transported. They take turns at choosing the films, by unspoken mutual consent avoiding anything with a contemporary war theme. The exception is *Waterloo Bridge*, Lachlan's choice, at which he weeps unashamedly. Robert Taylor's pained recollection, pacing the bridge, straining through the mist of amnesia to recall poignant instalments of his past love affair with Vivien Leigh, has Lachlan honking like a migratory goose into his handkerchief. Dramatic effect is deflated when the lights come up and he pragmatically states, 'I don't think that was an accurate portrayal of remission from amnesia.'

Franz thinks the tears were an anomaly till Lachlan's next choice. *That Hamilton Woman*, with Vivien Leigh as Lady Hamilton being again rendered inconsolable, this time by the death of Laurence Olivier as Nelson, leaves Lachlan equally tearful. In return for confidences, Lachlan has told Franz something of his own history, leaving out mention of his wife. The boy marvels that a man who has served in a theatre of war, who is confronted with disease as part of his everyday business, who has the constitution to return from a deathbed to his dinner, is reduced to tears by the situations counterfeited on the screen. His own preference is for action. He chooses *The Sea Hawk* and *Zorro*. The trip home involves Lachlan pontificating on the relative merits of what they have seen till the boy inevitably falls asleep. Tyrone Power as Zorro is a 'fop', only marginally better than 'that ham Fairbanks who did it before. Best thing about sound was that it got rid of him.' The only saving grace is Basil Rathbone. Errol Flynn as the swashbuckling privateer in *The Sea Hawk* is a 'posturing hormonal lout'. The only saving grace is Claude Rains. Lachlan chooses *Pride and Prejudice* to glimpse his screen sweetheart, confiding to his sleeping passenger that 'parts of me long dormant are quickened by Greer Garson. She is a fine, fine woman.'

Making another exception to their unspoken rule, they see *The Great Dictator*. Franz is enthralled, Lachlan only enjoying it because of the boy's delight. They see *His Girl Friday*, both enjoying the rapid-fire dialogue; *The Philadelphia Story* – 'That Cary Grant can teach the Americans something about diction'; *Rebecca* – 'Never trust a man with a moustache', 'But the bad man was clean-shaven', 'Don't trust them either'; *The Little Foxes* – 'You know, there are patients I've wanted to deny medicine to the way Bette Davis did today.'

They eat fish and chips out of paper in the car before the drive back and Franz falls asleep to Lachlan's running commentary and the pervasive smell of malt vinegar. Like exhaust fumes recalling his departure from Prague, it is one of the smells that will evoke for him exact reminiscences for the rest of his life.

Gail meets Murdo twice more on the way back from the harbour. They adjourn to the cupboard. Periods between meetings are sufficiently long to mark the occasions with the same urgency. In an attempt to convince herself that this is something more than a mercenary exchange she persuades him to stay with her one Saturday night in a hotel. Oban is too small, too local. Braving the possibility of more bombs, they choose Glasgow and travel separately. On the train she tries unsuccessfully to read. She sits in the room awaiting his arrival. He has been drinking by the time he arrives. They fuck without preamble. Getting up for a bath afterwards she catches sight of herself in the mirror. There is a bite mark on her shoulder and a dull bruise on one buttock where his hand cradled her. He lies sprawled on the bed behind, sleeping off the beer, his long muscular frame compressed by the perspective. She has not prepared herself for this scrutiny and in her face catches a look of complete misery. She wakes him while she dresses. He does not care where they eat, it is all fuel to him, as long as there is beer.

Over dinner she makes several attempts to get the conversation going, employing the prompts she has mentally rehearsed during the journey down when her book defeated her. She is trying to introduce an element of normality into the situation, to have the kind of exchange normal couples do, even though she knows normal couples don't rehearse inconsequential conversation in advance. She is desperately trying to help herself temporarily forget that she is having an affair with a married man since the thought of the wife she has only ever seen at a distance now insinuates itself between them, even during the act. It does not work. He is civil enough in his responses but each attempt is a cul-de-sac. He no longer employs the caustic humour of their first meetings because he has no need to: he has achieved his object and will continue to do so when she is near and the impulse is upon him. She realizes he is more interested in the beer and in the thought of resuming their activities.

As soon as the food is finished he pays quickly. On the way out he takes her arm and holds this at a height that leaves her heel on his side barely touching the ground. He walks too quickly back to the hotel. She is about to say something when she realizes she has no ground for complaint: it was this kind of handling she waited for at the crossroads. Despite having done this three hours before he again treats her with the same urgency he has shown in the schoolroom cupboard. He falls into a light doze afterwards. She can hear him swallowing loudly in his sleep. She begins to calculate how long it will be till she can remove her cap. She knows he will wake and want to do this again so it will all depend on that. Perhaps he will want to do this again before they have to check out. It did not seem to occur to him to provide condoms. The timing of the whole night has really been dictated by what he wants. What, she wonders, does she want, really want?

He duly wakes an hour later, roused by the proximity of a warm woman in his bed. As he moves across he notices the pillow is wet. This one has been crying, he surmises, as he turns her on to her face and kneels up.

50

Catriona Bone, wife of Gavin, is staring doggedly at Lachlan's sight chart, framed between her parted thighs, as was the molten globe Lucy witnessed emerge from the abortionist's floor before it expanded to render her visit redundant. From Catriona's supine perspective the arbitrary letters descend from knees to pubis in dwindling legibility, the bottom row being lost in the grey smudge of Lachlan's hair.

Her contrived preoccupation does not work either. Lachlan straightens, turning away as he does so to conceal the smile that he knows has formed itself on his face. He turns back when he has schooled his features.

'That, Mrs Bone, is what we in medical circles refer to as a chancre . . .'

51

Abandoning the idea of walking to the harbour, Gail turns from the schoolroom in the direction of the Campbells' farm. Although still drawing down early the evenings have lengthened. When not staying late at school she can get back in daylight, watch bright cold sunsets over a cup of tea from the kitchen window. Late-afternoon gusts hum in the fence wires, flattening her dress against her legs.

All concessions to discretion have been hers. When she returned, alone, from Glasgow, she found that Murdo had accepted a lift there and back from someone in the village. She has already concluded that he has made little attempt to conceal their meetings. She reasons that if she becomes common currency, as Lucy was, she has only herself to blame. She thinks of her exchanges with Lucy and considers herself a hypocrite. She once thought Lucy's moral development was as retarded as Angus's literacy. She lacks this excuse for her behaviour. Eileen Campbell has been more reserved of late. Perhaps she knows. If she does, it's a matter of time before everyone does. Eileen's opinion is of little consequence to her but Lachlan's isn't. Nor is the opinion of at least another dozen people she likes up here. Lucy could afford to be blasé. She didn't teach. Gail wonders how tenable her position will be. Behaviour like this has corroborated Gavin Bone's opinion. The night she spent with Murdo didn't dispel the qualms she felt on the way there, if anything it increased them. She had gambled that the pleasure of sexual release was sufficient antidote to the guilt of fucking another woman's husband, and she was wrong. She is struck by her own selfishness.

These thoughts are running through her mind when she hears her name being called, propelled by the wind behind her. She turns. Isabel Dougan is coming into sight round the bend. With one hand she is pushing a large creaking pram. The other holds the hand of a small boy, who must be no more than three, trotting beside her, trying to keep pace. With the wind at her back Isabel is having difficulty balancing the ensemble. They are on the stretch of road that runs out of the village. There are no diversions until the entrance to the Campbells' farm. There is no pavement. Continuous farm traffic has left the surface uneven. Isabel is struggling with the pram through the ruts. Hating herself, Gail turns away and starts to accelerate, her loose scarf a whirling plume before her. Her name is called again, high and plaintively. Worst of all, it is her Christian name. Refusing to turn she walks doggedly on, wondering what to do if this pursuit continues all the way to the farm. Perhaps she should continue walking past the entrance.

'Gail! Gail! Please don't make me run.' This is cut short by the sound of the boy crying. Gail turns. The child has fallen. Having suddenly stopped while still holding his hand, Isabel is trying to prevent the skewing pram veering into the ditch. Despite the gap Gail can see her crying. She runs back against the wind to where they are and stoops to the boy. His knee is bleeding. Her obvious thought is why is he wearing shorts in this weather? Picking him up and turning to Isabel, the answer is obvious. The pram is battered, the covers good, but Isabel is very shabby. What money she has been given has obviously gone to them. And that night in Glasgow he disdained her offer of dividing the bill and paid it all as a point of principle, paid it prematurely in a hurry to get back to fuck her.

She despises herself.

'You wouldn't want him if you knew. I've got the marks and I still want him.'

'Look . . . I'm . . .'

'Please don't take him. Please.'

Gail turns her attention to the knee, unable to look at the other woman's face. She takes her handkerchief and wipes the blood away. The scrape almost immediately turns bloody again. She wipes it again, and asking him to stand ties the handkerchief round in a loose bandage. The mother watches this, waiting for Gail to look at her.

'I don't know if he can walk back.'

'Say you won't see him again.' The boy limps to her and wrapping his arms round her legs buries his face in her thigh.

'I'll carry him.'

'I can see to the boy. Don't pretend to make this about the boy. Say you won't see him again.'

'I already decided . . .' This sounds limp. How insulting would it seem that she has already given up someone this woman is prepared to abase herself to keep? Better to let her think her appeal has prevailed. 'I won't see him again.'

'Promise.'

'I promise.'

At this Isabel turns her attention to the boy. She hauls the pram round to face the village. Facing into the wind it seems more steady till she lifts the boy and balances him sitting across the pram, knees crooked over the side rim. The whole thing gives a precarious lurch. Holding the handrail, she busies herself with the unseen baby. Satisfied with the arrangement, she braces the handrail against her stomach while using both hands to tighten her headscarf. The whole thing is done with intense preoccupation. Having got what she came for Gail feels herself dismissed.

'It'll be hard, all the way back . . . I'll carry him.'

The other woman turns. The face is ravaged. 'All the way back? To my house? To meet him and explain? You might even meet my mother-in-law.'

Leaning at an acute angle she pushes the pram forward into the wind. Progress is laborious. Gail watches till they approach the bend. No amount of standing on an exposed sea wall will wipe this away. The pram stops, Isabel leaning forward. She turns, holding the handkerchief, and throws it limply in Gail's direction. The wind snatches it and carries it high towards the sea.

52

Gavin's ablutions are in vain. The lengthier, the colder, the more rigorous, the more petrifying, all have been to no avail. Perhaps it is a sign, a test, he a latter-day Job. There is some comfort in this. But if so, would he not be informed? He is chastising himself to make atonement for a sin he cannot place having committed, but is that not the scheme of things? Iniquity covers its own tracks and it cannot be for nothing that these things have appeared where they have. Morning and night he mortifies his penis with cold water only to watch it slowly revive with its marks of sin still intact.

He has been tested in his faith before now and found wanting. Some time ago, when these symptoms first presented themselves, he had gone to that heathen doctor. The cough had been a pretext, an introduction to allow him time to assess the doctor's competence. The consultation had degenerated when the subject of that other heathen, the one who tried to pollute the children of their congregation with the heresy of evolution, came up. The whole incident had been a sign that he had no business seeking help from pagans. True succour only comes from Him.

If only he knew Lachlan would be delighted to measure the skull again, the last reading botched by Gavin's restless aggression, and say: 'That, Mr Bone, is what we in medical circles refer to as a chancre . . .'

53

Her manner in the classroom is subdued. Morning and lunchtime break the rain continues to pour. Confined indoors, the children are restless. The windows are covered in condensation. Her head feels like a pressure cooker. By two o'clock the rain has abated. Released for the afternoon break, they pour frenziedly into the playground, a little compound of puddles. She takes the window pole and opens each window in turn. The smell of wet vegetation after rain blows through, lifting the condensation, easing her headache. She leaves the children longer than normal before going out to sound the bell and eases the short remainder of the afternoon by reading aloud to them.

Franz approaches when the rest have dispersed. She is cradling her forehead in her hand and recognizes his shoes on the other side of the desk. Without looking up she says, 'Not this afternoon, please,' more abruptly than she intended. She looks up apologetically but by this time he has turned and is walking away. She thinks: 'Yet another thing I have misjudged.'

He is not offended but concerned, as he lugs his Gladstone bag towards home. His destination is next right, up the hill. He sees Murdo walking towards him. If he does not make the turn before Murdo reaches it they will pass each other on the pavement. He stands indecisively wondering whether to go back in the direction he has just come from. Over any distance Murdo will catch up. Summoning himself, he runs towards the turn-off, towards Murdo, and makes the junction before he does. He pants up the hill and turns back to look down and see him pass.

If Murdo has even seen him he shows no recognition. His face is set as he walks purposefully towards the school. Franz has seen him often enough at the croft to know what that look presages. Confused, he looks down at the bag. If he goes for Lachlan it will slow him down. If he gets Lachlan what will he do? He is old. Murdo is strong. Lachlan will call someone before he leaves. All this will take time. In a fit of indecision he drops the bag, runs half a dozen paces up the hill, stops, returns. His breathing is accelerating. Agitated, he opens the bag and looks in to reassure himself.

Gail is making her rounds with the pole, closing the windows, when she hears the outer door open and close. He walks in with as little forewarning as Gavin did that day. She knew the meeting would be inevitable but wanted more time. She would have preferred some other venue, somewhere she could have walked away from. It doesn't yet occur to her to be afraid.

'You didn't come.' There is no rising intonation, no incredulity or sense of disappointment, just a flat statement of fact.

'No. I'm sorry. And if I had come it would only have been to say we can't meet again.'

'You're upset because of your friend.'

'He was my fiancé.'

'I was thinking about the girl. Whatever he was it didn't stop you.'

'No. You're right. It was all wrong. I was wrong.'

'You're out of sorts.'

This elicits a surprised ironical laugh. The conclusion she came to, the self-reproach for suspending her conscience, the humiliating encounter with Isabel, all reduced to an evaluation that just might adequately describe an overtired child. Looking at him, she realizes he is serious.

'I thought I had an excuse. I was wrong. Other people have lost more and don't behave as badly as I did.'

'I think you should think more about yourself.'

'You mean about you and me.'

'Aye. At least with me you weren't miserable.' She forbears to tell him that this isn't true.

'You make it sound as if you were doing me a favour.'

'Maybe. You'll forget more easily – with me.'

'Sex as a miracle cure. Doctor Dougan. You missed your calling, Murdo. And what were you trying to forget?'

As she says this she turns away, missing the frown that has descended on him. No one ever practises sarcasm on him, least of all a woman. Looking up, she sees the cast of his features and for the first time feels wary. Nor does she like the solitude they have so recently sought. She was going to mention his wife but doesn't. What was it the poor woman said? Something about bearing marks. At the time she thought this was said for effect, figuratively. Now she is not sure. Somehow she senses that if she does say something he will take it out on Isabel. She looks at him resignedly, leans against the desk and sighs. He takes this as a concession and nods in the direction of the cupboard.

'I can't. You're married.'

'What the fuck has that to do with anything?'

'If you don't understand I can't explain.'

'Well, you better try. And you better explain how me being married last week and the week before that didn't matter then but does now.'

She only realizes he is angry as his voice gets quieter and quieter. In the otherwise silent classroom she has to strain to catch the last words.

'I wasn't thinking about your wife and children then, only about myself.'

'Well, don't think about them. Leave me to think about them. They've got fuck all to do with you.'

She realizes there is no reasoning with him.

'Murdo, please go. I'm sorry. I really am. I had no right to let you think . . .'

'Get in the cupboard.'

'It's finished.'

He walks past her towards the cupboard. Instinctively she expects a blow and shrinks. But he does not touch her. His left hand reaches the handle and wrenches the door open. He stands for a moment, as if committing the interior to memory. Looking back briefly to her, his right hand reaches across the gap and grasps her hair. He looks back towards the cupboard and in one convulsive movement yanks her towards him and propels her in.

Her head collides with the shelf of redundant slates. Momentarily dazed, it takes her a moment to grasp what is happening. He walks in, slamming the door behind him.

54

As Lachlan returns from a late house call he finds Agnes in the drive, ill-dressed for the cold, gesturing to him. He has not seen a similar look on her face since she handed him the Clydebank headlines. She shouts something that is obscured by the crunch of gravel as he stops the car in a skewed diagonal and climbs out.

'Franz.' She waves towards the house. He snatches his bag and hurries, making for the stairs. 'The lounge,' she says. He walks in. Franz is sitting in Lachlan's chair staring rigidly before him, rocking slightly. The intermittent blinking reminds Lachlan of the first time he met the boy, but a bat would not hear the surf from here. He takes both his hands and looks as intently into the boy's face as he did that first night, illuminated by car headlights on the clifftop.

The lips are forming a word, again and again, which he fails to enunciate. Pressing his hands, Lachlan nods in time with the rocking, agreeing with what he has not heard, teasing out the sound.

'Gail. Gail. Gail. Go to Gail.'

'Where?'

'Go to Gail.'

'Where is Gail?'

'Gail.'

He goes into the hall to the telephone and asks the operator to connect him to the Campbells'. Agnes dons her coat while he waits for the connection.

'Where are you going?'

'The school. If you go to the farm pick me up as you pass.'

The number rings out. When asked if he wants to hang on he drops the receiver and makes for the car. He would not leave the boy alone but there is no help for it. He is barely out of the drive when he comes across Agnes. She climbs in. He drops her at the bottom of the hill, a minute from the school, and accelerates off towards the Campbells' farm. The suspension protests at the same surface that rattled Isabel's pram. He is jostled so violently his foot leaves the accelerator. He drives straight into the yard, leaves the engine running and walks through the front door. He shouts from the threshold. No one responds. He walks to Gail's room, looks in just long enough to assure himself she isn't there, and goes back towards the car, absently noticing the trail of slurry his hurried entrance has left.

He swerves out of the yard. It is dark now. He puts the headlights on, shading the ruts in the same cratered road back. He stops with a screech in the playground. The door is locked. He bangs, shouting.

55

Having looked in his bag and overcome his indecision, Franz begins walking back down the hill towards the junction. Gravity helps. When he reaches the flat his resolve deserts him and he has to gather himself, pick up the bag and again begin walking. The outer door is closed. He pushes this open tentatively. Rows of vacant pegs are visible in the deepening gloom, each shadowed by light coming from the open door of the classroom beyond. He pushes this door further open and walks slowly inside. There is no one here. He had not known what he would interrupt but did not expect to find the classroom empty. He stands in the middle of the room and looks around. There is an added apprehension at the novelty of being here, alone, at this time.

He stops at the sound of a stifled concussion, tilts and slowly rotates his head, trying to discern the source. At the repetition he is utterly certain that it comes from the cupboard. He has been there once. The fact that this noise comes from some dark, unused alcove terrifies him. Walking slowly across, he pauses at the door. He hears something like a sob. Very gradually he turns the handle and lets the door swing inwards. It takes him a minute to assemble the image in his mind to realize what he is seeing. Murdo is standing with his back to him. His free hand is tugging at the opening of his trousers. His other hand is otherwise occupied, holding a dark coil mostly obscured by the bulk of the small of his back. Only when he sees the heels of the woman's shoes either side of the heels of Murdo's boots does he realizes he is witnessing the same spectacle he saw in the croft from another perspective. The man is standing between the woman's parted legs. The boy's next moves are very slow and deliberate. He puts the bag on the ground, opens its yawning mouth and reaches inside.

Straining bent across a broken trestle, Gail sees the light from the classroom on the far wall. Murdo doesn't. His eyes are closed. With the half-dozen or so women he has done this to he finds greatest arousal from the struggle. When they are subdued the remainder is automatic until the explosive conclusion. He has even found the need to galvanize himself through the passive interval until the urgency again takes over. His wife no longer offers the stimulation of resistance as she did on the first few occasions. The temporary suffocation that he improvised has turned out to be a happy experiment, the struggle for air simulating the same spasms he is about to enjoy again.

The first bang is so loud in the acoustics of the deserted classroom that it arrests even him. His first thought is that the roof has collapsed. Anyone coming in from outside could be forgiven for confusing cause and effect: the explosion of the display case, mounted on the classroom wall above the cupboard, coincides exactly with the detonation. Shattered glass rains down like ice, vivid fragments of butterfly wings spiralling through the smoke to come to settle on the littered floor. At the next roar the heel of Murdo's right boot blasts off to career against the opposite wall, taking with it an ellipse of bone and tissue from the base of Achilles tendon to rear instep. The force of this pivots him away from Gail to face in the direction of the light. He lets go of her hair and looks down. He thought there was something in the cupboard that had pushed him. He has automatically transferred the weight on his right foot to the ball to make allowance for the heel that is no longer there. In its place he sees a ragged bleeding concavity.

Looking up, he sees the smoke disperse to reveal that skinny little Jewish kid with eyes like saucers staring down the wavering barrel of the service revolver that he holds with erratic determination. The gun looks immense in his hands. Another report and the shelf to Murdo's immediate left fragments, driving splinters of wood into his shoulder and neck.

'You fucking little kike!' he screams. Only as an adult, when sufficient time has elapsed to allow him to look back at this emblazoned moment with some kind of impartial curiosity, does Franz wonder if Murdo was incensed at the loss of his heel, or the theft of his gun.

The next report detaches part of the doorjamb to Franz's immediate left. He is wavering violently. He could have just as easily hit Gail's heel. Now it looks as if he lacks the accuracy to hit anything within the frame of the door. Murdo attempts a step forward with his truncated foot and nearly falls when he transfers the weight to the other leg. The span of his huge arms is almost the breadth of the oblong cupboard. Spreading his arms to steady himself by touching alternate sides, he begins to slide towards the boy. Extending his damaged foot first and catching it up, he repeats this in jerking progress to the door.

He is now looming in the frame, completely obscuring Gail, presenting a larger target. He must be aware of the risk. He had wanted to fight. His idea of being under fire didn't encompass some fucking little yid making him a fucking cripple with his own fucking gun. He is screaming now, a hoarse, continuous ululation, his immense reserves of anger boiling to a state rendering him incapable of speech. Concentrating on the gun without looking up, Franz discharges the two remaining rounds in quick succession and continues to pull the trigger. The cloud before him seems to him enormous; the noise temporarily deafens. He anticipates Murdo lurching out the smoke to grasp him. He is too frightened to move, the paralysis complete with the exception of his hands.

The fifth shot dislodges one of the splinters sticking out of Murdo's shoulder without touching the flesh. At the sixth a crimson flower instantaneously blooms in his throat. The bullet passes clean through the larynx, windpipe and carotid artery and embeds itself in the wall behind, above Gail's cowed head, with a spattering of blood and tissue. Had she stood up more quickly it would have continued its trajectory through the back of her skull. Stopped dead by its puncturing momentum, Murdo clasps his throat. Blood spouts frivolously from the severed artery out the ragged hole in the back of his neck. His shattered foot, unable to take the sudden weight transferred to it, retracts. He slumps against the wall of the cupboard and slowly sits, the leg with the damaged foot folding unnaturally beneath him. The screaming stops abruptly with the disappearance of his vocal cords. The pierced whistle that escapes him descends in register to a gurgle. From his sitting position he leans forward, one hand to his neck, the second on the ground, as if intent on continuing towards the boy. The gurgling, after some moments, concludes in bloody frothing. He collapses, the impact of his forehead with the parquet twisting his head, forcing him to look back and upwards into the cupboard.

Gail stands slowly, trembling with shock. She pulls down the skirt he had forced over her hips and turns to see Murdo lying on the floor looking senselessly at the ceiling. A black puddle is radiating from the back of his head. Above this, framed in the doorway, Franz is disclosed through the dissipating smoke, holding some kind of monstrous gun. In the ensuing silence the only sound is the remorseless click of the hammer descending on empty chambers that slows to a stop as the boy's fingers cramp.

56

At his repeated banging Agnes opens the door and pulls him inside.

'For God's sake keep the noise down!'

'Is she here?'

'In there. Where's your bag?'

'In the car.'

'What use is it there?'

'Does she need help?'

'None that you can give without your bag. Go and get it.'

In the past she has inveigled money out of him for whatever cause she thinks he should subscribe to, she has cajoled him into providing assistance for this or that, she has implored, entreated, importuned, petitioned and persuaded, but she has never ordered him to do anything. Until now. If the case was not so desperate he would have a word with her about her tone. But instead he goes to the car. As far as he is concerned it is the work of a moment to retrieve the bag and return. Infuriatingly, she has locked the door again. Again he bangs.

'I said we had to keep the noise down.'

'Where is she?' This time he will not be deflected. He precedes her into the classroom. Gail is sitting behind her desk. From this distance there is an ominous semblance of normality, aside from the smell that reminds him of recently discharged fireworks. As he gets closer he notices her colour. She is paler than Franz.

'What happened?'

Agnes indicates a point on the floor. From his perspective this is obscured by the surface of a desk.

'Whatever you do, lock the door behind me.'

'Where are you going this time?' Despite the gravity of the situation he cannot keep the asperity from his voice. But she has already gone, and both infuriated and anxious he dumps his bag, goes back to obey her instructions and locks the door. As he approaches Gail again he is aware of crunching underfoot. Looking down, he sees glass fragments and some kind of coloured scraps he is walking through. Looking up, he notices some kind of stain radiating out beneath the closed cupboard door that Agnes had obviously been pointing to. Doing his best not to stand in this, he opens the door.

Very few things shock Lachlan. He says nothing, and forgoing his punctiliousness walks into the cupboard and lifts a wrist to take the expected reading. The blood has radiated out from the wound to the point of coagulation on the cold floor. Lachlan drops the wrist and steps back over the body blocking the doorway. He now adds congealed blood to the slurry on his shoes. His feet make sticking noises as he approaches Gail, still silent.

Looking up at him she whispers, 'He's dead.'

'Yes,' he says, not knowing if she is looking for confirmation, not knowing he also is whispering, and adds, 'Any death is a tragedy but I can't find it in myself to say I'm sorry.'

'He was shot while trying to rape me. I don't think it was the first time he's tried to rape anyone. Those poor women didn't have anyone to intervene. Where's Franz?'

'At home.'

'How is he?'

'His sole concern appeared to be you.'

The door sounds again. The sound seems very loud. They

exchange a startled look. Both begin to speak at once. Politely he defers.

'He saved me. That bastard would have raped me and then done God knows what. He's been through enough. He's not taking responsibility for this.'

'I couldn't agree more.' He stands stiffly and walks towards the door. Michael is alone. For the first time in his life Lachlan is frightened of a uniform.

'Agnes told me to come here. You look as if you were expecting someone else, Lachlan.'

'You'd better come in.'

Curiously, Michael locks the door at his back. He takes the same route as Lachlan's last entrance, crunching through the same glass, pulverizing the same friable wings. Attracted by the same stain, he opens the same door and stands in the same attitude of contemplation Lachlan did before checking for the pulse he knew he would not find. Deciding not to repeat the examination, he simply looks at Lachlan and says, 'Dead?'

The question is so ridiculous that in other circumstances Lachlan would laugh. But he cannot laugh. He merely nods assent. At the thought of due process taking its course he is, again for the first time in his professional career, crestfallen. Who knows what the law would decide would be appropriate punishment? The best they could hope for would be some kind of exoneration, mitigating circumstances, testimony of character witnesses . . . But any kind of investigation is likely to bring the boy's credentials to light. The only paperwork he has is a dead woman's impassioned plea in three languages. His being here cannot be legal, whatever that abstraction might mean in a world where each half of its population is intent on destroying the other. It is difficult enough to divine meaning in normal circumstances. From the colossal turmoil of the world beyond Rassaig Lachlan can only tease out one thread of sense and he cannot give rational account of it: for whatever reason the boy arrived and Lachlan was here to receive him. This is the only thing that matters. An enquiry will separate them. He has no doubt of it. Realizing his despondence is not helping the boy, he rallies.

'I know there has been a crime and therefore there is the question of accountability —'

'It was me,' Gail interrupts simply. Having said this she seems to think she has said sufficient to settle the issue. Michael is again looking into the cupboard. Holding the doorjamb, he leans forward without stepping into the stain. The question seems to come out of the cupboard.

'And how was this accomplished, miss?'

'He pushed me into the cupboard and bent me over . . . something. He was behind, trying to rape me when the weapon was . . . discharged . . .'

'I'm assuming he was shot in the heel first because the other wound looks like it finished him. It's interesting that you managed to shoot him in the heel when he was standing behind you.'

'She's overwrought. I'm prepared to take responsibility.'

'I've no doubt you are, Lachlan.' He straightens and turns, evidently satisfied with his scrutiny. His voice no longer comes from the cupboard. There is another bang at the door. 'This isn't just another thing you can shoulder or fix simply because you're the village doctor.' He begins to walk towards the entrance. Lachlan feels that unless they reach some kind of accommodation before the door opens, the boy's fate is sealed.

'Michael!' It is a shout. 'As long as it stops here, with me, I'll sign anything. If you agree I'll even write a statement at your dictation.'

'Everyone knows no one can read your writing, Lachlan.'

He has reached the door and unlocks it. Agnes comes in

with Fraser Laing, the harbour master, one of Lachlan's frequent chess opponents. Agnes locks the door at her back and gestures the two younger men towards her. They are both so much taller they have to bend as she talks in an intense undertone. Michael nods and turns to the classroom.

'Lachlan says he's prepared to take responsibility.'

Agnes says, 'Don't be so silly, man. It's not your responsibility to take.'

'And Gail over there shot a man who was standing behind her.'

Agnes continues, 'If we bring them in on it do you not think they'll put two and two together? Where's the gun either of you are happy to admit having used? Between here and the surgery or more likely in the Gladstone bag it came out of.'

'For God's sake!' He is speaking to them all. His tone is an entreaty. 'That boy's endured as much as it's humanly possible to take, more than could reasonably be expected of anyone three times his age. To institutionalize him now . . .' He falters, again a first, publicly at a loss. There is a brief silence. Agnes leaves Michael's side, walks across to him and touches his cheek.

'Lachlan dear, you're a bright man but sometimes you haven't got the common sense God gave you. No one's going to destroy that lovely boy's life. Certainly not for a fornicating wastrel like that. Much as I would have liked to settle this among ourselves I know we can't. Realistically there's a minimum number we need. We have to let some know to stop everyone knowing. What you'd call irony. That's why I brought my cousin.'

'I didn't know Michael was your cousin.'

'That's because he's not. Fraser's my cousin.'

'Michael's my cousin,' Fraser says.

'But to get rid of him effectively he's going to have to go in a boat,' Michael says.

'His boat,' Agnes says, with conviction that carries the moment.

Lachlan reflects that impoverishment of the genetic pool aside, he always knew there was advantage to be found from living in a small community.

57

At the combined insistence of all the cousins Lachlan is persuaded to go home. 'This is heavy work,' Michael insists, nodding to the cupboard.

'You're no spring chicken, Lachlan,' Agnes says.

'Neither of us are, Agnes. And tell me, do you intend heaving a corpse around in the night? You think an old woman and a cadaver won't attract some attention?'

'You're wandering again, Lachlan. As long as you've known you've taken care of everything and everyone you come in contact with. You've done more than anyone could expect. It's time for the younger ones. Go home. Take Gail. For once let someone else cope.'

The sense is obvious. Once he agrees, a great weariness possesses him. He has trouble picking up his bag. Seeing this, Michael picks it up for him and goes with him to the car. Agnes brings Gail. All four return to the house in Lachlan's car. Agnes puts Gail to bed. Lachlan administers a sedative. Agnes calls the Campbells to say Gail has been taken poorly on a visit and will stay at least the night. Agnes puts Franz to bed. Lachlan kisses him goodnight and tells him everything is being taken care of, that he will not let anything happen to him. From the doorway Agnes watches the exchange. Lachlan returns to the lounge where Michael is waiting. Agnes appears with three large whiskies.

Michael delves into the abandoned Gladstone bag and pulls out the revolver.

'Fortunate he shot that bastard on Friday. If it had been a

school day tomorrow we might really have been in trouble.'

When Lachlan is at last persuaded to go to bed Agnes goes to her kitchen and returns with a bucket, bleach and various cloths. She directs Michael to the linen closet to take what he needs.

'Have you any rope? Tarpaulin? Anything we could use.'

'Try the garage and the shed. Take anything.'

They return to the school, the headlights out. Michael parks a distance away. Fraser lets them in. They lock the door. The two men take what Michael has brought and go into the cupboard. Fraser goes to fetch his van. The last Agnes ever sees of Murdo is his shrouded figure being heaved out the schoolroom door, which she locks at their backs.

As she sweeps the glass and butterfly wings into a dustpan a rowing boat sculls quietly out. As she kneels down with cloths and bleach to the congealed stain, two boats, all lights out, throttle quietly out the harbour into the dark expanse.

She has to make repeated trips to the toilet to wring out the cloths and refill her bucket. With the forethought Lachlan has taken for granted all these years, she has stolen his penknife to prise what bullets she can find from the woodwork and masonry. Michael returns in the early hours for her. He stands on a desk to dismantle what remains of the mounted case. He will arrange for someone he knows to come and replace the shattered doorjamb and shelf. He drives her back, leaves the car in the driveway and walks down the hill, whistling. She rinses the bucket, brings her dressing gown to the kitchen and undresses in front of the iron range. Raking up the fire, she throws her clothes into the flames one item at a time, followed by the wrung-out cloths that hiss on contact. She wraps herself in the gown and goes upstairs to run a bath. Finally, clean by her own standards, she dries herself, dresses for bed and makes a quick inventory, looking in on all three before going to her own room. The last thing she does before putting out the light is to locate her bedside rosary. In the darkness she begins a decade for the repose of Murdo's soul. Her mind's eye sees a bundle, nestling in silt, fifty freezing fathoms down. The tarpaulin exudes a wraith that rises through the blackness, breaking the surface without a whisper of turbulence to be drawn further up, like morning mist sucked towards the sun, ascending to its luminous reckoning. She prays for an easy quietus, her mouth forming the words in little susurrations, slowing as she tires, sleep concluding her whispered conversation with God.

58

During a bright May morning in 1942 Dr Lachlan McCready stands near the edge of the platform contemplating the rails. At some distance, because he has detached himself from the little group, stand Agnes, Gail and Franz. The Gladstone bag is no longer the boy's constant adjunct. It has become a dispensable accessory. It sits on top of Gail's bags. It is on this forlorn little pyramid that Lachlan now concentrates, looking anywhere other than at the people he has just walked away from. The only other people on the platform are an elderly couple, awaiting a relative, who sit in the doorless waiting room in chatty conclave with the postman. He is regaling them with some shaggy dog story to the old man's sniggering amusement. The wife is pretending to be scandalized and casts reproving looks around to advertise her disapproval, lifting her hand to her mouth from time to time to conceal her smirk. Lachlan bets what he is saying is really unfunny, some seaside postcard toilet humour. At any other time he would take keen interest in the size and shape of the three skulls and perhaps even eavesdrop, correlating shape to the banality of the exchange. But he is too preoccupied. The three chortling from the booth are in marked contrast to the dismal silence that has descended on the good doctor and his companions. Lachlan walks back to the group who all look at him expectantly. Agnes is in the middle, holding the other two by an arm each.

'Franz, I want you to look out for the train's arrival and tell me the instant it comes into sight.'

'All right.'

He wants as much notice of the train's arrival as possible because he has still not decided what it is he wants to say. He wants to give the boy something to take with him, some appropriate distillation of what he feels, that encapsulates what they have gone through, something uplifting that will help sustain him.

It was Agnes who came and told Lachlan the boy would have to go, at least for a while. In doing this she merely articulated something he already knew. She started by saying, 'There's no going back from a killing,' and he sat, wordless, listening to the cards fall into place and her inexorable reasoning towards the conclusion he had already reached.

Morag Dougan bore the news of her son's disappearance stoically. Perhaps she had had an inkling of his behaviour and recognized it merely as a matter of time before something happened. Isabel accepted the news differently. By this time Franz had told Lachlan more of what he knew and Lachlan, this time summoned to the clifftop house by the mother for the benefit of her daughter-in-law, was again confronted with the full force of human despair. Again the inevitable sedative made an appearance. It defeated Lachlan that a woman could look deranged with grief, faced with the loss of a man who habitually raped her. He left the croft both confused and disappointed at the vagaries of the human heart.

The village rallied. Isabel was entitled to a pension. Materially she would be better provided for but her grief was so public as to give force to Agnes's argument. Having discussed the events of that evening with Agnes, Lachlan has gone over them again and again in his mind, looking for loopholes, some weak spot that will allow news to haemorrhage. Two boats left the harbour and one came back. Fraser could only pilot one. Michael was not in the second. That's someone else in the know. Michael found some tradesman to put the doorjamb and shelf to rights and plaster the holes in the walls. That's someone else. All it takes is some drunken unintentional divulgence. Agnes is right: there's no going back from a killing.

Since the incident he has kept Franz with him as much as possible. Is it his imagination or has the boy attained a quiet notoriety in the interim? He has tried to view the reaction of others as impartially as possible, which for him is impossible. He is a creature of prejudices and knows enough of himself to recognize this. He also knows he has become overprotective towards the boy. His custodial manner could eventually rouse suspicion. Perhaps Franz also senses a change in public attitudes towards him. Since the events in the schoolroom his manner to the world at large has become more withdrawn. He has compensated for it by becoming more forthcoming with those he trusts.

Gail wanted to leave almost immediately. She was only prevailed upon to stay by the combined efforts of Lachlan and Agnes. Lachlan wanted her to delay leaving until Murdo's disappearance ceased to invite speculation, clinching the argument by telling her that this would be in the boy's best interests too. It might come as news to her but her affair with Murdo wasn't a secret. If Murdo's wife knew, does she seriously believe that everyone else who's interested, who is everyone else, didn't? Eileen Campbell knew. That meant everyone knew. An affair, a death, a sudden departure: imagine herself impartial, what would she conclude? For the sake of burying the news with the body she should stay till the gossip subsides.

Lachlan's patronage is not extensive but select. He has written to the headmaster of his old school, giving an indication of Franz's abilities. He has followed this letter with a telephone call, reciting invented antecedents. Lachlan is only good extempore. The other man extends the courtesy of pretending the halting performance sounds plausible. A place is obtained. The boy will receive something like an education appropriate to his gifts. Lachlan does not want the boy to become a boarder. He does not want him swallowed by another institution, no matter how intentionally benign. He wants him to come back each night to something approaching a home, to be with someone he recognizes as a friend.

To this end he has arranged three interviews for Gail at different Edinburgh schools. The same headmaster he has already discussed Franz's education with can vouch for the calibre of these places. He has also arranged accommodation. He would have done as much for Gail anyway, the only difference being he would have consulted with her first.

And having convinced her to stay, he let a reasonable interim elapse and raised with her the topic of the public attitude to Franz. Is he being overprotective? If he is, she concedes, he has reason to be. He begins to reiterate Agnes's argument. She pre-empts him.

'Lachlan . . . This is difficult. I have been thinking about it a lot and I – I think Franz has to go. You can't leave. That would turn too many heads. I was always going anyway, sooner or later. I think he should go. I think he should come with me.'

And letting her know she has reached the same conclusion he and Agnes independently arrived at, he begins to talk to her about Edinburgh. She is a teacher. The city is bursting with schools – good schools. Why go back to England? England is full of memories. England is being bombed. Why risk it? Scotland has had its quota of bombs and even if it hasn't the next ones will land beside the last ones, in Glasgow. Edinburgh is not a munitions factory. Edinburgh is the city of the Enlightenment, of Scott, of Adam's visionary architectural symmetry, of Burke and Hare, of . . . of Greyfriars Bobby, of . . . of . . . of three teaching vacancies for each of which she has an interview.

Behind the well-intended coercion there is a persuasive logic to what he says. And she feels she owes it to Lachlan to keep the boy within visiting distance. She has no intention of going back to Winchester. She sits three interviews in two days and has her choice of two positions. She calls Lachlan to let him know the news and says she may stay another day or so to try to locate reasonable accommodation for her and Franz. He plays his trump card, reads the address over the phone and tells her the rooms are ready for habitation.

'You're a scoundrel, Lachlan. You've had it all worked out all along.'

'I'll call the headmaster I talked to and ask him his opinion on which of the two schools is better.'

'I think I'm capable of making up my own mind on this one.'

'It never hurts to be well informed.'

'You've thought of everything.'

'One tries.' In self-congratulation he blows a fragrant blue cloud from his cigar into the hall cornices.

'Have you thought of how you'll tell Franz?'

The consultation Lachlan has that evening is the most halting of his career. The hundreds of occasions on which he has had to confront the bereaved have polished his delivery. He has learned to speak slowly, expound clearly and with sympathy. While inference from personal experience leads him to understand what his listeners are often going through, he has developed a sense of professional detachment. Bad news seldom disturbs his constitution.

All of the inarticulate pauses that evening are his. Franz hears out without interruption the halting catalogue of reasons, and at the end says simply, without hint of complaint, 'But I don't want to go. I want to stay here. With you.'

On the kitchen side of the hatch Agnes stops in her

preparations and looks determinedly at the scarred table. After a moment of consideration she decides to make a novena for the two of them. Consoled by this solution, she continues chopping.

'The train is coming.'

Gail refuses Lachlan's help with the bags. Franz looks merely comfortable carrying his. He no longer has that obsessed, proprietorial air. As the train gets closer Lachlan becomes more agitated. He helps them both on. Franz immediately pushes down the window and, leaning out, kisses Lachlan. The old man steps back. This is the time to say what he has been preparing. But like Franz's father, attempting to put pen to paper on the eve of another departure, Lachlan finds himself unequal to the task. He says nothing at all and listens to the last-minute inconsequential exchanges between the women, confirming arrangements that have already been made for the sake of saying something. He and Agnes are to visit the weekend after next. They are to telephone tonight to let them know they are settled. They have the address of the Edinburgh Rabbi it has been arranged for Franz to meet. Gail is to provide Lachlan with the boy's school booklist. The doctor plans a jaunt with Franz round the same bookshops he used to haunt when he was nearer the boy's age than his own.

A succession of doors slam. The boy is going. Lachlan takes these concussions personally. A whistle blows. The boy is going, waving. Behind the regret Lachlan can see something else in his face. A sense of excitement at change, anticipation of seeing the place Lachlan has praised to mitigate the shock of yet another dislocation. The boy is going, in smoke, like a conjuror's trick. This is the difference between them: he is travelling forward into the future that is opening before him, Lachlan is going back to what remains. The boy is gone.

He stands until the train has turned out of sight and makes

no show of moving. Agnes stands with the patience of a monument. Finally she takes his arm.

'You will be seeing him in less than a fortnight.'

'It was delight in small things . . . daily exchanges . . . I can't explain.'

'You already have. You know, it's all right to cry.'

'Don't be foolish, Agnes.'

But she has steered him round and he looks at the car that will take them back to the village, suddenly impoverished, and a house without the boy's coat on the hall peg. Through the thickness of his sleeve she senses the spasm of grief.

'Just concentrate on the weekend after next, Doctor Mc-Cready. Think of it as twelve dinnertimes away. Speaking of which, I have made your favourite this evening.'

'Really?' She recognizes in him the anticipation he saw in Franz's departing face. He reflects that she is right. He should look at this as an interval till they next meet, not a farewell. The boy will fare better there. There is not enough substance here for one of his gifts. He would have reached a state of inertia that would have been painful to watch. Their absence will better qualify him to chart the boy's development than he would have been able to had they been in constant contact. Lachlan is prepared to be pleasantly surprised. The school has a chess club he looks forward to hearing Franz has over-whelmed. Or perhaps he is being too complimentary to his own game. Since his encounter with Franz he is now rec-onciled to the fact that there is stiffer opposition than the petrified tactics of a country doctor. It would be good if the boy excels, but all that matters is that he gets a chance and is happy. And it should not matter that she has made his favourite for dinner, but somehow it does. And there is that claret he has been keeping. In one of those extraordinarily rare moments of self-doubt Lachlan wonders if he is superficial to be cheered by such mundane home comforts. But he dismisses this thought almost as it arrives: life is made up of the quotidian, it is the warp and weft; only fools, or those who read too much, fail to take consolation from the texture of the everyday.

The tension in his arm slackens. She begins to guide him towards the car.

'And another thing, Agnes, after all this you can't go back to formal terms.'

'We'll see, Doctor McCready.'

With thanks to Christopher and Mary, agent and editor respectively, for having the foresight and taking the trouble when no one else would.